C000298882

Ireland

www.baedeker.com

Verlag Karl Baedeker

TOP ATTRACTIONS ★ ★

Spectacular cliff scenery and sleepy garden islands, picturesque towns and impressive ruins – Ireland offers a wealth of natural and cultural treasures. Here, we have put together the most beautiful destinations so you don't miss any of the highlights.

1 ✶✶ Giant's Causeway

The »Giant's Causeway« (approx. 40,000 basalt pillars) is considered the greatest natural wonder of Ireland. In 1986, the coastal strip was declared a UNESCO World Heritage Site. ► page 231

2 ✶✶ Antrim Coast & Glens

One of the most beautiful roads in the whole of Ireland leading to the Antrim Glens, a wild romantic area with plenty of charm. ► page 155

3 ✶✶ Ulster American Folk Park

This gives visitors an idea of the reality of emigration: from life in Ireland at the time, to the ship taking emigrants to the New World, to their arrival in Pennsylvania, USA. ► page 407

Landscapes of paradise
Around the most beautiful lakes in Ireland

4 ✶✶ Lough Erne

The most beautiful lake in Ireland is a paradise for water-sports lovers and fishing enthusiasts, and birdwatchers also get their money's worth. ► page 328

5 ✶✶ Céide Fields

Impressive, and not just for history buffs! The largest Neolithic excavation site in the world (15ha/37.1 acres) shows how people lived and farmed 5,000 years ago.
► page 177

6 ✶✶ Monasterboice

One of the most important sights in Ireland. The priests would use the extraordinary High Crosses in the monastic enclosure as props to explain the Bible to the faithful. ► page 396

7 ✶✶ Newgrange

The largest prehistoric ceremonial and burial site in Ireland was erected approx. 3,200 BC, which makes it older than Stonehenge and the Pyramids!
► page 210

8 ✶✶ Connemara

Thatched cottages, fields criss-crossed by stone walls, and on the coast, fine sandy beaches alternating with rugged peninsulas, draw visitors to this wild lonely landscape. ► page 245

9 ✶✶ Dublin

The metropolis of glaring social contrasts offers a rich and varied cultural life. Discover literature, contemporary music, splendid architecture and, of course, the cozy atmosphere of a pub! ► page 280

Young and trendy
Fresh faces and cheeky graffiti in the capital city

»Dine like an earl«
The Middle Ages come alive at Bunratty Castle.

Spectacular cliffs
Even shrouded in mist or whipped by storms, the Cliffs of Moher impress.

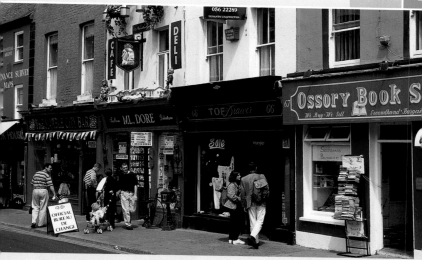

Charming city
Kilkenny's medieval lanes are great for leisurely strolls and shopping.

19 ✳✳ Irish National Heritage Park
Families with children in particular will enjoy this open-air museum, bringing to life 9,000 years of Irish history.
► page 456

20 ✳✳ Killarney Area
Stunning nature: with its lakes set in mountains and hills and scenic ruins, Killarney is one of the biggest tourist attractions in Ireland.   ► page 365

21 ✳✳ Ring of Kerry
The approx. 200km/124 miles of panoramic coastal road leading around the Iveragh Peninsula offer wonderful views. Schedule a full day for this!
► page 411

Flower island
On Garinish Island, magnolias, camellias and exotic trees thrive.

22 ✳✳ Garinish Island
It was only when the gardens were laid out between 1910 and 1920 that Garinish Island became a garden island. In good weather, look for basking seals during the crossing.   ► page 184

23 ✳✳ Skellig Islands
These two impressive rocky islands are completely given over to birds. Skellig Michael is not to be missed under any circumstances!   ► page 425

BAEDEKER'S BEST TIPS

From all the tips in this book we have compiled the most interesting for you here! Experience and enjoy the best of what the Emerald Isle has to offer.

⚡ Oul' Lammas Fair
Held in Ballycastle, this horse and sheep market with stalls is over 300 years old and probably the most famous in Northern Ireland. ▶ **page 157**

⚡ Aran Sweaters
With their creative patterns, these garments are some of the most popular souvenirs from Ireland. The off-peak season is the right time to find a bargain! ▶ **page 160**

⚡ Grace Neill's
Try wild duck with braised cabbage in the oldest pub on Irish soil. Even Peter the Great is said to have stopped here on his Europe trip. ▶ **page 165**

⚡ Irish »Wellness«
Relax in a seaweed bath in an old porcelain tub under Art Deco tiles … ▶ **page 178**

Kilkullen's Bath House

… offers relaxation and a trip to the past.

⚡ Crown Liquor Saloon
Gas lamps, a marble counter and a lot of mahogany lend the most beautiful pub in Belfast a very special note. ▶ **page 193**

Welcome
In the most beautiful pub of Belfast

⚡ Druamone Dolmen
We show you the way to the dolmen that is considered one of the most beautiful in Ireland. ▶ **page 208**

⚡ China on the Irish coasts
Watch china being made in the Donegal Parian China Pottery. ▶ **page 214**

⚡ Burren Smokehouse
Find out about traditional methods of smoking wild Atlantic salmon, before tasting and purchasing tasty delicacies. ▶ **page 218**

⚡ Irish Whiskey
Bushmills Distillery sells special sizes you can't get anywhere else. ▶ **page 231**

⚡ Sparkling crystal
Purchase beautiful crystal objects in the Cavan Crystal Showroom. ▶ **page 234**

🔲 Ring the Bell
Ring the bells of Cork before enjoying a sweeping view over the city.
► page 257

🔲 Butterfly House
Watch hundreds of tropical butterflies, exotic insects and reptiles at Seaforde Tropical Butterfly House ► page 276

🔲 Literary Pub Crawl
Join a walk around pubs and literary sites for some drama, recitals, singing and, of course, a pint. ► page 286

🔲 Iveagh Gardens
A small oasis of peace and quiet in the heart of Dublin, a breathing space from the hustle and bustle of the city.
► page 291

Faithful
The Claddagh ring is a popular souvenir

🔲 Claddagh-Ring
This ring, symbolizing friendship, love and loyalty, is found in Galway and all over the world. ► page 337

🔲 Irish Linen Tour
Visit the Irish Linen Centre, a flax mill and working linen weaving mill.
► page 390

🔲 Puck Fair
This merry fair in Killorglin even attracts visitors from overseas. ► page 414

🔲 Bog-standard discovery tour...
Hop on a small train weaving its way through numerous stations of geological, historical or botanical interest, and watch peat being cut. ► page 422

🔲 Quirke's Sculptures
How do fairies, giants and other mythical creatures come into being? In Sligo, watch chunky bits of wood being transformed into works of art. ► page 429

🔲 Butterstream Gardens
Beautiful small, hedge-lined gardens on the edge of Trim, each one of them with their own character. ► page 444

🔲 Waterford Crystal
One of the most renowned crystal workshops and one of the most popular tourist attractions in Ireland. ► page 449

Fragile
At Waterford Crystal, see how beautiful glass objects are made

The »wine of life« is dispensed behind fanciful façades
► page 96

BACKGROUND

PRACTICALITIES FROM A to Z

High Crosses bear witness to the country's rich history.
► page 59

TOURS

Kitted out in traditional Irish garb for Heritage Day in Ballina
► **page 175**

SIGHTS FROM A to Z

Phoenix Park – a green oasis on the edge of the capital
▶ **page 307**

Price Categories

▶ **Hotels**
Luxury: over €120 / £80
Mid-range: €80 – €120 /
£55 – £80
Budget: under €80 / £55
For a double room

▶ **Restaurants**
Expensive: over €20 / £14
Moderate: €10 – €20 / £7 – £14
Inexpensive: under €10 / £7
For a main course

Ormond Castle in Carrick-on-Suir
► page 222

Roundstone – one of the prettiest villages in Connemara
► page 252

Background

WHAT YOU NEED TO KNOW AND MORE
ABOUT THE EMERALD ISLE: THE
COUNTRYSIDE AND ITS PEOPLE,
THEIR CHEQUERED HISTORY AND RICH
AND VARIED CULTURE.

THE EMERALD ISLE

»Forty shades of green«, as the famous song goes. Well, green is indeed the dominant colour in this country, its many variations sustained by the gentle, moist climate. Meadows, pastures and hedgerows are offset by glorious touches of colour provided by rhododendron bushes and fuchsia hedges in lavish bloom.

The beauty of the landscape has to be the main attraction for anybody visiting Ireland. And of course most people would hope to enjoy the island in sunshine. But even if it does rain frequently, the weather changes reliably fast, and you can find all four seasons in one day; after a pelting shower the sky clears up quickly, the mild Irish sun bathing the undulating landscape in a beautifully soft light.

Green –
As far as the eye can see

Mind and Body

Alongside its magnificent natural beauty, Ireland has plenty of art and culture to offer. The bizarre shapes and figures of the country's Celtic prehistory, and the early Christian monuments, monasteries and High Crosses, are highlights of any trip to Ireland. Another striking feature of the landscape are the round towers, found nowhere else in the world. These, and other ancient ruins, blend harmoniously into the landscape to give a strong visual and spiritual impact.

For many visitors, a trip to Ireland provides a great opportunity for an activity holiday. Top of the list is golf – in Ireland, a sport for everyone. There are some 400 courses, including one third of the world's links courses, and more are being built all the time. Many tourists also appreciate the opportunity to explore the country on horseback or by bike, taking advantage of the attractive, varied landscape and the relatively low volume of traffic on the roads. But beware, bike tours in Ireland are a relentless up-and-down and do require a bit of stamina.

The island is a paradise for anglers too, drawn by the numerous unpolluted inland waterways and lakes teeming with shoals of fish, as well as by the rich fishing grounds of the coast, fed by the mild Gulf Stream. This classic fishing country offers the advanced angler plenty of opportunities for coarse fishing, game fishing and deep-sea angling.

Panoramic
The view from the scenic »Achill Drive« on the west coast of Achill Island peninsula

Romantic
For a long time, thatched cottages were the traditional dwelling in the countryside. Today, they are becoming scarce.

Prehistoric
The Kilclooney Dolmen north of Ardara bears witness to the country's rich past.

Heavenly
Swing your fishing rod over clear rivers and lakes rich in salmon and trout and relax...

Musical
Musicians often get together in the pub: everyone is welcome to contribute to the general fun.

Magnificent
On a clear day, standing on the summit of Slieve League, the highest sea cliffs in Europe, you should be able to see two thirds of Ireland.

Adventures on the Water

For a particularly rewarding experience, consider a holiday on a house-boat and discover Ireland on the Shannon and its tributaries – no boatman's license necessary! The Shannon-Erne canal connects Ireland's longest river with the scenic Erne Lakes in Northern Ireland, and, with the successful peace process, crossing the border is no longer an issue. In the past, Belfast and Derry used to be ghost towns come evening; today the restaurants, cinemas, theatres and of course, pubs, attract a lively crowd.

Beyond Pub Culture

Education has always been important to the Irish. Literature and teachers are held in high regard since the times when Irish schools were prohibited and »hedge school masters« used to illegally teach the countryside's children for a penny per week. The hedge school masters are said to have carried their ink well on a chain around their neck, and their copy of Virgil as well as an Irish primer in their pocket. Once Irish schools were allowed again, education and teaching passed mostly into the hands of teaching orders and lay priests. Today, school is compulsory from ages six to fifteen. Traditionally, the level of education on the island is high, and significant amounts of EU monies have been channelled into the educational system. The »Celtic Tiger«, the economic boom of recent years, would not have been possible without Ireland's highly qualified workforce, which has met the demand for employees in the financial services sector.

Georgian *Façades of Dublin residences on Merrion Square*

Welcome to Ireland

Visitors who want to get to know the Irish should try the pub, where a pint of Guinness is the perfect accompaniment to stories, debates and songs. Strangers are usually invited to join the conversation, which is why the first word that the visitor learns in the old Gaelic tongue is nearly always »Fáilte« – »Welcome«!

Facts

Ireland (Gaelic: Eire), split politically into the Republic of Ireland and Northern Ireland, forms part of the British Isles. However, the unresolved issue of whether the northern province should belong to the United Kingdom or the Republic of Ireland is continuing to be difficult.

Natural Environment

The interior of the island is dominated by extensive limestone plains with peat bogs, low hills and large and small lakes. About a fifth of the country is covered by the Shannon's extensive network of rivers and lakes. The central lowlands only extend to the coast in the Dublin area.

Central lowlands

Mountain ranges near the coast are characteristic of Ireland's landscape. One of the best examples is the Macgillycuddy's Reeks in the southwest, which reach up to 1,041m/3,415ft at Carrantuohill, the highest peak in Ireland. The mountains in the south are mainly comprised of red sandstone, those in Connemara, Donegal and Mayo mainly of granite and quartzite. Single conical, bare peaks jutting out of the plain are a typical feature of this type of landscape. Most of the northeast is covered by a basalt plateau, whilst the predominant rock in the Wicklow Mountains is granite. Of particular interest for geologists and botanists is the karst area of the Burren, on the western coast of County Clare. Ireland has experienced at least two Ice Ages; both left their traces in smoothly polished rocks and dark mountain lakes, and in the course of many valleys and numerous sediments, such as the drumlins (round low hillocks) between Sligo and Belfast.

Mountains

The coastline is a steady succession of steep cliffs and sandy bays, often with pronounced dunes. The most spectacular coastal scenery can be found at the Cliffs of Moher, Slieve League and the cliffs of Achill Island.

Across large swaths of the »Emerald Isle«, nature remains intact. In sparsely populated areas where organic agriculture – mainly cattle rearing – is practised, there are few problems. Over recent years however, in the wake of increasing industrial activity, much has changed, with important environmental legislation subservient to economic survival. The consequences have been water and air pollution, overfishing and the destruction of the peat eco-system through unregulated exploitation. However, an awareness of green issues is slowly gaining ground, not least because people understand its importance for the safeguarding of the natural environment as the very resource which makes the island so attractive to visitors.

Natural environment

Flora and Fauna

Ireland's flora and fauna is unusually poor in biodiversity. During the last Ice Age, the country was nearly completely covered by ice, allowing only a few Arctic plants to survive. When Ireland became an

Low level of biodiversity

← *The vertical Cliffs of Moher rising out of the Atlantic*

island at the end of the last Ice Age, the plants and animals struggled to take root here again. Only half of the flowering plants that visitors would expect to see in a country with Ireland's latitude and climate are actually found here. On the other hand, Ireland can offer all shades of the colour green – dependent on weather, cloud formation, amount of rain, direction of the wind and type of soil. This rich palette of greens has earned the island the nickname »Emerald Isle«.

No snakes   In the animal kingdom, the situation is similar: Ireland only has 28 different species of mammal living in the wild, and no snakes at all. The reptile family is only represented by the common lizard. To make up for this, there are many aquatic animals and birds.

Flora

Forests   Of the forests that once covered the whole island – made up of oak, holly, birch, ash and hazel – only a few remnants are left. A state reforestation programme is trying to reverse this trend by using, amongst others, the Sitka spruce; however, this species does not always thrive in Ireland.

Peat bogs   Some 16% of the land surface of Ireland is covered in peat bog. There are three different types: highland peat bog (c4%), reaching a depth of 7m/23ft, blanket bogs (c11%), only going down to a depth of 3.5m/11ft and covering both mountains and valleys, with the remainder made up of lowland peat bog. All types of bog are home to various species of bog moss, whilst heather, cotton grass, broom heather, bell heather and bog asphodel thrive here.

Tropical and subtropical shrubs that once used to be planted in the parks and gardens of stately homes have today spread over the whole country. In the warm southwest in particular, you frequently see palm trees and evergreen plants. Huge **broom and rhododendron bushes**, as well as fuchsia hedges in bloom, add touches of colour to all that green. In the nature reserves the spread of these plants is not always greeted with enthusiasm, as they often stifle the endemic vegetation. The foxglove and a dark bluebell with a particularly long stem grow well here.

In the southwest   In the southwest of the country and in the Burren, subtropical and arctic-alpine vegetation can be found within a confined space. These plants managed to survive here due to the cool summers following the last Ice Age.

Puffin on the bird island Little Skellig

Fauna

The island is rich in birdlife, with some 250 migratory birds joining **Birds** 135 local species. Many songbirds nest in hedges, and the bogs are home to larks, curlews and common snipe. In wetland areas, oyster-catchers – a shore bird like the puffin – may be seen inland. On the rugged Atlantic coast nest seagulls, guillemots, cormorants, and the agile gannets, dive-bombing their prey in the sea from great heights. The fulmar or the ocean swift are much more difficult to spot.

The water of the Irish lakes, rivers and brooks is often peaty brown, **Fish,** but clean and therefore rich in fish. Salmon and trout are the anglers' **seafood** favourite prey, with pike and rainbow trout only recently established here. Irish coastal waters are home to some 250 fish species; of importance for the fishing industry are herring, sprat, cod, mackerel, plaice, haddock, sole and monkfish. Various species of seal live on the coast and around the islands.

Facts and Figures Ireland

Geographical location
▶ Republic of Ireland, Northern Ireland
▶ Northwestern Europe
▶ 51°30' to 55°30' latitude and 5°30' to 10°30' longitude
▶ Longest distance from north to south: from Malin Head in the north to Mizen Head in the southwest: 486km/301 miles
▶ Longest distance between east and west coast: 290km/180 miles
▶ Coastline: 3,200km/1,988 miles

Surface and territory
▶ 84,403 sq km/32,588 sq miles, of which 14,120 sq km/5,452 sq miles in Northern Ireland, part of the United Kingdom
▶ Four historic provinces: Leinster, Munster, Ulster, Connaught
▶ 32 counties, of which 26 belong to the Republic of Ireland and six to Northern Ireland

Population
▶ 4.2 million (Republic of Ireland)
▶ 1.7 million (Northern Ireland)
▶ Population density:
Republic of Ireland – 60 inhabitants/sq km (155/sq mile);
Northern Ireland – 125 inhabitants/sq km (323/sq mile)
▶ Largest cities:
capital of the Republic of Ireland – Dublin 506,000 inhabitants;
capital of Northern Ireland – Belfast 276,000 inhabitants

Economy
▶ Gross Domestic Product (per capita): $45,700
▶ Unemployment rate: 4.6%
▶ Main sectors of economy:
agriculture 10%, industry 29%, services 61%
▶ Natural resources:
small quantity of minerals – ore, lead, zinc, silver, copper, mercury, pyrite; natural gas fields off Kinsale and, recently, Co. Mayo
▶ Main trade partners:
Great Britain, increasingly EU
▶ Other important trade partners:
USA, Germany, France
▶ Main exports: cattle, meat, machines, electronics, textiles, chemicals

Languages
▶ Irish (first official language, little spoken), English (second official language), Ulster Scots (regional)

Religion
▶ Approx. 90% Catholics, also Anglicans (Church of Ireland), Presbyterians and Jews

State

► Republic, (Poblacht na h'Éireann, Republic of Ireland): parliamentary democracy (based on the constitution of 1937)
► Head of state: a president (Uachtarán na h'Éireann) directly elected by the people, largely ceremonial role, term of office: 7 years
► Executive: prime minister (Taoiseach) and ministers
► Parliament: two-chamber system: lower house (Dáil Éireann), senate (Seanad Éireann)

Flag

► Republic of Ireland: green-white-orange tricolour. Green stands for the Catholic majority of the people, orange represents the Protestants (derived from the colour of King William of Orange), with white symbolizing peace between the two groups

Coat of arms

► Golden harp on blue (representing the great tradition of singers and bards), alongside a three-leafed clover (representing St Patrick and as symbol of the Trinity)
► National anthem: *A Soldier's Song* (1907), by Peadar Kearney, music by Patrick Heeney and Peadar Kearney, martial marching song

Northern Ireland

► The parts of the island belonging to the UK fly the Union Jack flag; the traditional symbol is the Red Hand of Ulster on a white background (dating back to the time of the Viking invasions and standing for the territorial claim)

Population · Politics · Economy

Population

The Republic of Ireland is one of the least-populated regions in Europe. As nearly a third of the country's population lives in Greater Dublin, vast areas can appear practically deserted.

Development

In the first half of the 19th century, Ireland was one of the most densely-populated countries in Europe. However, a wave of emigration started in the second decade, culminating in a veritable exodus during the Great Famine of 1845–49 (► History, Potato blight). Some 3.5 million Irish left their home country and tried to make a new life for themselves in the US or in Britain. Another marked wave of emigration started after the Second World War as, between 1951 and 1961, over 40,000 Irish emigrated every year. It was not until the 1970s that improved economic conditions led to an increase in population of 15.6% (Northern Ireland only 1.7%) and convinced ma-

Emigration

ny Irish to stay, even persuading some emigrants to return. High unemployment in the following decade however again boosted emigration. Whilst in the past, mainly poor farmers and workers with few qualifications had left the country, those years saw a dramatic increase in young Irish emigrants with a degree or high level of skills.

Immigration Since the mid-1990s, a massive economic boom has reversed that trend again. Today, alongside the Irish moving back to their country, many citizens from other European countries come to Ireland to take advantage of the good job opportunities. The island has also become increasingly attractive for asylum-seekers and other immigrants; from 1998 onwards people from Africa – Nigeria in particular – and Asia could be seen arriving, partly because, until new legislation took effect on 1 January 2005, Ireland was the last EU country to offer unqualified citizenship through birth. From a country with net emigration, Ireland has transformed itself into a country with net immigration, whilst the country's birth rate remains the highest in the EU.

1821	Population 6.8 million on 70,283 sq km/27,136 sq miles (Republic of Ireland)
1845	Population 8.5 million
1961	Population 2.8 million
2007	Population 3.9 million

The Irish in the US The Irish emigrating to the US mostly settled in the large cities of the north. Soon, unskilled Irish workers dominated the canal and railway construction sector, and turned into a political force to be reckoned with. In the years between 1870 and 1920, in every US city with a sizable Irish population, the Irish provided an important political leader, often the mayor, and large numbers of Irish immigrants worked in the police force and as firefighters. One famous American of Irish descent was playwright Eugene O'Neill (1888–1953), who in 1936 was awarded the Nobel Prize for Literature.

? DID YOU KNOW …?

■ When John F Kennedy (1917–1963) was elected in 1960, he was the first American of Irish descent to become president of the United States, and was also the first Catholic US president.

Travellers, Tinkers One underprivileged marginalized group in Ireland are the Travellers, also derogatorily called Tinkers. Similarly to the Roma, though not related to them ethnically, the Travellers have a semi-nomadic lifestyle. In the past, they earned their living mainly repairing pots and kettles. They have their own language too; however, it is now

Ireland Map

Republic of Ireland
Northern Ireland

DONEGAL
● Derry
DERRY
ANTRIM
ULSTER
TYRONE   BELFAST ●
FERMANAGH
DOWN
ARMAGH
● Sligo
SLIGO
MONAGHAN
MAYO
LEITRIM
CAVAN
ROSCOMMON
LONG-
FORD
LOUTH
CONNAUGHT
WEST-
MEATH
MEATH
GALWAY
Galway
● Athlone
DUBLIN
●
DUBLIN ●
OFFALY
KILDARE
LEINSTER
LAOIS
WICKLOW
CLARE
CARLOW
Limerick
TIPPERARY
KILKENNY
LIMERICK
WEXFORD
MUNSTER
KERRY
Waterford
● Killarney   CORK
WATERFORD
Cork ●

Shannon

state border
province border
county border

proven that the Travellers did not immigrate from elsewhere but are in fact Irish in origin. These days they have long swapped their brightly-painted horse-drawn carts, popular with tourists today, for modern mobile homes.

Anglo-Irish is the name given to those families whose English ancestors from around the 17th century were given the lands and properties of the dispossessed Irish. Where earlier English settlers had learned Gaelic and adopted the lifestyle of the native population, the new masters kept themselves to themselves. They continued to speak English, held on to their religion and shut themselves off from their Catholic Irish neighbours behind high walls. In the worst cases, they saw their lands purely as an asset to be exploited, hardly visiting Ireland and leaving their agents to collect the rent for the wattle-and-daub cottages of the people living on their estates. Later, the Anglo-

Irish landed gentry, as the ruling class, became the repository of cultural life in Ireland, also building castles and laying out large landscaped parks with many exotic plants.

Dwellings In Ireland, most people usually live in their own home, even if it is humble. It is only in the cities that more and more people are forced to rent. The traditional type of house is the cottage with a thatched

Traditional cottage

roof. Often, a cottage comprises just one big room, with a smaller room each side. Today you can still find families of six or more living on some 60 sq metres/650 sq ft, and some houses have no electricity or running water.

With the exception of the extremely barren regions of the West, travellers will not see so many people actually living in cottages of this kind. Those who can afford to often swap the cottage, that might seem so romantic to the tourist's eye, for a more comfortable bungalow or a simple farmhouse.

Cottages

State and society

The two major parties in Ireland, Fianna Fáil/FF (»Soldiers of Fate«, founded in 1926) and Fine Gael/FG (»Family of the Irish«, founded in 1933), have their roots in the Irish independence movement Sinn Féin. They have alternated in power since the founding of the state. Both have conservative policies, and both suffered major losses at the parliamentary elections in 1992. The general elections of 1997 brought a minority coalition of Fianna Fáil and Progressive Democrats/PD into government. FF under prime minister (or »taoiseach«) Bertie Ahern remained the largest party at the general elections of June 2007, but their coalition government now includes the Green Party too.

Political parties

To a large extent, the Irish legal system follows British law. The Old Irish Brehon Law (»Law of the Judges«) was based on the ideas of the rural clan system and was suppressed by the British as early as the 17th century.

Legal system

There is no conscription in Ireland, but some 10,500 men (plus 9,000 reserves) are under arms in the voluntary army, which has been successful in UN peace-keeping missions in many parts of the globe.

Military

Economy

After Ireland had become a Free State in 1922, most of the capital remained in the hands of wealthy Anglo-Irish families. In 1932, Fianna Fáil, led by Eamon de Valera, came to power, establishing a policy of economic self-sufficiency and favouring the manufacturing industry through the application of protection tariffs. Furthermore, the new Irish government refused to pay the British government's land annuities, a provision of the treaty of 1921. An economic war ensued, with the British government placing a 40% import duty on imports from Ireland, resulting in a dramatic downturn for the Irish export industry. The consequences of this »war« were softened by an agreement; as long as Ireland kept importing its coal from Britain, Britain

Developments up to 1945

would in turn import a large number of Irish cattle. The Anglo-Irish economic war only ended in 1938, when Britain dismantled its military installations in Ireland.

Up to the Second World War, the government's top priority was boosting the economy through the creation of numerous semi-state institutions such as the Agricultural Credit Corporation or the Electricity Supply Board, amongst others. Leaving the Commonwealth (1949) gave Ireland more economic freedom.

Current economic performance In recent years, the economic situation has shown a positive development, thanks not least to the supporting measures of the EU. With a low rate of inflation, a relatively high economic growth rate has been achieved. Whilst the rate of inflation in 1990–1998 stood at 2%, Gross Domestic Product in the same time period was 7.7%. Now, in

Lush meadows and herds of sheep are a common sight right across the island.

terms of per-capita wealth, the Republic of Ireland is one of the richest countries in the OECD!

Traditional branches of industry are food and beverage production, as well as tobacco and textiles. Since the late 1950s however, the government has been promoting the creation of new industries and inviting foreign companies to invest here, leading to more production of machinery, electro-domestic and electronic goods, pharmaceutical and chemical products, in addition to textiles and foods.

Overseas companies

Lured by tax breaks, relatively low salaries and low ancillary labour costs, almost 1,000 overseas companies have now set up a base on the »Emerald Isle«. Today, every fourth Irish worker has a foreign employer, mainly British, American, Dutch and German firms with subsidiaries in Ireland.

Some 70% of the country's surface is used for **agriculture**, mostly as pasture. The rearing of cattle is concentrated on meat production in the Midlands, and on dairy farming in the south. Alongside cattle, sheep, pigs and poultry are kept. Good pastures are used for breeding racehorses. The main crop is barley, used for beer brewing and as animal feed; other crops cultivated in Ireland are potatoes, sugar beet, wheat and oats.

? DID YOU KNOW ...?

■ One result of the occasionally absurd agricultural policy of the European Union has been the 11 million sheep grazing on Ireland's meadows. Though there is only money in lambs, nearly all sheep are allowed to live to a ripe old age as, every year, each animal brings in a €35 bonus. Today Ireland has seven times as many sheep as 20 years ago! Environmentalists are already warning against the overgrazing of some areas. Clever smugglers in the border country between the Republic and Ulster came up with yet another source of income: when the government's sheep counters are due, just borrow a herd from the other side.

One industry that was neglected for a long time was **fishing**, and the fishing fleet is visibly ageing. The country's rivers, lakes and bays, by and large still very unpolluted, are an important asset for the economy as well as for tourism. Here, over recent years, more fish farms have been set up, breeding game fish.

Energy

Roughly a third of energy demand is covered by production from hydraulic power and peat, some 60% by imported fossil fuels such as coal and petroleum. The power plant on the River Shannon is the largest of those working on a good number of the country's rivers. Recently, larger offshore wind farms have been set up. The huge bogs covering large parts of Ireland's central plain and the northern, western and southern coastline, provide a seemingly unlimited supply of peat. Peat has always been and still is the main Irish domestic fuel. Since the beginning of industrialization it has been extracted mechanically, but only in 1949 did the government found an organization, Bord na Móna, that took charge of the extraction, processing and use of the peat. Ireland has several power plants that are peat-fired, and it is also used in pellets as a domestic and industrial heating material. For this, peat is ground and pressed by machines. In addition, white peat is increasingly used in gardening. An institute based in Droichead researches peat exploitation, but the environmental costs of exploiting peat are only slowly beginning to dawn on the Irish. Every year, 36 sq km/14 sq miles of bog are destroyed, and the irreversible destruction of the Irish peat bogs is only a matter of time.

Tourism Despite its many ancient art treasures and monuments, picturesque landscape and friendly people, for a long time Ireland stayed a well-kept secret for a small number of travellers who wanted something different. However, by 1988 the government was trying to change this and a five-year plan was issued aiming to significantly improve the tourist infrastructure, both in numbers and in quality. This concept is paying off: whilst in 1987, for instance, 103,000 visitors came to Ireland, by 2006 the number had increased to 8.8 million for the whole island.

Peat cutter at work

The outbreak of the Troubles in Northern Ireland in the late 1960s hit tourism badly. After 25 years of a downhill trend, the mid-1990s marked a turning point. Along the coast in particular, the owners of B&Bs and small rural hotels are looking to attract a well-heeled clientele.

Tourism in Nor thern Ireland

Language

Two Languages

Irish (Gaelic) and English, the country's languages, have equal status in the Republic of Ireland. Irish is the country's official language; civil servants are required to have a degree of proficiency in it, and official documents and road signs are bilingual. In the Irish parliament, the Dáil, deputies (TDs) often start their speeches with a few words of Irish. The language of daily life however is English, a Hiberno-English conserving syntactic and vocabulary elements from the old language.

In some regions, called Gaeltacht, Irish is still the mother tongue of most inhabitants. Various institutions try to keep Irish from dying out. A Gaeltacht ministry is charged with protection of the minority language. Tax breaks and subsidies are in place to support the Gaeltacht areas.

Irish / Gaelic

The Irish language, often called »Gaelic«, belongs to the Celtic language family, and within that family, to the branch of island-Celtic languages. Alongside the Irish, the Gaelic family of languages comprises the Scottish Gaelic, as well as Welsh and Breton, the latter brought over to France by immigrants from the British Isles.

Originally, Celtic was spoken all over the British Isles. Raids by Germanic tribes in the 5th century brought Germanic languages into the region. The English language that developed out of those Germanic languages put so much pressure on the old language that it was only able to survive in remote regions – such as Ireland. From the time of English rule up to the establishment of the independent Republic of Ireland, Irish was more than just a means of communication – it signalled a commitment to national unity. The late 18th century saw a euphoric, often romantically-tinged revival of the Irish language. With increasing Irish confidence, the language gained in importance in terms of culture and history, to the extent that by the end of the 19th century it had become the expression of national identity and autonomy.

History of the language

Ogham Alphabet

From the 4th to the 7th century, the Ogham alphabet (► see diagram) was used for writing. Whilst its sounds are based on the Latin alphabet, the letters are completely different from the Latin script: the characters are points, as well as horizontal lines and slashes arranged in combinations of one to five along a vertical line, often carved into the side of an upright boulder.

Characteristics of the Language

To most people, the Irish language will initially seem completely foreign and unintelligible. There are few parallels to familiar structures or concepts. There is no such thing as High Irish or national standards; the three main regional dialects have equal status. Still, Irish does belong to the large family of Indo-European languages.

Gaeltacht

The areas where the language is spoken are shrinking, despite conscious efforts to preserve Irish over the last 200 years. Between 1851 and 1961, in a matter of about a century, the area where Irish was spoken decreased by nearly 80 per cent. Recent surveys show that only 1.5% of the population use Irish on a daily basis. The number of people living in the Gaeltacht continues to decrease, so that today, only some 35,000 have Irish as their mother tongue. Irish remains compulsory in all schools, but this is currently under threat. In contrast, the 28 secondary schools where teaching is completely or partly in Irish have become much *en vogue* with the upper middle class, who are also choosing to give their children old Irish names (such as Oisín for boys or Niamh for girls) again. In the summer holidays, city kids are bussed to the Gaeltacht areas, staying with families and learning Irish, whilst adults are taught in Irish Colleges. There are also quite a few foreigners – often with Irish ancestry – who enjoy learning the language in the Gaeltacht.

Gaeltacht *Map*

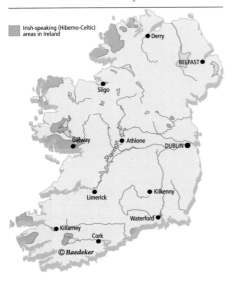

Irish-speaking (Hiberno-Celtic) areas in Ireland

© Baedeker

Religion

Celtic Christianity

Over the course of the 5th century, the Celtic Irish took on the Christian faith. The teachings of the early missionaries St Brendan and St Patrick were adopted without bloodshed; there were no martyrs. Often, whole clans decided to lead the monastic life, the leader founding a monastery and proclaiming himself abbot. His family, followers and charges took his example and submitted to the strict discipline of monastic life. Books of penitence and copies of monastic regulations tell of the hard life in the early monasteries.

Christianization

Alongside a church and cells, monasteries comprised a refectory, guest quarters, a scriptorium and workshops. People from England and the Continent as well as people fleeing the fallout from the great migrations came here. Latin was spoken alongside Gaelic, and the writings of Virgil, Cicero and Ovid read alongside religious texts.

Monasteries

As the faithful were denied the »red martyrdom« (laying down their life), many of them took on the »green martyrdom« of voluntary exile into remote areas. Whilst the hermits of the Middle East retreated into the desert, the Irish chose outlying small islands in the Atlantic that were difficult to reach. Visitors to Ireland can see what such hermitages would have looked like in the 8th-century monastic settlement of Skellig Michael; the tiny churches and stone cells reminiscent of beehives on the top rungs of this bare rock have survived to this day. Alongside the »green« martyrdom, a »white« martyrdom began – the »peregrinatio pro Christo«: leaving your home country behind for Christ. In light wooden boats tarred with animal pelts, Irish monks ventured into the »pathless« sea. Crossing England and France as itinerant penance preachers, they came to numerous European countries. Alongside a strong faith, they brought humanistic learning; in their leather satchels they carried valuable manuscripts and codices (books) that may already have been beautifully illuminated.

Green and white martyrdom

Amongst the saints of the early Celtic church, some personalities stand out, with their names cropping up again and again in Ireland. One of them is the nation's patron saint Patrick, who came to Ireland in 432 and whose life gave rise to numerous legends (►Baedeker Special p.34).

Irish saints

◄ Patrick

In 490, Saint Enda was one of the first to retreat to a remote and lonely place to dedicate his life as a hermit to study and renunciation. Soon, numerous students followed him to the Aran Island of Inishmór, establishing a large monastic settlement there. Its fame reached across the sea to the European continent.

◄ Enda

SAINT PATRICK

Ireland is said to be the only country where conversion to Christianity was not accompanied by bloodshed. This peaceful Christianization was by and large the work of Saint Patrick, apostle and patron saint of Ireland.

Ireland's patron saint was born in what is today Kilpatrick in Scotland, the son of a deacon. When Patrick was 16, he was captured by pirates and sold as a slave to Ireland, where he worked as a shepherd. After six years, he managed to escape and flee back to his home country. There, a vision commanded him to convert Ireland to the Christian faith. It is thought that Patrick received part of his teaching on the Mediterranean Lerins Islands off Cannes. There, he would have met representatives of Eastern faiths and been introduced to the idea of »religio arctior« (the hardest asceticism). In 432 Patrick returned as bishop to the island where he had been held captive, founding a string of schools, churches and monasteries. Establishing his episcopal see in Armagh, he managed to persuade many of the Celtic tribal lords and kings, together with their subjects, to take on the Christian faith. When Patrick died, the whole of Ireland was Christianized. Many legends surround the most successful missionary in Ireland.

St Patrick's Day

The cult of St Patrick is part of the Irish identity. Since the 17th century at the latest, St Patrick's Day has been celebrated on 17 March. It is said that wherever in the world three Irish

Standing at the foot of Croagh Patrick, the luminous white statue of Saint Patrick on a grey stone plinth marks the beginning of the pilgrimage path.

people live together, they will celebrate this feast day. In New York, the day is celebrated with a big parade on 5th Avenue. The Dublin parade attracts around 250,000 people each year, and there are smaller events all over the country. In the countryside, the pace is slower: with maybe just a ribbon or shamrock pinned to the lapel.

Pilgrimages

Every year, on the last Sunday in July, tens of thousands of people – some of them barefoot! – climb the rocky summit of Croagh Patrick. This mountain is said to be the site of a 40-day penance the saint undertook in 411. The bare quartzite cone with its sharp scree on steep slopes makes the climb hard work. People go on their own or in groups. The pilgrimage, involving school classes, sports clubs, military units, non-Catholics as well as foreigners, is not exactly an orderly affair.

Station Island in Lough Derg (Co. Donegal) near the border with Northern Ireland is also the site of an important pilgrimage. Back in pagan times, a cave on this island was thought to be the entrance to the underworld. The cave went on to become famous all over medieval Europe as »St Patrick's Purgatory«, the site where St Patrick is thought to have had a vision of Purgatory after 40 days of fasting. Erasmus, Rabelais, Dante and Calderón took inspiration from reports of visions of hell glimpsed there. This »hardest pilgrimage in Christendom« is undertaken between mid-June and mid-August nearly exclusively by the Irish. Alongside mass and prayers during their three days' stay on the island, the pilgrims have to perform numerous penances, mainly consisting in vigils and fasting. During the time of year when pilgrimages take place, the island may only be visited by the faithful.

Ciarán ► Of those men who came to join Enda, many went on to found monasteries themselves. One of those was St Ciarán, who settled in 548 on the Shannon. ► Clonmacnoise, which to this day continues to leave visitors spellbound, was soon called »University of the West« thanks to its monks' growing erudition.

Kevin ► St Kevin, born around the year 618, chose the hermit's life, retreating into the mountains and forests of Wicklow. His monastery in ► Glendalough went on to draw a large number of students, being equal in size and prominence to Clonmacnoise.

Brigid ► Amongst the women, St Brigid is the most important. Born around 453 in Faugher in the north of Ireland, in 490 she founded a large double monastery for monks and nuns in Kildare. Following a pre-Christian ritual, the eternal flame that burned in her Fire House was only extinguished during the time of the Reformation. Today still, St Brigid's Crosses woven from straw or rushes can be found in many Irish houses, as well as in cars and tractors, as a protective symbol.

Brendan ► St Brendan first founded a monastery in Clonfert, which was to attract many monks (► Ballinasloe), around the year 560. This saint became an inspiration for all who left their home to become a missionary and ventured out to sea, with an unknown destination (►Famous People).

Columba
the Elder ► Columba the Elder (521 or 543–597), called Columcille (»dove of the churches«), was, like St Kevin, of royal descent. He caused his own exile; born in Gartan in Ireland, Columba had secretly copied a book of psalms belonging to St Finian, who jealously guarded his books and claimed the copy for himself alone. As the two men could not come to an amicable agreement, Finian took the argument to the High King. The king ruled in favour of Finian, saying that a copy belonged with the book as a calf belongs to the cow. However, Columba and his followers were not prepared to accept the ruling, and Benbulben Mountain, north of Sligo, became the site of their fight with the king. Columba's victory resulted in the death of 3,000 people. In order to do penance for these deaths, Columba left his home country. Landing in 563 with twelve companions on the Hebridean island of Hy (today Iona), he founded a monastery there that became the base for his missionary activities. Despite his rigid faith, Columcille is said to have been a likeable person who loved nature, and animals in particular.

Columba
the Younger ► Columba the Younger, also called Saint Columbanus, was born in 540. He lived as a pupil of Comgall in the famous monastery of Bangor. Only when he had reached the age of 50 did Columba set off on a missionary voyage to the continent, taking twelve companions with him. At the Burgundy court, he became very influential, founding the monasteries of Annegrey and Luxueil. Columba is described as being strong in faith and charismatic, but also as irascible. Following a falling-out with the Burgundy king, Columba went up the Rhine via Lake Constance and the Alps to Italy, founding his last monastery in Italy and dying in Bobbio in 615. Through his monastic founda-

tions, Columba acquired followers all over Europe. His monastic rules were a decisive influence on occidental monasticism.

Some Irish missionaries, who were active abroad, are less known in their home country. Their tonsure – on the forehead rather than at the back of the head as was the custom in Europe – as well as their language, distinguished them from the other monks. They carried books with them in leather pouches and founded famous monasteries.

Irish missionarie

Gallus, one of Columba's companions, stayed at Lake Constance. The former monastery of St Gallen owns a number of beautiful manuscripts from the heyday of Irish book illumination.

Later, when the Vikings were already ravaging the island, Irish monks could be found as renowned scholars at many courts in Europe. »Irish« (»Scotus«) became an honorary title. Clemens Scotus followed Alcuin as head of the famous palace school at the court of Charlemagne, where Dicuil (grammarian, geographer and astronomer) was teaching too. Sedulius Scotus, a high-ranking scientist, came to Cologne via Metz. John Scotus Eriugena (»born in Ireland«), a towering mind of his era, belonged to the court of Charles II (the Bald) around 845.

Monks in science

The influence of Hiberno-Scottish missionaries extended far east, as evidenced by the **Scots monasteries** of Regensburg, Vienna and Kiev. The Irish church started early in passing on its faith and knowledge to other countries. The monasteries they founded became »repositories of the past and cradles of the future«.

Church and Popular Faith

No other people in Europe have so held on to the **tradition of their faith** – despite or maybe because of the religious strife of past centuries. As long as Catholics were banned from religious practice, the faithful celebrated Mass in secret, often outdoors at hidden rocks (Mass Rocks). Young men wanting to go for the priesthood had to travel ab-

Not an uncommon sight: a picture of the pope in a pub window

road for training and ordination, to France or Spain. And once the construction of churches was allowed again, they were initially only allowed to be built in inconspicuous side streets.

Influence of the church

Today, the influence of the Catholic church, which around 92% of the population profess to belong to, is evident in all areas of Irish life. On a Sunday, the many churches holding Mass are full to the brim, and saints remain popular as Christian names. Couples get married in church in the presence of extended family; there are very few registry office weddings. Divorce has only been legal since 1995, and abortion in Ireland is only possible when the life of the mother is in danger; at a referendum conducted in November 1992 (and confirmed in 2002), the majority voted for freedom of information in matters of abortion and the freedom to travel of pregnant women, but rejected any amendment of the core legislation.

Clergy

In large Irish families there was often a son or daughter who would decide to join the clergy or a religious order. Priests are still an integral part of Irish daily life, and clerics and nuns from Ireland can be found all over the developing world working as teachers, nurses and in other social sectors. The ethics of Christian welfare dominate daily life in Ireland, but these positive aspects have had a dark side too: censorship, for instance, used to be so strict that writers such as James Joyce or Sean O'Casey turned their backs on their home country. Until recently, the influence of the Catholic Church dominated the entire cultural sector. However, since the mid-1990s, the number of young men who train for the priesthood has decreased starkly. The rapid decline of the Catholic Church in Ireland is due in no small part to scandals such as the one involving Bishop Casey from Galway, who had to admit to fathering an illegitimate child.

❓ DID YOU KNOW …?

■ St Patrick is said to have explained the Trinity using the shamrock – today the Irish national symbol that visitors will encounter at every step: on jumpers and postcards, made from fur, plastic or yeast dough, as flowers and much more. For the national holiday on 17 March, St Patrick's Day, many Irish pin a shamrock to their lapel.

Knock

Knock in County Mayo, site of an apparition of the Virgin Mary in the last century, draws many pilgrims. Of the many sick coming to look for a cure, few are from abroad.

Pattern Day

Alongside the major pilgrimages, several local feast days are celebrated in the honour of a saint's anniversary (Pattern Day). For instance, on Inisheer, the smallest of the Aran Islands, every year on 14th June, the local population gather together in order to dig out the church of St Cavan, which is under constant threat of being engulfed by the sand dunes, and celebrate Mass there.

At many road intersections, Lourdes grottoes have been set up or built into the rock. Occasionally the visitor might stumble across wells with rosaries and coins, but also items of daily life placed on the ground around them. Bits of clothing are hung on shrubs or wooden posts standing close to each other. The water of such holy wells is credited with curative powers for certain diseases.

Holy wells

In the same way that monks were the first to write down the ancient folk tales, helping to preserve them, the Celtic church tolerated animist concepts. In Ireland, part of the »half-world of the spirits« were the »Sidhe« (fairies), dwelling in tree-covered hills, whilst the »leprechauns«, or »little people«, live under hawthorn bushes. According to popular belief in the West of Ireland, cutting down a hawthorn bush would carry dire consequences. A black animal called »Pooka« frightens lonely wanderers, and the wailing call of the »banshee« announces the impending death of a relative of a long-established local family.

Belief in spirits

History

It is not just with its Neolithic remains that Ireland puts visitors in touch with their ancestors. The Irish, symbol of peaceful Christianization in Europe, were themselves again and again overrun by violent waves of conquest, from the north as well as by the »arch enemy« England.

Prehistory and Antiquity

Humans Between Ice and Sea, Stone and Metal

6600 BC	First settlements in County Derry (Londonderry)
3500 BC	Wave of migration brings agriculture to Ireland, cairns and passage tombs appear
1750 BC	Metallurgy blossoms
400 BC	Conquest by the Celtic Gaels, rise of Tara to a political and cultural centre
from 300 AD	Ireland extends its influence to Wales and Scotland

Ice and stone ...

During the Ice Age, the whole of Ireland was covered in ice, making the region uninhabitable. Only with the melting of the glaciers did people, animals and plants from Scotland start arriving across the land bridge that still existed at the time. Around 6600 BC, the inhabitants of the first settlements in County Derry lived off hunting and fishing.

Some 3,000 years later, a new wave of migration brought **agriculture** to the land. Alongside wood, stone became an important material, as evidenced by stone axes, house foundations and the famous cairn and passage tombs.

? DID YOU KNOW ...?

■ Druids were Celtic priests who forecast the future, cured the sick, read the stars and sat in judgment. They were held in great esteem by the common people. The word »druid« comes from the Gaelic, meaning »the one who knows the oak«. In today's Ireland, only a few keep the memory of the Celtic rites alive, congregating in secret at dusk to say pre-Christian masses.

Mineral resources

Once, Ireland was rich in mineral resources. Gold, silver, and copper deposits enabled metallurgy to flourish from 1750 to 500 BC, with the necessary know-how brought to the island by migrants. The half-moon shaped »torc« collar became a popular export all over Europe.

Celts

The Celts owed their victory over the Irish to their better military equipment, their iron weapons proving superior to the Irish bronze swords and shields. From 400 BC, the Gaels, a Celtic tribe, started to subjugate almost the whole island. For nearly 800 years, Celtic culture dominated the country, with High Kings ruling over 150 king-

← *Ardmore monastery, with one of the most beautiful round towers in Europe*

doms, grouped together in provinces. During this time, Tara rose to be a centre of political power and the arts, ring forts secured the country, and druids, priests and legal scholars were held in high esteem.

Romans For centuries, it was claimed that the Romans never set foot on Ireland (as opposed to England). Archaeological finds, however, disprove this; settlers from the Roman province of Britannia did come to Ireland, gaining a foothold in some places near the coast. Whilst the Roman influence stayed limited both in duration and in geographical extent, after the fall of the Roman Empire, from AD 300 onwards, Ireland was able to extend its influence to Wales and Scotland.

Christians

from 432	Christianization by St Patrick
461	Death of St Patrick, Ireland is Catholic
from 500	Irish missionaries are active on the European continent

Pirates and saints It was a pirate raid that made Ireland one of the most Catholic countries in the world – the kidnapping of St Patrick. (► Baedeker Special, p.34) The kidnapping gave rise to the Christianization of Ireland; St Patrick's main achievement was to peacefully convert the Celtic chieftains and to integrate pre-Christian myths, customs and structures into Christian daily life.

»Scots« By the time of St Patrick's death in 461, the entire island had been converted to Christianity (► Religion, Christianization). Over subsequent centuries Ireland developed its own characteristic religious institutions and customs. Monasteries were established on the basis of Celtic tribal structures and headed by abbots of noble birth. The country experienced peaceful times, staying untouched by enemy incursions as well as by the developments of the Roman-Catholic church. Keeping their maxim of non-violent proselytizing, the Irish took their faith first to Northern England and Scotland, later on also to the Continent, where they were often erroneously called »Scots«. Their ecclesiastical foundations are today still called »Scots« churches or monasteries. The most famous Irish monasteries were established in St Gallen, Luxeuil, Bobbio, Regensburg and Vienna.

This lavishly decorated bell shrine said to belong to Saint Patrick is kept in the National Museum in Dublin

Medieval to Modern Times

»Norsemen«

from 800	Raids by Norwegian Vikings
from 840	The Vikings establish settlements
1014	Viking rule ends with the Battle of Clontarf
1172	Henry II of England claims Ireland
till 1250	The Normans conquer the country
1366	Statutes of Kilkenny: the Irish language and intermarriage between Irish and Anglo-Irish are banned

Around 800, the northern Irish coast saw frequent raids by Norwegian Vikings. The very belligerent and violent »Norsemen« first founded settlements in Ireland in 840. Of particular strategic importance were the estuaries on the east coast; Dublin, Wexford and Waterford, for instance, were founded by Vikings. From there, they sailed up the rivers, sowing fear and terror amongst the monasteries in particular, and slowly conquering the interior of the country. However, the monasteries were not just plundered by the Vikings, but also by the equally greedy Celtic tribal lords. Over time, the Vikings settled and converted to Christianity, whilst the Irish adopted improvements in shipbuilding, the military use of fleet and cavalry, as well as monetary commerce. As the tribal lords lost influence and the regional lords gained, a power struggle for domination of the country broke out. In 1014, Brian Boru led an army against the Vikings in the legendary battle of Clontarf. His victory, whilst paid for with his life, marked the end of the Viking era in Ireland. **Viking influence**

The subjugation of Ireland under Anglo-Norman rule was a political coup for the Vatican; the independence of the Irish monasteries had long been a thorn in the side of Rome. After the Cluniac reforms had tightened ecclesiastical hierarchies all over Europe and strengthened the influence of the pope on the monasteries, in the early 12th century they came to Ireland too, implementing new architectural styles and a new ecclesiastical philosophy. In order to tie the Irish church quickly and more permanently to Rome, the pope gave the English king Henry II the right to reform it, and thus the opportunity to intervene in Ireland. In 1172, Henry II had the pope confirm his authority over the Irish. **Between London and Rome**

In 1066, under William the Conqueror, the Normans had taken power in England. From 1169 onwards, they used Wales as a base to carry out raids in Ireland. Yet again, the Irish were defeated due to their inferior armoury, facing the Norman sword fighters and ar- **Anglo-Normans**

chers – kitted out in chain mail and iron helmets – in cotton tunics, wielding axes and stone slings.

By 1250, the Normans had conquered 75 % of the country. Imposing fortresses secured their rule, many new settlements were established, as well as churches and monasteries in the new Hiberno-Romanesque style. The arrival of the mendicant and preaching orders gave the church a new lease of life, founding the church's common touch that still endures today.

Within just 150 years, the Normans were nearly completely assimilated in Ireland. Fearing a loss of power, in 1366 England tried to secure its influence with the Statutes of Kilkenny, strictly banning mixed marriages and the Irish language.
Anglo-Irish

However, as England was busy dealing with political strife within and outside the country, it could not implement these segregation laws. The Anglo-Irish thus gained a large degree of autonomy, with the English influence from then on limited to small areas.

England's crown – England's whip

1541	Henry VIII becomes King of Ireland, implements the Reformation and dissolves some 400 monasteries
1607	Battle of Kinsale: the Catholics are defeated by the Protestants; the leaders leave the country.
till 1641	»Plantations«: lands are transferred to English ownership; resistance forms in the Confederation of Kilkenny
1649	Cromwell puts a bloody end to Irish resistance
1691	The Battle of the Boyne ends the bloody war of succession fought between James II and William III of Orange in Ireland
1695	»Penal laws«: Catholics lose their civil rights
1699	Economic and political colonization: installation of a viceroy, export bans
1769	Insurrection attempts fail, despite Spanish and French support.
1801	Act of Union: Ireland becomes part of the United Kingdom and no longer has a separate parliament.

Only with the beginning of Henry VIII's violent reign did England, from 1534 onwards, put its sights on Ireland again. Henry VIII crowned himself King of Ireland in 1541, introducing the Reformation and dissolving some 400 monasteries.
Henry VIII

← *The Irish were no match for the Normans with their superior battle gear.*

HOPE AT LAST

The events of spring 2007 in Belfast would have been completely unthinkable only a year before: Ian Paisley, the white-haired veteran leader of the Protestant Democratic Unionist Party, who had sworn he would »never negotiate with terrorists«, and Martin McGuinness of the Sinn Féin party, one of those very »terrorists«, took office at Stormont as equal heads of the government of Northern Ireland. Two former mortal enemies seemed to have made peace at last.

Early days: Cromwell

This historic moment possibly, hopefully, marked the end of a conflict that lasted nearly 40 years, costing over 3,600 lives and injuring over 30,000 people. The roots of the conflict date back to the 17th century, when, from 1610 onwards under the Stuart mo-

Every year, the Orange Order organizes a parade in honour of the Protestant king William of Orange, who defeated the Catholics on 12 July 1690, at the Battle of the Boyne

narchs and Oliver Cromwell, the »plantations« were mercilessly pushed ahead. Through the resettlement of predominantly Scottish Presbyterians, Ulster became a bastion of British rule in Ireland. In the struggle for the English crown between the Catholic James II and the Protestant William of Orange, the Catholics saw their chance and in 1689 laid siege to the Protestants in Derry for 105 days – in vain. The slogan given out at the time by the Orangemen, the supporters of William – »No surrender!« – can still be heard today, in particular every year in August in Derry (Londonderry) commemorating the »Relief of Derry«, and on 12 July to celebrate the victory at the Battle of the Boyne in 1691. With this victory, the Orangemen sealed their subjugation of the Irish-Catholic population, implementing their military success politically through the »penal laws« that barred Catholics from public

The occupation of the General Post Office in Dublin on 24 April 1916, Easter Sunday, was the start of the »Easter Rising« against British rule – and was to cost some 450 people their lives

other things. From then on, peaceful coexistence was no longer a real option; rebellions and unrest on the part of the Catholic Irish were violently put down.

Parallel Societies

In the North, a deep gulf separated the two religions, hatred and violence soon gaining the upper hand over peaceful coexistence. When the Irish **Home Rule movement** steered towards a separate state, the Protestant Northern Irish refused to accept the 1921 Anglo-Irish treaty, fearful of being swamped in a Catholic-dominated united Ireland and the loss of their strong economic position. In Northern Ireland (covering six of the historic counties of Ulster), the Protestants' strategy was to keep strong ties with the British mother country, marginalizing Catholics. Restrictions in the labour and housing market, and a law that tied voting rights in local elections to property ownership and tax revenue (»gerrymandering«) put the Catholics at a clear disadvantage. A Protestant and a Catholic society formed, where members of the one could live and work without ever having anything to do with the other side – unless they wanted to. In which case, however, any discussion

of political hot potatoes was avoided: »Whatever you say, say nothing.«, as poet Seamus Heaney put it.

Irish against Irish

Northern Ireland turned into a political and diplomatic issue. The Republic of Ireland felt obliged to come to the rescue of co-religionists in the North and to uphold the doctrine of a

»Whatever you say, say nothing.«

united Ireland that was enshrined in the constitution, whereas the United Kingdom supported, helped and protected its province. Whilst there were talks in the 1950s and 1960s, no settlement was reached. Both sides retreated to their respective positions and gave political, financial and military support to their own. The **»troubles«** were the bitter consequence.

Bloody Sunday

When, in the 1960s, the ideas of the international civil rights movement started to be discussed, they found fertile ground in the Catholic neighbourhoods. Voicing the demand »one man, one vote«, peaceful demonstrators gathered for the first time on 24 March 1967 in Dungannon. The

Riots in Belfast following the death of IRA activist and elected member of the British parliament Bobby Sands, who died on 5 May 1981 after a 66-day hunger strike

second protest march on 5 October in Derry was, however, brutally put down by police. On 14 August 1969, after further demonstrations had escalated into ever more bloody violence, bringing near-civil war to the streets of Northern Ireland, London sent over troops. The soldiers were initially welcomed by the Catholics as a neutral protecting power. This perception soon changed, after »Bloody Sunday« at the latest, when on 30 January 1972 paratroopers shot dead 13 unarmed participants in a Catholic demonstration. »Bloody Sunday« marked a turning point, in every way: for most Catholics, the British army was now the enemy, whilst moderate Protestants revised their views and demanded a tough stance. Most of all, however, the event radicalized young men on both sides, who joined the paramilitaries...

An Eye for an Eye

...who had regrouped, or were revived, from 1969 onwards, most prominently, the Catholic Irish Republican Army. The IRA inflicted a series of bombings and shootings on Northern Ireland, targeting civilians, military personnel and public institutions, eventually extending their campaign to London and even attempting to kill prime minister Margaret Thatcher. The British govern-

ment tried to counter the IRA terror by house searches and arrests, and, from August 1971 onwards, by interning suspects without trial. This provided the IRA with a ready-made propaganda tool. In 1981, some IRA prisoners started a hunger strike, demanding better conditions. When Bobby Sands died on 5 May 1981 after 66 days without taking food, the hunger strike campaign had its first victim – and the IRA a martyr. Nine more prisoners were to starve themselves to death before the action was called off in October 1981.

Whilst the Catholic paramilitaries aimed their attacks predominantly at the representatives and institutions of British rule (accepting the death of civilians as a necessary evil), the violence of the Protestant groups – Ulster Volunteer Force (UVF), Ulster Defence Association (UDA) and Ulster Freedom Fighters (UFF) – was aimed at Catholics, many of whom they accused of being members of the IRA. Alongside targeted killings, bomb attacks against Catholic pubs were a favourite strategy.

No End to Violence and Hatred

One attack would trigger another attack, one bombing another bombing. The violence had permeated daily life in the province – walls cutting straight through streets, metal

*Republican demand:
»Free Ireland«*

shutters put in place to keep bombs away from pubs and shops, helicopters patrolling the sky, roadblocks and armed patrols – and eventually gained its own tragic momentum. Nearly every Northern Irish person was affected by the »troubles«, numbering a victim in their family or circle of friends and acquaintances, until more and more Northern Irish, whether Catholic or Protestant, had had enough of the violence. The new thinking found expression in **Betty Williams and Mairead Corrigan**, the founders of the Community of Peace People, who, in 1976, were awarded the Nobel Peace Prize.

A new thinking also began to gain ground at state level: in the mid-1980s, when talks at the highest political level initiated a process of understanding, leading, in 1985, to a British-Irish agreement. This allowed Dublin a limited say in Northern Ireland – against the will of the hardliners. Fighting terrorism became a task to be shared, as the years 1991 and 1993 were marred by Protestant paramilitary murders and IRA bombs. In 1994, after 25 years, the **ceasefire agreement** marked the beginning of a process of change. The **Good Friday Agreement** of 1998 is considered a milestone, giving Northern Ireland semi-autonomous status, as well as the Nobel Peace Prize to the main

movers behind the scenes, **David Hume** and **David Trimble**. From that moment onwards, Northern Ireland politics became a constant rollercoaster between hope and fear. In 2001, the Northern Irish First Minister Trimble stepped down, as there was renewed violence and the IRA refused to hand over their weapons. In 2002, the British government suspended Northern Irish self-government. In 2003, regional elections were postponed; however, after the IRA had declared the end of the armed struggle in July 2005, handing in their weapons in September of that year, the negotiations started to get moving. Since 2007, a Northern Irish parliament has been sitting at Stormont once again, and the two former mortal enemies, Ian Paisley and Martin McGuinness, jointly lead the government of the province. Whilst some wounds will never heal, the future is looking brighter for Northern Ireland.

Flight of the Earls In subsequent years, the Irish made several unsuccessful attempts to shake off the English yoke, finding support with anti-English and counter-Reformation forces on the Continent.

The decisive Battle of Kinsale however was won by the English. In 1607, after the subjugation of even more provinces, the leaders of the insurrections left the country. The »Flight of the Earls« has since become a symbol of defeat, but also a symbol of choosing emigration over a life without freedom.

Plantations The English strategy of plantations marked the beginning of a creeping colonization. Large estates were given to English and Scottish settlers. As the owners often preferred to stay in their English homelands, they installed agents on their new estates. Pushing for maximum profits, the absentee landlords rented out the land to Irish farmers for high rents but showed little inclination to invest any money. Over the coming centuries, this system was to drag Ireland down until it became the poorhouse of Europe.

Cromwell Up until 1641, about 75 % of the land was still in Irish hands. Then, political and religious resistance formed in the Confederation of Kilkenny. These insurrections and revolts challenged the English to take a hard line. In 1649 Cromwell came to Ireland with 12,000 men, putting a bloody end to the resistance. In the following years, Cromwell ruthlessly implemented the plantations and confiscations, with the fertile northeast in particular coming under English rule. Within a few years, by 1665, the Irish only owned 25% of the land. In most cases, the Catholics' lands were restricted to small pockets in remote areas in the West of Ireland.

Jacobites and Orangemen The trigger for the final colonization of Ireland was the succession dispute between James II and William III of Orange. The Catholic Scot James had been driven from the English throne by his Protestant son-in-law. Following this, James left his French exile in 1689 to take an army to Ireland, which called William III into action in 1690. Led by Patrick Sarsfield, the Catholic Irish supported James II, resisting the Protestant Orangemen until 1691. After the Protestants' victory at the Battle of the Boyne, the Treaty of Limerick was negotiated, designed to grant Ireland freedom of religion. However, this apparent success proved deceptive, as the treaty was never ratified by the English parliament. The majority of Irish people were soon to feel the effect of the defeat through the full force of the new anti-Catholic discrimination laws, as they lost their rights and became second-class citizens.

Colonization and revolts By 1695, the »penal laws« were in force, banning Catholics from having their own schools and universities, from voting or holding higher office as well as from bearing arms. In the years to come, these segregation laws were implemented with the utmost rigidity.

Meanwhile, Irish culture, religion and traditions survived underground, strengthening the sense of national identity.

However, in the 18th century neither Catholics nor Protestants were prepared to just stand by and watch Ireland's decline. The Anglo-Irish Patriotic Party was propagating the model of an Irish-English dual monarchy and a relaxation of the anti-Catholic laws. Inspired by the autonomy movements of the American and French Revolution, the United Irishmen formed, under Wolfe Tone. When, in 1769, the French and Spanish wanted to lend armed support, the landing of their troops was foiled by the rough Irish Sea. England's reaction was unequivocal: with the »Act of Union«, Ireland became part of the United Kingdom for good, and the parliament in Dublin, which had shown itself to be independent- minded, was dissolved.

Wolfe Tone

Resistance and Foundation of a New State

The Fight for Survival

1829	Anti-Catholic laws repealed after mass protests led by O'Connell
1845–1849	Potato blight leading to the Great Famine; around one million Irish starve to death, another million emigrate
1870	»Home Rule« movement led by Charles Stewart Parnell
1880	First »boycott«; isolation of the English agent Boycott

Over the following years, Irish resistance carried on unbroken, finding charismatic leaders in Robert Emmet and Daniel O'Connell. The founder of the Catholic Association in 1823, O'Connell used »monster meetings« to call for non-violent protest. In 1829, unable to continue resisting this pressure, England repealed the anti-Catholic laws. O'Connell became the first Catholic to take a seat in the English parliament, while a revival of Irish arts and culture boosted the country's sense of national identity. However, this political and cultural success did little to improve the daily life for the majority of Ireland's impoverished rural population.

First steps

However, the biggest blow to Ireland was dealt not by wars, colonialism or repression, but by the potato blight that struck across Europe in the mid-19th century. In Ireland, the impact of the pest was devastating, leading, in 1845–49 to a massive famine.

Potato blight

Underlying this desperate situation was terrible poverty, exacerbated by English mismanagement: Irish leaseholders were pushed from the fertile east to the barren west while English estate owners switched much of the agricultural land to pastures, exporting grain and cattle to England on a large scale. Irish farmers were so poor that their diet was almost exclusively potato-based, complemented by milk or fish only on rare occasions. The potato blight therefore hit them extremely hard. By the mid-19th century, Ireland's population had nearly doubled; large families in particular were facing destitution. Potatoes were rotting on the stem, and several consecutive harvests were spoilt. Around one million people starved to death, while another million emigrated. Ireland continues to feel the effect of the loss to this day.

Invention of the »boycott« The fallout from the European revolutions of 1848 also reached Ireland, where several secret societies and political factions were founded. The protest movement even spread to the rural population: in 1880, their anger found a target in an English agent called Boycott (► Captain Boycott, Lough Corrib, Lough Mask), who despite terrible harvests insisted on collecting inflated rent from his tenant farmers. Boycott was faced down and the English government was forced to agree to land reform.

Home Rule The era of large estate owners was coming to an end. In 1869, discriminatory laws against the Catholic Church were also repealed. The call for Irish autonomy was becoming louder, and in 1870 became organized as the Home Rule movement under the leadership of Charles Stewart Parnell (► Famous People). As leader of the Irish Parliamentary Party, Parnell was able to push through land and social reform at Westminster. The northeastern province of Ulster,

Connemara – at the time of the Great Hunger

however, was strictly opposed to the reforms and Republican aims and wanted to remain part of the United Kingdom instead.

Before Parnell's private life embroiled him in media mud-slinging in 1890, the parliamentarian reformer carried the hopes of independence on his shoulders. His fall paved the way for more radical and nationalist factions, who rejected parliamentarianism.

Towards the Republic

1914	»Home Rule« suspended for the Protestant province of Ulster
1916	Easter Rising brutally quashed by British troops
1918	Election victory for banned Sinn Féin party
1920	Establishment of two Irish parliaments in Dublin and Belfast
1921	Ireland – excluding Northern Ireland – becomes a Free State; end of British colonial rule

The six northern counties continued to reject the »Home Rule« legislation and therefore, in 1914, these laws were suspended for six years for the majority Protestant areas. After the religious, economic and social divisions of past centuries, Northern Ireland commenced its political breakaway.

Northern Ireland breaks aways

The northern counties remained on the periphery of political developments up to 1920. In contrast with the rest of the country, their stated goal was to remain in the United Kingdom, rather than independence. The police tolerated the supply of arms to Northern Ireland, provoking the formation of the Irish Volunteers in 1913.

For Ireland, the outbreak of the First World War initially meant a pause in the fight for national self-determination. The Irish did not want to stab England in the back when the country was busy fighting a war. However, the various factions, parties and brotherhoods were becoming more radical, with their different philosophies and goals hampering the emergence of a united leadership. In Easter 1916, a badly organized revolt broke out: the »Easter Rising«. The Irish Republicans had already made a pact with Germany: Irish prisoners of war were to side with the Germans. In exchange, Germany would supply the revolution in Ireland with modern weaponry. The Germans did indeed send a shipload of arms to Ireland, but the *Aud* sank for reasons still unknown today; most probably the ship was sunk by the British. Without these weapons the Irish stood no chance and Britain brutally quashed the revolt.

The road to the Republic

Most of the leaders of the Easter Rising were executed, among them Patrick Pearse and James Connolly, shot in a wheelchair because he couldn't stand up. Eamon de Valera, who was born in America, was only spared because of confusion about his citizenship. Other participants of the rising were arrested. However, the executed leaders of the insurrection became idols of the independence movement, which reasserted its goals in the face of violence used by the British. In this sense, the Easter Rising meant the beginning of the end of British rule in Ireland.

Civil war The 1918 elections were won by the banned Sinn Féin party. However, the party's deputies refused to take their seats in Westminster, setting up an Irish national assembly in Dublin instead. Not prepared to accept this affront, London again tried to intervene using force. Compounded by bloody clashes in Northern Ireland, the situation escalated into civil war. In 1920, with victory by military means appearing impossible, England caved in and established two Irish parliaments: one in Dublin, another in Belfast. In 1921, a treaty gave Ireland the status of a Free State. This spelled the end of British colonial rule, but at a price: the isolation of Northern Ireland, which remains an open wound to this day.

The Young Republic

1937	Constitution makes Ireland a de facto republic
1939–1945	In World War II, Ireland remains neutral; air raids on Belfast
1949	Proclamation of the Republic of Ireland (ROI)
1955	ROI joins the United Nations (UN)
1968	Start of the »Troubles«, unrest in Northern Ireland
1973	ROI joins the European Union (EU)
1993 onwards	Peace initiatives for Northern Ireland
1998	Good Friday Agreement: semi-autonomous status for Northern Ireland
1999	ROI changes its constitution, renouncing its claim on Northern Ireland
2000	Ongoing efforts to bring peace to Northern Ireland
2004	Review of the Good Friday Agreement by the Irish and British governments
2006	The IRA announces an end to its armed struggle.
2007	Northern Ireland parliament reinstated at Stormont

De Valera The politician Eamon de Valera became the father of Ireland's statehood and neutrality (►Famous People). President of the illegal parliament and leader of the Sinn Féin party as early as 1919, de Valera was to shape the young republic as its prime minister and president, amongst other roles, until 1973. Rejecting violence as a means of achieving a united Ireland, de Valera founded the Fianna Fáil party in 1926. Fianna Fáil (»Soldiers of Fate«) and the Fine Gael party

(»Family of the Irish«), founded in 1933, were to shape the history of 20th-century Ireland. When de Valera took office as prime minister in 1932, he was an advocate of severing most ties with Britain. His main contribution was the drafting of a constitution that effectively made Ireland a republic.

The outbreak of the Second World War hindered its implementation: Ireland, strictly neutral, kept out of the war. Belfast though, due to its strategic shipyards and port, became the target of German air raids, whilst numerous Northern Irish fought on the side of the Allies.

After effectively breaking away from Great Britain, Ireland took the final official steps towards independence by proclaiming the Republic and leaving the Commonwealth in 1949. In the same year, the British »Ireland Act« sealed the special relationship between the two countries, cementing Northern Ireland's status as part of the United Kingdom, whilst at the same time allowing citizens of the Republic unrestricted entry to Britain.

»Special relationship«

The election of women to the office of president brought a new dynamic to Irish politics: Mary Robinson was elected in 1990, and succeeded by Mary McAleese, who was born in Northern Ireland. Mary Robinson pushed through social improvements, worked on behalf of Irish emigrants and marginalized communities such as gays and lesbians, and took the first steps towards a resolution of the conflict in Northern Ireland. Negotiations during her term of office brought about an IRA ceasefire from 1994 to 1996. A rapid succession of prime ministers in the 1990s mired the country in bugging and corruption scandals. Since 1997, Bertie Ahern, »Taoiseach« and head of the government, has been working towards resolving the conflict in Northern Ireland. With the changing of the constitution in 1999, the Republic renounced its claim to Northern Ireland, enabling the implementation of the 1998 Good Friday Agreement. A social pact was agreed to ease the worst social ills and tackle poverty. In 2006 the IRA announced an end to its armed struggle. In 2007 the Northern Ireland parliament reinstated at Stormont **under the Unionist first minister Ian Paisley and the Republican deputy first minister Martin McGuinness**.

Women against scandals

Ireland remains a conservative, Catholic country, where the two main political parties have only recently been forced to share power with smaller parties. However, political polarization is weakening and change is coming to the north: in a very short time, Ireland has become a modern country.

From past to present

Arts and Culture

Ireland possesses a wealth of treasures from pre-Christian times; flourishing Celtic art and culture reached a peak in Ireland. From tombs, High Crosses, monasteries and castles to illuminated manuscripts and literature: the breadth of Irish art and culture delights every visitor.

Art History

In Ireland, Celtic art and culture flourished in a way unrivalled else-where in the world. The island remained largely untouched by Ro-man influences, meaning that today's visitors find Celtic monasteries and High Crosses, metalwork and book illuminations of unique beauty here. However, through a lack of patrons and art-loving ru-lers, nothing similar has been achieved since the Middle Ages. From the 18th century onwards, the wealthy Anglo-Irish classes did leave their mark with classical country castles and »Georgian Houses«. However, while in most European countries such buildings were al-tered several times, in Ireland they mostly remained untouched – of-ten there was simply not the money. Many ruins have been left as they stand, although in recent years some churches and castles have been restored and revived.

Pre-Christian Period

During the Stone Age (c7000–2000 BC) megalithic tombs, shaped from large rough boulders, sprang up all over the island. Dolmens are some of the earliest megalithic tombs: several upright boulders form a narrow space covered by an extremely heavy cap stone, its lo-wer end sloping downwards towards the back end of the burial chamber. One of the largest dolmens can be admired in the grounds of Browne's Hill near Carlow.

Megalithic tombs
◄ Dolmens

Passage tombs feature a passage between high boulders to a central burial chamber. Soil was tipped over boulders decorated with spirals, zigzag lines and other ornamental designs. Often, these graves also have a cruciform ground plan, with three side chambers branching off from the main passage. The most famous passage tombs are situ-ated in the Boyne Valley.

◄ Passage tombs

By contrast, passage and chamber are not separated in a gallery grave. Wedge tombs (wedge-shaped gallery graves) have a burial chamber which is broader on one side than the other, surrounded by upright standing stones in a horse-shoe formation. These are the most common tombs in Ireland and one can be seen in Ballyedmon-duff near Dublin.

◄ Gallery graves

»Court cairns« (cairn = mound of stones), are burial mounds with a semicircular or oval forecourt and serving ritual purposes. One example can be admired north of Sligo, at Creevykeel.

◄ Court cairns

Stone circles, today preserved as impressive remains, were in use du-ring the Bronze Age (c2000 – 500 BC). They probably served reli-gious purposes. A good example is the Drombeg Stone Circle in

Stone circles

← *A prehistoric monument in the Burren*

County Cork. There are also single standing stones (Irish: gallain), called »menhirs« in Brittany.

Jewellery   Gold from the Wicklow Mountains gave rise to the production of valuable ornaments such as »lunulae« (crescent-shaped collars made **Enamel** from sheet gold). During the Iron Age, the Irish imported the art of **technique ▶** enamelling, probably from the Roman provinces, and used it to brilliantly decorate jewellery and everyday items.

Fortifications   In the Iron Age and the subsequent Christian period, c500 BC–400 AD, ring forts, surrounded by fortifications, were built. Ireland is believed to have over 30,000 ring forts; built from soil or stone, their Irish name is »rath«. A fortified version, erected on an elevation, served defensive purposes. One such hill fort (Irish: lis) is Dún Aenghus on the Aran Island of Inishmór.

Promontory forts ▶   Promontory forts (Irish: dún) are stone ring fortifications situated on steep cliffs or promontories jutting out to sea. One such construction is on the promontory at Dunbeg on the southwestern coast of the Dingle Peninsula. A »crannóg«, an artificial island erected on piles – though sometimes natural islands were used – served as served as the equivalent of a moated castle. Some of these were inhabited well into the Middle Ages.

Early Christian Period

The early Christian period (400–1170 AD) was the heyday of Irish arts. This was a time of lavishly illuminated manuscripts and carved High Crosses. Only a few stone buildings remain from this period, as wattle-and-daub technique dominated.

Beehive huts   Beehive huts are one of the most interesting architectural features of this period (Irish: clochán). The walls of these circular buildings are formed by corbelled stones stacked up without mortar. The top of the »false vault« is formed by a large keystone. Probably the most famous beehive huts are those built by the monks of Skellig Michael at the top of six hundred steps hewn into the rock.

Oratories   The first small churches were known as oratories. With two of the walls angled together to form a roof, an oratory chapel is shaped like an upturned boat. Apart from the door aperture, and later a narrow window above the altar, the interior is unlit.

Tomb slabs   The tomb slabs found in monastery grounds reveal an artistic evolution from simple to ornate decoration. In Clonmacnoise, an impressive selection of slabs and fragments has been set together into a wall. The four tips of the cross at the centre are finished with rich ornamental decoration. Standing stones from pagan times were »baptized«, by having a cross carved into them.

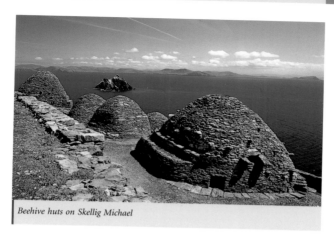
Beehive huts on Skellig Michael

Tomb slabs are probably the precursors of the famous Irish High Crosses. In Fahan and Carndonagh on the Inishowen Peninsula there are stones dating back to the 7th century bearing the outline of a cruciform, on which interlacing and primitive figurative relief can be made out. By contrast, the crosses of Ahenny feature a slim shaft rising up from the base, with a stone ring connecting the shaft and arms. The surface of these crosses is divided into individual panels and entirely covered in geometric patterns. The bases feature figurative representations; evidently scenes from monastic life. Given the stylistic similarities of their geometric motifs with those found in the Book of Kells, the Ahenny crosses probably date back to the 8th century.

High Crosses

In the following century, the ornamentation on High Crosses is replaced by figurative decorations. This change marks the dawning of the heyday of biblical crosses: as visible signs of piety and in the interests of instruction they are set up in monastic grounds. Their exquisitely carved figures, grouped inside rectangular panels, depict scenes from the Old and New Testament. In nearly all cases, a message of redemption lies at the centre of the imagery.

High Crosses were mainly made from local, fine-grained sandstone; examples can be seen at Kells and Monasterboice (Muiredach Cross, early 9th century). If no sandstone was available, then granite was used, such as in the Columban monastery of Moone in the southeast of Ireland, although the harder material required a simplification sometimes bordering on abstraction. The figures on the High Cross of Moone appear schematic, but their faces are not without expression. From around the 11th century onwards, the representation of biblical scenes, with the exception of Christ on the cross, was largely abandoned. Ornamental decorations covering the crosses were again favoured. Often, individual figures rise in high relief from a ring-less,

MONASTERIES

These imposing monasteries dating back to the 8th and 9th centuries are unique to Ireland. Testimonies to the past, with impressive round towers and elaborate High Crosses, they play a big part in creating the country's special atmosphere.

① Round Tower

The round tower, or bell tower, is an elegant structure tapering towards its conical stone roof at a height of around 20–30 metres/66–98 feet. The entrance was situated several metres above ground; the monks accessed the (usually five) floors by small ladders. Light only came in through a small window, used to spot the enemy coming. In peacetime, the monks working outside were called to mass with a hand bell.

② High Crosses

Up to the 8th century, High Crosses were decorated with ornaments; after that, they tended to feature figurative representations: Daniel in the Lion's Den, the Young Men in the Furnace, the Sacrifice of Isaac, David and Goliath. The desert fathers SS Paul and Anthony point to the Eastern models of Irish hermits; animal-like creatures on the short sides lend an oriental air. The centre is nearly always occupied by representations of Christ on the Cross or Christ in Glory on the day of the Last Judgment. The top of the cross is often finished off with a small stone house with a shingle roof, in the shape of a shrine.

1 Clonca
2 Carndonagh
3 Fahan
4 Ardboe
5 Donaghmore
6 Drumcliffe
7 Tynan
8 Termonfeckin
9 Monasterboice
10 Kells
11 Duleek
12 Tuam
13 Bealin
14 Clonmacnoise
15 Durrow
16 Kilcullen
17 Glendalough
18 Moone
19 Castledermot
20 Kilfenora
21 Dysert O'Dea/Ennis
22 Graiguenamanagh
23 Kilree
24 Killamery
25 St Mullins
26 Ahenny
27 Kilkeeran

© Baedeker

minated in purple, light red, emerald green, dark blue and yellow. In the individual chapters of the Gospels, the initials interlace and end in the heads of humans and animals; sometimes human bodies form the letter. Later, such initials fill entire pages of books. Countless bizarre creatures populate the pages of the Holy Scriptures: cats, mice, chickens, birds and fish appear above and below the lines.

Entire ornamental pages with elaborate decorations or representations from the salvation history show Irish book illumination at its peak. The similarities with motifs visible in metalwork and on wooden crosses are unmistakable.

Illuminated page of the Book of Kells

The four Evangelists, or their symbols, are a favourite theme. Here too, the artists were quite liberal in the implementation of their ideas: figures have their feet turned sideways (as on Egyptian tomb paintings), with two sets of hands, harlequin-like gowns, or blue hair.

In Dublin, the Royal Irish Academy exhibits St Columba's 6th-century *Cathach* (mentioned above), as well as the early 9th-century Stowe Missal. The Old Library at Trinity College possesses the 7th-century *Book of Durrow* (its earliest manuscript), the 8th-century *Book of Dimma*, the *Book of Ardagh* (dating from c807; with all four Gospels) and, of course, the undisputed masterpiece of Irish book illumination: the *Book of Kells* (► Baedeker Special p.64).

Thanks to missions by Irish monks, their manuscripts travelled to Britain and on to the Continent. Magnificent libraries and scriptoria were set up in the monasteries they founded. Many of the codices that subsequently emerged were written in a script that had originally evolved in Ireland. Occasionally, Irish scribes added personal notes in the margins of their work: poetry, observations of nature, pious (and sometimes less pious) thoughts. The fear of the Vikings is also expressed; and the raids of these Norsemen eventually did put an end to this flourishing period for the arts.

Romanesque Style

Ireland had to wait for the ecclesiastical reforms of the 12th century before the building of more monumental churches. Cormac's Chapel, on the Rock of Cashel, is a masterpiece of the emerging and distinctive Hiberno-Romanesque style. Consecrated in 1134, this was the first time that the nave of an Irish church had been given a tunnel vault and the choir a rib vault. Two square towers also form part of the structure. A pitched stone roof is typical of Irish-Celtic design, as are vividly carved mythical beasts and human heads. In Dysert O'Dea, for instance, moustached faces frame the main entrance.

At Clonfert Cathedral the ornate main entrance is topped by an extraordinary triangular tympanum featuring human heads. Zigzag

Ecclesiastical architecture

BOOK OF KELLS

On display in the library of Trinity College Dublin is one of greatest works of art in history: the Book of Kells. Every day a different, beautifully illuminated, page is shown from the 340 that make up this medieval Gospel Book.

Origin and Wanderings

To this day it is not known exactly when and where this marvel was produced. The most probable scenario is that the Book of Kells was written by monks towards the end of the 8th century on Iona, a barren island off the west coast of Scotland. In 791, the Irish **abbot Connachtach** assembled the best artists and calligraphers in Europe in his monastery, founded by Columbkille (St Columba) in 563. This was the mother house for monks travelling to the European mainland to leave their mark by founding monasteries in Würzburg/ Germany, in Luxeuil/France, Bobbio/ Italy and St Gallen/Switzerland.

Another pointer towards Iona as the probable place of origin for the Book of Kells is an illustration showing the Evangelist Luke, on page 201. In his right hand, the top part of the word »Jonas« can be made out, another name for the island of Iona. In 806, the Vikings landed on the island to plunder and pillage. The abbot of the monastery and 86 of his monks died. But research suggests that provisions had already been made for the book following the first Viking raid on Iona in 795. Shortly before their second attack, the book, still incomplete, is thought to have been shipped to the safe Irish monastery of Kells (Ceananus Mor), where it was completed in the early 9th century. It was stolen in the 11th century, but found again three months later – missing only its gilded cover.

According to a different theory, the book was produced in Ireland. In any case, the 12th century finds it at Kells monastery. We know this from the statutes of the monastic community, written on the white empty pages of this masterpiece. When Oliver Cromwell's marauding army came to attack Ireland, the book was taken to Trinity College Dublin for safekeeping.

Translation and Material

The text of the *Book of Kells* is based on the Vulgate, the Latin translation of the bible executed by Saint Jerome/ Hieronymus in the 4th century. The *Book of Kells* does not, however, follow this translation of the bible

In the Gospel of Matthew, at the beginning of the story of Christ's birth, a whole page (33x25cm/13x10 inches) is dedicated to the Chi-Rho monogram, the combination of the first two letters of »Christos« – »XPI« in Greek. Whilst the long curvilinear arms of the X reach across the page, the Rho can be seen in the lower right-hand half.

colour pigments were brought in from all over the world: ultramarine (via Persia and Constantinople) from the Hindu Kush mountains, carmine red from the south of France, purple and yellow orpiment from Spain. The variety of artistic styles points to the fact that several artists – probably four – worked on the book.

Illuminated Initials

Every paragraph of the four Gospels starts with an **illuminated initial**. There are over 2,000 of these and they are all different. Between the exquisitely illuminated ornamentation, surprisingly well-drawn figures and animal figures can be made out. The artistic work on the book page illustrated above is reminiscent of the most exquisite piece of gold work. The viewer cannot help but be fascinated by this blend of almost oriental and, at the same time, typically Celtic style elements. The interaction of decorative and figurative representation indisputably establishes the Book of Kells at the pinnacle of the great tradition of Irish book illumination.

word for word. The reason for this might be that several sources were used in its production.

Some say that this work of art was originally meant to be a **magnificent altar book**. This would explain the extraordinary degree of illumination and its format, which is larger than the other Gospel Books produced between the 7th and 9th centuries.

No expense was spared in the making of the *Book of Kells*. The hides of hundreds of calves were used for the fine soft vellum for the pages. The

Clonfert Cathedral

bands around doorways and ornately carved chancel arches characterize other Romanesque churches on the island.

In Mellifont, a master builder from Burgundy was responsible for a new type of monastery, which was to become a model for numerous other new buildings.

After their conquests, the Anglo-Normans erected various **fortifications**. A good example is the motte, a wooden tower on a hill, surrounded by a forecourt protected by palisades. Remains of the almost impregnable keep are often all that remains of larger structures. Rectangular towers with extremely thick walls usually form the centrepiece of large fortifications.

Over time, following English models, castles fortified by corner towers appeared, along with mighty crenellated stone walls.

Gothic Style

The Gothic style is not typical for Ireland. Brought over to the island from the 13th century onwards by Norman settlers or new monastic orders, uncertain times and limited means meant that Gothic cathedrals and monasteries appeared rather modest. Rosserilly, for example, with its tower and cloister, refectory with lecture recess, bakery and fish tank, appears like a Franciscan monastery in miniature.

Sculpture The Irish tombs of the Middle Ages, in common with their precursors, occupy a special place in the history of art. Rory O'Tunney was one of the most gifted stonemasons from the area around Kilkenny. Figures executed by him can be admired in the cloister of Jerpoint Abbey, on sarcophagi in the monasteries of Jerpoint and Kilcooley (near Urlingford) and also in Kilkenny Cathedral. In sculpted recesses, the likenesses of the dead in full armour rest on a stone sarcophagus. Particular attention was paid to hair and gowns, whilst the inscrutable gaze of the subject seems to be turned towards the hereafter.

Sheela-na-gigs ► Another typical feature of Irish art are sheela-na-gigs. These small, obscene figures are probably fertility symbols or were used to ward off evil. Carved from stone, they were mounted in discreet places in some churches.

Style Developments up to the Present Day

Due to the poor economic situation in Ireland, there are few outstanding examples of architecture or fine art.

In the 18th century, wealthy Anglo-Irish masters built houses and castles to reflect their social standing, mostly in the classical style and following the Italian architect Palladio and the Englishman Inigo Jones, such as Castletown House near Dublin. This castle, featuring wings and curved colonnades, was built for the Speaker of the Irish parliament, William Connolly, during 1722–1732 by Alessandro Galilei and Sir Edward Lovett Pearce. The stucco work was carried out by the Francini brothers. However, castle owners were usually more interested in the laying out and landscaping of parks than the decorations of their living quarters. Exotic trees, immaculate lawns and terraces (as in the park of Powerscourt) were more important than paintings, furniture or carpets. Some patrons realized their eccentric ideas in follies, enhancing their parks with Greek or Egyptian temples, obelisks or artificial ruins.

18th century

Mid-17th-century Dublin saw the beginning of a construction boom. Within 100 years, this fairly insignificant town was transformed into the second-biggest city in the British Empire. Four new bridges spanned the Liffey, quays lined its banks. Broader streets and planted squares framed the city centre. As early as 1670, architect Sir William Robinson was building the Royal Hospital as a home for retired soldiers, following the French model of the Invalides church in Paris. The construction activity reached a peak in the 18th century: Dublin Castle and Trinity College were redesigned, while Edward Lovett Pearce built a parliamentary building (today the Bank of Ireland). Architects from other countries also left their mark in Ireland and Dublin: Richard Castle (or Cassels, 1690–1751), a German, built Tyrone House and Leinster House, today the home of the Irish parliament amongst others. James Gandon (1743–1823), an Englishmen of Huguenot descent, built King's Inns in the north of Dublin, as well as the Custom House and the Four Court, two conspicuous landmarks on the north bank of the Liffey. Francis Johnston (1761–1829), a champion of the classical and neo-Gothic styles, was responsible for the chapel in Dublin Castle, as well as the General Post Office building, which was to be at the centre of heavy fighting in 1916 and was rebuilt as a symbol of the struggle for independence.

Dublin

Alongside the large public buildings, imposing residences were built for aristocrats and wealthy merchants, with stylish façades and front gardens behind cast-iron railings. This Georgian style takes its name from the rulers on the English throne at that time. High windows structure the well-proportioned brick façades of these Georgian houses; the only decorations are the numerous varieties of colourful painted doors with their shiny polished brass plates. The doors are framed by pillars or architrave (supporting beam resting on pilasters) and a semicircular fanlight with lantern and house number. The interior of these houses was often decorated by leading stucco craftsmen such as the Francini brothers.

Georgian style

Unfortunately, many individual houses or whole blocks have since been demolished to make way for modern housing. Only in recent times have conservation projects successfully preserved or skilfully restored some of the most beautiful streets and squares. The area around St Stephen's Green, Merrion Square and Fitzwilliam Square provides a cohesive ensemble of Georgian façades. In other cities too, Limerick and Cork in particular, three-storey and four-storey brick houses with their colourful doors catch the eye.

Stained glass In the 19th century, under the influence of Catholicism, numerous new churches were built, fostering stained glass painting of exceptional quality. The first workshops were soon turned into schools; artists experimented with new techniques and established connections to the continent, with art nouveau playing a significant role. Leading stained glass artists included Michael Healy, Harry Clarke, Sarah Purser and Evie Hone.

Trinity College – the oldest university in Ireland (1591)

Irish painting evolved mostly under the influence of international movements without producing really major artists. In the second half of the 18th century, portrait painter Robert Hunter (1748–1803) and James Barry (1741–1806) acquired national fame, the latter making his name with historical paintings, allegorical representations and etchings. The painters of the 19th century, such as Nathaniel Hone (1831–1917) and William Mulready (1786–1863), dedicated themselves primarily to landscape, history and genre painting. Around the turn of the century, naturalism and impressionism became the dominant styles in Ireland. William Orpen (1878–1931) was probably the most popular English society painter of his time. Jack Butler Yeats (1871–1957), the brother of the writer W B Yeats, started as an impressionist; his works however became successively more and more abstract (►Famous People). In their colour scheme, paintings by Roderic O'Connor (1860–1940) are reminiscent of the expressionists.

Today's architecture and fine art increasingly references style elements of the early period. Round churches are built with a layout reminiscent of prehistoric stone forts (Liam McCormick, amongst others). Inside these churches – new, or built on top of extant ruins – there are modern tabernacles, Stations of the Cross, baptismal fonts and doors (by Imogen Stuart, amongst others). Of particular interest are the secular buildings of architect Michael Scott, who designed Dublin's Abbey Theatre (1959) and the Bank of Ireland building (1973). The new library of Trinity College Dublin by Ahrends, Burton & Koralek (1963–1967) also merits a closer look.

Smaller bronze sculptures (by Edward Delaney and Oisin Kelly, amongst others) can be seen in public spaces; developed from works of early Celtic history, these have a style all of their own. They do however seem to share something with the brush drawings by Louis le Brocquy, Ireland's most expensive living painter, who has illustrated Thomas Kinsella's modern version of the *Cattle-Raid* saga (*The Táin*) and produced haunting portraits of Yeats and Joyce.

Irish Literature

400–600	Archaic period
600–1200	Early period
1200–1650	Middle period
1650–1850	Late period
1850–c1950	Modern period
c1950 onwards	Contemporary period

Archaic and early periods From the archaic epoch, some 360 short inscriptions (basically consisting of people's names) in Ogham alphabet (▶ Language), are mostly preserved on tombstones or boundary stones.

Filid ▶ The poets and singers from pre-Christian times, known as »filid«, had a high standing. As chroniclers they preserved the oral traditions of their tribes and ruling families. For their patrons, they would write songs of praise and laments, whilst composing insulting jibes against their protectors' enemies.

Heroic sagas ▶ The early period of Irish literature is the great time of heroic sagas. The oldest written records of these prose epics have been handed down as manuscripts from the 12th and 13th centuries. However, they still preserve the linguistic form of centuries earlier and reveal a pagan world still untouched by Christianity.

The Irish heroic sagas are classified in cycles. The Ulster Cycle, with its central story *The Cattle Raid of Cooley*, comprises, amongst others, the story of the tragic love of Deirdre (the Tristan and Isolde theme) and many archaic elements such as chariot battles, enemies' heads as trophies and the workings of the supernatural.

The Mythological Cycle describes the battle of mythical supernatural creatures, the Tuatha Dé Danann, and their king Dagdá against godlike creatures and demons. The Tuatha Dé Danann are probably meant to represent the native inhabitants of Ireland.

The legends and tales collected in the Cycle of the Kings are stories about individual historic kings, for instance *Cath Almain* (*The Battle of Allen*) or *Buile Suibhne* (*The Madness of Sweeney*).

Poetry ▶ The poetry from the early period has been preserved as historical poems, the more political poems of the Filid, and as religious poems such as the *Festology of the Saints of Ireland* (*Félire*, around 800) by Aengus Céile Dé.

This was also a time of saint's legends and gospel books such as the *Book of Kells*, an Irish national treasure (▶ Baedeker Special p.64), and medicinal as well as legal treatises (the *Séanchas Mar* Irish legal corpus). The *Dindshenchas*, a form of topography of Ireland that combines individually described locations with short stories and legends encapsulates examples of evolving religious and scientific prose.

Middle period
Bards ▶ During the course of the Anglo-Norman invasion in 1171, Ireland lost its political and cultural autonomy. At the newly established royal courts, bards replaced the Filid as court poets, even though the Filid had previously been higher placed on the social scale. Bards such as Muireadhach Albanach Ó Dálaigh, who lived in the first half of the 13th century, would mainly write songs of praise or satirical songs making fun of the enemies of their patrons.

Prose from the middle period is mainly represented by the fairy-tale-folkloristic Finn Cycle, the fourth great Irish cycle of sagas, centring around the *Acallam na senórach* (*Colloquy of the Old Men*) story.

The suppression of the Irish language by the English colonizers led to the disintegration of a unified literary language into various dialects. As the English prohibited the printing of Irish-language books, Irish literature became available only in longhand with a limited distribution. Dábhidh Ó Bruadair (1630–1698), who also partly followed the Bardic tradition still, was one of the most significant poets of this period.

In the 17th and 18th centuries, folk poetry written by farmers and workmen flourished, particularly in the southern Irish province of Munster. One of the most significant works of this »Munster poetry« is Brian Merriman's (1740–1808) *The Midnight Court* (*Cúirt an mhéanoiche*).

Since the 17th century, Irish writers have also written in English. The satirist Jonathan Swift (1667–1745), one of the most famous writers in Ireland, created his masterpiece *Gulliver's Travels* (1726) as a bitter satire against England. In later centuries, selective editing reduced the book to its fantastic, adventurous storyline until it was finally misinterpreted as a children's book.

Wit, humour and the joy of telling wonderful stories characterize both the content and style of the works of Laurence Sterne (1713–1768). The masterpiece of this rural clergyman is the comic novel *The Life and Opinions of Tristram Shandy*, published 1760–1767. A biography of the protagonist, embellished with digressions and ramblings, this is probably one of the finest books in the English language.

Oliver Goldsmith (1728–1774), a priest and author of the popular novel *The Vicar of Wakefield* (1766), mainly depicts the landscape of Athlone in his works. The area is called »Goldsmith Country« to this day.

The ongoing oppression of the Irish by the English, as well as the demographic and social consequences of the Great Famine of 1845–1850 led to the near annihilation of Irish literature. To this day, Irish artists of all persuasions continue to analyze the tragedy that shaped the further development of their country.

The »Gaelic Revival« kicked off a renewal of the Irish language and culture, triggered by the founding of the Gaelic League in 1893 by Douglas Hyde (1860–1949), who later became the first president of the Republic of Ireland. In numerous novels, James Stephens (1882–1950), one of the most popular prose writers of the Gaelic Revival, referenced the world of Irish legends.

The first Irish national theatre (»Irish Literary Theatre«) was founded in 1899 by Lady Augusta Gregory and W B Yeats (1865–1939), who also drew on Irish legend for the themes and plots of his plays. In 1901, the theatre premiered the first Irish-language stage play. With his realistic, poetic tragedies and comedies in stylised Irish language, J M Synge (1871–1909) is considered the strongest drama-

Marginal notes:
Late period
◄ Language
◄ Folk poetry
◄ English as literary language
The Great Hunger
Modern period
◄ Irish Literary Theatre

tic force of the time. Sean O'Casey (1884–1964) and Brendan Behan (1923–1964), who as an adolescent joined the IRA, used their plays and short stories to tell the story of the miserable social conditions in their home country and the ongoing Irish liberation struggle.

Irish theatre has produced a whole range of remarkable authors, including three Nobel Prize winners (►Famous People): W B Yeats in 1923, George Bernard Shaw in 1925 and Samuel Beckett in 1969, as well as the world-class playwright and author Oscar Wilde.

Prose ►

First and foremost it was the prose writers of the 19th and 20th centuries who gained international recognition for the literature of Ireland; their short stories and novels made an important contribution to English-language and European literature. James Joyce (1882–1941, ►Famous People) is considered the most important novelist Ireland has produced. His novel *Ulysses* (1921) – first planned as a short story – portrays Dublin and Ireland in the early 20th century (►Baedeker Special p.292).

With the novels, short stories and satires of Frank O'Connor (1903–1966), Seán O'Faoláin (1900–1991), Liam O'Flaherty (1897–1984) and M Ó Cadhain (1905–1970), whose work points to the increasing social ills and religious problems in Ireland, the spotlight of Irish literature turned increasingly towards political and social issues. The poet Máirtín Ó Diréan (1910–1988), who writes of the beauty and integrity of his native Aran Islands, at the same time criticised Irish society.

Bram Stoker

One of the most popular works of world literature was penned by Abraham (Bram) Stoker (1847–1912): *Dracula* (1897). In this sen-

sationalist novel, set far away from Ireland in the Transylvanian region of Romania, Stoker borrowed the name of his protagonist from the Romanian count Vlad Tepes. Infamous with his enemies because of his cruelty, the count, dubbed Dracula, lived in the 15th century. In *Dracula*, Bram Stoker used old Romanian myths and legends as well as the interest in vampirism and supernatural phenomena widespread in Europe in the second half of the 19th century. Bram Stoker did not live to see his work rise to become one of the most popular novels of the 20th century. It was only the screen adaptations of the vampire story – around 100 to date – that ensured world fame for the novel, the character of Count Dracula and, thereby, for its author.

Contemporary literature

In Flann O'Brien, real name Brian O'Nolan (1911–1966), Ireland boasts a writer whose work is a veritable firework display of comic wit. From 1929 to 1935, O'Brien studied Irish, English and German literature at University College Dublin. After spending 1934/1935 in

Germany, he worked until 1953 as a civil servant for the Dublin city administration. Under the pseudonym Myles na Gopaleen, he wrote satirical columns for the *Irish Times* between 1940 and 1960 that were almost feared by the Irish clergy and upper classes. The themes and structure of his first novel, *At Swim-Two-Birds* (1939), a satirical exploration of Gaelic culture, reveals an almost lifelong fascination with James Joyce and his work. Sadly, this extraordinary writer was to know little further success in his lifetime, remarking resignedly shortly before his death: »My fate as a man of letters seems to be to fail brilliantly and never know fame.« Since that time, Flann O'Brien has risen to become one of the best-known comic writers of the 20th century, with a cult following in Europe and the United States.

Novelists such as Patrick McCabe (*The Butcher Boy*, 1992), who was born in 1955, Eoin McNamee, born in 1961 in County Down, Northern Ireland (*Resurrection Man*, 1994), or Dublin-born (1963) Joseph O'Connor (*Desperados*, 1994) reveal a panorama of contemporary Ireland shaped by violent clashes between Catholics and Protestants.

Modern Ireland

With over 6 million copies sold world-wide, Frank McCourt's autobiography *Angela's Ashes*, published in 1996, has been a major success. Born in 1930 in New York, but raised in Ireland, McCourt relates his poverty-ridden childhood and adolescence during the 1930s and 1940s in the provincial town of Limerick with incisive humour.

The novels of Roddy Doyle (►Baedeker Special, p.248) also provide a keen insight into Irish life. Born in 1958 in Dublin, the former teacher landed a huge success with his Barrytown trilogy. *The Commitments* was made into a film by Alan Parker; *The Snapper* and *The Van* were filmed by Stephen Frears. Doyle's novel *Paddy Clarke Ha Ha Ha* was also very successful, earning him the prestigious Booker Prize.

The most important contemporary Irish poet is Seamus Heaney, born in 1939 in Northern Ireland. In his poems, considered to follow the tradition of WB Yeats, Heaney explores themes of Ireland's landscape and natural environment. At the same time, he takes on the political realities of his country, the rigours of poverty and oppression, and the violence between Protestants and Catholics. In 1995 Heaney was awarded the Nobel Prize for Literature and the Nobel committee praised his poetry as »works of lyrical beauty and ethical depth, which exalt everyday miracles and the living past«.

◄ Seamus Heaney

Famous People

Although the names of O'Connell or Parnell might mean little to a non-Irish person, even those who never pick up a book will have heard of Ireland's famous writers. Whether Samuel Beckett or Roddy Doyle, Irish literature appeals to the book-loving public as much as to the world of high literature.

Samuel Beckett (1906 – 1989)

Samuel Beckett became world-famous as one of the main exponents **Writer**
of the Theatre of the Absurd. Born and bred in Dublin, he studied
Romance languages and literature at Trinity College from
1923 – 1927, going on to teach English in Paris.
There, Beckett met James Joyce and the Existentia-
lists who were to become a major influence on his
work, alongside Dante and Descartes. In the early
1930s, Beckett taught French at Trinity College,
moving to London in 1933, where he started writing his first poems, short stories and essays in
English. In 1937, he moved back to Paris, writing
subsequent works in French and translating them
into English himself. Beckett had to wait a little
longer for his breakthrough; but the novel *Molloy*
(1951) made his name known, and his first stage
play, *Waiting for Godot* (1952) caused a major stir.
All his work shows a break with traditional form;
the action is reduced to a minimum. Using grotesque and burlesque elements, Beckett draws a
pessimistic picture of the absurdity of human existence. In 1969, Beckett was awarded the Nobel
Prize for Literature.

St Brendan (c484–c578)

So who really did discover America? Was it Christopher Columbus   **Monk**
in 1492? Viking Leif Erikson in 1000? The Phoenicians around the
late 7th century BC? Or was it after all an Irish monk?
Published in the 8th century, *The Voyage of St Brendan* was translated
into many western European languages and became a bestseller in
medieval Europe. The *Voyage* describes how the 6th-century Irish
abbot Brendan »the Navigator« discovers the »Promised Land«
beyond the Atlantic.
The Irish saint Brendan founded several monasteries in Ireland, including Clonfert in County Galway. Driven by missionary zeal, he
travelled through the Scottish isles and Wales. According to legend,
he took to sea in 540 with 17 companions and a well-equipped boat
after hearing of a »Promised Land« beyond the ocean, inhabited by
saints. It took him seven years to return.
In 1976, Timothy Severin proved that crossing the Atlantic in a leather boat of the type common in Brendan's time cannot simply be
dismissed as a crazy notion. Inspired by the similarity of place names
in the book and the actual topography on Labrador, the scientist sailed in a reconstructed boat from Ireland to Canada.

← *Statue of novelist James Joyce on O'Connell Street in Dublin*

Roger Casement (1864 – 1916)

Rebel

On 3 August 1916 Sir Roger Casement was hanged for conspiracy with the German war enemy and for preparing an Irish rebellion.

Born in Dublin, by the age of 20 Roger Casement was already travelling in Africa. From 1900, he was commissioned by the British government to research conditions in the Belgian Congo and Peru. Casement confirmed the rumours about mistreatment at the hands of white colonialists, bringing them to world-wide attention. From then on, Casement was considered an advocate of the poor, consequently held in high esteem internationally and given a peerage. Having damaged his health through his long stay in the tropics, Casement left the British civil service in 1913. From then on he dedicated himself to the fight for Ireland's independence from the English Crown and played a leading role in the »Irish Volunteers« resistance movement. Shortly after the outbreak of the First World War, he made contact with the German government in Berlin, with the aim of gaining Germany's support for the Irish independence movement – and weapons. The German Reich hoped to use the planned 1916 Easter Rising to weaken its enemy in war and agreed to smuggle 20,000 guns along with ammunition on board a fishing trawler to the Irish coast. When the ship was discovered by the British Navy, the captain was forced to sink it to prevent the cargo, essential to the war effort, from falling into British hands. Casement was taken by submarine in secret to Ireland, where he was immediately arrested.

These events showed the leaders of the rising very clearly that their insurrection was doomed to fail. But it was too late: on Easter Monday, 24 April 1916, the rising began, only to be violently quashed four days later by British armed forces. The British government accused Casement of chief responsibility, court-martialling him and condemning him to death by hanging for collaboration with Germany and initiating an insurrection against the Crown. In addition, a smear campaign aimed at tarnishing his reputation abroad used rumours about Casement's homosexuality and leaked his diaries (detailing his sexual exploits). As a result, the Archbishop of Canterbury and the US President Wilson both refrained from asking for clemency for Casement. In 1965, the mortal remains of Sir Roger Casement were transferred from England to Dublin and laid to rest in Glasnevin Cemetery.

James Joyce (1882 – 1941)

Novelist

While few will have read this world-famous author's masterpiece *Ulysses*, published in 1922, in its entirety, this book is the main reason behind Bloomsday, celebrated by fans every year on 16 June in Dublin (►Baedeker Special p.292).

After an education at Jesuit schools and at University College Dublin, Joyce went to Paris in 1902 to study medicine. From 1904 onwards, he lived in self-chosen exile in Trieste, Rome, Zurich and Paris, amongst other places. Ten years later, *Dubliners* was published: 15 short stories in which Joyce depicts Dublin society through different ages of life. The autobiographical novel *Portrait of the Artist as a Young Man* (1916) uses interior monologue to show the tensions between a young artist and his environment. In his last work, *Finnegan's Wake* (1939), Joyce tried – as in *Ulysses* – to harness the subconscious to language. Joyce's works owe much to the atmosphere of his home city of Dublin and, despite the many difficulties of interpretation, they were a significant influence on 20th-century literature.

In 1940, Joyce fled with his family from Paris to Zurich, where he died on 13 January 1941 following a serious illness. He lies buried in Fluntern cemetery.

Daniel O'Connell (1775 – 1847)

Daniel O'Connell was one of the best-known leaders of the Irish resistance against the English Crown. In the early 19th century, O'Connell was known as »Ireland's uncrowned king« but was ultimately defeated by the political realities.

Resistance leade

As the son of a relatively wealthy Catholic estate owner, O'Connell was able to study in France, where he witnessed the French Revolution – its ideals, but also its violence. Perhaps those experiences were responsible for the peaceful politics he later espoused. When O'Connell returned to Ireland, the English laws towards the Irish had been relaxed. O'Connell set up as a lawyer in Dublin, where his success soon made his name all over the country. Alongside work, O'Connell became increasingly active in politics. A complete severance of ties with the Union to Great Britain, in place since 1801, seemed for the time being unworkable to O'Connell. He therefore pursued two alternative goals: equal rights for Irish Catholics and the protection of small Irish tenants against the unreasonable English owners of large estates. With this in mind, O'Connell founded the Catholic Association in 1823. In only a short time, the association numbered over a million members: middle classes and peasants, nobility and liberals, clergy and highwaymen. With their help, O'Connell won the County Clare election to become MP, but it took an amendment of the English law to allow him, as a non-Anglican, to take his seat at Westminster. When the Conservatives returned to power in England, O'Connell lost his political influence. Initiating a new movement for Ireland's independence, he used mass meetings to call for the independence of Ireland and huge rallies to call for peaceful liberation. London became increasingly irritated. O'Connell was sentenced to prison but escaped when the House of Commons intervened on his behalf. The situation escalated again when the English governor proposed using the military to prevent a planned mass rally near Dublin. O'Connell cancelled the rally the evening before to avoid violence; most of his young supporters felt let down and turned their backs on him. Already in declining health, O'Connell went to Italy to recuperate, but died in Genoa in 1847.

Charles Stewart Parnell (1846 – 1891)

Politician

Born into a Protestant Anglo-Irish family, Charles Stewart Parnell became a figurehead for the Irish national movement. Parnell started his political career in the Home Rule League, a party founded in 1870 that demanded the independence of the Irish parliament but rejected violence against British supremacy. Parnell soon became party leader and the most important Irish politician, using peaceful means to fight the British government for concessions.

The first boycott in world history ensured his popularity. Parnell particularly detested British landowners who often cultivated the best soil and exploited the destitute rural population by using unscrupulous agents. It was against such an agent, Captain Charles Boycott,

that Parnell instigated an action of completely ignoring and refusing cooperation with him (► Boycott, Lough Corrib, Lough Mask). The situation became untenable and Boycott left Ireland for good.

However, Parnell's policy of peaceful rapprochement towards the liberal Home Rule policy of British prime minister Gladstone made him enemies. As it became apparent that Irish independence was unachievable within the framework of the constitution, his political opponents began a systematic campaign of character assassination. Parnell's affair with Katherine (Kitty) O'Shea, a married woman separated from her husband, was pilloried in the media as »immoral behaviour«, and more and more supporters crossed over to the enemy camp. Marrying Kitty O'Shea did not protect Parnell from being voted out as head of the party – and he died a few months after his deposition.

St Patrick

►Baedeker special p.34

George Bernard Shaw (1856 – 1950)

Author and critic

Cynicism, mockery and humour made George Bernard Shaw famous beyond his literary creations. Shaw was born in Dublin, the son of an English father and Irish mother. In 1876, Shaw moved to London, where he tried his hand as an estate agent. However, he soon turned to writing reviews of theatre, music and art that were admired as much as they were feared. Eight years later he assembled like-minded people to found the Fabian Society. This intellectual society supported evolutionary socialism rather than Marxist revolutionary ideals.

From 1891, Shaw turned to writing his own plays, which used critical cynicism to heap scorn on conventions and well-loved clichés as well as successfully coining witty paradoxes, polished dialogues and tremendous punchlines. His most famous plays include *Pygmalion* (1912) and *Saint Joan* (1923). In 1925, Shaw was awarded the Nobel Prize for Literature, but refused a knighthood.

As an individual, Shaw was equally full of wit, esprit and capacity for biting scorn. Once, a famous beauty said to him: »Just imagine, Mr Shaw, a child with your intelligence and my beauty!« Whereupon he replied: »And what is to become of him if he inherits your intelligence and my beauty?!«

Shaw's own views of Ireland only find expression in *John Bull's Other Island* (1904): »Ireland cannot be compared to any other country, in what's good and in what's bad; and nobody can touch its soil or breathe its air without becoming better or worse.«

G B Shaw at work (around 1940)

Jonathan Swift (1667 – 1745)

Satirist

Gulliver's Travels is one of the most popular children's books in world literature. However, this adventure story, written in 1726 by Jonathan Swift, is much more than just a children's book.

Swift describes the exploits of his protagonist Gulliver in different worlds: the land of the Lilliputs, the land of giants, the country where eternal life is possible, and in the realm of the horses endowed with reason who have created an ideal society with humans as servants. The book is a biting satire on contemporary English society, human stupidity and malice, as well as social ills. Irony is the hallmark of Swift's literary work; he is considered the most important satirist in English literature, world literature even.

In 1713, Swift returned to Dublin, holding the deanery of St Patrick's Cathedral up to his death. In 1729, he was given the freedom of the city, but when his companion Stella died, Swift's tone became more and more cynical; his contemporaries considered him to be disturbed. Jonathan Swift lies buried next to Stella in Dublin's St Patrick's Cathedral.

John Millington Synge (1871 – 1909)

Writer Born into an Anglo-Irish lawyer's family, the writer John Millington Synge studied at Trinity College Dublin. Travelling in Germany and Italy in 1892, he spent most of 1893 – 1898 in Paris. There, he met William B Yeats, who recommended a stay on the Aran Islands on the west coast of Ireland to study the way of life and the language of the islanders. Initially Synge only stayed for six weeks but in the following years he returned time and again, immortalizing the landscape and its people in *The Aran Islands* (1907). In 1904, Synge, who had settled in Dublin in 1902, became director of the newly-founded Abbey Theatre, which he managed up to his death.

In his works, Synge dealt with themes from the world of Irish peasants and fishermen. *Riders to the Sea*, one of his most important works, presents a fisherman's watery grave as inevitable. The black comedy *The Playboy of the Western World* (1907) is also famous as an homage to the islanders' tough but warm turn of phrase.

Eamon de Valera (1882 – 1975)

Politician Eamon de Valera is the most important personality of Irish 20th-century history. For six decades (1913 – 1973), de Valera dominated politics on the »Emerald Isle«; the Irish owe the creation of the Republic of Ireland first and foremost to him.

Born in New York on 14 October 1882, the son of a Spaniard and an Irishwoman, he grew up in Ireland with his grandmother, following the early death of his father. De Valera studied mathematics in Dublin and became a teacher. His political career started in 1913 as a

member of the recently founded Irish Volunteers, who demanded more autonomy for Ireland. As one of the leaders of the Easter Rising in 1916, de Valera was sentenced to death – but the sentence was not carried out. After being released, he stood for the British House of Commons and was elected. In May 1918, the English government had de Valera arrested again and interned in England, but he managed to flee to the United States. Whilst still in exile, de Valera became party chief of the Sinn Féin party, founded in 1906 and reformed in 1917, which won 73 of Ireland's 105 seats at Westminster. Aiming for Irish independence, the party wanted to win the majority of the Irish mandates in the British House of Commons. However, instead of taking their seats in Westminster, they founded the illegal Council of Ireland (Dáil Eireann) in 1919 under the presidency of de Valera, who returned to Ireland in 1920.

De Valera's goal was still the same: full independence for Ireland. In protest against the Anglo-Irish Treaty, which created the Irish Free State as a dominion of the British Empire but allowed Northern Ireland to opt out, he stood down from parliament. During the civil war of 1922/1923, he opposed the government. In 1926, de Valera founded the Fianna Fáil party, winning the 1932 elections as their candidate. Under his government, Ireland became a de facto republic, on the basis of the constitution of 1937, which he helped to draw up. During the Second World War, de Valera strictly maintained Ireland's neutrality, surviving a tricky time with a state that was not yet consolidated. Voted out of office in 1948 by his fellow Irish, he was nevertheless recalled to be »Taoiseach« (head of government) in the years 1951–1954 and 1957–1959. From 1959 to 1973, he represented his country as president. Eamon de Valera (known as »Dev« to his supporters and also as the »Long Fellow«) died on 29 August 1975, aged 93.

Jack Butler Yeats (1871–1957)

Jack Butler Yeats, the brother of writer William, dedicated himself to painting as his father had before him. Born in London, he spent his childhood in Sligo, returning there for his studies. Throughout his life, J B Yeats painted Irish landscapes and daily life, such as scenes from the pub, variety theatre or the racecourse.

Painter

William Butler Yeats (1865–1939)

The writer William Butler Yeats was the founder and guiding spirit of the Gaelic Revival. This movement, closely linked to the struggle for Irish independence, aimed to revive Irish-Celtic traditions in the arts and culture.

Poet

Yeats spent his childhood in Dublin, London and Sligo, remaining strongly attached to the landscapes of the west coast of Ireland, its legends and folktales, all his life. From 1884 to 1886, Yeats attended art college with a view to becoming a painter. However, from 1886 onwards he dedicated himself to literature, becoming, in 1899, one of the founders of the Irish National Theatre.

After the proclamation of the Irish Free State, Yeats became senator and used his term in office (1922–1928) to propose the decoration of Irish coins with animals already mentioned in the Book of Kells: hare, dog, fish and bird. Yeats' entire oeuvre is suffused with Irish-Celtic legends, fairytales and myths. Whilst his early work still shows the influence of French symbolism and »fin-de-siècle« aesthetics, the author later became interested in magic and occultism, rites and symbols. His plays resemble epic poems, with a symbolic plot and protagonists representing types rather than individuals. Yeats' most beautiful poems are collected in two volumes of poetry: *The Tower* (1928) and *The Winding Stair and Other Poems* (1933). Yeats was awarded the 1923 Nobel Prize for Literature.

Practicalities

MUST-HAVES FROM HOME
THE SPEED LIMIT ON
IRELAND'S ROADS
WHAT YOU NEED TO KNOW
ABOUT IRISH FOOD
FIND OUT BEFORE YOU GO!

Accommodation

Bed and Breakfast

Bed and Breakfasts (B & B's) offer relatively good value for money accommodation (approx. €25/£20 – €50/£35 per person per night) in Irish homes, which serve the famous Irish breakfast, sometimes in the company of the owners.

Tourist information offices can supply the *Accommodation Guide* in the Republic of Ireland, and the *Where to Stay* guide in Northern Ireland, which list all B & B's. The same offices can often make reservations for you, and you can also purchase accommodation vouchers as part of any package tour.

Camping and Caravanning

Republic of Ireland
There are 137 officially recognized Camping and Caravanning sites in the Republic of Ireland, which are graded according to their facilities. The best have four stars, the most basic have one star, but most Irish campsites do not bear comparison with their continental counterparts in terms of conditions or facilities. Find out more in the *Caravan and Camping Parks* brochure supplied by the Irish National Tourist Board.

Northern Ireland
Camping is also common in and you can find out more in the »Where to Stay« brochure supplied by the Northern Ireland Tourist Board.

Camping Wild
In the old days, no one was bothered by unofficial camping, but today camping or staying the night on roadsides, at car parks, rest stops or in fields is generally prohibited. If you are on private land, you must always clear things with the owner first.

Country Houses

Country Houses Association
In the Republic of Ireland former estates and manors have often been turned into hotels and restaurants and are listed in »Ireland's Blue Book«, published by the Irish Country Houses and Restaurants' Association. However, they are normally also included in the general listings provided by the Irish Tourist Information. »Hidden Ireland« **Hidden Ireland** is a brochure covering a variety of private and exclusive country houses offering small-scale accommodation. This ranges from castles by the sea to luxury farmhouses and you can get the full listing either directly from the Association or from the Irish Tourist Board.

IMPORTANT ADDRESSES

COUNTRY HOUSES

► **Ireland's Blue Book**
c/o Hilary Finlay
8 Mount Street Crescent
Dublin 2
Tel. (01) 67 69 914
Fax (01) 63 14 990
www.irelandsbluebook.com

► **The Hidden Ireland**
P O Box 31, Westport, Co. Mayo
Tel. (098) 6 66 50
/(01) 6 62 71 66
www.hidden-ireland.com

HOLIDAY HOUSES

► **Irish Cottage Holiday
Homes Association**
4 Whitefriars
Aungier Street
Dublin 2

Tel (01) 4 75 19 32
www.irishcottageholidays.com

HOTELS AND GUESTHOUSES

► **Resireland**
Tel (00 800) 66 86 68 66
Fax (00 353) 6 69 79 21 16

YOUTH HOSTELS

► **AN ÓIGE Irish Youth
Hostel Association**
61 Mountjoy Street, Dublin 7
Tel. (01) 8 30 45 55
www.anoige.ie

► **Hostelling International
Northern Ireland (HINI)**
22 Donegal Road
Belfast BT12 5JN
Tel. (0 28) 90 32 47 33
info@hini.org.uk

Holiday apartments and houses

Holiday apartments and houses are rented out all over Ireland. Irish cottages usually have a thatched roof, are fully furnished, and offer accommodation for between five and eight people. Information is available at both national tourist boards.

Hotels and Guesthouses

The Republic of Ireland offers a great variety of hotels and the range spans everything from castles to simple accommodation. Alongside hotels, holidaymakers can also make use of guesthouses, which are smaller than hotels and usually have a more personal service. Hotels (H) are officially categorized into five groups, from luxury hotels with five stars and standard hotels with two or three stars, to simple accommodation with one star. Guesthouses are categorised into four groups, ranging from four stars to one. Prices for both hotels and guesthouses are significantly higher in Dublin and major tourist resorts than in the rest of the country, and there are also significant seasonal differences in pricing. For this reason, tarriffs for hotels listed in this guide can only be very rough guidelines. The table lists prices per person per night in a double room, including breakfast.

In Northern Ireland hotels are officially classified according to their facilities, ranging from luxury hotels (four stars) to basic accommodation with one star. Guesthouses are only divided into two groups: A and B. Accommodation in Belfast tends to be at the upper end of the price scale and significantly higher than in the rest of Northern Ireland, where prices tend to be at the lower end in rural areas.

Reservations In high season especially, it is recommended that you book accommodation in advance via a travel agent or directly with the hotel itself. Reservations can also be made via Tourist Information Offices(▶Information) which also offer a free booking service.

Youth Hostels

Youth hostels offer younger travellers value-for-money accommodation. An international youth hostel card is required (but can be taken out on arrival) and making reservations is recommended.

Arrival • Before the Journey

Getting there

By air There are plenty of options for British visitors. The Irish airline Aer Lingus offers direct flights several times a week from London and Cardiff, to Dublin and Shannon. British Airways (Loganair) connects Glasgow and Derry/Londonderry. Irish budget carrier Ryanair has inexpensive flights to Dublin and Shannon from London Stansted and Glasgow (Prestwick) airports, among others, while their rival Easyjet connects Belfast International with Bristol, Liverpool, London Stansted and London Gatwick, Newcastle, Edinburgh and Glasgow. Aer Arann serves the airports of Waterford, Galway and Kerry from Bristol, Cardiff, Edinburgh, Leeds Bradford, London Luton and Manchester.

For US visitors, Aer Lingus offers the biggest range of connections from Boston, Chicago, Dallas, Denver, Los Angeles, New York JFK, Orlando, San Diego, San Francisco, Seattle, St Louis and Washington Dulles to Dublin or Shannon Airport. American Airlines offer a non-stop service to Dublin from Boston, Chicago and LA. Delta flies to Dublin and Shannon from Atlanta, US Airways flies to Dublin and Shannon from Philadelphia and Continental flies daily to Belfast from Newark. Ryanair are planning to serve Ireland–US routes in the near future. Air Canada has non-stop summer flights from Toronto to Dublin (and on to Shannon), and Canadian budget carrier Zoom has seasonal daily direct flights to Belfast from Halifax, Toronto and Vancouver and to London Gatwick from New York JFK, Ottawa, Toronto, Vancouver and Winnipeg. London, Paris or Frankfurt

Heading towards Ireland from Swansea port.

are the usual gateways for visitors from Australia, New Zealand and South Africa. From Dublin, there are good connections to Cork, Kerry (Killarney), Shannon, and Galway, as well as Sligo and Donegal. For Continenal European travellers, the traditional way to get to the Northern Irish capital of Belfast is via Dublin, London, Amsterdam or Paris, but Easyjet also now offer direct flights from various European cities, such as Amsterdam, Berlin Schönefeld, Barcelona, Cracow, Faro and Malaga.

Additional information ►Transport

By car and ferry

There is a ferry service to Ireland from six British ports. It is advisable to book the crossing in advance.

By car and ferry

By bus and rail

Taking the train to Ireland is expensive and takes a long time. Visitors opting for this mode of transport have to travel via London by train and ferry (Hoek van Holland – Harwich and Oostende – Dover) or through the Eurotunnel. In London, change for the train to Holyhead (in Wales), the terminal for ferries to Dublin, Dun Laoghaire or Rosslare (www.sailrail.co.uk).
Coach trips through Ireland are offered by various companies. For more information, visit your local travel agent or check online.

Travel documents

Travel
documents
Driving Licences ▶

Entry to the Republic of Ireland and Northern Ireland is normally granted to travellers holding a full passport. National driving licences and insurance papers should be carried and are recognised in both the Republic of Ireland and Northern Ireland. Be sure to carry the International Insurance Card or »Green Card«. Vehicles must carry an EU sticker or the relevant blue oval country sticker.

 CAR FERRIES, BUS AND RAIL

FERRIES FROM BRITAIN

▶ **Cairnryan (Scotland)–Larne (Northern Ireland)**
approx. 2hr: P & O

▶ **Stranraer (Scotland)–Belfast (Northern Ireland)**
1hr 30min: Stena Line

▶ **Holyhead (Wales)–Dublin/Dun Laoghaire**
3hr 30min: Stena Line

▶ **Fishguard (Wales)–Rosslare**
2–4hrs: Stena Line

▶ **Fishguard (Wales)–Cork**
10hr: Swansea (Wales) Cork

▶ **Liverpool–Belfast and Dublin**
8hr: Norse Merchant

FERRY COMPANIES

▶ **Irish Ferries**
Ireland: tel. (0)8 18 300 400
www.irishferries.com
UK: Tel. 08 70 5 17 17 17
Agent for US/Canada:
Scots American Travel Advisors
825 13th Lane
Tel. 7 72 563 28 56

▶ **Britanny Ferries**
Tel. (0 21) 42 77 801
www.britanny-ferries.com
UK bookings: Tel. 08 70 9 076 103

▶ **Stena Line**
Ireland: Tel. (01) 20 47 77 77
outside Ireland: Tel. (01) 20 47 77 77
www.stenaline.com

▶ **P & O**
Tel. (08 70) 24 2 47 77
www.poirishsea.com

▶ **Norse Merchant Ferries**
Tel. +44 (0) 8 70 6 00 43 21
www.norsemerchant.com

▶ **Swansea Cork Ferries**
Tel. +44 (0) 17 92 45 61 16
www.swansea-cork.ie

BUS COMPANIES

▶ **National Express/Eurolines**
Tel. (08 705) 80 80 80
www.nationalexpress.com

▶ **Bus travel Ireland**
Bus Éireann/Eurolines
Tel. (0 1) 8 36 61 11
www.buseireann.ie

RAIL

▶ **National Rail**
Tel. (08 45) 48 49 50
www.nationalrail.co.uk

▶ **Irish Rail (Iarnród Eireann)**
Tel. (18 50) 36 6 222
www.irishrail.ie

Import permissions are required for dogs and cats and a six-month quarantine is mandatory, though it is waived for arrivals from England as long as British import conditions have been met.

Personal effects and goods can normally travel without customs duty within the EU, though there are limits. For example, the individual limit for people aged 17 and over is 800 cigarettes, 10 bottles of spirits and 90 bottles of wine.

For travellers from outside the European Union the limits for individuals aged 17 and over are set at 200 cigarettes or 100 cigarillos, or 50 cigars or 250gr of loose tobacco and for alcohol at two bottles of wine and one bottle of spirits. (This applies both to the Republic of Ireland and Northern Ireland).

Travel Insurance

British and other EU citizens are entitled to free emergency medical care in hospitals and with general practitioners. Make sure to carry the EHIC (European Health Insurance Card), which replaces the old E111 forms and can be picked up from post offices or applied for online (www.ehic.org.uk). Emergency services are usually free, but US, Canadian, etc. citizens may have to pay for some medical services and reclaim at home with their health insurance provider.
It is worth checking the details of your travel insurance policy.

Electricity

Adaptors required! Without them you will not be able to use your appliances anywhere in Ireland. The Republic of Ireland's electricity functions on 220 volt, with a frequency of 50 hertz. Northern Ireland functions on 240 volt, also with a 50 hertz frequency.

Emergency

Car Assistance

In the case of a breakdown contact the nearest garage or one of the Irish automobile clubs mentioned below. In the case of hired cars always contact the hire firm in the first instance. In the case of accidents resulting in personal injury the police must always be informed at once.

▶ EMERGENCY SERVICE CONTACT NUMBERS

EMERGENCY IN IRELAND

▶ **free in all of Ireland**
999 or 112
(Police, fire brigade, ambulance
and sea rescue)

**BREAKDOWN
ASSISTANCE**

▶ **Breakdown Assistance**
Tel. 18 00 66 77 88 (free of charge)

▶ **Cork**
12 Emmet Place
Tel. (021) 4 27 69 22
Fax (021) 4 27 60 87

▶ **Dublin**
23 Suffolk Street
Tel. (01) 6 17 95 40
Fax (01) 6 77 49 42
aa@aaireland.ie

▶ **Dundalk**
Newry Road
Tel. (042) 3 29 55
Fax (042) 3 13 73

▶ **Galway**
Headford Road
Tel. (091) 56 44 38
Fax (091) 56 57 86

▶ **Limerick**
Arthur's Quay
Tel. (061) 41 82 41
Fax (061) 41 19 85

▶ **Sligo**
Broderick's Travel Agency
21 O'Connell Street
Tel. (071) 6 20 65
Fax (071) 6 22 53

▶ **Waterford**
11 The Quay
Tel. (051) 87 37 65
Fax (051) 85 03 93

▶ **Northern Ireland**
Automobile Association (AA)
Tel. (08 00) 88 77 66
www.theaa.com
Royal Automobile Club (RAC)
Tel. (08 00) 82 82 82
www.rac.co.uk

Etiquette and Customs in Ireland

Irish society is characterized by large families and family networks: most of today's over thirties come from families with five or more children. This has significantly informed the Irish character and the family lies at the root of their typical tendency to assertiveness, but also respect and submission regarding their parents, easy social skills and a willingness to talk to anyone, even to the degree of gossip. One should also never forget that many Irish are strict Catholics.

Greetings The standard greeting formula is »how are you« and signifies nothing more than »hello«. The speaker certainly does not expect a full report of your day or week, but a simple »how are you« in return.

The Irish are a friendly and sociable nation, famous for their hospitality. There is usually no point in declining an invitation out of politeness. Yet the Irish can be quite shy as guests, so if you have an Irish person visiting, you may have to insist several times before he or she will help themselves to tea and cakes. Generally, courtesy dictates that you offer at least a cup of tea when inviting somebody to the house. Note that Irish time-keeping has its own rules. For example, if you invite people to your house

Invitations

Smoking Prohibited

- Smoking in Irish pubs and restaurants has been prohibited since March 2004, and anyone who ignores this law risks a fine of up to 1900 Euros.

for 8pm, you can be sure they will not arrive before 8.30pm or even later, and any time arrangements accompanied by the phrase »ish« after the time specified are definite agreements to an unspecified later hour. For example, a suggestion to meet »at 8ish« in the evening guarantees that no one will be there on the dot of 8pm. This vague phrase of »ish«, which means much the same as »roughly«, can also be used to describe other things, such as age and income.

The Irish love to make fun and are not shy of using the popular sport of »slagging« with foreigners either. **Slagging** is never meant to be malicious so please don't take this light-hearted banter the wrong way. A healthy portion of humour is expected and visitors do well to join in the spirit of fun intended. The Irish are very sociable and even nosy people and a bit of »chat« is always popular, whether you know those involved or not. Careful, or you might become the object of gossip yourself!

Humour

The Irish love talk and debate of any kind

Travelling The weather in Ireland is always an important conversation topic with the locals and you should always come prepared for rain on excursions. On the other hand, the weather can change so quickly in Ireland that a little rain is never a reason to cancel a trip. Lots of interesting hiking routes partly cross private land, so it is a good idea to check your planned route with farmers, as not all of them relish seeing ramblers on their land.

Directions All travel directions should be treated with care. In addition to the often unsatisfactory and even misleading road signs in rural areas, many locals appear to have a problem with giving directions. Often they either confuse the traveller with well-meant but highly complicated instructions, or they send you off just anywhere, with the advice to ask again later, because they don't want to admit ignorance.

Queueing Queueing is standard procedure in Ireland and normal at bus stops, in supermarkets and at cashpoints at the weekend. Queue-jumping is frowned upon. A small tip: if you are going out at the weekend in Dublin and don't want to queue at cash tills, you should get your money in the afternoon or outside the city centre.

Fun To enjoy »the craic« (pronounced »crack«) basically means to have fun. The story goes that two Irishmen in America wanted to have some »craic«, so they approached a policeman and asked him for some, whereupon he immediately arrested them for soliciting crack cocaine …

Festivals, Holidays and Events

Bank Holidays These moveable holidays are called »Bank Holidays« in Ireland and they usually fall on a Monday.

 FESTIVALS AND HOLIDAYS

FESTIVALS

▶ **Republic of Ireland**
1 January (New Year's Day)
17 March (St Patrick's Day)
Good Friday
Easter Monday
1 May (Labour Day)
June Bank Holiday (First Monday of the month)
First Monday in August (August Bank Holiday Weekend)
Last Monday in October (Autumn Bank Holiday)
25 and 26 December (Christmas)

▶ **Northern Ireland**
1 January (New Year's Day)
17 March (St Patrick's Day)
Good Friday
Easter Monday
First Monday in May (Bank Holiday)

Last Monday in May or first Monday in June (Bank Holiday)
12 July (Orangeman's Day; to commemorate the Battle of the Boyne, 1690)
Last Monday in August (August Bank Holiday)
25 and 26 December (Christmas)

EVENTS IN JANUARY

► **Horse Racing**
There is horse racing across the entire country during January, from Leopardstown near Dublin to Naas in Co. Kildare and the Temple Bar Traditional Music Festival (www.templebartrad.com) at the end of the month.

EVENTS IN FEBRUARY

► **Rugby**
The Six Nations Championship (between Ireland, England, Wales, Scotland, France and Italy) starts this month and two or three matches are held in Ireland, usually at Lansdowne Road, currently being refurbished.

EVENTS IN MARCH

► **Belfast Music Festival**
Up-and-coming spoken word, drama and music talent show what they are made of in the first two weeks of March

► **St Patrick's Day**
The St Patrick's Day parade is held every year on 17 March (or a day closely following that date) (Baedeker Special p.34).

EVENTS IN APRIL

► **Dublin International Film Festival**
This festival in honour of Irish and international film is held for ten days every year in April.

► **Gaelic Football League Final**
Venue: Croke Park, Dublin

► **Irish Grand National**
Horse racing at Fairyhouse, Co. Meath

► **World Irish Dancing Championship**
This championship for Irish dancers is held in a different city each year. (Please see Board Fáilte under Information).

EVENTS IN MAY

► **Dublin Agricultural Spring Show**
An agricultural show is held on the Royal Dublin Society Showground.

► **Fleadh Nua**
This traditional music and dance festival is held at the end of May in Ennis, Co. Clare.

Fun at Fleadh Nua in Ennis

► **International Choral and Folk Dance**
Location: Cork

► **International Football Association Cup Final**
Matches at Lansdowne Road Stadium in Dublin.

EVENTS IN JUNE

► **Bloomsday**
On 16 June, the day James Joyce describes in his novel *Ulysses*, many fans wander in the footsteps of Leopold Bloom, one of the main characters of the book. (Baedeker Special p.292)

► **Fiddler's Stone Festival**
A small festival of Irish music in Belleek, Co. Fermanagh.

► **International Fishing Festival**
Venue: Rathmullen, Co. Donegal.

► **Irish Derby**
Famous horse race at the Curragh in Co. Kildare

► **Jazz and Blues Festival**
in Hollywood (Co. Down)

► **Pettigo Pilgrimage**
From the beginning of June to mid August pilgrims take a boat from Pettigo (Co. Donegal) to a small island in Lough Derg.

► **Writer's Week**
This literature festival takes place every year in Listowel (Co. Cork).

EVENTS IN JULY

► **Cork Arts Festival**
is held in mid-July.

► **Fishing**
Various championships and festivals are held in Athlone and Mayo. For more information, contact Bord Fáilte for the *Angler's Guide to Ireland* brochure.

► **Galway Arts Festival**
This festival of the arts, that begins in mid-July, encompasses art, music and much more, and a parade is also held.

► **Galway Film Fleadh**
Beginning of July, this is one of the largest film festivals in the county of Galway.

► **Reek Sunday**
A pilgrimage journey up Croagh Patrick, Ireland's holy mountain, which takes place on the last Sunday of the month.

EVENTS IN AUGUST

► **Connemara Pony Show**
in Clifden, Co. Galway

► **Dublin Horse Show**
This annual horse show, held on the Royal Dublin Society Show-ground during the second week of the month, counts as a major social event.

► **Féile**
Ireland's largest rock festival is held in Thurles (Co. Tipperary) during the August Bank Holiday (around the weekend of the first Monday of the month).

► **Féile an Phobail**
Large and popular art festival and street carnival in West Belfast, held at the beginning of August.

► **Fleadh Cheoil nah Eireann**
The three-day festival of traditional Irish music that is held in a different town each year.

► **Kilkenny Arts Week**
Towards the end of August each year, the whole town is filled with

exhibitions, concerts and the atrical shows.

▶ **Oul' Lammas Fair**
This market is held during the last weekend of the month (Baedeker Tip p.157).

▶ **Puck Fair**
A traditional festival with lots of merriment in Killorglin, Co. Kerry (Baedeker Tip p.414).

▶ **Rose of Tralee Festival**
Internationally famous beauty contest

EVENTS IN SEPTEMBER

▶ **All-Ireland Hurling and Football Finals**
Both games are held at Croke Park in Dublin: hurling during the last weekend in August and football on the third Sunday in September.

▶ **Matchmaking Festival**
»Marriage market« in Lisdoon-varna, Co. Clare

▶ **Sligo Arts Week**
Annual Arts Week in Sligo

▶ **Waterford International Festival of Light Opera**
The whole town shares in this festival of musicals and operettas,

including competitions, during the last two weeks of September.

EVENTS IN OCTOBER

▶ **Ballinasloe Horse Fair**
The largest Irish horse and cattle market is held in Ballinasloe, Co. Galway.

▶ **Cork International Film Festival and International Jazz Festival**
This jazz festival attracts many, including an international audience.

▶ **Dublin Marathon**
on the last Monday in October

▶ **Dublin Theatre Festival**
Irish and international productions are shown for two weeks in Dublin.

▶ **Gourmet Festival**
in Kinsale, Co. Cork

▶ **Wexford Opera Festival**
This renowned opera event draws visitors from all over the world.

EVENTS IN NOVEMBER

▶ **Belfast Festival at Queen's**
This three-week cultural festival counts as the second largest in the United Kingdom, after Edinburgh.

Food and Drink

Few people travel to Ireland for the food. Traditionally, the Irish are in the habit of overcooking their vegetables and home cuisine is heavy on meat, potatoes and cabbage; and if you are hoping for fancy salad dishes on this Emerald Isle, you will be bitterly disappointed. Yet that certainly does not make Ireland a culinary desert. There are a number of very good restaurants (several with star awards), though

No need to fear Irish cooking!

All over the world, Guinness is associated with cozy Irish pubs

GUINNESS IS GOOD FOR YOU

The heart of Ireland beats at St James's Gate in Dublin – the place where Guinness is brewed. Every Irish person knows the »wine of life«, as James Joyce calls the dark beer in his *Ulysses*, as a medicine, staple food and mood enhancer.

Seen in the cold light of day, Guinness is a dark, top-fermented beer brewed in a special way. For their beer mash the brewers on the River Liffey use, apart from roasted malt, a little grain roasted over beech-wood logs but not malted, to get the dark colour. Then they make a hearty blend of several beer mashes and hops in order to achieve the taste, which is surprisingly bitter for a dark beer. The result is an »Extra Stout« which, despite its name, only has an alcoholic content of 4.3%, as opposed to the roughly 5% of a regular beer. Today, »Stout« refers to the strong colour rather than the strength of the beer. In Ireland, »Draught Guinness« has the most intensive and fresh taste, as the rapid turnover means the beer does not have to be pasteurized.

If you have tried Guinness at home, you will be surprised not just at the taste, but also at the colour of the original version of the beverage: it is much darker, with a nearly-white head. Depending on the country where it is to be sold, Guinness is brewed to a different recipe, the strongest selling as »Foreign Extra Stout« in the tropics.

A family business

However, Guinness is much more than just a beer and the national tipple; it is also the success story of

one family and its product, becoming a worldwide brand and legend. In 1759, Arthur Guinness I came to Dublin from Celbridge, Co. Kildare, with 100 pounds he had inherited. Buying a small brewery, he brewed the »Entire« Beer, a blend of several beer mashes very popular with the drinking classes at the time, who demanded blended beers. As this strong beer was a favourite with the porters, it soon came to be called by that name. When Arthur Guinness I handed over the brewery to his son, also called Arthur of course, he was already dominating the Irish beer and grain market – at one time, nearly the entire Irish grain harvest ended up in the Guinness Brewery.

Arthur Guinness II started wooing the English beer drinkers, and soon even the British upper class partook of the former proletarians' brew. The population's increasing thirst for Guinness increased the family's fame and wealth. Benjamin Lee, the third in the dynasty, even became Mayor of Dublin, promoted the arts, and – his

»Is Ireland sober, is Ireland stiff.«

(James Joyce in »Finnegans Wake«)

most important deed in a global context – introduced bottled Guinness. His successor Edward Cecil who, in 1899, floated what was by that stage the largest brewery in the world on the stock market, was made a peer. Since then, the head of the Guinness dynasty is entitled to use the title Earl of Iveagh. Not stopping there, James Joyce immortalized Edward Cecil as Noble Buniveagh in *Ulysses*! Cecil also gave the Australian South Pole ex-

plorer Douglas Mawson a few bottles of Guinness to leave behind in the ice. Naturally, when the bottles were found again 18 years later, they were perfectly drinkable. On his Eleveden estate in Phoenix Park, Edward Cecil had a tower built next to his palace, climbing it every morning after his early-morning tea. The idea was to check whether the chimneys of his brewery at the other end of town were still smoking. To this day, every member of the Guinness family has been able to climb down again, reassured.

Edward Cecil was a hard act to follow; his successor Rupert only took to the limelight once as a member of parliament, in an issue regarding his own company. When the disfigurement of the landscape by Guinness billboards proclaiming »Guinness is Good for You« was debated, Sir Rupert stood up to reply »But Guinness *Is* Good For You!«

Publicity

This advertising slogan, originally conceived by (crime writer) Dorothy Sayers, stands for the hugely successful Guinness publicity in the 1920s and 1940s.

> *»Guinness Is*
> *Good For You«*

Alongside well-known writers, no less famous artists such as Rex Whistler, H M Bateman or the cartoonist »Vicky« worked for Guinness, illustrating the advertising slogans. The most popular was a series about a zookeeper who recovers with a glass of porter from the surprises the animals constantly hold in store for him (»My Goodness – My Guinness«).

This campaign was so successful that in 1953, Guinness had publicity posters printed for the coronation of

A perfect draught Guinness can be enjoyed in McDaid's in Dublin.

Elizabeth II, with no slogan and no mention of beer, just a sea lion, a toucan and a kangaroo – everybody knew the story.

Guinness today

Over time, »porter« lost its popularity, and has not been brewed in England or Ireland since 1973. The last barrel was drunk in a mourning ceremony in a Belfast pub in May 1973. However, Guinness had started to back the stronger »stout« in good time, to fill the gap left by the demise of porter. Today, Guinness is not only the largest brewery in Europe, but also a multinational group with interests in the car and food industry, a company that owns chains of stores, runs a fleet of cabin cruisers on the lakes and rivers of Ireland and, of course, also publishes the *Guinness Book of Records*. Family members have married into the European aristocracy and have not had to deal with money worries for a long time. Many simple Irish folk, at least the males, still harbour a desire for the dream job: taster at Guinness – they do exist!

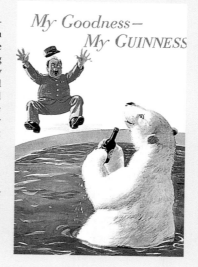

My Goodness— My GUINNESS

their prices are pretty steep. Typical dishes, such as Irish stew and lamb in mint sauce, taste very good when prepared well, and Irish salmon is rated as one of the best in the world. Luxury seafood, such as mussels, lobster and more are also comparatively affordable. Poultry, especially chicken, is available almost everywhere in a variety of guises. However, be careful of misunderstandings: »Black Pudding« is in fact a sausage made from congealed blood!

From breakfast to dinner

Breakfast, lunch, tea time and dinner make up the four most important mealtimes of the day. In the old days there was also »high tea«, an early supper, but that is rarely on offer now.

A full Irish breakfast is a real challenge: cornflakes or porridge are followed by eggs, bacon and sausages accompanied by toast, plus brown bread, butter and jam. Coffee, tea or fruit juice are the standard drink options.

Not surprisingly, this heart attack on a plate is normally followed by a light lunch, which usually just consists of sandwiches and tea. Value for money tourist lunches can often be found, though the quality of the food is often reflected in the low price. Many pubs offer pub grub at lunch time and a full pub often signifies good food.

In the afternoons, around 4pm, the Irish are in the habit of **taking tea**, which is usually served with delicious scones (small buns with raisins) or other pastries.

Dinner is always comprised of several courses. Sherry, whiskey or gin is taken as an aperitif, and German or French wine is usually drunk with the meal itself. (Note that not all restaurants hold a license to serve beer).

Specialties

A dish famous beyond the shores of Ireland is »Irish Stew«, a casserole of mutton, potatoes, onions and spices which is simmered for several hours. »Coddle« is another casserole of potatoes, sausage and bacon. »Leg of Lamb with Mint Sauce« is also often found on menus, while »Colcannon« is very rarely found, because this dish of cabbage, mashed potatoes, carrots and turnips is to this day considered poor man's fare. A tasty snack comes in the shape of potato cakes, prepared with mashed potato, flour, butter and milk, which are covered in butter and eaten warm. An unusual dessert is »Carageen Moss Jelly«, which is made from edible seaweed, milk, sugar and lemon rind. Less adventurous eaters should choose lemon meringue pie, hot apple pie with ice cream or fruit salad with fresh cream for dessert.

No »tea time« is complete without scones.

Drinks

Next to tea, which is drunk at any time of day, preferably with fresh milk, beer and whiskey are the Irish tipples of choice. There is a wide variety of beer, from English Ale to dark »Guinness stout« brewed at the famous Guinness brewery. Bottled beer, meanwhile, is on a par with Central European brands. Irish whiskey differs from Scottish and American varieties, not only in spelling, but also in its milder taste, and in Ireland it is usually drunk straight or with water.

Restaurants
◀ Alcohol License

»Full License« indicates that a restaurant is entitled to serve the full range of alcoholic beverages during official opening times. »Wine License« indicates that only wine may be served.

Pubs

In general pubs are principally for drinking in. Drinks are bought and paid for at the bar, and it is customary to return the favour if someone buys you a drink. It is very easy to get chatting to locals in pubs, so an evening visit can continue long into the night!

◀ Opening Hours

Most pubs are open Mon–Wed, from 10.30am to 11.30pm, Thu–Fri, from 10.30am to 12.30am, and Sun from 12.30pm to 11pm (plus half an hour of »drink up time« after last orders). When the landlord calls out »last orders« you should take it literally, as »closing time« is rigorously adhered to. In Northern Ireland Sunday opening times are 12.30pm to 2.30pm and from 7pm to 10pm. By the way, there has been a complete ban on smoking in Irish pubs since 2004.

◀ Singing Pubs

In so-called singing pubs vocalists and musicians meet for informal music sessions and the general public can also join in.

Information

● USEFUL ADDRESSES

THE REPUBLIC OF IRELAND

▸ **Board Fáilte,**
Irish Tourist Board
Baggot Street Bridge, Dublin 2
Tel. (01) 6 02 40 00
Fax (01) 6 02 41 00
www.discoverireland.com

▸ **Tourism Ireland**
Beresford House
2 Beresford Road
Coleraine
BT52 1GE
Tel. (028) 70 35 92 00
Fax (028) 70 35 92 21
www.discoverireland.com

NORTHERN IRELAND

▸ **Northern Ireland**
Tourist Board
59 North Street
Belfast BT 1 NB
Tel. (0 28) 90 23 12 21
Fax (0 28) 90 24 09 60
www.nitb.com

IN ENGLAND

▸ **Tourism Ireland**
Tel. (02 0) 7 51 8 0800
103 Wigmore Street
London W1U 1QS
Fax (0 20) 74 93 90 65
www.irelandtravel.co.uk
www.tourismireland.com

IN SCOTLAND

▸ **Tourism Ireland**
Tel. (01 41) 5 72 4030
James Millar House
7th Floor, 98 West George Street
Glasgow
Fax (01 41) 5 72 40 33
www.irelandtravel.co.uk
www.tourismireland.com

IN USA

▸ **Tourism Ireland**
345 Park Avenue
New York, NY 10154

Tel. toll-free 1-800 223 64 70
Tel. (2 12) 418 08 00
(information, brochures)
info@irishtouristboard.com

IN CANADA

▸ **Tourism Ireland**
Tel. (0 800) 223 64 70
2 Bloor St West, Suite 3403
Toronto
M4W 3E2
www.tourismireland.com

IN AUSTRALIA

▸ **Tourism Ireland**
Tel (0 2) 92 99 61 77
Level 5, 36 Carrington St

Sydney
NSW 2000
www.tourismireland.com

IN NEW ZEALAND

► **Tourism Ireland**
Tel. (0 9) 977 22 55
Level 6, 18 Shortland St
Auckland 1
M4W 3E2
www.tourismireland.com

IN SOUTH AFRICA

► **Tourism Ireland**
Tel. (0 11) 3 39 48 65
c/o Development Promotions
Everite House, Level 7
20 De Korte Street
Braamfontein 2001
Gauteng
www.tourismireland.com

EMBASSIES • CONSULATES

IN USA

► **Ireland**
Embassy of Ireland
2234 Massachusetts Ave. NW
Washington, C 20008
Tel (2 02) 2 462 3939
www.irelandemb.org
Consulate General of Ireland, New
York
Ireland House
345 Park Avenue
17th Floor
New York NY 10154-0037
Tel. (2 12) 319 25 55
congenny@AOL.com
Consulate General of Ireland, San
Francisco
100 Pine St, 33rd Floor
San Francisco, CA 94111
Tel. (4 15) 392 08 85

Consulate General of Ireland,
Boston
535 Boylston Street
Boston MA 02116
Tel. (6 17) 267 93 30
irlcons@aol.com

► **Northern Ireland**
British Embassy
3100 Massachusetts Avenue

Washington DC, 20008
Tel. (2 02) 588 78 00
www.britainusa.com

IN CANADA

► **Ireland**
Embassy of Ireland
Suite 1105
130 Albert Street
Ottawa
K1P 5G4 Ontario
Tel. (01) 6 13 233 62 81

► **Northern Ireland**
British High Commission
80 Elgin Street
Ottawa
Ontario K1P 5K7
Tel. (01) 6 13 237 1530
www.britainincanada.org

IN AUSTRALIA

► **Ireland**
Embassy of Ireland
20 Arkana Street
Yarralumla, Canberra, ACT 2600
Tel. (0 2) 62 73 30 22
irishemb@cyberone.com.au

► **Northern Ireland**
High Commission

Commonwealth Ave
Yarralumla, Canberra, ACT 2600
Tel. (02) 62706666

► **Ireland**
Consulate General of Ireland
7 Citigroup Building
23 Customs Street East
Auckland
Tel. (09) 9772252

► **Northern Ireland**
The British High Commission
44 Hill Street, Thorndon
Wellington 6011
Tel. (04) 92888
www.britishhighcommission.
gov.uk

► **Ireland**
Embassy of Ireland (Pretoria)
1st Floor, Southern Life Plaza
1059 Schoeneman Street Cnr Festival & Schoeman Street
Arcadia, 0083
Pretoria
Tel. (012) 3425062
www.embassyireland.org.za

Embassy of Ireland (Cape Town)
12th Floor, LG Building
No. 1 Thibault Square, Long Street
Cape Town 8000
Tel. (012) 4190636
www.embassyireland.org.za

► **Northern Ireland**
High Commission of the United
Kingdom of Great Britain &
Northern Ireland
»Her Britanic Majesty's High
Commission«, »Greystoke«
255 Hill Street
Arcadia, 0083
Tel. (012) 4217500
www.britain.org.za

► **Britain**
British Embassy Dublin
29 Merrion Road
Ballsbridge, Dublin 4
Tel. (01) 2053700
www.britishembassy.ie

► **USA**
American Embassy of the
United States
42 Eglin Road, Ballsbridge
Dublin 4, Ireland
Tel. (01) 6680777

► **Canada**
Canadian Embassy
7–8 Wilton Terrace, Dublin 2
Tel. (01) 4174100
www.geo.international.gc.ca/
canada-europa/ireland/
menu-en.asp

► **Australia**
Australian Embassy Ireland
7th Floor, Fitzwilton House
Wilton Terrace, Dublin 2
Tel. (01) 6645300

► **New Zealand**
Consulate General
PO Box 9999, Dublin 6
Tel. (01) 6604233
nzconsul@indigo.ie
Or contact the High Commission
in London (see below).

► **South Africa**
South African Embassy
Alexandra House, 2nd Floor
Earlsfort Centre, Earlsfort Terrace
Dublin 2, Tel. (01) 6615553
www.dfa.gov.za

► **USA**
US Consulate General
Danesfort House

223 Stranmillis Road
Belfast BT9 5GR/
Tel. (028) 9038 6100
www.london.usembassy.gov

► **Canadian High Commission**
Macdonald House
38 Grosvenor Street
London W1K 4AA
Tel. (020) 7258 6506
www.canada.org.uk

► **Australian High Commission**
Australia House
Strand London WC2B 4LA
Tel. +44 (20) 7379 4334
www.australia.org.uk

► **New Zealand High Commission**
New Zealand House
80 Haymarket
London SW1Y 4TQ
Tel. +44 (20) 7930 8422
www.nzembassy.com/uk

► **South African High Commission**
South Africa House
Trafalgar Square
London WC2N 5DP
Tel. +44 (20) 7451 7299
www.southafricahouse.com

⏵ INTERNET INFORMATION

► **www.discoverireland.com**
Website of the Irish Tourist Board
»Fáilte Ireland«; check this for
information on entry require-
ments, accommodation and travelling within the whole island of
Ireland.

► **www.discovernorthern
ireland.com**
Website of the Northern Irish
Tourist Board. Information and
attractive pages.

► **www.eventguide.ie**
Events, entertainment, concerts,
cinema programmes.

► **www.visitdublin.com**
Online guide to Dublin.

► **www.irishdancing
directory.com**
All about Irish dance, from show
dates, dress makers, to contacts of
dance schools for Irish Dance all
over the world.

► **www.gaelchultur.com**
Irish-language classes in Dublin
and Cork.

► **www.irish-music.net**
Lots of information and links.

► **www.ireland-information.com/
engine**
Excellent search engine for all
things Irish, including a recipe
collection.

► **www.luminarium.org/
mythology/Ireland**
All about Irish mythology, stories
and fairytales, with links to Irish
newspapers, online Irish diction-
aries and much more.

Language

English is the most commonly used language throughout Ireland, though you might have difficulties with some words originating in Gaelic.

The **Gaelic alphabet** has a few less letters than its Latin counterpart; k, v, w, x, y and z are missing. Other letters have orthographic differences. For example, an accent on a letter indicates emphasis. A recommended English-Irish dictionary **dictionary** (Eng: dictionary, Irish: foclóir) is published by the Talbot Press Ltd. in the Republic of Ireland, with many distinct words and geographical names, as well as information on grammar. It has been updated several times.

Irish language courses

For an overview of Irish language courses, contact the tourist boards or see www.irishlanguage.net.

Gaelic Dictionary

abha	river
ard	height
áth	ford
béal	mouth (river)
ben	mountain
bord	Office
bun	end
burren	stone
cahir	stone fort
cashel	stone fort
cavan	cave
cill	church
clochán	beehive shaped stone hut
cnoc	mound
croagh	pointed hill
drum	chain of hills
derry	oak
dún	mountain fort
éireann	irisch
ennis (innis)	island, meadow
gal	river
grianán	palace
lis	stone castle
lough	lake, sea channel
mac	son
monaster	monastery

ráth	wall circle
skerry	rock
slieve	mountains

Literature

Binchy, Maeve: *Circle of Friends*. Dublin: Arrow 2006.
In her books, the best-selling popular novelist describes daily life in Ireland with a keen eye and warm heart, with the plot often revolving around friendships between young women, town and country, love and innocence.

Novels, short stories

McCabe, Patrick: *The Butcher Boy*. London: Picador 1993.
An unsettling read, though fascinating in its language and dramatic vibrancy, about the life of a murderer from the Irish provinces who, in everything he did, was only looking for love. Neil Jordan made the novel into a successful film

McNamee, Eoin: *Resurrection Man*. London: Faber & Faber 2004.
The story of recent conflicts in Belfast, narrated succinctly and poetically as a man becomes a member of a Protestant terror organization. Also available as a film noir on DVD.

Eds. John Somer/John J. Daly. New York: *New Irish Writing*. Anchor 2000.
A collection of stories by authors as diverse as Elizabeth Bowen, John Banville, Joseph O'Connor and Anne Enright – a treasure trove of the legendary Irish storytelling with a contemporary twist.

O'Brien, Flann: *The Best of Myles*. London: Harper Perennial 2007.
Under the pseudonym of Myles na gCopaleen, from 1940 to his death in 1966, Flann O'Brien gave the readers of his column for the *Irish Times* advice on all the vital questions of life; from bureaucracy to booze and unforgettable Dublin vignettes, this is a hilarious read.

McCourt, Frank: *Angela's Ashes*. London: HarperPerennial 2005.
This bestselling memoir, telling the story of an impoverished childhood in Limerick, was made into a successful film.

Biographies, journals

Sands, Bobby: *One Day in My Life*. Cork: Mercier 2001.
The IRA prisoner Bobby Sands was 27 when he died in 1982 on hunger strike, following nearly nine years of imprisonment. In his diary, written on toilet paper and smuggled outside, he describes the cruelty

of prison life, the inmates' fight for political prisoner status in the infamous Belfast »Maze«, and the IRA's armed struggle for a free Ireland.

Sayers, Peig: *An Old Woman's Reflections*. Oxford Paperbacks 1977.
Fisherwoman Peig Sayers describing her life on the bleak Blasket Islands, this has become a classic of Irish storytelling.

Dames, Michael: *Mythic Ireland*. London: Thames and Hudson 1996.
An archaeologist's engaging illustrated exploration of Ireland's sacred locations, legends and mythological figures.

McCarthy, Pete: *Mc Carthy's Bar: A Journey of Discovery in Ireland*. London: Hodder & Stoughton 2000
The late Anglo-Irish writer's hilarious exploration of the country, through visiting all bars bearing his family name on a quest to find his Irish roots, is not without deep undertones.

Hawks, Tony: *Round Ireland with a Fridge*. London: Ebury Press 1999 / New York: St. Martin's Griffin 2001.
The story of a drunken bet to hike around Ireland with a fridge, told with a comedian's skill.

Non-fiction **Arnold, Bruce:** *Irish Art*. London: Thames & Hudson 1995.
Compact and beautifully illustrated overview of Irish art from the Celtic era up to the late 1970s.

Feeney, Brian: *O'Brien Pocket History of the Troubles*. Dublin: O'Brien 2007.
The Northern Ireland conflict – where does it come from, who are the main players, and what might the future hold? Revised edition of a clear and non-partisan overview of a complex issue, published in a breakthrough year for the peace process.

Somerville, Alexander: *Letters from Ireland during the Famine of 1847*. Ed. K D Snell. Dublin: Irish Academic Press 1995.
An engaging read based on the dispatches of a journalist who travelled in Ireland during the Great Hunger.

Irish Fairy Tales **Stephens, James:** *Classic fairytales from the Emerald Isle*, available as an e-book on www.gutenberg.org/etext/2892.

Sterry, Paul: *Complete Irish Wildlife*. London: Collins 2004.
In-depth photoguide of the country's flora and fauna.

Young readers **Parkinson, Siobhán:** *Cows Are Vegetarians*. Dublin: O'Brien 2002.
The story of city girl Michelle's eventful visit to her country cousin Sinéad is an engaging children's variation on the classic theme of town versus country, or »Dub« versus »culchies«.

Money

The euro has been the only acceptable currency in the Republic of Ireland since 1 January 2002.

Republic of Ireland

In Northern Ireland the working currency is the pound sterling (£), divided in 100 pence (one penny or pence). There are bank notes to the value of £5, £10, £20 und £50. Coins come in denominations of £1, as well as one pence, two pence, five pence, and ten, 20 and 50 pence.

Northern Ireland

EXCHANGE RATES REPUBLIC OF IRELAND

► €1 = £0.68
£1 = €1.47
€1 = US$1.37
US$1 = €0.73

EXCHANGE RATES NORTHERN IRELAND

► £1 = €1.47
€1 = £0.68
£1 = US$2.02
US$1 = £0.49

CREDIT CARD COMPANIES ROI

► **American Express**
(01) 6791200
www.americanexpress.com

► **Diners Club**
(0818) 300026
www.dinersclub.co.uk

► **MasterCard**
(0044) 2075575000
www.mastercard.com
Call your issuing bank for assistance.

► **Visa**
(1800) 558002
www.visaeurope.com

CREDIT CARD COMPANIES UK

► **American Express**
(01273) 696933
www.americanexpress.com

► **Diners Club**
(0870) 1900011
www.dinersclub.co.uk

► **MasterCard**
(020) 75575000
www.mastercard.com
Call your issuing bank for assistance.

► **Visa**
(0800) 891725
www.visaeurope.com

Customs   EU citizens are allowed to bring (and take out) an unlimited amount of EU currency to the Republic of Ireland and Northern Ireland.

Credit cards   Standard international cards, such as Visa, Euro-/Mastercard, and American Express can be used almost everywhere.

Post and Communications

Post   In the **Republic of Ireland** letter boxes and postal service vehicles are painted green. Stamps can be purchased at post offices, at machines and in some newspaper kiosks. The standard rate for a letter or card under 50gr is 55 cents within Ireland (including Northern Ireland), and 78 cents to Great Britain, Europe and worldwide.
In **Northern Ireland**, letter boxes and postal service vehicles are red. British stamps and rates are required here, which means letters and cards up to 20g to the rest of the UK require a 27p stamp, EU countries need a 48p stamp and those to non-EU countries need a 78p stamp.
Post Offices are open from 9am to 5.30pm, Monday to Friday, and from 1pm to 5pm on Saturdays. (Some open from 2.15pm).

Telephones   **Telephone boxes** in the Republic of Ireland are grey or green and white. In Northern Ireland, they are red or metal with plexiglass. Public telephones accept coins or alternatively phone cards (Call-Card), which can be purchased in post offices and at newspaper kiosks. Check with your mobile phone **Mobile phones** provider for their roaming services which should allow you to use your phone in the normal way while travelling.

▶ DIALING CODES

► **To the Republic of Ireland**
Tel 0 03 53

► **To Northern Ireland**
from outside UK: Tel. 0 48
from the the UK
(area code): Tel. 0 28

► **To the UK**
Tel 00 44

► **To the US and Canada**
Tel 00 1

► **To Australia**
Tel 00 61

► **To New Zealand**
Tel 00 64

► **To South Africa**
Tel 00 27

Prices and Discounts

Some visitor attractions are free, but occasionally very steep entrance fees are charged, even for churches. For those planning on visiting several cultural heritage sights in Ireland it might be worth buying the »National Heritage Card«, which gives access to over 70 attractions, including Dublin Castle, Rock of Cashel, Newgrange and others. The card is valid for one year and can be purchased in almost all of Ireland's tourist centres (www.heritageireland.ie). Visitor
attractions
◄ Heritage Card

The National Trust (www.nationaltrust.org.uk) in Northern Ireland maintains over sixty buildings or areas of outstanding natural beauty which typically cost around five pounds to visit. Included are Castle Ward, Giant's Causeway and Strangford Lough Wildlife Reserve. Members of the National Trust are entitled to free entrance to all their properties. ◄ National Trust

In general, it is customary to leave a 10–15% tip on restaurant bills. Many hotels and restaurants add the tip onto your bill automatically. Tipping

 WHAT DOES IT COST?

3-course meal
from €25

Simple meal
from €10

Cup of coffee
€2

Hire care
from 35 per day

Simple room
from €30

1 pint of Guinness
from €4

Shopping

Opening Hours

Opening times for chemists in Ireland are Mon–Sat, 9am (or 9.30am) to 5.30pm (or 6pm) and Sun 11am–1pm. Outside these opening times an emergency service is offered in towns, details of which are posted in the window. Chemists

Shops in the Republic of Ireland do not have fixed opening times, but in general they are in business from 9am or 9.30am to 5.30pm Shops or 6pm. Outside Dublin, shops are shut on either Wednesday or Thursday afternoons, but shopping centres and supermarkets remain open until 9pm on those days. In some places, shops are open till 8pm or 9pm on Saturdays, and even on Sundays there is almost always a grocery store to be found open somewhere. In Belfast shops are open 9am–5.30pm from Mondays to Saturdays, and many large shopping centres are open till 9pm. In many of the smaller towns in Northern Ireland a lot of shops close for half a day during the week (the day varies), and are also usually closed during lunchtime.

---

i Best Buys

- Craft work from Ulster: Craftworks Shop in Belfast
- Crystal: Waterford Crystal in Waterford
- Woodwork: Quirke's Sculptures, Wine Street in Sligo
- Porcelain: Factory in Belleek
- Aran jumpers are best value on the islands themselves
- Whiskey specialties: Bushmills Distillery in Bushmills

Banks In the Republic of Ireland banks are open Mon–Fri, 9.30am–4.30pm. In Dublin banks are open until 5pm on Thursdays. On Saturdays, Sundays and Bank Holidays, only the banks at Dublin, Shannon and Cork airports are open (Dublin, daily 8am–10pm; Shannon and Cork: daily 6.30am–5.30pm, from 7.30am during the winter). Money can be exchanged at the general post office in Dublin, Mon–Sat, 8am–8pm, Sun, 10am–6pm.
In Northern Ireland banks are open Mon–Fri, 10am–12.30pm and 1.30pm–3.30pm. In smaller places banks are often only open three days a week.

Petrol Stations Petrol stations are normally in business 9am-6pm during the week, but one should fill up for the weekend, as there is only a limited service on Sundays. There are just a few 24-hour petrol stations in Dublin and Cork.

Artwork In many parts of Ireland craftsmen still follow their traditional trades of pottery, basket weaving and glass blowing. If you want to get creative yourself there are many opportunities provided by holiday courses. Information can be found at:

► **The Administrator**
I. C. A.
Grianan Adult Education College
Termonfeckin, Co. Louth
Tel. (0 41) 9 82 21 19
www.edunet.it/angrianan

► **Crafts Council of Ireland**
The Castle Yard
Kilkenny, Co. Kilkenny
Tel. (0 56) 776 18 04
www.ccoi.ie

▶ READY-TO-WEAR SIZES

▶ Ladies					
D	36	38	40	42	44
IRL/GB	34	36	38	40	42
	10	12	14	16	18

▶ Men						
D	46	48	50	52	54	56
IRL/GB	36	38	40	42	44	46

Souvenir shopping

Typical Irish products are hand-woven tweed, as well as fine lace, jumpers, pipes, porcelain, ceramics, silver, and handcrafted crystal. The most popular gifts are smoked salmon and hand-knitted Aran jumpers. Beautiful antiques can also be found in antique shops, at auctions and at flea markets (Dublin, Cork and Limerick). The larger tourist information centres sell artwork, jewellery and books, and can also provide information on nearby shops.

Salmon and woo

Sport and Outdoors

Fishing

Thanks to its numerous lakes, rivers and coastal areas, Ireland is a classic fishing destination. Options include coarse fishing, game fishing (trout and salmon) and deep-sea angling.

As the Irish themselves are predominantly only interested in fishing for salmon or trout, holidaymakers do not generally require a permit for coarse fishing, either in the Republic or in Northern Ireland. (The exception is the region along the north bank of the Shannon, where you need a »Share Certificate«). There are no closed seasons, but fishing with more than one rod and the use of live bait is forbidden. The best fishing region is made up by the »Irish Lake Plateau«, comprised of parts of the counties of Westmeath, Longford, Cavan and Monaghan. The county of Clare also has an appealing lake district. Best times of year are: all year round for pike (Nov–Mar in the large lakes); April–Aug for bream; May–Sep for tench; April–Sep for rudd; April–Sep for roach; and all year round for perch, carp and eel.

Coarse Fishing

ℹ Fishing Board

- Central Fisheries Board
  Swords Business Campus
  Swords, Co. Dublin
  Tel. (01) 8 84 26 00
  www.cfb.ie

Lough Corrib – fishing heaven

Salmon fishing requires a licence which is issued in the fishing districts, and can be purchased in fishing shops, many other shops and also in hotels. Most salmon grounds are in private hands and an additional fee may be charged (information available locally). The closed season, from the end of August to the beginning of January, should be strictly observed. The most common trout species are brown trout and rainbow trout, and the best stocks are in the lakes to the west, in Lough Corrib for example. Most demand is for salmon of course, which can be found in the mouths of almost all rivers running into the sea.

Deep Sea Angling
Due to the mild Gulf Stream, superb deep sea angling grounds can be found, especially off western and southern Ireland. Among others, you will find shark, stingray, Atlantic cod, haddock, pike, sea bass, sea carp, grey mullet, and sea bream. The season goes from spring to autumn and major deep sea angling centres are at Youghal, Kinsale, Courtmacsherry, Cahirciveen, Galway, Westport, Killala, Killybegs, Dungarvan, Baltimore, Schull, Valentia, Cleggan, Rosses Point, Mullaghmore und Bunbeg.

Package tours
Numerous travel agents offer fishing package tours and an overview of individual companies can be found in listings supplied by the Irish National Tourist Board.

Cycle Touring

As long as cyclists don't mind the changeable weather, Ireland's great variety of landscape, its relatively short distances and low traffic density make it an ideal cycle touring destination. **Bringing your own bike** Many airlines will transport your bicycle as a normal part of your 20kg allowance, or charge a very small fee. As Irish sizes for spare parts may differ to the ones you need, it is advisable to bring your own spare parts, such as inner tubes and tyres. Transporting bicycles by train will cost you 25 % of a standard ticket. Cross country buses will also take bikes for an additional fee.

Bike hire
Several bike hire companies have offices in a number of towns, and since bicycles are purchased new each season, they are normally in good condition. As a rule, three to five-gear bikes are hired out, but you can also rent mountain bikes and sporting bikes with 12 or 18 gears. Booking ahead with plenty of time is advisable for July and

⏵ DUBLIN BY BICYCLE

▶ **Raleigh Rent-a-Bike**
Raleigh House
Kylemore Road, Dublin 10
Tel (01) 6 26 13 33
www.raleigh.ie

IRELAND BY BICYCLE

▶ **Irish Cycling Safaris**
Belfield Bike Shop
UCD, Dublin 4
Tel. (01) 2 60 07 49
www.cyclingsafaris.com

August. The weekly rental fee, including insurance, generally lies at around €50, depending on bike and firm. For an additional fee, bicycles can usually be returned at the rental outlet of your choice.

The brochure *Cycling Ireland*, available from the national tourist board, gives short guidelines for 23 cycle tours of between 200 and 300 kilometres in length. Another brochure also provides an overview of tour companies that offer cycle touring packages.

Bike tours

Golf

In Ireland golf is a national sport. At the end of the working day or during the weekend many Irish people can be seen playing golf in unpretentious clothing. There are more than 400 golf clubs and half of those have 18-hole courses. Casual golfers, including beginners, are welcome without a reservation almost anywhere. Equipment can often be hired. Most package tour hotels are located near golf courses.

⏵ IMPORTANT GOLF ADDRESSES

INFORMATION

▶ **Speciality IrelandGolf Tours**
Gortnafleur Business Park
Clonmel, Co. Tipperary
Tel. (052) 7 06 29
www.specialityireland.com

DUBLIN • EAST

▶ **Druids Glen Golf Club**
Newtownmountkennedy
Co. Wicklow
Tel. (01) 2 87 36 00
www.druidsglen.ie
18-hole course in park with many lakes; visitors welcome daily

▶ **Edmondstown Golf Club**
Rathfarnham, Dublin 16
Tel. (01) 4 93 10 82
www.edmondstowngolfclub.ie
18-hole course. Visitors welcome: Mon, Thu and Fri mornings, as well as afternoons during the weekend.

▶ **Hollystown Golf**
Hollystown, Dublin 15
Tel. (01) 8 20 74 44
www.hollystown.com
18-hole course. Visitors welcome daily

Golfers at the Royal Portrush Golf Club in Derry

▶ **Kilkea Castle Golf Club**
Arnosford Ltd.,
Castledermot, Co. Kildare
Tel. (05 9) 9 14 51 56
www.kilkeacastle.ie
18-hole course in park landscape.
Visitors welcome daily

▶ **Knockanally**
Golf & Country Club
Donadea
North Kildare
Tel. (0 45) 86 93 22
www.knockanally.com
18-hole course. Visitors welcome
daily.

▶ **Luttrellstown Castle**
Golf & Country Club
Castleknock
Dublin 15
Tel. (01) 8 60 95 00
www.luttrellstown.ie
18-hole course. Visitors welcome
daily.

▶ **Mount Wolseley**
Golf & Country Club
Tullow, Co. Carlow
Tel. (05 9) 9 18 01 00
www.mountwolseley.ie
18-hole course in park landscape.
Visitors: daily

▶ **Portmarnock**
Hotel & Golf Links
Strand Road
Portmarnock
Co. Dublin
Tel. (01) 8 46 24 42
www.portmarnock.com
18-hole course in park landscape
with sand dunes. Visitors: daily

▶ **Powerscourt Golf Club**
Powerscourt Estate
Enniskerry, Co. Wicklow
Tel. (01) 2 04 60 33
www.powerscourt.ie
18-hole course in a park landscape
with views of the mountains and
the coast. Visitors: daily

► **Rathsallagh Golf Club**
Dunlavin, Co. Wicklow
Tel. (0 45) 40 31 12
www.rathsallaghhousehotel.com
18-hole course. Visitors: weekday
afternoons and weekends

► **Seapoint Golf Club**
Termonfeckin, Co. Louth
Tel. (0 41) 9 82 23 33
www.seapointgolfclub.com
18-hole course in a park landscape. Visitors: daily

► **St. Margaret's**
Golf & Country Club
St. Maragaret's, Co. Dublin
Tel. (01) 8 64 04 00
www.stmargaretsgolf.com
18-hole course. Visitors: daily

SOUTHEAST

► **Co. Tipperary**
Golf & Country Club
Dundrum, Co. Tipperary
Tel. (0 62) 7 11 16
www.dundrumhousehotel.com
18-hole course in a park landscape. Visitors: daily

► **Mount Juliet Golf Club**
Thomastown, Co. Kilkenny
Tel. (0 56) 7 77 30 00
www.mountjuliet.ie
18-hole course in a park landscape. Visitors: daily

► **St Helen's Bay & Golf Club**
St Helen's Bay
Kilrane, Co. Wexford
Tel. (0 53) 91 3 32 34
www.sthelensbay.com 18-hole
course in a coastal landscape.
Visitors: daily

► **Waterford Castle**
Golf & Country Club
The Island

Ballinakill, Waterford
Tel. (0 51) 8 78 203
www.waterfordcastle.com 18-hole
course, sand dunes and park.
Visitors: daily

► **West Waterford**
Golf & Country Club
Dungarvan, Co. Waterford
Tel. (0 58) 4 32 16, 4 14 75
www.westwaterfordgolf.com
18-hole course in a park
landscape

SOUTH

► **Adare Golf Club**
Adare, Co. Limerick
Tel. (0 61) 60 52 74
www.adaregolfclub.com
18-hole course located in Adare
Manor park, which was designed
by Robert Trent Jones. Visitors:
daily

► **Fota Island Golf Club**
Carrigtwohill, Co. Cork
Tel. (0 21) 4 88 37 00
www.fotaisland.ie
Visitors: Sat / Sun,
10.30am – 12.30pm and
2pm – 5pm, Mon – Fri,
9am – 12.30pm and 2pm – 5pm

► **Kenmare Golf Club**
Killowen, Kenmare, Co. Kerry
Tel. (0 64) 4 12 91
www.kenmaregolfclub.com
18-hole course in a park with
views of Kenmare Bay. Visitors:
daily, but reservations recommended at weekends.

► **Kilkee Golf Club**
Kilkee, Co. Clare
Tel. (0 65) 9 05 60 48
www.kilkeegolfclub.ie
18-hole course in coastal area on
the Atlantic. Visitors: daily

▶ **Lee Valley Golf & Country Club**
Clashanure, Ovens, Co. Cork
Tel. (0 21) 7 33 17 21
www.leevalleygcc.ie
18-hole course in a park landscape. Visitors: daily, but reservations recommended at weekends.

▶ **Limerick County
Golf & Country Club**
Ballyneety, Co. Limerick
Tel. (0 61) 35 13 84
www.limerickcounty.com
18-hole course in a park landscape. Visitors: daily

MID WEST

▶ **Esker Hills Golf & Country Club**
Tullamore, Co. Offaly
Tel. (05 7) 9 35 59 99
www.eskerhillsgolf.com
18-hole course in hilly park landscape. Visitors: daily

▶ **Glasson Golf & Country Club**
Glasson
Athlone, Co. Westmeath
Tel. (09 0) 6 48 51 20
www.glassongolf.ie
18-hole course in a park landscape by Lough Ree. Visitors: daily, but reservations are recommended

▶ **Rosapenna Hotel & Golf Links**
Downings, Co. Donegal
Tel. (0 74) 91 55 3 01
www.rosapenna.ie
18-hole course in a coastal park landscape. Visitors: Mon, Thu, Fri and during holidays

▶ **Slieve Russell Hotel,
Golf & Country Club**
Ballyconnell, Co. Cavan
Tel. (0 49) 9 52 6 4 44
www.quinnhotels.com
18-hole course in a park landscape. Visitors: daily

▶ **Westport Golf Club**
Westport, Co. Mayo
Tel. (0 98) 2 82 62, 2 70 70
www.westportgolfclub.com
18-holes at Clew Bay, one of the most beautiful golf courses in Ireland. Visitors: daily

NORTHERN IRELAND

▶ **Ardglass Golf Club**
Castle Place
Ardglass
Tel. (0 13 28) 44 84 12 19
www.ardglassgolfclub.com
18-hole course on the coast. Visitors: best visit Mon–Wed

▶ **The Blackwood Golf Centre**
Crawfordsburn Road, Bangor
Tel. (0 12 28) 91 85 27 06
www.blackwoodgolfcentre.com
Two 18-hole courses in a park landscape. Visitors: anytime

▶ **Castle Hume Golf Club**
Castle Hume, Enniskillen
Tel. (0 28) 66 32 70 77
www.castlehumegolf.com
18-hole course. Visitors: anytime

▶ **Castlerock Golf Club**
Circular Road, Castlerock
Tel. (0 28) 70 84 83 14
www.castlerockgc.co.uk
18-hole and 9-hole course in a dune landscape. Visitors: Mon–-Tue

▶ **City of Derry Golf Club**
Victoria Road, Londonderry
Tel. (0 28) 71 34 63 69
www.cityofderrygolfclub.com
18-hole and 9-hole course and park. Visitors: ideally weekdays before 4.30pm

▶ **Clandeboye Golf Club**
Tower Road

Conlig, Newtownards
Tel. (0 28) 91 27 17 67
Two 18-hole courses in a park and
heather landscape. Visitors: ideally
weekdays.

▶ **Foyle International
Golf Centre**
Alder Road, Londonderry
Tel. (0 28) 71 35 22 22
www.foylegolfcentre.co.uk
18-hole and 9-hole course in park
landscape.
Visitors: anytime

▶ **Massereene Golf Club**
Lough Road, Antrim
Tel. (0 28) 94 42 80 96
www.massereene.com

18-hole, partially sandy course and
park. Visitors: daily, except Sat.

▶ **Royal County Down**
Newcastle
Tel. (0 28) 43 72 33 14
www.royalcountydown.org
18-hole course in a dune landscape. Visitors: Mon, Thu and Fri.

▶ **Royal Portrush**
Bushmills Road, Portrush
Tel. (0 28) 70 82 23 11
www.ramadaportrush.com
18-hole course in a dune landscape. Visitors: ideally weekdays,
except Wed and Fri.

Houseboats

Wonderful boat trips are possible on the Shannon, Shannon-Erne
Waterway, Grand Canal, and on Lough Erne in Northern Ireland.
The captain needs to be at least 21 years old. A boating qualification
is not required, but a minimum of two people have to be on board.
Houseboat facilities depend on the size of the boat and provisions
need to be ordered in advance from the rental company or purchased before the trip. Most people renting have never handled a
boat before, so it is not difficult, but a reasonable level of care is
needed. Speed restrictions are an average of 10km per hour, and
most Shannon cruisers cover approximately 50km in one day. Each
cruiser holds the Shannon Guide which informs about specific
routes, petrol stations, water supplies and shops. Life belts, life jack-
ets (one per bed), a first aid box and emergency flares should be carried, and it is very important to listen to the weather forecast. In
principle, always steer on the right, especially on narrow bends in
the river, and always steer to the right of black markers in the water,
such as buoys or poles.

*Renting
houseboats*

The Shannon has six locks which are usually in operation from April
to September, generally from 9am to 6pm (or 8pm) on weekdays,
and from 9am to 6pm on Sundays. At other times an extremely
limited service can be expected, and all boat traffic is prohibited after
dark. From 31 October to 15 March, all boats are out of service due
to excessive water levels.

Shannon River

Gently down the stream on a Shannon cabin cruiser

Shannon-Erne Waterway   The 62.5km/39 miles long Shannon-Erne Waterway connects Ireland's two large rivers. Completely restored in 1994, the canal has been fitted with six new moorings. Leisure cruisers have to pass 16 completely automated locks in order to get from Leitrim in the Republic of Ireland to Belturbet in Northern Ireland, but there are no border formalities.

Grand Canal   The Grand Canal is an idyllic and, in comparison to the Shannon, noticeably quieter waterway. The large cabin cruisers of the Shannon cannot travel here, because the 130km/81.2 miles long canal is never wider than 12m/13.1 yards. Instead special narrow boats are used, that are between 10m/32.8ft and 14m/45.9ft long, although of course their interiors are significantly less spacious.

Package tours   Numerous travel agents offer organised cabin cruising holidays and the Irish tourist board publishes an overview of services available.

Medieval Banquets

Several old castles and one converted church regularly host medieval banquets. Knaves and ladies dressed in courtly clothing serve wine and hearty dishes during meal times, and guests are entertained by performances of ancient ballads and medieval music. As a rule, there are two events per evening, one at 5.30pm and another at 8.45pm. At the Bunratty Folk Park in County Clare they also put on »Traditional Irish Nights«, with Irish dishes, wine, music, song and dance. (May–Oct daily at 5.30pm and 8.45pm).

Irish nights ▶

► MEDIEVAL BANQUET RESERVATIONS

Reservations can be made via every tourist information office and also via:

► **Shannon Castle Banquets & Heritage Ltd.**
Bunratty Folk Park, Co. Clare
Tel. (061) 361511
fax (061) 472523
reservations@shannon-dev.ie

► **Bunratty Castle**
Bunratty, Co. Clare
Banquets all year round

► **Knappogue Castle**
near Quin, Co. Clare
Banquets: May–Sept

► **Dunguaire Castle**
Kinvara, Co. Galway
Banquets: May–Sept

► **Killarney Manor Banquet**
Killarney, Co. Kerry
Tel. (064) 31551
fax (064) 33366

Horseriding

Ireland offers ideal conditions for an equestrian holiday for beginners as well as advanced riders. It is possible to book package tours, where experienced teachers offer courses for novices, but advanced riders can ride out independently, and there are also courses in jumping and dressage, which normally last 14 days. The horses are usually good as they are used to strangers.

 Equestrian Holidays Ireland
■ www.ehi.ie, info@ehi.ie

One-week riding tours, which usually involve around four hours per day in the saddle, are known as »pony-trekking« holidays. The most interesting treks are in Connemara, on the Dingle peninsula, in Sligo and around Killarney. Ireland, the great horse breeding country, organises many races each year. More than 250 race meetings are held on 28 courses maintained and sponsored by the »Turf Club« and supervised by the »Racing Board«. The most famous race course is the »Curragh« in the county of Kildare.

Pony-trekking

◄ Horse racing

Sport

The desire for independence from the English in everything, including sport, led to the foundation of the Gaelic Athletic Association in 1884, the largest sporting club in the country, and also to the energetic promotion of Gaelic football, similar to traditional European football. On quiet roads in southern Ireland one occasionally comes across village bowling teams competing with a heavy steel ball, but first prize for the most typically Irish sport in the country goes to hurling. Already mentioned in the oldest legends, this 15-a-side national game is played with wooden sticks, approximately one metre/3.3ft long, similar to hockey sticks, and is also known as »the world's fastest grass sport«. The annual finals held in Dublin's Croke Park are watched by more than 80 000 fanatical spectators. Very popular all over Ireland, not least for the betting, is greyhound racing. The dogs are bred in Ireland and races are held in many places all year round.

Travellers with disabilities Disabled travellers interested in sport can get contact addresses for organisations and associations, such as the Irish Wheelchair Association and National League of the Blind, from the Irish tourist board. They can advise on the best opportunities.

Hiking

Long-distance footpaths Hiking is a relatively new invention for the Irish, but in recent years successful efforts have been made to develop a larger, well-marked network of trails that is continuously being expanded. The brochure entitled *Walking Ireland*, published by the Irish tourist board, provides an overview of signposted long distance footpaths by which one can explore virtually all corners of the country. Circular routes offered, for example, are the »Kerry Way« (215km/134.3 miles) and the »Slieve Bloom Way« (66km/41.2 miles).

The 900km/559.2-mile »Ulster Way« is a long-distance footpath taking you through Northern Ireland. Information is supplied by the Field Officer of the Sports Council for Northern Ireland (www.walkni.com).

Short rambles The eleven Forest Parks, as well as National Parks, such as Killarney, Connemara, Glenveagh, Burren, and the Wicklow Mountains, are ideally suitable for strolls and shorter walks. Beyond these parks and the official long-distance footpaths there are hardly any marked trails. Existing paths mostly serve the needs of agriculture and rural tracks are predominantly paved. Often it is impractical to head off cross-country anyway. Good maps, such as the »Ordnance Survey Maps«, are essential.

Hiking basics In principle, it is never a good idea to go hiking alone as most walking routes go through thinly populated areas. Other hikers are rare, which means solitary walkers would be entirely dependent on their own resources should an accident occur. Taking dogs is not advisable due to the many sheep. As a rule, farmers don't mind people crossing their land, but doors and gates should always be shut on the way out.

The Irish tourist board publishes a list of travel agents offering walking holidays in Ireland.

Watersports

The Atlantic Ocean and the Irish Sea are excellent sailing territory. For longer jaunts, the southwest of Ireland is especially popular, but Ireland's lakes are also gaining more and more sailing fans. Various sailing schools and centres offer courses for beginners and experienced sailors and you can book these courses via the organisers listed in the relevant publication provided by the Irish tourist board. An overview of options is also provided by the Irish Sailing Association.

There are good opportunities for water skiing on the rivers and lakes, and especially along the flat coastal areas. Necessary equipment and boats can be rented at, among other places, Farran, Castleblayney, Macroom and Sligo.

In Ireland surfing is possible just about anywhere where there is water. As a rule there is always plenty of wind. In many places, such as Kinsale, Killaloe, Rosslare, Caherdaniel, Schull and Carlingford, surfboards are rented out and courses are offered. The Irish Windsurfing Association offers more details. For experts the west coast of Ireland offers ideal conditions, as waves between one and four metres high are virtually guaranteed all year round. There are board rental outlets in Doolin, Strandhill and Rossnowlagh.

► IMPORTANT WATERSPORTS ADDRESSES

CANOEING

► **Irish Canoe Union**
Sport HQ, 13 Joyce Way
Park West, Dublin 12
Tel. (01) 6 25 11 05
www.canoe.ie

ROWING

► **Irish Amateur Rowing Union**
Long Mile Road
Walkingstown
Dublin 12
Tel. (01) 4 50 98 31

SAILING

► **Irish Sailing Association**
3 Park Road
Dun Laoghaire, Co. Dublin

Tel. (01) 2 80 02 39
info@sailing.ie

SCUBA DIVING

► **Irish Underwater Council**
78A Patrick Street
Dun Laoghaire,
Co. Dublin
Tel. (01) 2 84 46 01
www.scubaireland.com

WATER SKIING

► **Irish Waterski Federation**
Mount Salus
Knocknaree Road,
Dalkey, Co. Dublin
Tel. (01) 4 50 21 22
www.iwsf.ie

Scuba diving

Scuba diving conditions are excellent. The warm Gulf Stream ensures relatively pleasant temperatures, even at greater depths, and a tremendous variety of underwater flora and fauna can be observed. Several diving centres rent out equipment, including at the Bay View Hotel on Clare Island, at Dolphin Diving in Ballyvaughan, Valentia Diving Centre on Valentia Island, and Skellig Aquatics Dive Centre in Caherdaniel.

Rowing

The country's numerous rivers and lakes are ideal for rowing and the use of inflatables. Information is available from the Irish Amateur Rowing Union.

Canoeing, kayaking

Furthermore, white water rafting, canoeing and kayaking is possible on the country's many waterways. The most suitable rivers are the Liffey, Barrow, Nore, Boyne, Slaney, Lee, Shannon, Suir and Munster Blackwater. Rental kayaks are available; for more information contact the Irish Canoe Union.

Gypsy Wagons

Those who love horses and would enjoy exploring Ireland at a slow pace can rent a »gypsy wagon«. Drawn by powerful carthorses, these barrel-shaped wagons are about 4m/13.1ft long and 2.5m/8.2ftwide, and have room for a maximum of four people. Inside they offer seating and sleeping facilities, as well as a cooking niche with double gas burners (using propane gas). Starting points for tours are at Wicklow, Portlaoise or Tralee, and the rental companies provide route maps marked with all overnight stops. Average daily distances covered should not exceed 10–15 km/6.2–9.3 miles. The horse needs feeding once a day (don't forget the oats!) and taking to pasture overnight. Deposits are customary on taking up a rental agreement, and are refunded after the safe return of horse and wagon. An overview of travel agents offering gypsy wagon holidays can be had from the Irish tourist board.

Transport

By car

Road network in the Republic of Ireland

Except around Dublin, there are no motorways in the Republic of Ireland. The main routes are designated either as national roads (»N«) or regional roads (»R«). Many roads are extremely narrow, but usually have very little traffic. However, as visibility on many roads is difficult and the roads themselves often in less than perfect condition, driving is a slow business. For example, the 300km/187.5

miles distance between Dublin and Killarney can take a good five hours. The road network in Northern Ireland is more modern. There are motorways (»M«) near Belfast, as well as long distance country roads designated as A (major) and B (minor) roads.

◄ Road network in Northern Ireland

Road signs are sometimes insufficiently clear. Place names appear twice, in English and in Irish, and distances on the older signs are still indicated in miles (1 mile = 1.6km); on new signs they are indicated in kilometres.

Road signs

Driving is done on the left in the whole of Ireland, and overtaking on the right. If not indicated otherwise, however, the rule of »right has priority« still applies. On the numerous roundabouts, traffic already on the roundabout has priority.

Driving left

Apart from driving on the left, more or less the same rules apply in Ireland as for the rest of continental Europe, including the obligatory use of safety belts and helmets (for motorcycles). In general, road signs match international norms.

Traffic regulations

In both the Republic of Ireland and Northern Ireland a speed restriction of 30mph/48kmh applies in built-up areas. On country roads it is 60mph/96kmh; and on motorways in Northern Ireland the maximum speed allowed is 70mph/113kmh. Beware of fines for speeding as they are very high.

Speed restrictions

On the road with a gypsy wagon

Alcohol levels — In both the Republic and Northern Ireland the maximum level of alcohol permitted while driving is 0.8g of alcohol per litre of blood.

Parking restrictions — Parking is prohibited on roads signposted with »NO WAITING« signs. Continuous double yellow lines by the side of the road mean 'no parking', and a single yellow line indicates parking is permitted at certain times shown on nearby signs.

 IMPORTANT ADDRESSES

CAR RENTAL IN DUBLIN

▶ **Avis**
1 East Hanover Street
Tel. (01) 6 77 52 04
Dublin Airport
Tel. (01) 8 44 52 04
www.avis.com

▶ **Budget**
1 Lower Drumcondra Road
Tel. (01) 8 37 98 02
Dublin Airport
Tel (01) 8 44 59 19
www.budget.com

▶ **Enterprise**
Tel. 18 90 22 79 99
Dublin Airport
Tel. (01) 8 44 58 48
www.enterprise.com

▶ **Hertz**
149 Upper Leeson Street
Tel. (01) 6 60 22 55
Dublin Airport
Tel. (01) 8 44 54 66

▶ **Sixt**
Old Airport Road, Santra
Tel. (01) 8 62 27 15
Dublin Airport
Tel. (01) 8 44 41 99
www.e-sixt.com

CAR RENTAL IN BELFAST

▶ **Avis**
69–71 Great Victoria Street
Tel. (0 90) 24 04 04
City Airport
Tel. (0 90) 45 20 17
International Airport
Tel. (0 94) 42 23 33
www.avis.com

▶ **Budget**
96–102 Great Victoria Street
Tel. (0 90) 23 07 00
www.budget.com
City Airport
Tel. (0 90) 45 11 11

▶ **Enterprise**
Building 10, Unit 3
Central Park, Mallusk
Co. Antrim, BT36 4FS
(pick-up from airport)
www.enterprise.com
Tel. (028) 90 84 58 65

▶ **Europcar**
6–24 Agincourt Ave
Tel (0 90) 31 35 00
City Airport
Tel. (0 90) 45 09 04
International Airport
Tel. (0 94) 42 34 44
www.europcar.com

▶ **Hertz**
City Airport
Tel. (0 90) 73 24 51
International Airport
Tel. (0 94) 42 25 33
www.hertz.com

BUS

► **Europa Bus Centre**
10 Glengall Street, Belfast
Tel. (0 28) 90 33 30 00
as well as at the Belfast Central
Rail Station

RAIL

► **Iarnrod Eireann**
Tel. (18 50) 36 62 22
www.irishrail.ie
in Ireland: at all C.I.E. offices and
larger stations

► **National Rail**
Tel. (08 45) 36 48 49 50
www.nationalrail.co.uk
in Ireland: at all C.I.E. offices and
larger stations

AIRLINES
AER LINGUS

► **Ireland**
Reservations
Tel (08 18) 365 000
www.aerlingus.com

► **UK, incl. Northern Ireland**
Reservations
Tel. (08 70) 876 50 00

► **USA/CANADA**
Reservations
Tel. 1-800-IRISH AIR /
1 8 00 47 47
424 www.aerlingus.com

► **AUSTRALIA**
Reservations Sydney
(World Aviation)
Tel. (0 2) 92 44 21 23
aerlingus.sydney@
worldaviation.com.au

► **NEW ZEALAND**
Reservations
World Aviation Systems Level
12A Sofrana House, 396 Queen St

Auckland Tel. (0 9) 3 08 33 55
reservations@worldaviation.co.nz

► **SOUTH AFRICA**
Reservations Johannesburg
Green Islands Aviation
Unit A, 2nd Floor
Hanover Sq., Cnr Hendrik POTG
Edenvale, Johannesburg
Tel. (0 11) 6 09 24 67

AMERICAN AIRLINES IRELAND

Tel. (01) 60 20 55 0
www.americanairlines.ie

CONTINENTAL AIRLINES IRELAND

Tel. (1890) 92 52 52
www.continental.com

DELTA AIR LINES IRELAND

Tel. (01) 40 73 16 5 /
(1850) 88 20 31
www.delta.com

US AIRWAYS IRELAND

Tel. (1890) 92 50 65
www.usair.com

BRITISH AIRWAYS IRELAND

Tel. 18 90 62 67 47
www.britishairways.com

BRITISH AIRWAYS UK

Tel. 08 70 85 09 85 0
www.britishairways.com

AIR CANADA IRELAND

► **Premair Marketing Services**
Tel. (01) 6 79 39 58
www.aircanada.com

AER ARANN

1 Northwood Avenue
Santry, Dublin 9
www.aerarann.com

Fuel Alongside diesel, almost all petrol stations sell »super plus unleaded« (unleaded 98-octane petrol) and »unleaded premium« (unleaded 95-octane petrol). Prices are somewhat lower than those common in continental Europe.

See also ►Hire cars and ►Emergency numbers

Hire cars

Rental conditions Irish and international car hire firms maintain offices throughout the land, but especially at airports and ferry ports, as well as in the larger cities. The minimum age for hiring a car varies depending on the company and the type of vehicle required, but is usually 26. The maximum age can be as low as 69, but there is some flexibility for those between the ages of 23 and 26, and those between 71 and 74. Enterprise has the most senior-friendly policy, with no upper age limits. Most car hire firms do expect you to have had your licence for at least one year, however.

By rail and bus

Ireland does not have much of a rail network and only the larger towns are connected by train. The bus network, on the other hand, is very extensive and also significantly cheaper. The Irish Explorer Ticket is valid both for rail and bus journeys, though it cannot be used within the cities of Dublin, Cork, Limerick and Galway. Northern Ireland also offers opportunities for value for money travelling. For example, the Emerald Card entitles you to unlimited bus and rail journeys in both the Republic and Northern Ireland within a period of eight or 15 days.

By air

Airports There are four international airports in the Republic of Ireland (Dublin, Cork, Shannon and Knock), and one at Belfast in Northern Ireland (Aldergrove). The regional airports at Galway, Killarney (Farranfore), Waterford, Sligo, Derry and Londonderry, are mostly used by smaller internal carriers and private aircraft. Aer Lingus is the state airline, which flies both regional and international routes.

Time

All Ireland uses Western European Time (WET), meaning in summer it is one hour ahead of Greenwich Mean Time (GMT), and the same as GMT at other times.

Travellers with Disabilities

The Irish Tourist Board can provide a comprehensive list of accommodation suitable for disabled travellers.► Information • Important addresses) With the relevant identification card all disabled travellers can park for free at any parking metre in Ireland.

● PRACTICALITIES

► **RADAR (Royal Association for Disability and Rehabilitation)**
12 City Forum, 250 City Road
London
London EC1V 8AF
Tel. (020) 7 25 03 22
www.radar.org.uk
This umbrella organization publishes a useful annual *Holidays in Britain & Ireland* brochure.

► **Access Able USA**
www.access-able.com
(online information provided by travel-loving disabled couple)

► **SATH (Society for Accessible Travel & Hospitality) US**
347 Fifth Ave., Suite 605
New York, NY 10016–5010
Tel. (2 12) 4 47 72 84
www.sath.org
(professional resources for members and non-members, links to specialized tour operators)

► **The National Disability Authority/Rehabilitation Centre**
Access Dept., 25 Clyde Road
Dublin 4
Tel. (01) 6 08 04 00
www.nda.ie, nrb@iol.ie
Contact this organization for a county-by-county fact sheet.

► **Irish Wheelchair Association**
Blackheath Drive,
Clontarf, Dublin 3
Tel. (01) 8 18 64 58
www.iwa.ie, info@iwa.ie

► **Disability Action**
Head Office/Portside Business Park
189 Airport Road West
Belfast BT3 9ED
Tel. (028) 90 29 78 80
www.disabilityaction.org
There are other offices in Carrickfergus, Derry, Dungannon and Newry.

Weights and Measures

In line with the establishment of the Single European Market, Ireland has been officially metric since 1 January 1993. Only the »pint« remains current, though other old measures are also often used.

Weights and Measures

► **Length Measures**
1 inch = 2.54cm
1 foot = 30.48cm
1 yard = 91.44cm
1 mile = 1.61km

► **Liquids and Weights**
1 pint (pt) = 0.568 l
1 gallon (gal) = 4.546 l
1 ounce (oz) = 28.35g
1 pound (lb) = 453.59g

When to Go

The tourist season generally runs between the end of March and the end of October. The warmest months are July and August, so this is often the best time for a beach holiday, though in many places you will have to compete with large crowds. May and June offer the best chance of sunny days, while autumn is also a pleasant time for a holiday to Ireland, as the weather during the months of September and October is often mild and relatively dry. Ireland lies in an area of mild southwesterly winds which is influenced by the warm waters of the Gulf Stream. Its island nature favours a relatively stable climate, with cool summers and mild winters, though the Atlantic currents ensure the weather is very changeable so rain gear should always be carried. Long downpours are less frequent than in Central Europe, however. Rainy days regularly end with a brightening sky towards evening and rainbows can often be seen. Snow rarely falls in Ireland and when it does, it only settles on high ground in hilly areas, and even there it does not survive for long. Seasonal temperature variations are small. During the coldest months, in January and February, temperatures range between 4°C/39.2°F in the northeast and 7°C/44.6°F in the southwest, while the warmest months of July and August enjoy an average temperature of 14–16°C/57.2–60.8°F. Temperatures of 25°C/77°F and above are rarely reached. The southeast of the country enjoys the most sunshine, while the west of the island is directly influenced by Atlantic winds, and heavy showers often pelt the coastal mountains. On average there are 250 rainy days in western Ireland, with 3000mm/118.1in of precipitation, while Dublin, on the sheltered east coast, only has 190 rainy days on average, with a precipitation of only 750mm/29.5in. Air humidity is relatively high in the whole country.

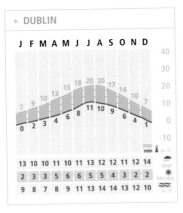

► DUBLIN

J F M A M J J A S O N D

40
30
20
10
0
-10

7 9 10 13 15 18 20 20 17 14 10 7
0 2 3 4 6 8 11 10 9 6 4 1

max / min in °C

13 10 10 11 10 11 13 12 12 11 12 14   days
2 3 3 5 6 6 5 5 4 3 2 2   h/day
9 8 7 8 9 11 13 14 14 13 12 10   in °C

The atmosphere of a genuine »singing pub« or festival is unmistakable. Come and discover the magic of Irish music…

SINGING IN THE RAIN

Why is it that beer tastes so good in the pub, and why is it so easy to while away the evening chatting in a pub? Some of this is to do with a place brimful of people sharing the »craic«, but a lot of it is down to the music. There seems to be some magic involved here…

Since times immemorial, the Irish have enjoyed a song. In Celtic times, bards played an important role, handing down language, culture and history, and rising to advisors of rulers. As today, the most important instruments, alongside the singing, were the Celtic harp and the flat »bodhrán« drum. To the English colonizers of the 17th century, these musical traditions seemed subversive, and they sensed dangerous revolutionary notions. Cromwell had hundreds of harps burnt at the stake and harpists executed. Today, the Celtic harp is seen as a national symbol and forms part of the official Irish coat-of-arms.

The old and the new

For centuries, Irish music was only transmitted orally. Therefore old songs and melodies can often not be dated with certainty. During English rule, the English viceroy and some aristocratic families promoted international musicians. Georg Friedrich Händel stayed in Dublin in 1741/2, conducting the world premiere of his *Messiah*. Alongside famous composers such as Francis Ireland, all-rounders such as Richard Poekrich enriched the musical landscape of Ireland. The latter invented the glass harp, presenting it to the public at a concert in 1744. The majority of the Irish however, stayed excluded from this music for the elite.

Out into the world

Also since times immemorial, music has been a remedy for homesickness. For emigrants in their new home country, to carry on making music together played an important role. The Irish influence in the US and

In »singing pubs«, folk music is played, the audience is welcome to join in, and sometimes events of the day are woven into the evening's songs. The traditional heart of Irish folk music beats in Doolin, which has three atmospheric music pubs to its name.

Canada continues to be considerable, the Irish elements in folk, pop and rock music unmistakable.

On the path to national independence, traditional music was a means of identifying with the cause. The »Comhaltas Ceoltóirí Éireann« organization has been promoting Irish music since 1950, with increasing success. Main attractions are open-air festivals in the summer, the »Fleadh Cheoil« music competition in particular (every August in different towns). Alongside the official programme, a main draw is the relaxed atmosphere: people meet their friends and old acquaintances, camp or just roll out their sleeping bag wherever there's space; and whoever is not on stage, is probably making music in one of the pubs or somewhere else.

Pub folk

An infectious rhythm and melodious ballads made Irish music popular worldwide. The roots of this tradition may be experienced every night in Ireland's »singing pubs«, where musicians with a fiddle, tin whistle, guitar, banjo, »uillean pipes« (Irish bagpipes) or accordion congregate. The audience joins in with refrains of well-known songs, and the lyrics might be changed to suit events of the day. The spectacular liberation of IRA prisoners from a Northern Irish jail, for instance, became the subject of a song that same night all over the country.

Irish folk music also has high currency in radio stations around the world – not least since the successes of the Dubliners and the London-based Pogues. Whilst the earthy Dubliners stand for traditional tunes, the Pogues sound as if they've drunk all the whiskey and beer they sing of themselves. In the 1960s, Christy Moore started his career as a »traditional folk« singer-songwriter and musician. The Chieftains are classic performers of Irish instrumental music. Starting back in the 1960s, they blazed a trail for the world-wide revival of Irish Folk. Clannad, a band singing in Irish, impresses with wonderful a cappella songs.

Contrary to popular belief, the Kelly Family does not hail from the Eme-

rald Isle; Papa and Mama Kelly had Irish ancestors, but started their musical conquest from the United States.

Music in the blood

Considering its small population, Ireland has produced a disproportionately high number of musicians. Gary Moore and Rory Gallagher are two of the biggest names in blues, Chris de Burgh one of the most successful singer-songwriters. Innovation came in the shape of bands such as Them and Thin Lizzy; the latter landing a big hit with their version of the folk song *Whiskey In The Jar*. One member of Them, Van Morrison, started his solo career in 1967 and became a cult figure, much as Gilbert O'Sullivan did, whereas the Boomtown Rats had to wait to get to London for their breakthrough. In the 1980s, the Rats' front man Bob Geldof, organizing massive charity concerts such as *Band Aid* and *USA for Africa*, rose to be »Saint Bob«. The biggest international success story however has been U2. Star producer Brian Eno had the right flair for the combination of good lyrics and the charismatic voice of band leader Bono – who has since taken Bob Geldof's mantle of tireless charity promoter. The Cranberries and Sinéad O'Connor are also influenced by Irish pop history. If you have Irish roots, count yourself lucky: you are likely to have music running through your veins!

Tours

NATURE TRIPS ALONG THE COAST
OR ART AND CULTURE
IN THE INTERIOR? QUIET FISHING
VILLAGES OR PULSATING
CITIES? WE SUGGEST
THE BEST ROUTES.

EXPLORING IRELAND

There are several ways to explore the Emerald Isle. Visitors who want to see as much as possible should take to the road by car. Here, we show you the most beautiful routes through the country.

TOUR 1 Stone Trail
From Dublin via Belfast to Derry: an attractive tour via Newgrange to Northern Ireland, up to one of the most spectacular coasts in Ireland. ► **page 140**

TOUR 2 Forests, Monks and Long Beaches
From Dublin via Arklow to Wexford: lush forests with lingering patches of fog and tranquil coastal scenery await on the east coast. ► **page 142**

TOUR 3 Magnificent Views and Clear Lakes
Round trip from Cork to the Ring of Kerry: see the bizarre cliffs of the south western tip and the magnificent lakes in Killarney National Park. ► **page 144**

Relaxing after the drive
Long beaches near Galway

TOUR 4 Broad Shannon and Wild West
From Dublin via Athlone to Galway: from the peaceful Midlands towards the west coast and Galway, springboard to the wilds of Connemara and the beautifully barren Aran Islands. ► **page 146**

TOUR 5 Towards the Northern Lights
From Dublin via Carrick-on-Shannon to Derry: a varied tour past the Shannon and picturesque lakes up to the rugged northern coast. ► **page 147**

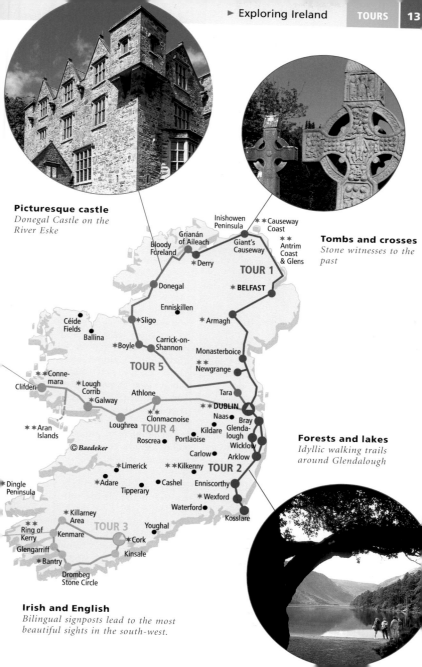

Picturesque castle
Donegal Castle on the River Eske

Tombs and crosses
Stone witnesses to the past

Forests and lakes
Idyllic walking trails around Glendalough

Irish and English
Bilingual signposts lead to the most beautiful sights in the south-west.

Inishowen Peninsula

Causeway Coast

Grianán of Aileach

Giant's Causeway

Bloody Foreland

Antrim Coast & Glens

Derry

TOUR 1

Donegal

BELFAST

Enniskillen

Céide Fields

Sligo

Armagh

Ballina

Carrick-on-Shannon

Boyle

Monasterboice

TOUR 5

Newgrange

Conne-mara

Lough Corrib

Athlone

Tara

Clifden

Galway

DUBLIN

Clonmacnoise

Naas

Bray

Aran Islands

Loughrea

TOUR 4

Kildare

Glenda-lough

© Baedeker

Roscrea

Portlaoise

Wicklow

Carlow

Arklow

Limerick

Kilkenny

TOUR 2

Dingle Peninsula

Adare

Cashel

Enniscorthy

Tipperary

Wexford

Killarney Area

Waterford

TOUR 3

Youghal

Kosslare

Ring of Kerry

Kenmare

Cork

Glengarriff

Kinsale

Bantry

Drombeg Stone Circle

Travelling in Ireland

Driving is not a problem

There are many ways to explore the Emerald Isle: by bike, on foot, by houseboat or gypsy wagon (please see Practicalities for options). Those with little time or who wish to see a great deal should use a car, though driving in Ireland is significantly different to what you

Rainy days can be fun in castles, galleries and museums.

may be used to. People drive on the left here and some roads are pretty narrow and littered with potholes. Sheep or cows regularly block the road and, while fuchsia hedges are wonderful, they also obscure the view. Road signs are sometimes more enervating than edifying, but that should stop no one from venturing onto the charming byways. Just bring time, don't rush, and stop every now and then. Of course the wealth of sights means this happens almost naturally and thanks to the ubiquitous bed and breakfasts, those who wish to stay in a different place every night will find simple, relatively cheap options almost everywhere. Don't let the rain spoil a good mood. That is just part of every Ireland journey and the rain rarely lasts long. Ideally such times can be put to good use to dedicate a few hours to art and culture, and some of the most wonderful experiences along the road include ending up in a characterful pub by chance and witnessing a spontaneous music session.

The tempting southwest coast

The wild southwest coast is Ireland's trademark, drawing nature lovers in particular, who take pleasure in thundering surf, crystal clear lakes, jagged coastal strips and rainbows over the hills. The Ring of Kerry, the Dingle Peninsula, and the wonderful tip of this green island's southwest captivate with their mild Gulf Stream climate, magnificent scenery and continuously changing panorama of images and colour. When the weather plays along, the attractive beaches that open up here and there to form an amphitheatre of cliffs can be used for swimming. However, during the high season it is entirely possible for visitors to the southwest to become surrounded by tourist hordes, and in Killarney, gateway to the Ring of Kerry, as well as in neighbouring Kenmare, it is advisable to book accommodation ahead during July and August.

The landscape turns a little more monotonous in the west, but many are thrilled by just such barrenness and spaciousness as that of Connemara or the treeless wilderness of the Burren, a stone tortoise shell of limestone; and the pubs of Galway have something to offer every evening. The rough, sparsely populated coast of the north counts as a paradise among hikers and for all those who prefer isolation to immersion in the crowd and there is no lack of magnificent natural monuments, such as the Giant's Causeway, for example, whose photogenic basalt pillars rise like organ pipes out of the sea north of Belfast.

The barren wes and lonely nort

The east coast has a completely different character. Calm, temperate, and often flat, the east and southeast are more for the experienced Ireland visitor, or for all those who really want to enjoy the wealth of Ireland to the full. In particular, the forests around the Wicklow Mountains, an hour south of Dublin, tempt, as well as Glendalough Monastery and beautiful places such as the Viking town of Wexford, and also Arklow. Of course, Dublin itself, the urbane heart of Ireland, is the best starting point for further tours into the back country. Worth the journey for culture fans are visits to the world famous cultural heritage sites of Newgrange, a grave for unknown Irish rulers, and to the monastic settlement of Clonmacnoise, on the shores of the Shannon in the Midlands, the centre of the island.

Art and culture i the east

Time to take it easy and have a chat on the Aran Islands

Tour 1 Stone Trail

Start C 5

Length of Tour: approx. 380km/240 miles

Ideal tour for fans of ancient stones of every kind, such as the Newgrange megaliths with their spiral decorations, the delicately worked High Crosses of Monasterboice or the basalt pillars of the spectacular Giant's Causeway high up in the North, where nature itself was the creator. The tour begins in Dublin and ends in Derry.

From ✶ ✶ **Dublin** The N1 leads north towards Swords, an old town with a ruined castle and a round tower. The coast of the Irish Sea is then reached at Balbriggan (water sport opportunities). From there the N1 heads northwest towards **Drogheda**. North of there the route leaves the N1 and follows the N51 due east, towards the Boyne Valley, where the 5,200-year-old burial mounds of ❶ ✶ ✶ **Newgrange** lie.

DON'T MISS

■ Newgrange
■ Monasterboice
■ Giant's Causeway

After this detour, the journey continues with a return to Drogheda, where the route follows the N1 to Dunleer. About half way there, to the left of the road, the former monastic settlement of ❷ ✶ ✶ **Monasterboice** spreads out, which is famous for its High Crosses.

From Dunleer the N1 leads to the port of **Dundalk**, which lies just a few kilometres/miles from the border with Northern Ireland. Beyond the border, in Northern Ireland, the A1 leads in the direction of Belfast. It is worth making a detour towards the northwest by Newry, on the A28, into beautiful ❸ ✶ **Armagh**, the religious centre of Ireland whose surrounding area is well-known for its apple trees. The main route towards ❹ ✶ **Belfast** is then reached via the A3 at Lisburn.

North of Belfast, along Antrim's coast, the A2 traverses a genuine picture-postcard landscape of Ireland: jagged cliffs, wild sea, and inland, lovely valleys known as Glens. In the far north, the A2 turns off towards the ✶ **Causeway Coast**. The swinging rope bridge at Carrick-a-Rede, the impressive ruins of Dunluce Castle and the legendary ❺ ✶ ✶ **Giant's Causeway** with its bizarrely formed basalt pillars are considered highlights here.

Continuing along the A2 in a westerly direction, the tour finally reaches its destination. ❻ ✶ **Derry** is the second largest city in the north of Ireland and worth seeing for its massive and exceptionally well-preserved town walls alone.

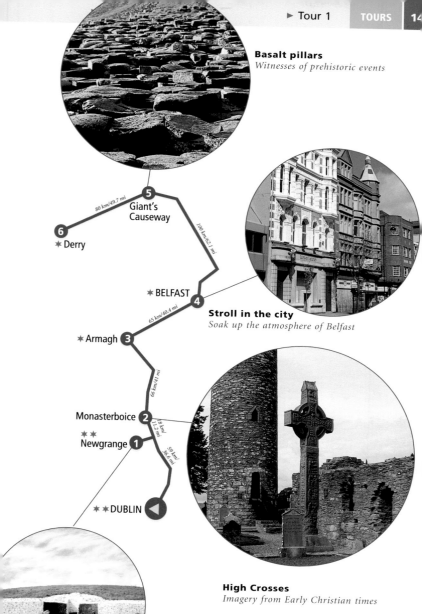

Basalt pillars
Witnesses of prehistoric events

5
80 km/49.7 mi
Giant's
Causeway

6
✳ Derry

100 km/62.1 mi

✳ BELFAST **4**

Stroll in the city
Soak up the atmosphere of Belfast

65 km/40.4 mi

✳ Armagh **3**

99 km/61.4 mi

Monasterboice **2**

✳✳
Newgrange **1**

18 km/11.2 mi

59 km/36.6 mi

✳✳ DUBLIN ◄

High Crosses
Imagery from Early Christian times

Royal tomb
Walking in ancient vaults

Tour 2 Forests, Monks and Long Beaches

Length of Tour: approx. 170km/110 miles

Ireland is not usually associated with deep forests. However, this tour, that begins in Dublin and follows the Wicklow Mountains, will introduce the unknown side of the country. The traveller will also discover the extensive sandy beaches of a whole row of seaside resorts along the flat southeast coast.

Just a few kilometres/miles after ✳ ✳ **Dublin,** along the coast road, **Dun Laoghaire** is reached, the destination for ferries coming from

Holyhead on the Isle of Anglesey. Following the spit of land to Dalkey, which encompasses the southern tip of Dublin Bay, the road turns inland on the N11. A secondary road turns off to ❶ **Bray** one of Ireland's largest seaside resorts. Those wishing to visit the legendary monastic ruins of ❷ ✳ ✳ **Glendalough,** a jewel made of stone set in a deep valley, can do so via the R755 and R756. The hiking opportunities all around are terrific! The main tour route can be rejoined via Rathnew using the R755 and R752.

Well worth the detour: Glendalough

The N11 runs along the eastern side of the Wicklow Mountains-Wicklow Mountains, from Bray to Rathnew, passing scenically beautiful landscapes and forests via Ashford, which is very close to the magnificent Mount Usher Gardens.) From there the R750 leads to the coast and ❸ **Wicklow,** continuing on to Wicklow Head (Lighthouses). The resort of ❹ ✳ **Arklow,** where the Avoca River runs into the sea, is then reached via the coastal road (Brittas Bay, Mizen Head). (Take a detour to the north-easterly Vale of Avoca).

From Arklow the N11 continues via Gorey through landscape with limited scenic appeal to ❺ **Enniscorthy,** an attractive little town on the banks of the Slaney. From there the route continues on the N11 to the picturesque coastal town of **6** ✱ **Wexford**, where the Slaney runs into the sea. (Wexford can also be reached from Gorey via the R741 and the R742 running close to the coast). South of Wexford the tour reaches the resort of **7** **Rosslare** and the ferry port of Rosslare Harbour.

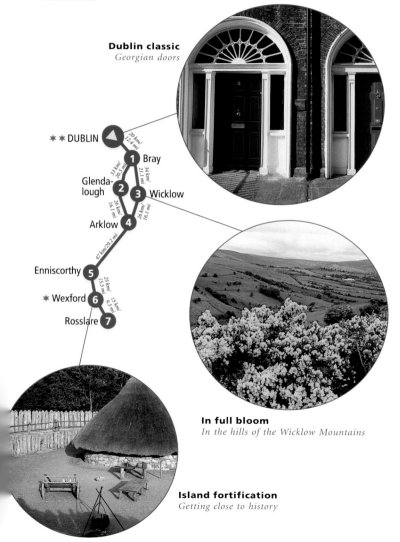

Dublin classic
Georgian doors

✱✱DUBLIN
1 Bray
20 km / 12.4 mi
32 km / 20.5 mi
34 km / 21.1 mi
Glenda-lough **2** **3** Wicklow
26 km / 16.1 mi
26 km / 16.1 mi
Arklow **4**
47 km/29.2 mi
Enniscorthy **5**
25 km / 15.5 mi
✱ Wexford **6**
15 km / 9.3 mi
Rosslare **7**

In full bloom
In the hills of the Wicklow Mountains

Island fortification
Getting close to history

Tour 3 Magnificent Views and Clear Lakes

Length of Tour: approx. 295km/184.3 miles

The wild, often lonely, southwest tip of Ireland really does offer plenty of unforgettable roads. West of Cork, the N71 first follows the country's Riviera and then turns up towards the Killarney Area, which thanks to its clear lakes and spectacular gorges is one of the most visited regions in Ireland.

For all those who arrive by ferry in ✱ **Cork**, this road will be a wonderful introduction to their Ireland journey. The main route is easy to find, just keep following the N71. An early detour to the appealing port of ❶ ✱ **Kinsale** for a pit stop suggests itself, not least because the local restaurateurs make a great effort to offer fine dining. Fur-

Take a break
The lanes of Killarney

Desolate, wild and beautiful
Ring of Kerry coast

✱ Killarney Area
❻
27 km
Kenmare ❺
27 km
Glengariff ❹ 18 km
❸
✱ Bantry 52 km 56 km
❷
Dromberg Stone Circle
87 km
23 km
▸ ✱ Cork
❶ Kinsale

Live like an earl
Staying at Bantry House

ther along the N71, the beautiful sandy beaches of Clonakilty are reached, from which a detour to the ❷ ✳ **Drombeg Stone Circle** via the R597 should not be missed. The effects of the Gulf Stream can especially be noted in the parks of Skibbereen and later, Bantry House near ❸ ✳ **Bantry**, where the almost Mediterranean climate can quickly change the weather. Rainbows arc above sparkling meadows and flame-red fuchsia hedges. The N71, in the direction of Killarney, touches on the **Ring of Beara**, and a possible access point onto this

✔	DON'T MISS
	■ Kinsale
	■ Dromberg Stone Circle
	■ Garinish Island
	■ Killarney Area
	■ Gallarus Oratory auf Dingle

very narrow circular road by the coast is offered by ❹ **Glengarriff**. From here, why not take a very enjoyable boat tour to ✳ ✳ **Garinish Island**, to see the tireless effects of gardeners, and sleepy sea lions?

The N21 then winds north, past Beara peninsula, in tight serpentine curves, heading for ❺ ✳ **Kenmare**. This is where the famous panoramic highway known as the ✳ ✳ **Ring of Kerry** begins, which largely follows the coast and offers any number of viewpoints, though in high season it is almost choked in bus traffic. Nevertheless, this drive around the Iveragh peninsula belongs to the highlights of every Ireland journey. (Time required: 2 – 3 days).

Art in Cork
On Rory Gallagher Square

From Kenmare the N71 leads directly due northeast to ❻ **Killarney**, the capital of tourism in the ✳ ✳ **Killarney Area**. The town lies in the attractive and much-visited Lake District and offers an ideal break in the form of magnificent hiking tours for those who have had enough of driving. Meanwhile, the Ring of Kerry can also be reached from Killarney. Those who wish to make the return journey from here can quickly reach lively Cork – which some consider the secret capital of the entire island – via the N22.

An alternative to the Inveragh peninsula is offered by the ✳ **Dingle Peninsula**, an as yet little visited area of the southwest, which can be accessed through its gateway at Castlemaine by driving via the N72 to Killorglin and then along the N70. Not to be missed here is the ✳ **Gallarus Oratory**.

Tour 4 Broad Shannon and Wild West

Length of Tour: approx. 230km/145 miles

This tour travels through the heart of the country along the Shannon and deep into the forested country of Connemara, and those who want to go one step further can visit the barren Aran Islands, where Gaelic is still spoken.

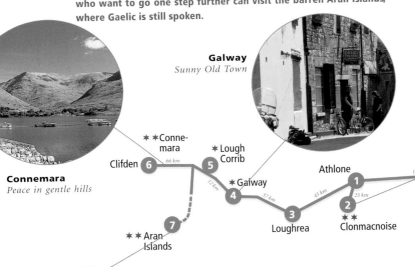

Galway
Sunny Old Town

Connemara
Peace in gentle hills

★★Connemara

Clifden **6** *66 km*

5 ★Lough Corrib

Athlone

1

12

★Galway

4 *12 km*

37 km *45 km*

25 km

3

Loughrea

2

★★ Clonmacnoise

7

★★Aran Islands

Dún Aenghus
Ireland's most beautiful stone fort

A gentle journey westward is promised by the N4, which goes from ★★ **Dublin** to Kinnegad via Maynooth, and closely follows the Royal Canal in parts. From there, the route follows the N6 via Killbeggan and Moate to **1** **Athlone**, where the River Shannon flows out of Lough Ree.

South of town, idyllically situated on the eastern banks of the sluggishly flowing Shannon are the ruins of the famous monastic settlement of **2** ★★ **Clonmacnoise**, which is particularly famous for its unique High Crosses. From Athlone the walled grounds can be reached either by boat or via the road to Shannonbridge.

From Shannonbridge the R357 leads to the N6, which travels via **Ballinasloe**, ❸ **Loughrea** (possible detour to the Turoe Stone) and Oranmore to ❹ ✳ **Galway**. With its dynamic atmosphere and attractive centre, western Ireland's most important city is an inviting place to join the crowd and take a stroll. From here it is also worth taking tours around ❺ ✳ **Lough Corrib**, for example, and to Connemara, the wildly romantic landscape with numerous picture book beaches on the Atlantic where Gaelic is often still spoken. The beach towns of ❻ **Clifden** and Roundstone should not be missed! Furthermore, from Galway it is possible to take a ferry to the ❼ ✳ ✳ **Aran Islands**, though they can also be reached by air.

Walled monastic enclosure
Ruins, tombs and High Crosses from Early Christian times

✳ ✳ DUBLIN

Tour 5 Towards the Northern Lights

Start C 5

Length of Tour: approx. 360km/225 miles

A special treat for culture fans is the Hill of Tara, where the Irish High Kings once had their seat. From there the tour travels to the moors and table mountains of County Sligo and up to the storm-whipped coast of Donegal.

Meadows and gently undulating plateaus characterize the first part of the tour. From ✳ ✳ **Dublin** the drive is via the N3 to Dunshaughlin. Turn off left at about the half way point between Dunshaughlin and **Navan**, by the village of Taranach, to find the ❶ ✳ **Hill of Tara**, once seat of the Irish High Kings. From there the N51, and from Delvin the N52, lead to **Mullingar**. There is no reason to stop here, so continue straight on northwest on the N4, via Longford to ② **Carrick-on-Shannon**, the departure point for cabin cruises on the Shannon.

It is worth making a stop-over in ③ ✳ **Boyle** for the sake of the beautiful Cistercian Abbey and – for walkers – for the sake of the Lough Key Forest Park. The sea is reached at last at ④ ✳ **Sligo**. The beautiful birthplace of W. B. Yeats is also worth a visit because of the many pubs. Lough Gill stretches out towards the east, set in attractive countryside; 5 km/3 miles further south lies the largest cluster of megalithic graves at Carrowmore Megalithic Cemetery, while Yeats fans can spend some time at the poet's grave at Drumcliff.

The N15 then follows the storm-battered coast past several resorts to ⑤ ✳ **Donegal** with its famous tweed mill, Magee's. From here the tour continues to follow the N15 through partly forested hill country northeast, to Ballybofey.

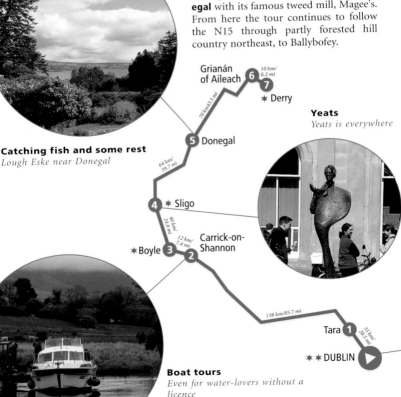

Catching fish and some rest
Lough Eske near Donegal

Grianán of Aileach ⑥ ⑦   10 km/6.2 mi
✳ Derry

70 km/43.5 mi

⑤ Donegal

64 km/39.7 mi

④ ✳ Sligo

40 km/24.8 mi

12 km/7.4 mi   Carrick-on-Shannon

✳ Boyle ③ ②

Yeats
Yeats is everywhere

138 km/85.7 mi

Tara ①   33 km/20.5 mi

✳✳ DUBLIN ▶

Boat tours
Even for water-lovers without a licence

The prehistoric stone fort of Grianán of Aileach leaves a lasting impression

The spectacular high coast of Ireland's northern tip is reached via Letterkenny on the N13 and the N56, and is particularly beautiful at **Horn Head**, and at the **Fanad and Rosguill Peninsula**.

In contrast, if you stay on the N13 you will reach ❻ ✳ **Grianán of Aileach** (»sun palace«), a massive stone fort with a fantastic view. A detour can also be made from there to the attractive peninsula of ✳ **Inishowen**. Following the N13, the tour then crosses the border into Northern Ireland and immediately reaches ❼ ✳ **Derry**, a port on Lough Foyle, with a walled historic centre. From here one can add on the journeys from Tour 1.

Lively big city
Point of departure and a destination in its own right

Sights
from A to Z

BREATHTAKING LANDSCAPES,
MYSTERIOUS RUINS,
MAGNIFICENT ART TREASURES,
COZY PUBS ? THE EMERALD ISLE
ENTICES THE VISITOR
WITH MANY HIGHLIGHTS.

Achill Island (Oileán Acaill)

B/C 1/2

Republic of Ireland, province: Connaught **Population:** 3,500	**County:** Mayo **Information:** Tel. (098) 4 73 53 (July–Aug)

With a surface area of 142 sq km/55 sq miles, Achill Island is the largest island off the Irish coast. The narrow Achill Sound, spanned by a swing bridge, separates it from the mainland. Almost the entire island is covered with heather and bog.

Europe's highest cliffs
For splendid cliff scenery, head to the northern and western coast: the Cathedral Rock Cliffs in the west rise up to 670m/2,198ft, making them the highest cliffs in Europe. A spin on the scenic Atlantic Drive reveals the island's most beautiful places and viewpoints.

Drive around Achill Island

Achill Sound
Not far from the bridge, Achill Soundvillage is the island's main shopping centre, where you can swim, hire boats or start out on a deep-sea fishing expedition. Take the Atlantic Drive around the southern tip of the island, to see the 15th-century ruins of Carrickkildavnet Castle, which used to belong to Grace O'Malley (►Baedeker Special p.451).

Dugort
11km/7 miles northwest of Achill Sound, on the northern coast of the island, lies Dugort. Standing on the main road is the house where Heinrich Böll and his family used to live, intermittently, from the mid-1950s onwards. The cottage was already little used in the last years of the German writer's life; today, writers and artists can use it as part of a scholarship programme. Dugort also boasts a fine sandy beach, and, nearby, some remains of megalithic graves (cairns) and dolmens.

Slievemore
A climb or hike around Slievemore (661m/2,169ft), is well worth the effort, rewarded by wonderful views. Passing the deserted village of Slievemore, spare a thought for its inhabitants who abandoned it in the mid-19th century, during the Great Famine. The seal caves below the mountain are only accessible by sea and in good weather; it is best to ask experienced boatsmen to take you there from Dugort, 3km/1.8 miles away.

Keel
Situated at 6km/3.6 miles southwest of Dugort, Keel is an attractive holiday resort with a sandy beach stretching 3km/1.8 miles southeast to the foot of the steep Minaun Cliffs. 5km/3 miles to the west of Keel, Dooagh, with its white thatched houses, is the most beautiful village on the island.

Feel the force of the roaring sea all around on the circular Atlantic Drive.

Adare (Áth Dara)

D 3

Republic of Ireland, province: Munster
County: Limerick
Population: 900

This attractive if fairly touristy village lies in the southwest of Ireland, on the forested western shores of the River Maigue. It is no coincidence that the thatched roofs and ancient grey church walls appear reminiscent of English villages – the Earl of Dunraven had Adare's picturesque Thatched Houses built in the 19th century in the English style.

In the early 18th century, German refugees from the Palatinate region were settled between Adare and Rathkeale, earning the area the name of »Palatine«. German traditions were upheld for a long time, and today still, German names can be encountered here.

German refugees

▶ VISITING ADARE

INFORMATION
Church View
Tel. (061) 396255
open: April–Oct

WHERE TO EAT
► Expensive
Wild Geese
Main Street
Tel. (061) 396451
Fine gourmet restaurant in a typical cottage.

► Moderate
Blue Door
Main Street
Tel. (061) 396481
One of the most beautiful cottages in town, serving typical Irish fare (Irish stew, lamb, salmon, etc.)

WHERE TO STAY
► Luxury
Dunraven Arms
Tel. (061) 396633, fax (061) 396541
www.dunravenhotel.com

Stylishly furnished rooms with antique furniture, a good restaurant, as well as a fine garden with stables.

Baedeker recommendation

► Mid-range
Carrabawn House
Killarney Road (N21)
Tel. (061) 396067, fax (061) 396925
Pretty guesthouse with very nice rooms, a well-kept garden, and good breakfast

Adare Heritage Centre
The Adare Heritage Centre has information on the history of the village, using models and a short film. (Opening times: May–Oct 9am–5pm.)

Adare Manor ✳
Adare Manor, the former manor house of the Dunraven family, has for several years been run as a luxury castle hotel (with restaurant). The park surrounding the neo-Gothic building today serves as a golf course, but determined visitors can access the romantic ivy-clad ruins of the 13th-century Desmond Castle. Also in the park, look for the relics of a Franciscan friary, with notable stalls on the southern choir wall and a tall yew tree at the centre of the cloister.

Churches in Adare
Catholic Holy Trinity Abbey in the village used to belong to the only Trinitarian monastery in Ireland. Dating from the 13th century, it only took on its current size and shape in the 19th century. At the eastern end of Adare, near the bridge over the River Maigue, stands

the 14th-century Augustinian abbey, used since the 19th century as the Protestant church and school. The cloister has served as a mausoleum for the Earls of Dunraven since 1826.

Around Adare

Some 11km/7 miles southwest of Adare, on the Deel River, lies the little market town of Rathkeale. Nearby, the beautifully restored Castle Matrix (c1440) displays antique furniture and art pieces.

Matrix Castle

The Celtic Park & Garden was established on the site of a former Celtic settlement in what is today Kilcornan, 7km/4.5 miles northwest of Adare. Reproductions of a stone circle, a dolmen, and a holy well aim to make the past come alive.

Celtic Park & Garden

★ Antrim Coast & Glens

A/ B 5/6

Northern Ireland, province: Ulster   **County:** Antrim

North of Belfast, one of the most beautiful roads in Ireland hugs the coast, past the famous Glens of Antrim up 90km/55.9 miles to the ► Causeway Coast. The attractions on this route are coastal scenery, wooded glens, the little port of Ballycastle and a visit to the island of Rathlin.

Along the coast, heading north from Belfast on the A2, the stretch between Larne and Carnlough already gives an idea of the beauty of the landscapes of the North. The highlight, however, is the following 16km/10 miles, where the road clings to steep slopes near the shore, before turning towards Red Bay at Waterfoot. Here is the turn for Glenariff, one of the most spectacular glens that have carved themselves into the basalt of North Antrim.

★
Glens of Antrim

The Glens of Antrim stretch between Larne and Ballycastle, with every one of the narrow valleys having its own character and its own coastal village. From south to north these are: Ballygally, Glenarm, Carnlough, Cushendall and Ballyvoy. All in all, this is a wild and romantic area shrouded in legend, with murmuring brooks and waterfalls, wooded mountain slopes and small villages.

> ! **Baedeker TIP**
>
> **Panoramic view**
> Particularly fine is the panorama from Fair Head, accessible from the third parking opportunity at Murlough Bay (to Coolanlough and back, count 3.5km/2.2 miles). From the viewpoint, at an elevation of over 180m/590ft, Rathlin Island is visible on the left, sometimes even the outline of the Isle of Arran in Scotland. The path leads past Lough na Cranagh, with an old Crannóg at its centre.

Glenariff Forest Park

Coming from Red Bay, a coastal strip with spectacular sandstone cliffs, the magnificently scenic valley of Glenariff branches off just before Cushendall. The visitors' car park at Glenariff Forest Park is the starting point for various signposted trails; particularly beautiful is the 5km/3-mile Waterfall Trail. The coastal village of Glenariff is known for its Feis na NGleann, a summer festival with music, dance and the Irish national sport: hurling.

Ossian's Grave

Back on the coast road, past the village of Cushendall, some 1km/0.6 miles to the north, lie the ruins of Layde Old Church, originally founded by Franciscans. Following the A2 inland (approx. 5km/3 miles south of Cushendun) and taking a left turn, small backroads lead to Ossian's Grave on the slopes of Tievebulliagh Mountain. According to local legend, the megalithic burial site holds the grave of the poet-warrior Ossian, son of Finn MacCool.

Cushendun

The pretty village of Cushendun, nestling among fuchsia and honeysuckle hedges, is famous for the houses designed by Clough Williams Ellis (1883–1977) for Lord Cushendun. Also, the village is a popular stop with hikers, lying on the route of the Ulster Way, running northwards inland in front of Murlough Bay and then along the coast to Ballycastle, southwards towards Cushendall.

Murlough Bay

Murlough Bay is often called the loveliest of all the bays on the Antrim coast; on clear days, the view stretches all the way to the Scot-

The Glen at Cushendall

⏵ VISITING ANTRIM COAST & GLENS

tish Mull of Kintyre. Unfortunately, the A2 diverges a little from the coast here, leaving a minor road to hug the bay. The best thing to do is leave the car in one of the three car parks and take a walk to really appreciate the landscape in peace and quiet. From the second car park, the remains of a cross commemorating Robert Casement (► Famous People) are visible. Casement's family came from this area; shortly before his execution in 1916 in London he asked to be buried at Murlough Bay.

Ballycastle

A picturesque port surrounded by forests is Ballycastle (pop. 4,000), where the Atlantic and the Irish Sea meet. Ballycastle is mainly used as a practical base for trips around the area.

Rathlin Island

From Ballycastle, it is a 40-minute ferry trip to Rathlin Island. This small island, inhabited by around 100 people, lies 9km/5.5 miles off the coast of Ballycastle. At the harbour, there is a pub, a restaurant, shops and accommodation. Find out about the history, flora and fauna of the island at the Boathouse Centre. Rathlin Island is popular for its near-untouched nature, in particular with sea anglers, divers and birdwatchers.

Thousands of seabirds live on the cliffs; the best location to watch them from is the Kebble Nature Reserve to the west of the island. One of the local caves was made famous by Robert the Bruce. In 1306, he is said to have hidden here after his defeat at the hands of the English. After regrouping, Robert the Bruce went on the counter-attack at the Battle of Bannockburn, an important victory in the Scots' wars of independence.

❗ *Baedeker* TIP

Oul' Lammas Fair

Arguably the most famous market in Northern Ireland, this horse and sheep fair with stalls set up around the Diamond is over 300 years old and held on the last Monday and Tuesday in August in Ballycastle. The local specialities, »dulse«, sun-dried seaweed, as well as iron-hard honey sweets called »yellow man«, may be an acquired taste.

★ ★ Aran Islands (Oileáin Árainn)

C 2

Republic of Ireland, province: Connaught
Population (in total): 1,600

County: Galway

The main draw of the three Aran Islands, jutting out of the Atlantic Ocean southwest of Galway, is their wind-torn aspect and barren, untouched natural environment. Their inhabitants hang on to many elements of the Irish culture, which has disappeared in so many other places, and the majority continue to speak Irish.

Islands of fishermen and artists

The Aran Islands consist of the three rocky islands of Inishmór, Inishmaan and Inisheer, as well as four tiny uninhabited islets. In order to make the karsty soil yield anything at all, the inhabitants of the islands have collected sand and seaweed and laid it down layer by layer on small plots of land protected by dry-stone walls. Locally, these man-made patches of soil are called »gardens«. Towards the sea, the rocky coast descends in terraces; there are few beaches. As with the Burren, various rare plant species have survived here.

Old traditions

Whilst tourism has continued to gain in importance over recent years – several private rooms, holiday homes and small B&Bs are available – the inhabitants have held on to many old traditions. Numerous writers have portrayed the islands' tough fishing folk. Up to this day, fishing and lobster fishing is the second-most important source of income after tourism. For this, the locals still sometimes use the curraghs, light boats made from wooden laths covered with tarred canvas.

Aran Islands Map

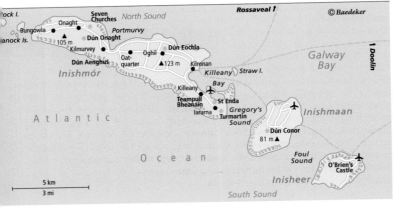

The biggest attraction on Inishmor are the magnificent sheer cliffs.

The Aran Islands are accessible by plane or boat. Aer Arann fly several times daily from the Connemara Regional Airport at Inverin (38km/24 miles west of Galway) to all three islands. There are several ferry connections to Inishmór from Rossaveal (around a 75-minute drive from Galway, past the airport, or by shuttlebus), as well as in the summer months once daily from Doolin, Co. Clare. There is also a ferry to Inisheer from Doolin. Currently, there are no services departing from Galway.

Getting there

Today, some 900 people live on Inishmór island, 12km/7.5 miles long and up to 3km/1.8 miles wide; a hundred years ago it was twice as many. Life focuses on the island capital Kilronan, where the ferries put in.

Inishmór

The main sight of the Aran Islands is the stone fort Dún Aenghus on the southwestern coast of Inishmór. This is one of the mightiest prehistoric fortifications in Europe, three semi-circular stone walls and a fourth (nearly completely destroyed) outer wall enclosing a space of 45m/50yd diameter immediately at the edge of the vertical sea cliffs. A defensive belt made from thousands of spiky stones set upright and close together into the ground in the style of today's anti-tank defences (»chevaux-de-frise«), was intended to deter potential attackers. From the cliff edge, there is a breathtaking view of the surf down below and beautiful views over the sea.

★ ★
Dún Aenghus

Kilmurvey

North of Dún Aenghus, near the hamlet of Kilmurvey, stand the churches of St Brecan, dating back to the 9th century, and Temple MacDuagh. There is a fine beach here too. On a ridge to the north-west rises the stone fort of Dún Eoghanachta. On the way back to Kilronan, watch out for seals in the sheltered bay of Port Chorrúch. Further east stands Dún Eochla (Oghil Fort), a stone fort with two circular walls, as well as the Early Christian church of Teampall Chiaráin with a High Cross. Take a walk out to the spectacular fort of Dun Duchatair (Black Fort); a hike along the coast from the fort is a fantastic experience. Take sufficient water and food and wear a hat in summer.

ARAN ISLANDS

INFORMATION

Aran Kilronan
Tel. (0 99) 6 12 63

Killeany

Some 3km/1.8 miles south of Kilronan, the area around Killeany contains numerous sacred sites, amongst them Tighlagh Eany, the remains of a monastic settlement. Its church holds a particularly beautiful cross shaft with interlacing and a horseman in relief. This area also boasts one of the smallest churches in the world, St Benan's Church (Teampull Benan's, Church Bheanáin).

Fort Dún Conor

Rising on a steep elevation, Fort Dún Conor has some stone huts within its grounds and good views from the walls. Also worth seeing are Cill Cheannannach church and Dún Fearbhaigh fort.

The house where poet and playwright John Millington Synge spent some holidays is lovingly kept. With his book, »The Aran Islands« (1907), Synge was the first to draw attention to this little archipelago. He is said to have spent much time at Synge's Chair on a cliff in the west of the island, which affords good views across Gregory's Sound.

! *Baedeker* TIP

Aran Sweaters

... are one of the favourite souvenirs from Ireland. On the islands, the fancifully patterned garments can be found on every corner. The story goes that the fishermen were able to identify the drowned by their family knitting pattern, but this is all it is: a story. In fact, the »typical« sweaters were only introduced here at the end of the 19th century.
Out of season is the right time for a bargain!

At 3km/1.8 miles in diameter, is the smallest of the Aran Islands. **Inisheer**
However, it has several monuments of interest to the visitor:
O'Brien's Castle, a medieval structure with a tower visible from afar,
St Gobnet's church (Cill Gobnet), with the characteristic features of
early Irish architecture, and St Cavan church. Every year on 14 June,
shovels are taken to this church, to free it from the sand threatening
to bury it.

Ardara (Árd na Rátha)

B 3

Republic of Ireland, province: Ulster   **County:** Donegal
Population: 650

**The fame of the tweed fabrics and knitwear from Ardara, near
Loughros More Bay, has reached far beyond the town. »Nancy's« is
said to be one of the best pubs in all Donegal. Nearby, enjoy lakes
with fish aplenty and great hiking territory.**

In most cases, today's tweed fabrics are no longer spun on the loom   **All about**
at home, but some factories encourage visitors to watch tweed being   **tweed**
made and buy it at much lower prices than in the shops in the towns
and cities. The Ardara Heritage Centre has further information on
the history of Donegal and tweed weaving.

Around Ardara

Around 11km/7 miles northeast of Ardara, on the Owenea River
amidst a forested region of lakes with plenty of fish and fine hiking
trails, lies the village of **Glenties**. To the northeast, Aghla Mountain
rises 589m/1,932ft above long Lough Finn, source of the Finn River.

Some 3km/1.8 miles southwest of
Ardara, a road turns off to the
west, winding its way in narrow
bends through a landscape of impressive and barren heights up to
Glengesh Pass and leading on to ►
Glencolumbkille.

West of Ardara, the long narrow
Loughros Peninsula is great for
walks or bike tours. There are
splendid views from its western
tip, Loughros Point . From the
northern shore of Loughros Beg
Bay, the **Maghera Caves** are acces-

One of the last hand looms

sible at low tide. Footpaths lead from the point along the coast or via the heights of the Slievetooey (460m/1,509ft) to ►Glencolumbkille. North of Ardara, the R261 turns off west from the N56. At Kilclooney, look out for a huge dolmen in a pasture. The twin villages of Narin and Portnoo consists of two holiday villages in a sheltered position on the southern shore of Gweebarra Bay. Narin has an 18-hole golf links and 2.5km/1.5 miles of sandy beach. At low tide, take a walk across – usually it will have to be barefoot – to the islet of Inishkeel, with a ruined chapel standing at its shore. The quiet seaside resort of Rosbeg, 5km/3 miles south of Portnoo, boasts a sandy beach and trout fishing.

Kilclooney ►

Narin and Portnoo ►

Rosbeg ►

Ardmore (Ard Mór)

E 4

Republic of Ireland, province: Munster
Population: 440

County: Waterford
Information: (024) 9 44 44
(June–Sept)

Looking for old buildings and modern villas, as well as beaches and steep cliffs? The popular beach resort of Ardmore, halfway along the southern coast of Ireland, fits the bill here. A mysterious erratic (boulder) on the beach is said to cure rheumatism.

✱
Round tower

The 12th-century round tower of Ardmore is one of the best-preserved in Ireland and very photogenic. Inside the tower, which is nearly 29m/95ft high, look out for corbelled stones with grotesque faces.

✱
Cathedral

Next to the tower stand the ruins of a 13th-century cathedral. The Romanesque reliefs on the west gable are particularly impressive. Despite the damage wrought by the elements, it is possible to make out, in the top row, Archangel Michael Weighing the Souls, below Adam and Eve, the Judgment of Solomon, as well as the Adoration of the Magi. The choir has two Ogham stones. The church was named after bishop St Declan who is said to have founded a Christian congregation here before the arrival of St Patrick.

St Declan's Well

St Declan's Stone ►

Some 800m/875yd east of the cluster of buildings stands the ruined Dysert Church, formerly of great prominence. Close by, pilgrims used to take a bath in St Declan's holy well. The erratic (boulder) lying at the southern tip of the beach is St Declan's Stone. The story goes that sinless sufferers of rheumatism who crawl under it will be cured from their ailment.

Cliff walks

There are various cliff walks to choose from: to the sea caves of Ardmore Head and Ram Head to the east and south of the town, also to Whiting Bay (west of Ardmore) and the bay of Monatray.

✴ Ards Peninsula   (Ain Aird)

B 6

Northern Ireland, province: Ulster   **County:** Down

In the northeast of County Down, large Strangford Lough pushes into the flat countryside, parallel to the Irish Sea, cutting off the Ards Peninsula. This quiet peninsula, an hour's drive from Belfast, boasts beautiful beaches.

The two roads stretching along the shore of this 35km/22-mile-long peninsula, show the different sides of the area: the A20, on the lough, is sheltered from the wind, whereas the route facing the sea (A2) appears wind-ravaged. What strikes the visitor is the wealth of tower houses, of which, however, only remains are left today. In the 15th and 16th centuries, numerous buildings of this type were erected, as King Henry VI, in 1429, offered a reward to everyone building this kind of fortification to protect the borders.

Tower houses and ostrich farms

The Ards Peninsula is an agricultural region; in recent times, traditional farming methods have diversified to include ostrich rearing and daffodil cultivation.

The best starting point for a drive around the Ards Peninsula is the nice market town of **Newtownards**. The top of the 41m/134ft Scrabo Tower, standing 2km/1.2 miles southwest in Scrabo Hill County Park, offers a wonderful view of Strangford Lough. The tower was erected in 1857 in honour of the third Marquess of Londonderry. (Opening times: June–Sept Sat–Thu 11am–6.30pm.)

Scrabo Tower, famous landmark on the Ards Peninsula

Some 3km/1.8 miles north of Newtownards on the A21, the Somme Heritage Centre commemorates the First World War's Battle of the Somme (1916), in which many Irishmen died. The historical events are presented from the perspective of soldiers from Ireland and Ulster. Close by, the Ark Open Farm is open to the public, displaying its rare breeds of sheep, cattle and poultry. (Opening times: Mon–Sat 10am–6pm, Sun 2–6pm.)

Somme Heritage Centre

Mount Stewart House and Gardens

Mount Stewart House and Gardens lie 8km/4.8 miles south of New-townards on the A21. The splendid 18th-century manor house boasts an important art collection, but the real attraction are the imaginative gardens, which were in large part laid out in the 1920s following the vision of Lady Edith, the wife of the 7th Marquess of Londonderry.

Divided into 17 different sectors, the garden shows a varied range of landscapes, comprising a natural-looking parkscape with many exotic trees and shrubs, a bizarre border featuring the Red Hand of Ulster, as well as a yew tree pruned into the shape of an Irish harp. Also fairly unusual are the statues of dinosaurs and mermaids. The octagonal »Temple of the Winds« banqueting house with views of Strangford Lough was erected in 1780. (Opening times gardens: April daily 10am–6pm, May–Sept daily 2–8pm, Nov–March daily 10am–4pm. Manor house: May to June Mon/Wed/Fri 1–6pm, Sat/Sun noon–6pm, July–Aug daily noon–6pm. Sept daily except Tues noon–6pm, mid-May–April and Oct Sat/Sun noon–6pm.)

Mount Stewart House and Gardens

Only 1.5km/1 mile southeast of here lies the village of Greyabbey, with the ruins of the old **Grey Abbey** amidst a fine park. Founded in 1193 by John de Courcey, his wife Affreca, daughter of the King of the Isle of Man, gifted it to the Welsh Cistercian monastery Holm Cultram. In 1572 the abbey was destroyed, but the church was restored and remained in use until the construction of a new building in 1778. Look out for the three-light lancet windows, very reminiscent of English cathedrals, and the preserved western doorway. Also of interest are the medieval monastery gardens, with over 50 different medicinal and culinary herbs. (Opening times: April–Oct Tues–Sat 10am–7pm, Sun 2–7pm.)

Portaferry

In the quiet town of Portaferry (pop 2,350), on the furthest tip of the peninsula, the A20 ends. From here, a ferry takes five minutes to cross over to Strangford on the western shore (► Downpatrick, Around), for some diving, fishing or to continue the tour following the eastern route.

The names of Strangford Lough describe its character: the Old Norse »Strangford« refers to the strong current of the narrows, the Irish name »Loch Cuan« to the calm waters of the mud flats. The lough is said to be one of the maritime areas of Europe with the most biodiversity, as the current brings huge amounts of plankton into this deep inlet on a daily basis. This is an opportunity to spot rare waterbirds, seals and sometimes even whales and sharks. Thanks to this wealth of interesting wildlife, the famous marine biology station likes to use the shore region as a field lab; the Strangford Lough Wildlife Scheme offers boat tours and ornithological excursions. A large flock of wild geese regularly spends the winter in this large bird and wildlife reserve; greylags and Greenland white-fronted geese cackle, various birds roam the mudflats, and seagulls and sea swifts often spend the summer here.

Strangford Lough

The diverse fauna of Strangford Lough and the Irish Sea is also explored in the **Exploris Aquarium** in Portaferry, situated near the small 16th-century tower house. Children in particular enjoy the various tanks, where they can touch sea urchins, sea anemones and other animals. There is also an orphanage for baby seals. (Opening times: March–Aug Mon–Fri 10am–6pm, Sat 11am–6pm, Sun 1–6pm; Sept–Feb only to 5pm.)

The stone wall leading out to sea at Millisle (approx. 20km/12 miles north of Portaferry and 12km/7.5 miles east of Newtownards), is a good vantage point for spotting eider ducks and wild geese. The popular coastal resort boasts an amusement park, shops, pubs, a swimming pool and campsites.

Millisle

Standing only 1.5km/1 mile to the northwest, on Moss Road (B172 towards Newtownards), the late 18th-century Ballycopeland Windmill is a popular subject for holiday snaps and one of the last two working windmills in Ireland. Take a guided tour to learn about flour production and what the miller's work involves. (Opening times: April–Sept Tues–Sat 10am–7pm, Sun 2–7pm.)

Ballycopeland Windmill

A bit further north, the nice port of **Donaghadee** is the point of embarkation, in summer, for boats to the three Copeland Islands. For nearly 50 years, seabirds have been the islands' only inhabitants.

> **!** *Baedeker* TIP
>
> **Grace Neill's**
> Grace Neill's, on the High Street in Donaghadee, happens to be the oldest pub on Irish soil; it was opened as far back as 1611. Peter the Great is said to have stopped off here on his European travels in 1697. The sausages with red onion or the wild duck with braised cabbage come highly recommended.

Arklow (An tInbhear Mór)

D 5

Republic of Ireland, province: Leinster
Population: 8,520

County: Wicklow

It is said that Saint Patrick chose Arklow to come ashore. Today, the town attracts visitors with pleasing sandy bays and charming potteries. In spring, the nearby Vale of Avoca is transformed into a dream of cherry blossoms.

History At Arklow, the Avoca River, which gave the valley its name, flows into the Irish Sea. Over the course of history, the town has changed owners several times. A monument in front of the Catholic parish church commemorates the last battles that took place there, including one of the bloodiest encounters during the rebellion of 1798. Apart from the Marine museum, Arklow has few sights. Shipyards and a fertilizer factory provide employment.

 ARKLOW

INFORMATION
Grand Parade
Tel. (0402) 3 24 84
open: mid-June–Aug

Around Arklow

From Woodenbridge, the R752 leads north to the **Vale of Avoca**, a valley much praised for its scenic beauty. The springtime wild cherry blossom is stunning. However, as various industries have now established themselves in the region, some parts of the Vale of Avoca have lost their charm.

Meeting of the Waters Some 5km/3 miles upriver, Castle Howard looks down from a cliff onto the famous »Meeting of the Waters« , where the Avonmore and Avonbeg become the Avoca River. Lion's Bridge is a particularly good vantage point to watch the two rivers converge.

! *Baedeker* TIP

Avoca Handweavers
A trip to Avoca in the south of the Wicklow Mountains is well worth making: visit Ireland's oldest hand-weaving mill, buy nice textiles and enjoy the good restaurant. The whole country has branches of the Avoca Handweavers, in Dublin, Bunratty and Molls Gap (Ring of Kerry) amongst others. For more information, see www.avoca.ie

Another 3km/1.8 miles further along, Avondale Forest Park is an extensive forest park, with the birthplace of Charles Stewart Parnell (► Famous People) open to the public. The interior of the building, built in 1779 after plans by James Wyatt, is beautiful, and a video provides information on the life of the Irish freedom fighter. (Opening times: May–Sept daily 10am–6pm, Oct–April 11am-5pm.)

✱ Armagh (Ard Mhacha)

B 5

Northern Ireland, province: Ulster   **District:** Armagh
Population: 14,600

Armagh, one of the most interesting towns in Northern Ireland, lies amidst the Garden of Ulster, southwest of ►Lough Neagh. The countryside is particularly attractive during Apple Blossom Time in May. A signposted Apple Blossom Trail begins and ends in Armagh.

Armagh is the seat of a Protestant and a Catholic archbishop and holds great significance for the ecclesiastical life of the province. Many buildings are in pink, yellow or reddish limestone called »Armagh Marble«. The material was very popular with local architect Francis Johnston (1761–1829), who designed several public buildings and Georgian town houses along the Mall, Armagh's main street. Important economic sectors are textiles and meat processing.

Religious centre of Ireland

The Irish name for the town is Ard Macha (»Macha's Hill«), as in the 3rd century BC, the legendary Queen Macha had a fort built on a hill some 3km/1.8 miles west of Armagh (see Around, Navan Fort). The place became important in Early Christian times, when St Patrick had a monastery and a church built here around 445, laying the foundation for Armagh becoming a centre of missionary activity. The famous 9th-century »Book of Armagh« manuscript was written in the monastery. Over the course of the centuries, the town was burned down and rebuilt several times.

 ARMAGH

INFORMATION
40 English Street
Tel. (028) 37 52 18 00

Sights in Armagh

The Protestant St Patrick's Cathedral (Vicar's Hill) stands on the site where St Patrick founded a church in the 5th century. This Church of Ireland cathedral owes its current appearance to a restoration carried out in the 19th century by Lewis Cottingham. Inside, the original crypt and several monuments – for Sir Thomas Molyneux,

Protestant St Patrick's Cathedral

amongst others – are worth seeing, as well as a bust of Archbishop Richard Robinson. From June to August, guided tours are available, at 11.30am and 2.30pm.

On the outer wall, a plaque points out that in 1004 the Irish king Brian Boru, after his death at the Battle of Clontarf, was buried in the grounds of the cathedral, according to his wishes.

Armagh Public Library When the Armagh Public Library (Robinson Library) was founded nearby in 1771, it was the first public library outside Dublin. An inscription above the main entrance calls it »the medicine shop of the mind«. The library comprises a valuable collection of books, mainly from the fields of theology, sciences and archaeology. The institution also possesses the »Claims of the Innocents« (petitions addressed to Oliver Cromwell), some wood engravings by the English painter and engraver William Hogarth (1697– 1764), as well as a copy of Jonathan Swift's »Gulliver's Travels« with handwritten annotations by the author. (Opening times: daily 9am–5pm.)

Armagh *Plan*

In the northwest of town, **St Patrick's Roman Catholic Cathedral**, a neo-Gothic building (1840–1873) with mosaics, stained glass windows and marble panelling executed by Italian artists, occupies a commanding position. During modernization works in 1981, Liam McCormick redesigned the chancel, including a tabernacle and crucifix made from a light polished stone. Both seem strangely out of place in this otherwise lavishly decorated church.

In the centre of town, below both cathedrals, the former Presbyterian church (next to the tourist information) and several new buildings

St Patrick's Trian were turned into St Patrick's Trian, a visitor centre looking mainly at the history of Armagh since the Celts and the Christian tradition. In »The Land of Lilliput«, children enjoy the huge model of Gulliver tied to the floor, ready for the little ones to clamber over. The centre also features various shops, galleries, restaurants and a multi-storey carpark. (Opening times: Sept–June Mon–Sat 10am–5pm, Sun 2–5pm; July and Aug Mon–Sat 10am–5.30pm, Sun 1–6pm.)

The Mall Back on English Street, have a look at the Shambles Market at the corner with Cathedral Road. Then onto the Mall – a finely laid-out park, where horse races and cockfights used to take place. Today, war memorials appear to stand guard over the flower beds. Standing at the northwestern end of the Mall, the Court House was built between 1805 and 1809 by Francis Johnston. Today however, the visitor encounters a reconstruction, as the original building was destroyed by a bomb in 1993.

A former school house on the Mall houses the **County Museum**, boasting interesting exhibits on archaeological, natural and local history of the region, as well as an excellent library. One gruesome feature is the cast-iron skull that used to adorn the Armagh gallows. The museum also has paintings by George Russell (1867–1935) and James Sleator (1889–1950), who portrayed numerous important Armagh personalities (opening times: Mon–Fri 10am–5pm, Sat 10am–1pm and 2–5pm.)

Archeological find in the County Museum

Royal Irish Fusiliers Museum ⏲

The Royal Irish Fusiliers Museum in Old Sovereign's House shows military artefacts and commemorates historic battles in which the fusiliers took part. (Opening times: Mon–Fri 10am–5pm.)

Armagh Observatory & Planetarium

Carry on northwest from Court House on College Hill, passing the Royal School, founded by James I in 1608, on the right-hand side, to reach the Armagh Observatory. Carrying on a bit further, the path leads to the Planetarium with the Hall of Astronomy, displaying astronomical instruments (touching allowed!). Furthermore, there is a replica of the Gemini rocket, spacesuits worn by American astronauts, models of the Space Shuttle and Voyager, as well as various telescopes. (Opening times: Mon–Fri 10am–4.45pm, Sat/Sun 1.15–4.45pm. Presentations weekdays 3pm, at weekends 2, 3 and 4pm, in July and Aug every hour.)

Franciscan Friary

To the south of town, the grounds of the former archbishop's palace (Friary Road) hold the remains of a Franciscan friary founded in 1266. With a length of nearly 40m/130ft, the church is said to be the longest Franciscan church in the country. Today, it houses the municipal administration.

Palace Stables Heritage Centre

Follow the street turning off at this point to reach the Palace Stables Heritage Centre standing in the grounds of the Palace Demesme built for Archbishop Robinson. Robinson's private chapel, in the shape of an Ionic temple, is also open to the public. In the former stables, an exhibition documents life in the palace, which the archbishops of the Church of Ireland occupied until the 1970s, over the course of the year 1776. (opening times: April–Sept Mon–Sat 10am–7pm, Sun 1–7pm; Oct–March Mon–Sat 10am–5pm, Sun 2–5pm.) ⏲

Around Armagh (northwest)

Navan Fort On the A28, some 3km/1.8 miles west of Armagh, the tree-lined grass mound of Navan Fort (Emain Macha) occupies the centre of a 7ha/17-acre area of mysterious hill forts and holy lakes from the Bronze and Iron Ages. Navan Fort was chosen for its destiny around 300 BC, when the legendary Queen Macha is said to have built a wooden palace here, serving as the base for the Red Branch Knights. Around AD 450, the palace and the surrounding town were destroyed by looters from Connaught. Today, the only reminder of the site's illustrious past are some ditches and ramparts; however, the hill commands a splendid view of the surrounding area.

Visitor centre ► Walk for five minutes to reach the award-winning visitor centre, which is designed to look like a green hill, blending in wonderfully with the landscape. The centre has information on the history of the town, explaining the archaeology and introducing the visitor to the Celtic myths and the epic literature of Ulster. (Opening times: daily except Christmas: Mon–Fri 10am–5pm, Sat 11am–5pm, Sun noon to 5pm; last show at 4pm.)

? DID YOU KNOW …?

■ For over six centuries, Navan Fort was the seat of the Kings of Ulster – an Irish Camelot, which the geographer Ptolemy called »Isamnium« when he drew up his map of the world as early as the 2nd century. It is said that Queen Macha gave birth to twins here after a horse race; hence the name Emain Macha, meaning »Twins of Macha«.

Benburb Valley Park, approx. 11km/7 miles northwest of Armagh, cuts through the Blackwater, very popular with anglers (salmon) and kayakers. Lying within the park, Benburb Castle was used by US troops during WW II as a hospital; A former linen mill houses the Benburb Valley Heritage Centre. (Opening times: April–Sept Mon–Sat 10am–5pm.)

The **Orange Order Museum** in the village of Loughgall, 10km/6 miles north of Armagh, commemorates a skirmish that took place in 1795 between Catholics and Protestants around 5km/3 miles northeast at

Blackwater is popular for salmon fishing.

Diamond Hill. Subsequently, the Protestant farmers in the area decided, in the Loughgall pub, to found an order taking its name from William of Orange: the Orange Order.

Ardress House 5km/3 miles northeast of Loughgall (14.5km/9 miles from Armagh), Ardress House was a modest manor house until 1760, when it was converted into an imposing stately home. Look out for the classical stucco work in the drawing room and the precious 18th-century furniture. The farm belonging to the estate, with pig breeding and a smithy, is still working; the garden has been planted with various traditional apple varieties, and there are old-fashioned varieties of Irish roses in a small rose garden. (Opening times: April and Sept: weekends and bank holidays 2–6pm; June–Aug: Wed–Mon 2–6pm.) 🕐

Further north, on Derrycaw Road (off the B28, 3½km/2.2 miles northwest of Moy), a hill overlooking the Blackwater, look out for the The Argory, a pretty country house. The furnishings, original murals and an organ – dating from 1824 and still used – are very well-preserved. The rose garden (opening times as Ardress House) is a marvel.

The Argory

Around Armagh (south)

Children in particular will love a trip to Gosford Castle Forest Park near Markethill (approx. 10km/6 miles southeast of Armagh). Admire various poultry, red deer and other animals; there are also nice nature trails and places for a picnic. Jonathan Swift is said to have stayed at Gosford Castle several times.

Gosford Castle Forest Park

Southern Armagh, alleged hideout for smugglers and partisan fighters, is also known as Bandit Country. It is true that the armed battles between the IRA and the British army were particularly fierce here. The town has few sights as such, but does boast a few nice places for a day trip, starting at Armagh or Newry (►Mourne Mountains).

A trip into »Bandit Country«

From Armagh, take the A28 south and drive some 20km/12 miles on the A25 to Camlough, where a sign points south to the remains of the two Killevy Churches, 5km/3 miles away. Here, medieval Augustinian nuns erected a new convent on top of the ruins of a convent founded in the 5th century and destroyed in 923 by the Vikings. The eastern church dates from the 15th century, the western one is some 300 years older. The western door's solid lintel is even said to date back to around 900.

◄ Killevy Churches

Only a few miles further west, Slieve Gullion (577m/1,893ft) lies at the centre of the Ring of Gullion, a particularly scenic landscape in the hills and mountains of south Armagh. Legend has it that it was here that the Irish hero Cú Chulainn stopped the armies of Queen Maeve. The area abounds in legends; the southern cairn on the mountain summit is said to be the house of Caillech Bhérri, the huge old witch and incarnation of the winter and death aspects of the Irish god-mother. Nearby, the northern cairn has two Bronze Age cists. 13km/8 miles of panoramic road lead through the conifer forest on the southern slopes of Slieve Gullion Forest Park.

◄ Slieve Gullion Forest Park

Discover traditional music in the Thí Chulainn Cultural Centre in the village of Mullach Ban, west of Slieve Gullion. Here, and in neighbouring Forkhill, regular folk music sessions are held.

◄ Thí Chulainn Cultural Centre

Crossmaglen ▶ Another place known for its music is Crossmaglen, approx. 5km/3 miles southwest; a horse fair also takes place here in early September. Visitors who have studied the Northern Ireland conflict will remember that during the Troubles, over 20 British soldiers were killed by Provisional IRA bombs and attacks in and around the town.

Athlone (Baile Átha Luain)

C 4

Republic of Ireland, province: Leinster
Population: 24,000

County: Westmeath

Athlone lies close to the geographical centre of the island, on the shores of the Shannon. The town is a lively rail and road hub, as well as featuring a marina for the sailing and nature paradise of the Shannon and Lough Ree.

Disputed bridgehead
The Shannon crossing at Athlone has been of strategic significance since time immemorial. A wattle-and-daub bridge stood here as early as the end of the first millennium. In the 13th century, a bridgehead was established, with a castle and shore fortifications that through the centuries were to be fought over, destroyed and rebuilt again. North of Athlone, the ▶Shannon flows through the large Lough Ree.

Athlone Castle & Museum
In 1210, King John of England commissioned the building of Athlone Castle. King John's Castle took on most of its current aspect in the early 19th century. Today, the group of buildings house a visitor

St Peter and Paul's Church opposite Athlone Castle

cated to the life and work of Athlone-born tenor John McCormack (1884–1945), who was very successful on the opera stages of the world. The museum also offers a glimpse of the flora and fauna of the Shannon area. (Opening times: May–Sept Mon–Sat ⊘ 10am–4.30pm).

Around Athlone

North of Athlone stretches the large, reed-lined Lough Ree, famous for the Early Christian monastery ruins on its many islets, and for excellent trout fishing. Many migrating birds nest here, mainly swans, mallards and curlews. There is also very good sailing to be had here.

Lough Ree

Northeast of Athlone, the N55 leads through Goldsmith Country, the literary landscape of Oliver Goldsmith and John K Casey. Goldsmith was born and bred in Lissoy. The area is also very well suited to bike rides, in particular the route along the »Lough Ree Trail«.

Goldsmith Country

At Moate, half-way between Athlone and Kilbeggan on the N6, lies the Dún na Sí Heritage Park, which aims to give visitors the experience of life on a 19th-century farm and opportunities to research family history.. In summer, traditional Irish evenings are held here on Fridays, with music, dance and storytelling.

Moate
◄ Dún na Sí Heritage Park

▶ VISITING ATHLONE

INFORMATION
Athlone Castle
Tel. (0902) 649 29 12
Open: mid-April–Oct

WHERE TO EAT
► Moderate
The Olive Grove Restaurant
Bridge Street/Custom Place
Tel. (0902) 647 69 46
The colourful Olive Grove Restaurant offers delicious dishes for every taste. At weekends, many people come here for a quiet breakfast and to browse the newspapers and magazines.

WHERE TO STAY
► Luxury
Shamrock Lodge Hotel
Clonown Road

Tel. (0902) 649 26 01
Fax (0902) 649 27 37
A great source of pride for Shamrock Lodge, established in 1951, are its celebrity guests, such as Prince Rainier and Grace of Monaco.
Now, there is also a conference centre here.

► Mid-range
Hodson Bay Hotel
Roscommon Road
Tel. (0902) 648 05 00
Fax (0902) 648 05 20
The Hodson Bay Hotel on Lough Ree offers a wide range of sports facilities (golf course, tennis courts, etc.), but is also well suited as a conference centre.

Athy (Baile Áth Í)

Republic of Ireland, province: Leinster
County: Kildare
Population: 5,300

Athy occupies a scenic position on the shores of the gently flowing River Barrow. The town's most conspicuous building is its bulky 15th-century tower. Visible from afar, it signals the end of this particular leg of the journey to all hungry and thirsty houseboat skippers.

Important ford

The fact that the ford of the River Barrow has been of significance for Athy since time immemorial is shown by the Irish name for the town, meaning »town of the ford of Ae«, after a second-century AD chieftain killed on the river crossing. One branch of the ►Grand Canal joins the river here. Athy lies in the east of Ireland, southwest of Dublin and south of Portlaoise. The most conspicuous building in Athy is **White's Castle**, a bulky rectangle with corner towers, built by the Earl of Kildare in the 15th century to protect the bridge over the River Barrow. The bridge has the unusual name of Crom-a-boo, derived from the war cry of Desmond's followers (one Earl of Desmond was English governor around 1420). Another defence of the river crossing was Woodstock Castle (800m/0.5 miles north on the R147).

Around Athy

Ballitore
⊙ Opening times: daily 10am–1 9pm.

10km/6 miles further east, Ballitore was once a vibrant Quaker settlement with a school whose fame extended beyond the region. A reminder of this time is the Quaker Meeting House, housing a small museum. Another sight is the Crookstown Mill and Heritage Centre. The former mill has been restored, its wheels are working again, and numerous exhibits document the process of milling and baking bread in past centuries.

Rath of Mullagast ►

Rath of Mullagast, an Iron-Age fort, lies only 2km/1.2 miles to the west. One of the legendary »monster meetings« led by the Catholic freedom fighter Daniel O'Connell is said to have taken place here in 1843.

★
High Cross of Moone

South of Ballitore, near the N9 at Moone (coming from Dublin, to the right-hand side of the road) stands a ruined church. Here, the visitor finds a slim Celtic High Cross, at nearly 6m/18ft high the second-tallest in Ireland. Its stylized bas-reliefs have a strong visual impact, showing scenes from the Bible, such as the Sacrifice of Abraham, the Twelve Apostles, the Miracle of the Loaves and Fishes, the Flight to Egypt and Daniel in the Lions' Den.

East of Moone, **Baltinglass**, situated on the N81, houses the remains of the 12th-century Cistercian monastery Valle Salutis. Its stonemasonry works (nave and choir) display a mix of Hiberno-Romanesque and Cistercensian forms. Parts of the cloister are more recent, the tower and east window are 19th century.

Northeast of the village rises **Baltinglass Hill** (377m/1,237ft). On its summit stand the stone walls of a hill fort enclosing Neolithic passage tombs. A pleasant panoramic view can be enjoyed from here.

Take the N9 south from Moone to reach, after 8km/5 miles, **Castledermot**. Look out for the remains of a very ancient monastery, amongst them a Romanesque archway, a round tower and two granite High Crosses. The scene with David playing the Harp is of particular interest, being one of the few representations of an Irish harp. In the southern part of the village, the remains of a 14th-century Franciscan monastery are all that survived its dissolution in the 16th century.

Look for the harps depicted on the High Crosses of Castledermot.

On the way back to Athy (driving northwest from Castledermot), after 5km/3 miles the road passes Kilkea Castle, which was built in 1180, but suffered extensive alterations in the 19th century. Today, the castle is occupied by a nice hotel with health spa.

Kilkea Castle

Ballina (Béal an Átha)

B 2

Republic of Ireland, province: Connaught
Population: 8,200

County: Mayo

Ballina, the largest town in County Mayo, is an ideal base for anglers. But for those not in the mood for salmon and trout fishing, try sampling the friendly town's cozy pubs and good restaurants.

Paradise for anglers

Ballina lies far in the northwest of Ireland, in the boggy terrain on the River Moy, where the river widens into its Atlantic estuary at Killala Bay. In this fishing paradise, keen anglers flock first and foremost to the River Moy, as well as to the fish-rich lakes of Lough Conn and Lough Cullin. Apart from the stained glass in the 20th-century Catholic cathedral and the nearby remains of a 15th-century Augustinian abbey there aren't that many sights around here. Not far from the railway station, a dolmen serves as tomb for four brothers said to have murdered their foster father, a bishop, in the 6th century.

Around Ballina

Rosserk Abbey

Take the R314 until, after approx. 6km/3.5 miles, you reach a sign. Follow this and turn left at the next crossroads to reach 15th-century Rosserk Abbey. The lavishly sculpted western doorway of this Franciscan abbey leads into the single-aisled church, with one south chapel. The windows are particularly impressive. The choir features a double piscina (baptismal font), with a round tower and a square tower carved into one of its pillars.

✱ Moyne Abbey

Back on the main road, take a left-hand turn after another 3km/1.8 miles just past the village; this side road leads southwest to the 15th-century Moyne Abbey right on the seaside. Many parts of this Franciscan abbey are preserved if only as ruins.

Killala

Another 6km/3.5 miles to the north, in Killala (pop. 710), a 25m/82 ft well-preserved round tower stands opposite a small 17th-century church. French forces who landed in Kilcummin Bay in 1798 to support the rebels, held on to Killala for a while as a bulwark against the British.

▶ VISITING BALLINA

INFORMATION
Cathedral Road
Tel. (0 96) 7 08 48
Open: April–Oct

WHERE TO STAY

▶ **Mid-range**
Downhill Inn
Sligo Road
Tel. (0 96) 7 34 44
fax (0 96) 7 34 11
Angling, golf, swimming pool, squash, sauna, tennis – all these options are on offer at this comfort-

able establishment situated 1km/0.6 miles outside the town.

Baedeker recommendation

▶ **Budget**
Castle Arms Hotel
Enniscrone, Co. Sligo, tel./fax (0 96) 3 61 5[
At some 15km/9.3 miles from Ballina, Enniscrone has the Castle Arms Hotel, wit several golf links, a spa and leisure centre, seaweed and steam baths, tennis courts an other amenities nearby.

Baedeker TIP

Tír Sáile

The North Mayo Sculpture Trail (Tír Sáile) runs along the coast, from Ballina via Killala, Ballycastle, Belderrig and Belmullet to finish in Blacksod. For the celebrations of Mayo's 5,000 year-history, 15 international artists were commissioned to create sculptures reflecting the wild beauty of the region. For more information, see www.ballina.mayo-ireland.ie.

Past Ballycastle, it is worth taking the east coast byroad via Rathlackan; take a right turn in Carrowmore towards Lackan Bay. The road leads past the remains of RathfranFriary; a signposted path points to the 2.5m/8 ft Breastagh Ogham Stone.

Kilcummin, Rathfran Abbey and Breastagh Ogham Stone

The R314 leads northwest to Ballycastle; however, the drive along the coast via Downpatrick Head is also very scenic, with its shore rocks, shaped into bizarre formations by the sea. Jets of water gush up where the surf pushes the seawater through narrow openings.

Ballycastle
◄ Downpatrick Head

At 10 sq km/3.8 sq miles, Céide Fields is the largest Neolithic archaeological site in the world. The village, 5,000 years old, lies 8km/5 miles west of Ballycastle on the R314. The settlers cleared the forest, laid out pastures and lived in free-standing farmsteads, with walls dividing the plots of land from each other. The remains of walls excavated from under a thick layer of turf may not seem very impressive to the lay visitor, but a visitor centre provides the necessary background to the sensational discoveries made here. (Opening times: mid-March–May and Oct: daily 10am–5pm, June–Sept daily 9.30am–6.30pm, Nov daily 10am–4.30pm; the excavation site itself is accessible at any time.)

★★
Céide Fields

It is a quick 16km/0.6-mile drive on the N57 to reach **Foxford** south of Ballina. In the past century, the hydropower of the River Moy, snaking through the little town, was harnessed to power mills for spinning wool. The **Foxford Woollen Mills Visitor Centre** shows wool production then and now. There is also a chance to take a short break in the teashop and browse for crafts. (Opening times: Mon–Sat 10am–6pm, Sun 2–6pm.)

Baedeker TIP

Irish »Wellness«

Looking for a relaxing experience? Why not visit Kilcullen's Bath House in Enniscrone (Inishcrone), 15km/9 miles north of Ballina, and enjoy a seaweed bath. Alongside steam baths and massages, the »Hot Sea Water and Seaweed Bath« has been offering a trip into the past since 1912: the enamel tubs, art-nouveau tiles and an old-fashioned steam box have been preserved. The Tea House offers more pampering. For more information call: Tel. (0 96) 3 62 38.

Angling The River Moy is considered one of the most salmon-rich rivers in Europe. Going south, the R310 leads to the narrow strait between Lough Conn (famous for its trout and pike) and Lough Cullin. Both lakes allow fishing without permits. The R315 leads around Lough Conn to the popular angling base of Pontoon.

Ballinasloe (Béal Átha na Sluaighe)

`C 3`

Republic of Ireland, province: Connaught
Population: 5,800

County: Galway

Ballinasloe is a busy commercial town, famous for its horse, cattle and sheep fairs. The October Fair is the largest in Ireland, and, at a time when there were no cars but lots of cavalry, was considered the most important horse fair in Europe.

Terminal of the Grand Canal Once, Ballinasloe – in the heart of Ireland, southwest of Lough Ree, on the N6 – had a significant strategic position. Ballinasloe is also the western terminal of the ▶ Grand Canal, which is, however, not navigable on its last stretch. Above the River Suck, 19th-century Ivy Castle stands on earlier defensive structures.

Ponies for sale at the Ballinasloe horse fair

Around Ballinasloe

On the R355, 8km/5 miles south of town lies the ruined Augustinian monastery of **Clontuskert Abbey**. The abbey, one of 130 houses established by the Augustinians following the church reforms of the early 12th century, probably occupied the site of an earlier monastery dating from the 8th century. The western entrance of the church, erected in 1471, is worth seeing for its ornate carvings: Michael Weighing the Souls, saints, a pelican, and a mermaid holding a mirror amongst others.

BALLINASLOE

INFORMATION
Kellar Travel
Tel. (0905) 42604
open: July–Aug

From the monastery, take a byroad via Laurencetown to reach **Clonfert Abbey**, 21km/13 miles southeast of Ballinasloe. The former abbey's famous main doorway, dating from the 12th century and sumptuously decorated with human heads and triangles, is considered the peak of Hiberno-Romanesque sculpture. The eastern choir windows count among the most important examples of late-Romanesque art in Ireland. Inside, look out for the decorations of later sections – the supporting arches of the tower, featuring angels and a mermaid, the chancel arch and the 15th-century window.

Ballybunion (Baile an Bhuinneánaigh)

D 2

Republic of Ireland, province: Munster

County: Kerry

Population: 1,450

Sea caves, jagged cliffs, bays, little hideouts and a seemingly endless sandy beach offer a varied and attractive holiday experience in and around Ballybunion. Many tourists come just for the golf – even US president Bill Clinton was here in 1998, his visit commemorated by a sculpture outside the Garda (police) Station.

This popular family resort lies in the southwest of Ireland, where the Shannon meets the Atlantic. The northern coastal strip has many caves that are accessible from the sea, some of them by boat, others, at low tide, on foot. A path of approx. 5km/3 miles leads along the top of the cliffs between Doon Cove and Doon Point, both with remains of promontory forts, and past the old fortress of Lick Castle. East of Ballybunion rises Knockamore Hill (264m/866ft), which offers a magnificent panoramic view.

Coastal caves

Around Ballybunion

Ballylongford Carrigafoyle Castle, Lisloughtin Abbey ▶

Northeast, the R551 leads to Ballylongford. On the western side of the narrow inlet stands Carrigafoyle Castle, dating from the 15th century; there are splendid views to be had from the top of the 26m/85ft tower. East of the town lie the ruins of the Franciscan Lisloughtin Abbey, also dating from the 15th century. Note, in particular, the west window of the church. The Ballylongford Cross, today kept in the National Museum in Dublin, was made at this monastery.

Tarbert

Continue on the R551 from Ballylongford for 8km/5 miles to reach Tarbert (pop. 680), which is the embarkation point for a car ferry to Killimer (▶ Kilkee), crossing the Shannon. The Tarbert Bridgewell Courthouse & Jail highlights the criminal justice system in the 19th century, telling the story of Thomas Dillon in recreated scenes. Tarbert Island has a lighthouse and an old gun battery.

Listowel

Some 14km/9 miles southeast of Ballybunion, Listowel (pop. 3,350) is a small up-and-coming town, with, some say, more pubs than residential buildings! Listowel became famous for its Writers' Week taking place every year in June. Another event is the harvest festival at the end of September, which to this day operates simultaneously as a marriage fair.

✶ Rattoo Round Tower

A good 12km/7.5-mile drive west of Listowel, in the grounds of the early monastic foundation of Rattoo, stand a 15th-century church and the very well preserved 28m/92ft Rattoo Round Tower.

✶ Bantry (Beanntrai)

E 2

Republic of Ireland, province: Munster
Population: 2,900

County: Cork

Giant fuchsia hedges and palm trees are a common sight in the famously beautiful Bantry Bay in the furthest southwestern corner of Ireland, as the influence of the Gulf Stream can indeed be felt here.

Lively holiday resort

Bantry itself is fairly busy if not that attractive – not helped by the oil terminal on Whiddy Island, with facilities for supertankers. French fleets invaded the bay twice: in 1689, to support James II, and in 1796, to help the Irish rebels. They failed, however, on both accounts. Conscientious visitors may prepare their visit to Bantry House at Bantry Museum, located behind the fire station which has exhibitions mainly on matters of local interest.

Feel like an earl for once – a wing of Bantry House offers affordable accommodation.

On the southern edge of town, in a magnificent park, Bantry House awaits. This Georgian building, begun in 1740, was extended in 1840 by two wings to form a harmonious broad ensemble. Bantry House boasts a valuable art collection with exhibits from all over Europe, including icons, tapestries and French furniture, and mosaics from Pompeii adorning the hall. The pretty tearoom is a good place to linger. The most beautiful feature though is the park with its Italianate terraces and sculptures seemingly leaning against the ascending slopes. The last scenes of »Moll Flanders« were filmed here. (Opening times: daily 9am–6pm, summer to 8pm.)

✱
Bantry House & Gardens

⊙

Opposite Bantry House, visit the 1796 French Armada Exhibition Centre. In the winter of 1796, a French fleet of 43 ships with 16,000 men aboard sailed to Ireland to support the United Irishmen in their insurrection against the British. However, as only 16 ships reached Bantry Bay, the French had to retreat after only a few skirmishes. Unfavourable winds prevented the larger part of the force from landing, although it was in Tone's words »close enough to toss a biscuit ashore«. A model of the sunk French frigate »La Surveillante« is on display at the Armada Museum. (Opening times: Easter–Sept daily 10am–6pm.)

1796 French Armada Exhibition Centre

⊙

▶ VISITING BANTRY

INFORMATION
Tel. (0 27) 5 02 29
Open: June– Sept

WHERE TO STAY

▶ **Mid-range**
Westlodge Hotel
Tel. (0 27) 5 03 60, fax (027) 5 04 38
www.westlodgehotel.ie
Families in particular like to stay at
this hotel, offering plenty of leisure
activities: pools, sauna, jacuzzi, fitness
room, aerobics, squash, tennis and
leisurely strolls.

Gougane Barra Hotel
Gougane Barra, Ballingeary
Tel. (0 26) 4 70 69, Fax (0 26) 4 72 26
gouganebarrahotel@eircom.net
A quiet, idyllic little place at Gougane

Barra Lake, source of the River Lee
and considered one of the most
beautiful in Ireland. This area is good
for hiking, biking and as a base for
trips into Cork and Kerry.

Baedeker recommendation

▶ **Budget**
Vickery's Inn
New Street
Tel. / fax (0 27) 500 06
www.vickerys.ie
vickerys-inn@westcork.com
This good-value guesthouse is a handy base
for trips into West Cork. In the summer, the
bar has live music.

Around Bantry

Stones and waterfalls

Kilnaurane Pillar Stone ▶

Around Bantry, there are several nice options for tours to explore
the scenic area. One route leads to the Kilnaurane Pillar Stone, featuring one of the rare representations of the boat allegedly used by St
Brendan to sail to America in the 6th century. To find the stone, take
the N71 in the direction of Cork. At the Westlodge Hotel, 2km/1.2
miles out of town, turn left; after 800m/0.5 miles, you will pass a
sign pointing to a gate. Drive straight on past the sign until the stone
appears behind the brow of the hill.

Cousane Pass

Particularly nice to explore are the roads to Macroom (▶ Cork,
Around) and on to Glengarriff (▶ Beara Peninsula) along the coast,
with beautiful vistas of the sea and mountains.

Donemare Waterfalls

North of the town, on the road to Glengarriff, visit the impressive
Donemare Waterfalls of Mealagh River, which, together with Drom-
brow Lough above, and Lough Bofinna, offers anglers good fishing
grounds.

Sheep's Head Peninsula

Stretching southwest from Bantry, the long, scenic Sheep's Head
Peninsula has attractive beaches on its southern coast, at Kilcrohane
and Ahakista. It is worth driving all around the peninsula, pushing

on as far as Sheep's Head. The road from Kilcrohane to Gouladoo runs below Seefin mountain (alt 340m/1,115ft), with particularly fine views.

✴ Beara Peninsula

E 1/2

Republic of Ireland, province: Munster   **County:** Cork

The Beara Peninsula in the southwest of Ireland, with its many small lakes, has a unique wild beauty. Jutting out some 60km/40 miles to sea between the bays of ►Bantry and the Kenmare River, it is strewn with great viewpoints.

On the Beara Peninsula, the coast road (Ring of Beara) winds its way behind Bantry Bay around rocky bays and promontories, past beautiful sandy beaches and charming fishing villages, whilst the inland route leads through barren mountain scenery.

Peninsula with varied scenery in the southwest

✴ Ring of Beara

Glengarriff, in Irish An Gleann Garb (»the barren valley«), is a small village in the southwest of Ireland at the end of a 10km/6-mile valley, where the Glengarriff River flows into Bantry Bay. The village (pop 250) is completely given over to tourism, with numerous guesthouses and B&Bs. Day trippers mainly come here to visit Garinish Island just offshore or to start their drive around the Ring of Beara. Due to the favourable climate nurtured by the warm Gulf Stream, an almost tropical vegetation of fuchsia, yew trees, holly and strawberry trees (arbutus) covers the rocky slopes down to the sea. Also recommended is a visit to Glengarriff Woods, a huge oak and pine forest, the entrance to which lies about 1km/0.6 miles north of town on the Kenmare road (N71).

Glengarriff

Of the many small islands in the bay, Garinish Island (Ilnacullin), east of the R572, is most worth a visit. During the 15-min trip out to the island, the boat passes a rock with seals basking in the sun. The fine gardens on Garinish Island, with magnolias, rhododendrons, camelias and many exotic trees, were only laid out between 1910 and 1920. All other buildings on the islands, blending in well with

✴ ✴
Garinish Island

? DID YOU KNOW …?

■ One of the most famous visitors of Garinish Island, George Bernard Shaw, wrote large parts of his play »Saint Joan« here in 1923.

the park landscape, were built at the same time – apart from one Martello tower from the Napoleonic era.(Opening times: July–Aug

Gougane Barra Lake, one of the most beautiful mountain lakes in Ireland

Mon–Sat 9.30am–6.30pm, Sun 11am–7pm; April, May, June and Sept Mon–Sat 10am–6.30pm, Sun 1–7pm; March and Oct Mon–Sat 10am–4.30pm, Sun 1–5pm.)

Drive around the peninsula

From Glengarriff, start exploring the peninsula jutting out west into the sea, the Ring of Beara. Less well known than the Ring of Kerry, this stretch (of approx. 135km/85 miles) offers scenery that is no less spectacular. The interior of the peninsula is traversed by the bleak ranges of the Caha and Slieve Miskish mountains (400m/1,312ft to 700m/2,296ft).

Castletownbere ▶

The R572 initially wends its way between the Caha Mountains and the sea along Bantry Bay, around the bay of Adrigole Harbour, to the fishing village of Castletownbere (pop. 920), which also has some shops. Lying off the shore of Castletownbere, Bere Island has an interesting shape and boasts a sailing school and good hiking.

Bere Island ▶

⏵ VISITING BEARA PENINSULA

Some 3km/1.8 miles to the southeast, visit the picturesque ruins of Dunboy Castle, the former residence of the O'Sullivans, which burned out in 1602. Close by, look for the remains of the castle of the-Puxleys, who prospered here in the 19th century by exploiting the local copper mines. Daphne du Maurier, in her novel »Hungry Hill«, an astute analysis of the social conditions of the time, allegedly based her protagonists on individual members of this family.

◀ Dunboy Castle & Puxley Mansion

Dursey Sound separates the furthest point of the peninsula from the island of the same name. Only a dozen people live on Dursey Island. Daring visitors can take the »Dursey Cable Car«, the only cable car in Ireland. A short ride in this tiny tin cab dangling between two masts (which is licensed to carry three people and a cow!) will leave lasting memories.

◀ Dursey Island

Between 1810 and 1962, the small village of Allihies was a centre for copper mining; some stone cottages and chimneys are reminders of the time when almost 1,300 men, women and children worked here.

Allihies

Follow the road northeastfor 12km/7.5 miles, past fuchsia and rhododendron hedges, to the small village of Eyeries. Continuing on towards Lauragh, a sign to the right-hand side points to the Ardgroom Stone Circle set in a scenic location.

Eyeries

From Eyeries, the road runs northeast across the border with County Kerry to Lauragh, where the fine Derreen Gardens are worth a visit. (Opening times: April–Sept daily 11am – 6pm.)
Mossy paths lead through a forest landscape, past tall rhododendron, eucalyptus and bamboo groves, yielding splendid vistas of the sea. From Lauragh, one option is to drive south to return to Glengarriff via Healy Pass (325m/1,066ft) and Adrigole.

◀ Lauragh
⏱

★ Belfast (Béal Feirste)

B 5/6

Northern Ireland, province: Ulster   **District:** Belfast
Population: 300,000
(Greater Belfast 600,000)

Belfast has been the capital of Northern Ireland since 1920 – nearly a third of all the inhabitants of the province live here. Since 1994, the Northern Ireland conflict has calmed down a lot, and an ever increasing number of visitors can be seen strolling through the shopping streets between Donegall Square and Royal Avenue.

Capital of Northern Ireland

Belfast (Béal Feirste means »sandy ford at the river mouth«), with its position on the estuary of the Lagan, is an important industrial and port city. Outside the city centre, the university quarter on the western shore of the River Lagan is attractive too: narrow, quiet streets with old trees, small Victorian houses, little shops and galleries dominating the scenery. The main attractions of North Belfast are Belfast Castle and the Zoological Gardens in Cave Hill Park. For those interested in the recent history of the city and the »Troubles«, a Black Cab tour through West Belfast should prove illuminating.

Festivals

Belfast has various festivals to offer, most of all the Belfast Summer City Fest and the Belfast City Folk Festival featuring local and international stars, as well as the Féile an Phobail in West Belfast (► Events).

History

1177	Destruction of the medieval castle
17th century	Huguenot immigration
1800	Union with England
1969	Sectarian violence against the Catholic population
1994	The »peace process« begins
2007	Formation of a government for Ulster by Protestant and Catholic parties

Belfast already had a fortress in the early Middle Ages, but by 1177 it was destroyed. The castle erected subsequently was much fought over between the English conquerors and Irish owners. Since the early days, linen production played an important role in Belfast; the sector was boosted significantly with the arrival of the Huguenots fleeing France in the late 17th century. These immigrants not only introduced better methods of production, but also gave the city a little French flair and enriched it culturally. After the union with England (1800), Belfast grew to be a major industrial city, its magnificent 19th-century buildings earning it the epithet of »Athens of the

North«. Alongside linen weaving, rope manufacture, shipbuilding and the tobacco industry rang in Belfast's economic heyday. Belfast never quite recovered from the economic crisis between the two world wars; today still, the rate of unemployment remains very high.

Belfast has always been at the centre of violence in the Northern Ireland conflict. The »Troubles«, as the violent clashes between Republicans and Unionists are euphemistically called here, dominated the daily life and the development of the city to a large extent. On the face of it, the issue revolves around whether Northern Ireland should stay within the United Kingdom or ultimately join a »united Ireland«; the spiral of sectarian violence which cost the lives of over 3,500 people was triggered by social discrimination against the Catholic minority in the late 1960s and the authorities' heavy-handed reaction to these grievances. Since the beginning of the »peace process« in 1994, the situation in Belfast has settled down. Whilst the social segregation of the population in Catholic and Protestant neighbourhoods continues in schools, pubs, etc., there has been an increasing focus on projects to bring Catholics and Protestants closer together. At the political level this finally happened in May 2007, when Ian Paisley of the Protestant Unionist party and Martin McGuiness of the Catholic Sinn Féin were sworn in at Stormont as joint heads of government for the province.

Northern Ireland conflict

Iconic landmark: Belfast's City Hall

Belfast Map

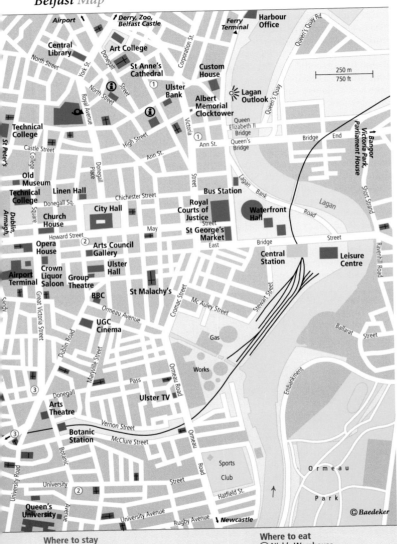

©Baedeker

Where to stay
① Mc Causland Hotel
② Dukes Hotel
③ Malone Lodge

Where to eat
① Nick's Warehouse
② Restaurant Michael Deane
③ Cayenne

City Centre

The hub of the city centre is Donegall Square. From here, it is a five-minute walk to The Entries, an old commercial quarter with narrow streets and plenty of atmosphere. Along the shopping mile of Royal Avenue lies the city's biggest shopping mall, Castlecourt Centre. An ultra-modern Belfast is growing up around the Waterfront Hall on the shores of the Lagan River. This is also where some of the most beautiful buildings of the city can be found, dating from around 1900. Look out for the lavishly decorated Scottish Provident Building, for instance, the Pearl Assurance Building and the Robinson & Cleaver Building, formerly seat of the Royal Irish Linen Warehouse.

Unmissable, the impressive City Hall is an imposing building with four towers and an enormous dome, erected 1898–1906 in the Renaissance style after designs by Sir Brumwell Thomas. Guided tours last around 45 minutes and have to be booked in advance. (Guided tours June–Sept: Mon–Fri 10.30am, 11.30am and 2.30pm, Sat 2.30pm; Oct–May Mon–Sat 2.30pm; tel. 0 28 / 90 32 02 02) Worth seeing in particular are the 50m/164ft splendidly furnished banqueting hall, the marble-lined entrance hall, as well as the wall painting by John Luke (1951) showing important trades that played a major role in the development of the city: rope-making, shipbuilding, weaving and spinning. In front of City Hall stand statues of Queen Victoria and distinguished citizens, and on the western side, in the Garden of Remembrance, a war memorial. A cluster of sculptures commemorates the »Titanic« disaster of 1912; the ship had been built by Harland and Wolff (see p.194).

★ **City Hall**

Situated on the northwestern corner of Donegall Square, the Linen Hall Library (1788) is Belfast's oldest library. Irish literature occupies the whole of the first floor. Unusual here is the Political Collection, containing over 100,000 works dealing with different aspects of poli-

Linen Hall Library

Highlights Belfast

City Hall
Belfast landmark is located on Donegall Square
▶ page 189

Botanic Gardens
Relax under palm trees in a glass palace
▶ page 192

Golden Mile
Nightlife around Great Victoria Street
▶ page 192

Ulster Museum
End of the line for a Spanish galleon
▶ page 193

Stormont
Seat of the Parliament
▶ page 194

? DID YOU KNOW ...?

■ Above the entrance to the library look for the symbol of Ulster, the »Red Hand«. Its history dates back to the time of the Viking raids, when a group of Norsemen had already settled the country and another group came to take it. The leader of the first group decreed that whoever put his hand on it first should have it. He then cut off his hand and threw it on to the land, thereby »winning« the challenge.

tical life in Northern Ireland since 1966. Moreover, some of the first books to be printed in Belfast belong to the Linen Hall Library, for instance »Paddy's Resource« (1796), an early collection of patriotic Irish songs. The first librarian here, Thomas Russell, was a founding member of the United Irishmen and a close friend of Wolfe Tone's; after Robert Emmet's failed rebellion, Russell was hanged in 1803. ⏱ (Opening times: Mon–Fri 9.30am–5.30pm, Sat 9.30am–4pm.)

The Entries & High Street
From Donegall Square, the roads lead north to the oldest part of Belfast, which suffered extensive damage during the Second World War. Narrow alleyways, called »Entries« branch off from High Street and Ann Street towards the pedestrianized zones. There are some fine old pubs and bars here, such as the Morning Star in Pottinger's Entry, which also serves good food, The Globe in Joy's Entry and the oldest pub in Belfast, White Tavern in Winecellar Entry. The United Irishmen, lead by the Protestants Wolfe Tone, McCracken and Samuel Nielson, were founded in 1791 in Peggy Barlay's Tavern in Crown Entry. In the area, Samuel Nielson also published the Northern Star, a magazine dedicated to the revolutionary ideals of freedom, equality and brotherhood. At the end of Ann Street, the five pedestrianized streets meet on Arthur Square. The square features a small stage for buskers; often, snack-food sellers, vendors and preachers ply their trade here.

Albert Memorial Clocktower
On Queen's Square, where High Street and Victoria Street meet, stands the Albert Memorial Clocktower, which was erected in 1869 in memory of Albert, consort of Queen Victoria. Due to its similarity to the famous Big Ben in London, the tower is often called »Big Ben of Belfast«. Once tilting dangerously, it has now been restored.

On the shore of the Lagan River
To the east, there is a good view of the River Lagan and the huge cranes of the Harland & Wolff shipyard. In this area, visitors can discover some important works by architect Sir Charles Lanyon, such as the Queen's Bridge with its ornate lamps and, on Donegall Quay, **Custom House**, completed in 1857 in the Corinthian style. Its pediment features the figures of Britannia, Neptune and Mercury. To the west, look for the Georgian **Clifton House**. The former poorhouse

was erected in 1774 after designs by Robert Joy and is considered the most beautiful of the preserved buildings from that period.

At Lagan Weir & Lookout

South of the **Lookout**, boat tours are offered in summer. Directly behind Custom House, look for the results of the ambitious Laganside Development Project for the protection of the harbour area and other parts of the shore. In order to protect the city from flooding, a start was made with the **Lagan Weir**; the river was dredged and new fish stocks released. Pick up more information on the project, as well as on the role of the docks and trade in the history of Belfast, from the Lagan Lookout. (Opening times: April–Sept Mon–Fri 11am–5pm, Sat noon–5pm, Sun 2–5pm; Oct–March Tues–Fri 11am–3.30pm, Sat 1pm–4.30pm, Sun 2–4.30pm.)

Waterfront Hall & Odyssey

Two impressive event venues have completely changed the river skyline. In late 2000, the Odyssey Arena was opened on the other side of the Lagan, with an indoor arena seating 10,000, cinemas, the W5 Science Centre as well as bars, restaurants and shops. Further south, on the other bank, the Waterfront Hall seats 2,000 concertgoers.

Around the Ulster Bank

Following Victoria Street north leads to Waring Street, with the impressive Italianate Ulster Bank building (1860). Note the fluted pillars, Greek urns and female warriors on the balustrade, as well as the Victorian street lamps. Looking very elegant amidst a range of eclectic buildings is the art deco building of the Bank of Ireland at the corner of North Street / Royal Avenue.

At the northern edge of the city centre rises St Anne's Cathedral, begun in 1898 after designs by Sir Thomas Drew and now the main church of the Anglican Church of Ireland. The building, in the style of a neo-Romanesque basilica, has three notable western doorways with archways and sculptures. The mosaic ceiling in the baptismal chapel consists of hundreds of thousands of small glass stones. Lord Carson, the redoubtable opponent of Home Rule and leader of the Irish Unionist Party (died 1935), lies buried there.

? **DID YOU KNOW …?**

- Old seadogs will immediately feel at home in Sinclair's Seaman's Church. The pulpit of the church, built in 1857 near the Harbour Office, was constructed from the bow of a ship, the bell came from »HMS Hood«, whilst ship lamps and other maritime accessories complete the impression of a curiosity shop.

Architecture around the Bank of Ireland

South Belfast

The University Area takes up that part of South Belfast called the **Golden Mile**. Starting at the Grand Opera House at the northern end of Great Victoria Street, the Golden Mile continues south of the university towards Lisburn, Malone and Stranmillis. Over the past years, various restaurants have opened up along the Golden Mile; nice accommodation options are located in the smaller side streets. The fine **Grand Opera House** offers opera, theatre, musicals and ballet and is also the venue for the events of the annual Belfast Festival.

In contrast to the cosmopolitan world along the Golden Mile, not far from Great Victoria Street, along **Sandy Row**, discover a Protestant working-class neighbourhood with Loyalist murals and kerbstones painted in red-white-blue. Fans of Van Morrison are bound to remember the line from his album »Astral Weeks« (1968), where he sings about roaming «up and down the Sandy Row«.

University Area Continuing on from Bradbury Place, University Road passes the late 19th-century Crescent Church, with its skeletal bell tower. The focal point of this area is Queen's University (1845–1894), built in red-brick Tudor-style following designs by Charles Lanyon. Its central tower is very reminiscent of the Founder's Tower of the more famous Magdalen College in Oxford. Today, the university, independent since 1909, has 8,000 students, who meet in the many cafés in the smaller streets around the campus.

Botanic Gardens To the south of the campus, the nicely laid-out, popular Botanic Gardens are a good place to take a breather from the city. Beautiful examples of Victorian garden design are the Palm House, erected around 1850, and the Tropical Ravine, with exotic plants such as orchids or banana plants and a basin full of turtles. At the gate near the road to Stranmillis stands the statue of Lord Kelvin, who was born in Belfast and went on to develop the Kelvin scale measuring temperatures from 0° to 273°C/32° to 523° Fahrenheit. (Opening times: gardens daily 8am–dusk, Palm House and Tropical Ravine Mon–Fri 10am–noon and 1–5pm, winter 4pm, Sat, Sun and bank holidays 1–5pm.)

Also in the grounds, visit the Ulster Museum, showing finds from the Celtic and Early Christian period. Look out for the gold and silver treasures salvaged in 1968 from the »Girona«, a Spanish galleon sunk in the 16th century off the Northern Irish coast. The Art Gallery shows European painters of the 17th/18th centuries and Irish artists of different periods, as well as Irish glass and silverware. Just how many Irish emigrated over the course of the centuries, to the United States in particular, is highlighted by the portrait gallery of famous emigrants, including presidents whose families came from Northern Ireland. (Opening times: Mon–Fri 10am–5pm, Sat 1–5pm, Sun 2 5pm.)

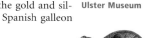
★
Ulster Museum

After a 15-minute stroll from the Botanic Gardens along Strandmillis Road, Lockview Road turns off to the left, leading to the river and to the start of the Lagan Towpath, where many people meet for Sunday lunch at Cutter's Wharf. Signs point the way to the Lagan Meadows. A trail of approx. 10km/6 miles leads to Lisburn, past locks, forested areas and marshland.

Lagan Towpath

Passing the ring road, visit Malone House, a late-Georgian manor house in the grounds of the Barnett Demesne, today part of the Lagan Valley Regional Park. Receptions and readings are often held here, and there is also an excellent restaurant and gallery. Particularly beautiful are the azaleas and rhododendrons in the surrounding gardens. Ulsterbus 70 or 71 also go to the building on the Upper Malone Road. (Opening times: Mon–Sat 9.30am–5.30pm.)

Malone House

! *Baedeker* TIP

Crown Liquor Saloon

The most famous pub in Belfast has to be the Crown Liquor Saloon opposite the Europa Hotel on Great Victoria Street. On the outside, the pub is richly decorated with tiles, while inside there are gas lamps, a marble counter and lots of mahogany, lending the place a special flair. The food – typical dishes from Ulster, sometimes even oysters – is very good. A side entrance leads to Flannigan's, a quieter bar above the Crown Liquor Saloon, where some exhibits on the »Titanic« are on display.

East Belfast

Harland & Wolff Shipyards

Lagan Lookout is an excellent vantage point for »Samson and Goliath«, as the second- and third-largest cranes in the world at the Harland & Wolff Shipyards are called. These shipyards, founded in 1859, possess the world's largest dry dock, once employing tens of thousands of people. The main type of ship built here used to be oil tankers and freighters, but faced with commercial pressures, the company has been diversifying into other structural work, such as building bridges. As the shipyard is not open to the public, tourists usually only come out to East Belfast to visit the birthplace of Van Morrison (125 Hyndford Street).

> **? DID YOU KNOW ...?**
>
> ■ The reputation of the Harland & Wolff Shipyards rests mainly on cruise liners made here in the early 20th century, of which the most famous was the »Titanic«, built in 1912.

✳ Stormont

The former Northern Irish Parliament is located 9km/5.6 miles east of the city in Stormont. Approaching by road, the classical white building (1928–1932) catches the eye amidst extensive parkland. The Parliament of Northern Ireland sat here until 1972, and in 1999/2000, for 72 days only, there was a Northern Irish cabinet, before it failed over the lack of verifiable IRA weapon decommissioning. After many discussions, false starts and setbacks, a Northern Ireland Assembly has been working once again since May 2007, under the Unionist first minister Rev Ian Paisley and the Republican deputy first minister Martin McGuinness, former sworn enemies. The building is also home to a power-sharing cabinet made up of nationalists and unionists. The Parliament Buildings are not open to the public, but visitors can stroll around the park undisturbed. Also closed to the public and hidden behind trees is Stormont Castle, the headquarters of the British Secretary of State for Northern Ireland.

North Belfast

Cave Hill Country Park

In the north of Belfast, Cave Hill Country Park takes up nearly 300ha/741 acres of space near Belfast Lough. This is a great place for long walks, visits to Belfast Zoo and Castle, or to climb Cave Hill itself (360m/1,181ft), also called »Napoleon's Profile« due to a passing resemblance to the profile of the French emperor. On a clear day, the hill offers a fantastic view over the city, across to Lough Neagh to the west and towards the coast, and the Isle of Man to the east. In 1795, Wolfe Tone and the northern Irish leaders of the Uni-

> **? DID YOU KNOW ...?**
>
> ■ A legend says that the inhabitants of Belfast Castle would be blessed with good luck only as long as a white cat was living here. This explains the many representations of cats in the garden – as mosaics, painting, sculpture and even as pieces of furniture.

ted Irishmen met here to join forces plotting a rebellion against England. To get to Cave Hill, catch buses 8–10 or 45–51 from Donegall Square West.

Halfway up Cave Hill rises Belfast Castle (1870), the former manor of the Earl of Shaftesbury. Today, it houses the Cave Hill Heritage Centre, highlighting the history of the region, as well as two restaurants, a bar and a small antiques shop. (Opening times: daily ⊕ 9am–6pm.)

◄ Belfast Castle

The road carries on towards Belfast Zoo, sitting prettily on the slopes of Cave Hill and covering nearly the whole forest. Particularly popular with children are the red pandas, the long-tailed monkeys and the lemurs with their black-and-white striped tails. (Opening times: ⊕ April–Sept daily 10am–6pm, Oct–March daily except Fri 10am–3.30pm, Fri 10am–2.30pm.)

Belfast Zoo

West Belfast

When the Troubles started in Northern Ireland (troubles, ►Baedeker Special p.46) in 1968, murals sprang up in the Catholic Falls Road and the Protestant Shankill Road in order to document allegiance to political groups. Kerbs, posts and gates, among other things, were painted in the colours of Ireland (green, white, orange) or the British Union Jack (red, white, blue).

Murals

The gates of the wall – today called »Peace Wall« – might be open now, but the past is visible in many places: heavily protected schools and youth centres, pubs with CCTV cameras and many plaques and black flags commemorating brutal attacks. Despite all this, the area is now perfectly safe for visitors.

The Shankill Road starts near St Anne's Cathedral and runs northwest in the direction of Crumlin Road. There are several impressive Protestant murals; the most interesting shows how the Apprentice Boys of Derry locked the city gates in 1689.

Shankill Road

SIMPLY THE BEST

! *Baedeker* TIP

Black Cab Tours

Today, with the »peace process« going strong, visitors can take tours through working-class areas in West Belfast, once locked in irreconcilable enmity. Black cab drivers explain the historical background and show the area, their political murals, the Peace Line and much more. The tours may be booked through hotels or by calling (077) 54 09 57 36 or www.blackcabtoursni.com.

The first murals were painted as early as 1908 by Loyalists to celebrate the anniversary of the Battle of the Boyne (1690). Later, too, they continued using militaristic motifs to express their belief in Northern Ireland's role as a part of the United Kingdom. Most of their murals feature masked members of the Ulster Volunteer Force in black battle gear, armed with machine guns, and the vow »No Surrender«. Often they also show the Red Hand of Ulster or the British Union Jack. Loyalist murals can also be seen on the Crumlin Road (A52), in East Belfast in the area around Newtownards Road, and to the south of town in Sandy Row and Donegall Pass.

Fernhill House: The People's Museum ☼　Behind the Shankill Road, at the end of Glencairn Road, lies Fernhill House (The People's Museum), which looks at the history of the Shankill district, focussing on the Home Rule crisis of 1886 and both world wars. (Opening times: Mon–Sat 10am–4pm, Sun 1–4pm.)

Falls Road　West of the city centre of Belfast, Castle Street becomes Divis Street and then Falls Road. To the southwest lies Lower Falls, with the Sinn Féin offices located in the renovated Conway Mill building. Around Falls Road stretches the Catholic sector of this working-class neighbourhood. Many of the murals here refer to the Republican support for a united Ireland, or the hunger strike of 1981.

Mural commemorating Bobby Sands

The most famous of those murals, near the Sinn Féin office, honours the memory of Bobby Sands, who at the time was the first to die. Some images have a military theme dealing with the armed struggle, others with the history of Ireland and the country's Celtic past. Very beautiful is the mural off the Falls Road which commemorates the Great Famine, and the one in Braemar Street, dedicated to women, children and workers. More republican murals are on display around Beechmount Ave and Donegall Road in West Belfast.

»Peace Line«　To get to the »Peace Line«, take one of the side streets turning off north from the Falls Road. This iron curtain was put up (temporarily) in September 1969, to separate the Catholics from their Protestant neighbours. Today, the gates are open (at least in the daytime), some »crossings« however remain under CCTV surveillance. Near the hospital look for the Cultúrlann MacAdam ÓFiaich arts centre, with a bookshop, Irish music and a café. Behind Lower Falls, **Milltown Cemetery** ► visit Milltown Cemetery, with the graves of many famous Republicans who died on hunger strike or at attacks during the Troubles.

● VISITING BELFAST

INFORMATION
35 Donegall Place
Tel. (0 28) 90 24 66 09
Fax (0 28) 90 31 24 24

WHERE TO EAT

► Expensive
② *Deane's Restaurant*
34 – 40 Howard Street
Tel. (0 28) 90 33 11 34
One of the best restaurants in Belfast, with a nice atmosphere.

► Moderate
③ *Cayenne*
7 Ascot House, Shaftesbury Square
Tel. (0 28) 90 33 15 32
Popular, relaxed and fashionably elegant restaurant, with a careful selection of Asian-influenced dishes.

► Inexpensive
① *Nick's Warehouse*
35 Hill Street
Tel. (0 28) 90 43 96 90
www.nickswarehouse.co.uk
Modern Nick's Warehouse in the Cathedral Quarter is always busy, serving a selection of creative and varied dishes.

PUBS

Crown Liquor Saloon
44 Great Victoria Street
Tel. (0 28) 90 32 53 68
Pub with Victorian furnishings, wood-panelled booths, tinted glass and faïence tiles.

Kelly's Cellars
Bank Street
Tel. (0 28) 90 32 48 35
One of the best old pubs in the city, offering live folk and blues music at weekends.

WHERE TO STAY

► Luxury
① *McCausland Hotel*
34 – 38 Victoria Street
Tel. (0 28) 90 22 02 00
Fax (0 28) 90 22 02 20
www.mccauslandhotel.com
Since 1998, this wonderful Italianate building has been the home of the luxury McCausland Hotel, with the Merchants Brasserie, where you can try modern Irish cuisine.

Baedeker recommendation

► Mid-range
③ *Malone Lodge Hotel*
60 Eglantine Avenue
Tel. (0 28) 90 38 80 00
Fax (0 28) 90 38 80 88
www.malonelodgehotel.com
Town house in the leafy university suburb in the south of Belfast. The Malone Lodge Hotel is famous for its friendliness. Enjoy the culinary delights of the Green Door Restaurant, where you will experience cuisine unrivalled in Northern Ireland.

► Budget
② *Dukes Hotel*
65 – 67 University Street
Tel. (0 28) 90 23 66 66
Fax (0 28) 90 23 71 77
A nice modern hotel housed in one of Belfast's most beautiful Victorian buildings. Queen's University, Ulster Museum and the Botanic Gardens are close by.

Around Belfast

★
Ulster Folk & Transport Museum

Some 5km/3 miles north of West Belfast, near Cultra, visit the Ulster Folk & Transport Museum, an open-air museum set within attractive scenery. An entire Irish village with shops, workshops, a school and church was relocated here stone by stone and now showcases traditional crafts and agricultural methods all year round. The A2 runs between the Folk Museum and the Transport Museum. Here, a large hall houses the Irish Railway Collection. Worth seeing are the Pullman car of the train running from Portrush to the Giant's Causeway, ⏱ and the De Lorean prototype. (Opening times: Mon–Sat 9.30am – 6pm, Sun noon – 6pm, in winter to 4pm.)

Belfast Lough

To the north and south of Belfast Lough, the wide bay forming the estuary of the River Lagan, the coast boasts several popular seaside resorts. The northern coast is particularly beautiful. (▶Antrim Coast & Glens).

Greater Belfast Map

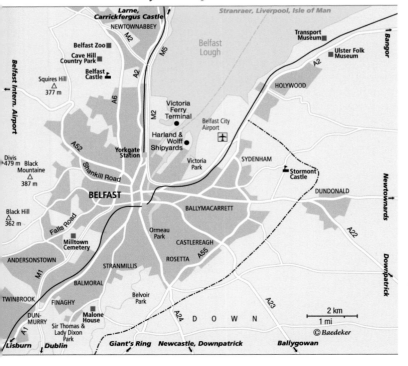

Family outing to Carrickfergus Castle

11km/7 miles north of Belfast, Carrickfergus was an important sea-port before Belfast took its place. It is famous for its very well preserved Norman castle, one of the most beautiful in Northern Ireland. The castle occupies a rocky outcrop which was originally surrounded by water on all sides except the north. This position lent it an important strategic significance for nearly 750 years. The Norman John de Courcy began the building between 1180 and 1204, for King John to capture it in 1210 after a near year-long siege. In 1316, the castle fell into the hands of the Scottish, and the French were the last to capture it in 1760. In the 18th century, Carrickfergus Castle served as a prison, later as an army depot and armoury (up to 1928).

The main sights are the bulky keep, a small museum of military history, on the third floor a magnificent Norman hall with nice views from the top, a twin-turreted gatehouse, and in the eastern tower a room

★
Carrickfergus

> ! **Baedeker TIP**
>
> **Trip to the Gobbins**
>
> From Carrickfergus, a particularly beautiful section of the coast road leads via the popular seaside resort of Whitehead to the promontory of Island Magee. Don't miss the Gobbins, 77m/253ft basalt cliffs, comprising several caves and surrounded by many legends.

Carrickfergus Castle *Plan*

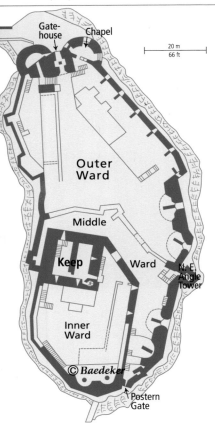

Gate-house
Chapel
20 m
66 ft
Outer Ward
Middle
Keep
Ward
N. E. Angle Tower
Inner Ward
© Baedeker
Postern Gate

called »chapel« for its unusual window, as well as several cannons dating from the 16th–19th centuries. (Opening times: Oct to March Mon–Sat 10am–4pm, Sun 2–4pm, April–Sept to 6pm, July and Aug also Sun noon to 6pm.)

Quarries and cement works mar the road from Whitehead to **Larne**, the busy industrial town on Larne Lough which still doubles up as a seaside resort. Worth seeing are the remains of the three-storey Olderfleet Castle defensive tower. From Larne, a ferry service runs to Island Magee; there is also a connection with Scotland (Stranraer and Cairnryan).

A very romantic and attractive proposition is the **coast road leading from Larne to Cushendun**. First, drive through the Black Cave Tunnel, then round Ballygalley Head with its mighty basalt rocks. Ballygalley is a popular spa resort, with the former castle turned into a hotel. White limestone cliffs line the road to Glenarm. The next resort along is Carnlough, where a small harbour and nice sandy beach provide a pleasant place to stop.

Waterfoot   The village of Waterfoot occupies a charming position close to the shoreline of Red Bay on the Antrim coast. Its sandstone cliffs resemble an amphitheatre. From there, one of the most beautiful glens of Antrim, Glenariff, stretches southwest. Drive north from Waterfoot to discover Cushendall and Cushendun (►Antrim Coast), and from there on to the ►Causeway Coast.

Holywood   Continue on from Belfast on the southern bank of Belfast Lough and discover other beautiful landscapes and some lovely villages. One suburb of Belfast, Holywood, has remains of the 12th-century Franciscan friary of Sanctus Boscus (»holy wood«).

Via Crawfordsburn the road leads to Bangor, the most popular seaside resort in Northern Ireland, with many options for entertainment and sports, long sandy beaches and fine promenades. The castle and Castle Park are worth seeing. The Abbey Church stands on the site of a monastery founded in 555. Driving on from Bangor following the coast, the bird sanctuary of Copeland Island becomes visible just off the coast.

Bangor

Garden lovers should ignore the route along the Lough and instead choose the one taking in the village of Saintfield, where the Gardens of Rowallane entice with a wealth of rare plants. (Opening times: mid-March–late Oct Mon–Fri 10.30am–6pm, Sat, Sun noon–6pm, Nov–March Mon–Fri 10.30am–5pm.)

✱ **Gardens of Rowallane**

Belfast is also a good base for lovely trips to the nearby ►Ards Peninsula and Strangford Lough. A day trip to Lisburn to see the interesting Irish Linen Centre (►Baedeker Tip p.390) is recommended.

Day trips

✱ Birr (Biorra)

C 4

Republic of Ireland, province: Leinster
Population: 3,400

County: Offaly

Birr, a flourishing market town in the centre of the country, is worth a detour, especially for amateur astronomers and lovers of fine parks. West of Birr, the rivers Little Brosna and Camcor converge, both teeming with fish.

Four main roads, starting from Emmet Square, form the basic layout of Birr. The attractive street façades are dominated by buildings from the 17th and 18th centuries, particularly in Oxmanlown Mall and St John's Mall. This is also the site of a monument to William Parsons, third Earl of Rosse and famous astronomer.

Provincial town with astronomer

Birr Castle, built in the early 17th century by Sir Laurence Parsons, suffered various sieges and was altered and enlarged several times. The castle is not open to the public, but the magnificent park, laid out in the mid-18th century on the Camcor River, is. Over 1,000 different species of trees and shrubs thrive here.
A particular source of pride are the approx. 12m/39-ft-high box tree hedges said to be over 200 years old. To find the sculpture of »Sweeney«, the very well hidden figure of a Celtic king, amongst them, follow the Sweeney Trail. The best times to visit are spring when the magnolias are in bloom, or autumn when the trees glow in a blaze of colours. (Opening times: daily 9am–6pm.)

✱ **Birr Castle**

► BIRR

In the gardens of Birr Castle

Around 1840, William Parsons, the third Earl of Rosse, designed and built a huge telescope, setting it up in his park. For some 80 years, the »Leviathan« was the biggest telescope in the world, and using it, the earl was the first to discover the spiral structures in galaxies. The restored telescope may still be admired today; there is also an exhibition of optical devices and drawings.

Around Birr

Some 13km/8 miles northwest of Birr, on an elevation on the eastern shore of the Shannon, lies **Banagher** (pop. 1420). The English gun batteries opposite date from the 17th century. 8km/5 miles northeast of Banagher stand the impressive ruins of 16th-century **Clonony Castle**. The road there passes Shannon Harbour, where ► Shannon and ► Grand Canal meet. Old warehouses and a hotel dating from 1806 are evidence of the former importance of the place.

East of Birr rise the Slieve Bloom Mountains, with, at their foot, the pretty village of **Kinnitty**. Continuing on southwest from here, look out for St Ciaran's Bush, a hawthorn growing in the middle of the road just past the Clareen crossroads. This is the site where the saint founded a monastery in the 5th century. A few kilometres further south, **Leap Castle** burned down in 1923, though the castle of the O'Carrolls remains an impressive building.

✳ Blarney (An Bhlarna)

E 3

Republic of Ireland, province:
Munster
Population: 2,000

County: Cork

A flurry of souvenir shops and coaches are evidence of pretty Blarney's pole position on the route map of organized tours around Ireland. Visitors queue to kiss the famous stone at Blarney Castle.

Blarney, 8km/5 miles northwest of ► Cork, near the south coast, is one of the most popular tourist destinations in Ireland. However, in the wake of daytrippers, the traditional wool industry has also been revived in recent years, and a crafts centre (Blarney Woollen Mills) has opened in an old restored mill.

Wool and crafts

Blarney Castle is a 15th-century romantic castle set in an extensive park. With its walls 5.5m/18ft thick and a 25m/82-ft-high tower, this was the best-fortified castle in the province of Munster. A part of the park, Rock Close, features boulders in interesting shapes, as well as a stone circle set up in the 18th century.

Blarney Castle

Having fun kissing the stone

Blarney Stone It is said that kissing the Blarney Stone confers the gift of eloquence, or the famous Irish »gift of the gab«. And sure enough, today visitors queue to kiss the stone set in the battlements. To do this, lie on your back, helped by a guard, bend your upper body downwards above the abyss (covered by a gate) and try to kiss the underside of the Blarney Stone.

»Talking Blarney« »Talking Blarney« means something like »flattering talk« or »blah-blah«. The expression was coined by Queen Elizabeth I. She had asked the Lord of Blarney to stop getting himself elected by the chieftains and have his lands loaned to him as a Crown fiefdom instead. Lord Cormac McCarthy, pretending to accept this demand, kept coming up with excuses to drag out actually complying with it, until the Queen called out in anger: »This is all Blarney; what he says, he never means!«

Blarney House Blarney House south of Blarney Castle was completed in 1874 and is surrounded by extensive lawns and flower beds. A collection of furniture, family portraits, tapestries and works of art can be seen on conducted tours from June to Mid-September.

Blarney House

● VISITING BLARNEY

INFORMATION
(021) 4 38 16 24

WHERE TO STAY
► **Mid-range**
Blarney Park Hotel
Tel. (021) 4 38 52 81Z
Fax (021) 4 38 15 06
www.blarneypark.com
The hotel includes a nicely designed
bathing landscape with pool and
sauna, as well as tennis courts. Visit
the Castle and the Woollen Mills or

take a trip to the Ring of Kerry,
Waterford Crystal, or Cork and the
Lee Valley.

► **Budget**
Blarney Castle Hotel
Tel. (021) 4 38 51 16
Fax (021) 4 38 55 42
www.blarneycastlehotel.com
Tastefully furnished inn, some 7km/
4.5 miles outside Cork, with restau-
rant and bar.

Bloody Foreland (Cnoc Fola)

A 3

Republic of Ireland, province: Ulster   **County:** Donegal

**Bloody Foreland, in Irish Cnoc Fola (»bloody mountain«), the broad
headland high up north, takes its name from the red colour of the
rocky coastline at sunset. The waters also take on a rosy hue, and
Tory Island off the coast turns into a glowing dream island.**

Bloody Foreland, the area between Ballyness Bay in the north and
Gweedore in the south, is one of the Gaeltacht regions of Ireland
where Irish is still the main language. It is taught at two Irish summer schools, at Bunbeg and Gloghanheely.

Irish schools

In the southeast of the area, on salmon-rich Lough Dunlewy lies the
village of the same name. Study traditional wool production at the
Lakeside Centre – the region is famous for its sheep farming and its
tweed and woollens.

Dunlewy

Climbing Mount Errigal (740m/2,428ft), north of the lake does not
take an experienced mountaineer (ascent: 1½–2 hours). The marked
path from the east starts at a car park on the R251. There is a magnificent view from the top: north towards the wild and lonely Altan
Lough, with Mount Aglamore rising up over 400m/1,312ft, east to
the Derryveagh Mountains, south to the rocky canyon of Poisoned
Glen (named after the spurge growing there) and west to the Atlantic
coast.

**Mount Errigal &
The Poisoned
Glen**

View of Gweedore Bay from Bloody Foreland Drive

Gweedore Bay   From Bunbeg, take a boat trip to the islands off Gweedore Bay: Innishinny, Gola and others; with their rocks and cliffs, all have scenic appeal. There are fine beaches along the coast too, such as the extensive Magheraclogher Strand.

Mount Muckish   In the north of Bloody Foreland, Gortahork and Falcarragh on Ballyness Bay are starting points for climbing Mount Muckish (670m/2,198ft). The steep climb is rewarded by a splendid view.

Around Bloody Foreland

Tory Island   Between June and September – weather permitting – there are daily ferry connections to Tory Island from Bunbeg, Maheraroarty, Portnablagh and Downings. Often the crossing cannot be made due to rough seas, and in the winter months there are fewer boats.

Despite its barrenness, Tory Island, north of Bloody Foreland, has been settled for over 4,000 years. For the 160 inhabitants, the highlight of the week is the ceilidh, an evening of music and dance put on every Saturday night in the two villages on the island. Apart from a few scant remains of buildings, there are not many sights on Tory Island, but local painters have created powerful works portraying life on the island. View or buy them in the Dixon Gallery at the harbour. An interesting collection by the way is also on display at Glebe House & Gallery (►Letterkenny).

★ Boyle (Mainistir na Búille)

C 3

Republic of Ireland, province: Connaught
Population: 1,700

County: Roscommon

The Irish name for Boyle, Mainistir na Búille, means »monastery of the pasture river«. Today, the ruins of the former Cistercian abbey are the main sights in town. Children will be thrilled with King House.

Boyle lies in the northwest of Ireland on the northern banks of the Boyle River connecting Lough Gara with Lough Key, and at the foot of the Curlew Hills. Today, its market makes Boyle one of the main towns of County Roscommon.

Market town in the northwest

At the northern end of Boyle stand the ruins of Boyle Abbey, founded in 1161 as a Cistercian daughter house of Mellifont Abbey. Of the roofless cruciform church, the nave, choir and transepts are well-preserved, as are the guesthouse and kitchen of the monastic buildings. Particularly fine are the capitals with figurative and foliage decorations, amongst them the representation of a cockfight, dogs and two men holding a tree. (Opening times: Easter–Nov daily 9.30am–6.30pm.)

★ Boyle Abbey

In the centre of Boyle stands the lavishly restored **King House**. Built in 1730, this was the country seat of the Kings, Protestant lords of the manor who made themselves unpopular with the Irish through their harshness, but who were elevated to Earls of Kingston by King George III in 1768. Later, the building was used by the Irish Army. Today, the visitor centre is a lot of fun for the kids too, offering interactive features alongside interesting audiovisual exhibitions on the history of the region. Children can, for instance, learn to write using a quill, or try on old Irish capes, brooches and leather shoes. (Opening times: May–Sept daily 10am–6pm, April and Oct weekends only.)

> ▶ **BOYLE**
>
> **INFORMATION**
> Courthouse
> Tel. (079) 6 21 45
> Open: Jun–Aug

Impressive Frybrook House (1750) in the town centre near Shambles Yard was once known for its luxurious furnishings and the hospitality of its owners. It is said that a bell was rung daily to invite everybody who wanted to share food. Due to the huge demand, a tent was specially erected in the garden. In the house fine plasterwork and an Adam fireplace remain. (Opening times: June–Aug Mon–Sat 2–6pm.)

Frybrook House

Around Boyle

Lough Key Forest Park

✳ Northeast of town lies Lough Key, lined by forest and featuring many small bays, peninsulas and islets. Along its southern shore stretches Lough Key Forest Park, its amenities including a very well equipped camping site, a restaurant, a water playground for children and picnic areas. Visitors also have the opportunity to hire a rowing or motor boat, or go fishing and hiking. The Bog Park is worth seeing too, and an island on the lake holds the ruins of a former abbey, lined by ⊙ picturesque greenery. (Opening times: daily 10am–7pm.)

Strokestown

Strokestown (approx. 28km/17 miles southeast of Boyle) is a little town laid out around the year 1800 along a central axis with workshops showcasing old Irish crafts. In the middle of an extensive park stands Lord Hartland's wonderful manor house (Strokestown Park House), the home of the Mahon family until 1979. The garden boasts the longest herbaceous border in Ireland or Great Britain. The fruit and vegetable garden has restored Georgian glasshouses, in which old varieties of fruit and vegetables are cultivated using traditional methods. A guided tour of the estate gives interesting insights into the world of the rich landed gentry. The disused church today houses the Heritage & Genealogical Centre where visitors can search for their Irish ancestors. (Opening times: June–Aug Tues–Sun 11am to 5.30pm.)

> **! Baedeker TIP**
>
> **Druamone Dolmen**
>
> One of the most beautiful dolmens in Ireland is located very close to Boyle, following Patrick Street westwards out of town. After 2km/1.2 miles, a sign points to the left to Ballina; after a further kilometre/0.6 miles, the road goes under a railway bridge, and shortly afterwards, there is a path crossing the tracks to a sheep pasture containing the dolmen.

The former stables of Strokestown Park House today house the **Famine Museum**, which poignantly shows the terrible consequences of the potato blight in Ireland: photographs, documents and furnishings recall the Great Famine (1845–1849) and the involvement of the local landowning family Mahon. At the same time, parallels are drawn to hunger in the developing world.

Douglas Hyde Interpretative Centre

Some 15km/9 miles southwest of Boyle, in Frenchpark on the R361, the Douglas Hyde Interpretative Centre commemorates the first President of the Republic of Ireland. (Opening times: May–Sept Tues–⊙ Sat 2–5pm.)

Monasteraden

West of Lough Gara, already in County Sligo, at Monasteraden stands the most famous of the many holy wells of the region; this one is dedicated to St Attracta. The well is lined on three sides by walls; one of them shows a relief of Christ on the Cross.

Boyne Valley

C 5

Republic of Ireland, province: Leinster   **County:** Meath

On the east coast of Ireland, between Belfast and Dublin, in the valley of the River Boyne, lies the cradle of Irish civilization. Archaeologists reckon that the royal tombs in the Boyne Valley are around 5,000 years old. The magnificent megalithic site of Newgrange is world-famous; there are others at Knowth and Dowth.

✳ ✳

Newgrange

Newgrange, which is only accessible as part of a guided tour, is the largest of the three burial sites. Up to 1962 however, it was hidden by an earth mound that could hardly be distinguished from its surroundings. The excavations were completed in the late 1970s, followed by an extensive restoration of the grounds on the basis of the findings.
The megalithic complex consists of a heart-shaped stone-and-earth mound of over 90m/100yd diameter and a height of nearly 11m/36ft. The foot of the mound is formed by reclining stones that stop the roof cover from slipping; the kerb is a reconstruction: all around, there used to stand 97 boulders.

The entrance, marked by a kerb-stone with spiral decorations, is formed by 43 orthostats (upright stones) between 1.5m/5ft and 2.4m/8ft high and topped by capstones. A passage leads to the splendid main chamber, with a vault of some 6m/19ft in height. Three side chambers branch off from the main chamber, forming a cruciform ground plan. In the shallow stone bowls of the side chambers, traces of ash and bone have been found. Many of the stones are decorated with impressive carved spirals, lozenges, wavy lines or zigzag ornaments.

▶ BOYNE VALLEY

INFORMATION

Newgrange, Bru na Boinne Visitor Center
Dunor, Co. Meath
Tel. (041) 9 88 03 05
Open: mid-April–Oct

Just a few hundred yards away, have a drink at the coffee shop of Newgrange Farm, or pass the time in the grounds, as sometimes there is a wait for visiting the burial site.

◀ Newgrange Farm

Other Sights

Whilst the excavations in Knowth still continue, the grounds may be visited (except for the interior of the tomb).
In Knowth, a mound, 10m/33ft high and with a diameter of approx. 85m/95yd covers two passage tombs. As on the site of Newgrange,

Knowth

NEWGRANGE

✱ Around 150 prehistoric passage tombs are known to exist in Ireland – Newgrange is the most famous of them all. Every year, thousands of visitors flock to the Boyne Valley to see this 5,000-year-old mausoleum. In 1962, the burial complex was extensively restored, showing what the cairn (burial mound) originally looked like. The mound is 11m/36ft high, its front lined with white quartz stones, a shimmering wall visible from afar. A circle of 97 mighty megaliths surrounds the entire mound.

⏱ Opening times:
In summer daily 10am-6/7pm; in winter daily
10am–4.30/5pm

① Entrance
In the south-eastern part of the cairn, the entrance leads into a passage, 19m/62ft long and only 1m/3.2 ft wide. The passage is formed by 43 uprights (between 1.5m/5ft and 2.4m/8ft) topped by capstones. One of Newgrange's secrets was discovered in 1969: at winter solstice, light enters the burial chamber through a small slit in the rectangular »box« above the entrance.

② Burial chamber
In the earliest Irish literature, Newgrange, once called »An Brug« (dwelling), is considered the home of the most ancient gods. When, at winter solstice, light shines into the chamber for 17 minutes, the decorations on the stones seem

35 to 38 upright undressed standing stones once surrounded the cairn in a wide, slightly erratic circle – possibly designed to form the border of a holy area.

aflame, the light reflected by the ground, penetrating the furthest recess. During guided tours, this impressive spectacle is recreated using an artificial light source.

③ Vault
The magnificent main chamber has a vault, reaching a height of about 6m/20ft. This corbelled dome was constructed in 3,200 BC, with such precision that it has lasted to the present day, not letting in any water even after extensive periods of heavy rain

④ Side chambers
Three side chambers branch off from the main chamber, forming a cruciform plan. In the shallow stone basins in the side chambers, traces of ash and bones have been found belonging to 5 individuals. Which position these people occupied – kings, priests? – is unknown. Many of the stones are decorated with impressive spirals and lozenges, wavy lines or zig-zag patterns.

Newgrange *Plan*

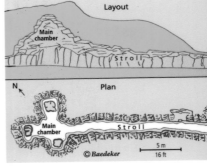

Layout

Main chamber

Stroll

N

Plan

Main chamber

Stroll

5 m
16 ft

© Baedeker

was laid out in the late 17th century and has managed to hang on to most of its original character to the present day. The winter garden was added in the 19th century. (Opening times: May, June and Sept daily 1–5pm.)

! Baedeker TIP

Fine woven fabrics for sale

On the way to the Great Sugar Loaf Mountains, stop at Kilmacanogue at the shop of the Avoca Handweavers, selling fine woven fabrics.

Some 4km/2.5 miles west of town, the River Dargle forms a **romantic valley** with dense forest and wild rock formations. A narrow path follows the river.

Around Bray

8km/4.8 miles south of Bray, in a forested area, the seaside resort of Greystones features tennis courts and an 18-hole golf links. The bay is good for swimming; sailing and motor boats may be hired too. | **Greystones**

South of Bray, a hiker's paradise stretches around the Great Sugar Loaf Mountains. The summits of both Little Sugar Loaf (337m/ 1,105ft) and the Great Sugar Loaf (496m/1,627ft) offer fine views. | **Great Sugar Loaf Mountains**

Bundoran (Bun Dobhráin)

B 3

Republic of Ireland, province: Ulster
Population: 1,500

County: Donegal
Information: (0 72) 4 13 50 (June–Sept)

Surfers in particular appreciate the lively seaside resort of Bundoran to the far north of the Irish Atlantic coast on Donegal Bay. There are many other options for sports and leisure too. Visitors have the opportunity to watch china being manufactured nearby.

The main thoroughfare (N15 from Donegal to Sligo) is lined with hotels and restaurants. The chief attraction of the resort is its fine sandy beach. Bundoran is an ideal base for various walks: a good one leads north to the cliffs and caves of Aughrus Head; the Puffing Hole blowhole is only one of the interesting features. From there, carry on to Tullan Strand, which has a cairn, dolmen and a stone circle. | **Fine sandy beach**

Around Bundoran

North-east of Bundoran, on the Lough Erne esturary, lies the busy town of Ballyshannon. The poet William Allingham (1824–1889) was born here and lies buried in Ballyshannon churchyard. Allingham is best known for his lines »Up the airy mountains/Down the rushy glen« from »The Fairies«. | **Ballyshannon**

BUNDORAN

INFORMATION
Main Street
(072) 4 13 50
Open June–Sept

! *Baedeker* TIP

China on the Irish coasts
Anyone wanting to see how china is made, or maybe purchase a specimen of these very delicate beauties, can visit the Donegal Parian China Pottery on the road between Ballyshannon and Bundoran. (Opening times: Mon–Sat 9am–6pm, Sun 10am–6pm.)

Visit a restored mill (**Water Wheels**) with film showings, and a craft shop and café on the north-western edge of town, very close to the ruined Cistercian abbey of Assaroe.

Nearby, a sign points to **Patrick's Well**, a popular pilgrimage site. Look out for the strips of fabric blowing in the breeze; they are fastened all year round to the hedges surrounding the well to honour the saint.

Approx. 5km/3 miles northwest from here, on the coast, stand the ruins of **Kilbarron Castle**, once the seat of Michael O'Clery, the principal of the Four Masters (► Donegal) and co-author of the famous »Annals« chronicling the history of Ireland.

★ Burren (Boireann)

C/D 2/3

Republic of Ireland, province: Munster   **County:** Clare

Burren (Boireann) means »stony place«, and the name alone should prepare the visitor for this strange karst landscape on the southern side of Galway Bay. Into this grey desert of rock, the water has dug bizarre holes and grooves where rare flowers thrive.

Bizarre karst landscape
The Burren, this landscape unique in Europe, roughly at the centre of the Irish west coast, is dominated by mountain tops of porous grey rock and bare terraces, brooks that disappear into the cracked earth, and subterranean streams, caves and holes. Lakes that fill up today may be drained empty tomorrow, but the nooks and crannies where the rich humus soil is able to cling on, shelter a unique flora. Seeing this area for the first time, Cromwell's officers are said to have exclaimed: »Too few trees to hang a man, too little water to drown them, too little soil to bury them in.« All this might not sound so attractive, but explore the Burren at a leisurely pace to discover that the beauty of this landscape lies in fact in this unrivalled barrenness. A visit to this region can easily be combined with a trip to the ►Cliffs of Moher.

At first glance, the Burren may appear inhospitable to visitors.

From Ballyvaughan to Liscannor, a 45km/28-mile signposted hiking trail, the Burren Way, leads past major Burren sights.

Burren Way

Drive through the Burren

There are three different routes through the area: the N67 running straight from Ballyvaughan in the north east to Lisdoonvarna in the south west, the R480/R476 running east or the R477 (recommended for travelling back from Lisdoonvarna to Ballyvaughan) running mostly along the coast.

Take the road from Ballyvaughan for approx. 6km/3.5 miles and follow the sign to the ruins of Corcomroe Abbey, formerly a Cistercian abbey, founded in 1180 and situated in a peaceful, green valley. The church is worth seeing with its cruciform ground plan, in particular its rich decorations, the fine vault and the interesting tombs.
A few miles south of Ballyvaughan, to the right of the N67, look for the unusual tower of Newtown Castle, a cylindrical body rising from

To Lisdoonvarna
◄ Corcomroe Abbey

a pyramid-shaped foundation. After a steep climb, the road then reaches its highest point, Corkscrew Road (220m/722ft). To the west rises **Slieve Elva** (340m/1,115ft), boasting the longest cave in Ireland, Pollnagollum Cave. Shortly before reaching Lisdoonvarna, to the left of the road, the stone fort of **Cahermacnaghten** spreads out, featuring a ring wall of 31m/34yd diameter, with the remains of a castle.

2km/1.2 miles south of Ballyvaughan, the R480 turns off south from the Corkscrew Road. This road leads to Ailwee Cave. Of the miles of cave passages, a small part is accessible to visitors. At the entrance of the cave system is an information centre with restaurant and

✳
Ailwee Cave ► shop. Take a guided tour to discover impressive stalactites and stalagmites and a subterranean river, which swells to a torrent after heavy rains. The guides also show visitors the place where the soil shows evidence of the presence of bears hibernating before the last Ice Age in this cave, which has held its constant temperature of 10°C/
⏲ 50°F. (Opening times: mid-March–Nov daily 10am–5pm, till 6pm in summer.)

Gleninsheen Wedge Tomb ► Further south, the R480 runs past the Gleninsheen Wedge Tomb (also called »Druid's Altar«). This is where, in 1930, one of the most beautiful examples of prehistoric Irish craftsmanship was found: a golden torc, which today can be seen in the National Museum in Dublin.

✳
Poulnabrone Dolmen To the left of the road, after 800m/0.5 miles, look for the Impressive Poulnabrone Dolmen, a mighty megalithic tomb and one of the most popular holiday snaps in Ireland. The tomb was erected around 3000 BC; excavations have yielded the bones of 17 adults and 16 children.

Carran Some 5km/3 miles east of there, Carran (Carron) is famous for its aromatic essences derived from wild flowers. Here, a minor signposted road turns off towards Temple Cronan, a small Early Christian church approx. 2km/1.2 miles away, with grotesque Romanesque heads in the exterior walls.

Cahercommaun ► From Carran, follow the road in the direction of Killinaboy (Kilnaboy) and then, after 1.5km/1 mile, take the path to the left, to get to the impressive stone ring-fort of Cahercommaun on the edge of a steep valley.

Leamaneh Castle ► At the junction of the R480 and the R476 rises the imposing ruined Leamaneh Castle, consisting of a tower house and added residential

Most popular location for a holiday snap in the Burren: Poulnabrone Dolmen

quarters. Máire Rua, the wife of the man who built the manor house, is the subject of numerous legends. Immediately after her husband was killed in battle, she is said to have married one of Cromwell's soldiers to save the land and castle for her little son.

Past Killinaboy, the R476 leads past the lovely Inchiquin Lough, bordered by forested hills, and the ruined Inchiquin Castle (1459), on towards Corofin, in a pleasant location at the centre of an area where numerous lakes and the River Fergus offer good sports fishing. ◄ Corofin

Visitors who prefer to carry on without a detour can take the R476 at Leamaneh Castle, heading west to Kilfenora, which used to be an episcopal see up to the 18th century. Alongside the fine 13/14th-century tombs in the modest cathedral, built in 1189 on the site of a monastery, don't miss the High Crosses. One of them stands 100m/110yd apart in a field used as pasture for cattle; it shows a lavishly decorated Crucifixion scene. The most beautiful of the five crosses is the Doorty Cross (in front of the cathedral's western wall), featuring on its east face three bishops and a two-headed bird. ◄ Kilfenora

! Baedeker TIP

Sheela-na-gig

A detour to Killinaboy, 4km/2.5 miles east of Kilfenora, reveals the ruins of an interesting 16th-century church, with a well-preserved Sheela-na-gig figure above the southern entrance. This is the representation of an old Celtic fertility goddess, a tradition which survived Christianization. Most of these figures of a naked woman openly presenting her private parts used to be set above the entrances of churches.

Baedeker TIP

Burren Smokehouse

In the attractive Burren Smokehouse Visitor Centre, west of Lisdoonvarna on the road to Doolin, find out what lies behind the story of the »Salmon of Knowledge« and hear all about the traditional smoking of wild Atlantic salmon, try and purchase some tasty tidbits. Shrink-wrapped, they can also be mailed abroad (open: daily 10am–6pm, longer in summer).

Burren Display Centre ▶

⏲

Also in Kilfenora, the Burren Display Centre has a small exhibition room with good displays on the Burren region, its origin, geology, flora and fauna, as well as a video. There is also a tea room and shop here. (Opening times: mid-March–Oct daily 10am–5pm, in summer till 6pm.)

Lisdoonvarna

At the foot of the Burren, 7km/4.5 miles northwest of Kilfenora, Lisdoonvarna (pop. 650) is the only spa in Ireland and a popular holiday destination with the Irish, offering tennis, mini golf, a fun fair and more. The town is also famous for its radioactive springs containing sulphur, magnesium, iron and iodine. The Spa Wells Health Centre is open from June to October. However, Lisdoonvarna is most famous for its traditional Matchmaking Festival in September, a kind of marriage fair where lonely hearts meet. This derives from the meetings of farming families after the harvest festival.

Along the coast

Some 8km/4.5 miles west of Lisdoonvarna, the fishing village of Doolin (pop. 200) offers the holidaymaker swimming and angling opportunities. In good weather, several boats a day leave from Doolin Pier to the ▶Aran Islands. However, Doolin is most famous for its pubs, playing Irish folk music every night in the summer months. Some tourists come from afar to take part in the folk music sessions. The drive from Lisdoonvarna along the coast is very rewarding. The R477 initially winds northwest, past Ballynalackan Castle (on the Burren Way), towards the coast and then northwards. To the left, the Aran Islands rise out of the sea, to the right is the flank of the mountains with Slieve Elva, and ruined churches scattered in-between.

▶ BURREN

PUB

O'Connors
Doolin
Tel. (0 65) 7 07 41 68
One of the most important music pubs in Ireland, famous for its rousing folk music sessions. The food is very good too.

The most northerly point of the coastal route offers a sweeping view over Galway Bay from windsweptBlack Head. From here, the road runs southeast along Ballyvaughan Bay, passing, to the left, 16th-century Gleninagh Castle – a four-storey tower house with round corner turrets – before reaching Ballyvaughan.

Black Head

★ Cahir (An Cathair)

D 4

Republic of Ireland, province: Munster
Population: 2,100

County: Tipperary

The former garrison town of Cahir in the south of Ireland is today a lively market town. The splendidly restored Cahir Castle in particular makes visiting the town an attractive proposition. Castle Street, lined with pubs, leads to the River Suir, Cahir Castle and the thatched Swiss Cottage. To the west, the Galtee Mountains rise to a height of 900m/2,950ft.

Cahir Castle, one of the largest castles in the country, was built in the mid-12th century and has repeatedly been used as a backdrop for films. The current building dates mainly from the 15th and 16th centuries. Following a chequered history of destruction and rebuilding, the castle has been extensively restored over past decades. It consists of the bulky three-storey tower house with hall, and a further hall building; both are surrounded by tall strong curtain walls, fortified by towers. The living quarters of the fortification are furnished to look as they would have done 500 years ago. (Opening times: mid-June–mid-Sept daily 9.30am–7.30pm; mid-Sept–mid-Oct and April–mid-June daily 9.30am–5.30pm; mid-Oct–March daily 9.30am–4.30pm.)

★ Cahir Castle

Something is brewing over Cahir Castle....

Amidst Cahir Park, situated in a pretty location by the water, stands Swiss Cottage, which got its name through a remote resemblance to a Swiss chalet. The small reed-thatched country house was built in 1810 by John Nash, the architect of English royalty in the regency period, and is open to the public. (Opening times: May–Sept daily 10am–6pm; mid-March–April and Oct–Nov Tues–Sun 10am–1pm and 2–4.30pm.)

Swiss Cottage

Around Cahir

6km/3.5 miles north of Cahir, look for a cluster of notable medieval buildings: the **Knockgraffon Motte**, a 12th-century Anglo-Norman fortress guarding the ford crossing the Suir, as well as the ruins of a church and a 16th-century castle. The lovely Glen of Aherlow northwest of Cahir offers good hiking country. Between Cahir and Michelstown, south of the N8 at Burncourt, visit the **Mitchelstown Caves**, three caves with impressive limestone formations. (Opening times: daily 10am–6pm.)

▶ CAHIR

INFORMATION
Castle Street
Tel. (0 52) 4 14 53
Open: March–Oct

Carlow (Ceatharlach)

D 5

Republic of Ireland, province: Leinster
Information: Tel. (0 59) 9 13 15 54

County: Carlow
Population: 12,000

Due to its strategic position on the River Barrow, Carlow was for a long time a fortified Anglo-Norman base. Today, the town does not have that much to offer tourists, who usually only pass through on their way to Browne's Hill Dolmen.

Market and industrial centre

Carlow, at the junction of the N9 and the N80, lies southwest of Dublin. The capital of the county is today considered the market and industrial centre of the region. In 1361 Carlow was walled, and since then has been heavily fought over, the last time in 1798 when 640 rebellious Irish died. A monument in the shape of a modern Celtic-style High Cross in the churchyard commemorates the dead.

Carlow Castle

Castle Hill Street leads to Carlow Castle. Of the core building, only the eastern side with two strong round 13th-century corner towers survives. The interior is currently not open to the public. At the junction of Athy Road and Dublin Road, look out for the splendid Court House, built in 1830 in the classical style. Visit the Carlow County Museum in the town hall for insights into the local history. Outside the town, on the N9, magnificent Oak Park boasts an 18-hole golf course.

? DID YOU KNOW …?

■ The largest dolmen in Ireland stands in the grounds of the manor house Browne's Hill, 3km/2 miles east of Carlow. The capstone of the 4000-year-old dolmen weighs 100t. The gigantic roof is supported by three blocks at the front, and at the rear it is lower, lying on the ground.

Around Carlow

4km/2.4 miles west of Carlow , in the cemetery of the village of Kil-   **Killeshin**
leshin stands a Romanesque 12th-century church; its doorway is
worth seeing for its sculptures and pointed gable top. From the cemetery, there is a fine view across the plain all the way to the Wicklow Mountains in the distance.

Carrick-on-Shannon (Cora Droma Rúisc)

C 3

Republic of Ireland, province:
Connaught
Population: 2,000

County: Leitrim
Information: Tel. (078) 20170
(April–Oct)

**Carrick-on-Shannon is the starting point for leisurely cabin-cruiser
trips on the ►Shannon and the Shannon-Erne Waterway. Situated
to the north of the Midlands, the town is the capital of County
Leitrim.**

In Carrick-on-Shannon, not much remains of the buildings from   **Tiny**
previous centuries. Look out for the Courthouse and Costello Cha-   **chapel**
pel, measuring only 5 x 3.6m/5.5 x 3.9yd, at the end of Bridge Street.

Around Carrick-on-Shannon

A few kilometres north of Carrick-on-Shannon, the Shannon-Erne   **Shannon-Erne**
Waterway branches off from the Shannon. This waterway connects   **Waterway**
two of the most popular European boating grounds: the Shannon
and the Erne Lake Area in Northern Ireland. The canal, inaugurated
in 1860, turned out to be an economic failure and was closed again
in 1869. After extensive repairs, it now has an overall depth of at

Marina in Carrick-on-Shannon

CARRICK-ON-SHANNON

INFORMATION

The Old Barrel Store
Tel. (078) 2 01 70
Open: April–Oct

least 1.5m/5 ft, making it a very attractive playground for amateur skippers. With an average house boat, the 78km/49-mile stretch from Carrick to Belturbet (► Cavan) can be mastered in a good 16 hours.

The R280 leads northwards via the picturesque village of Leitrim, which gave the county its name, to Drumshanbo, a holiday resort for anglers at the southern tip of **Lough Allen**. Driving on along the western shore, the road passes the quarry area of Arigna.

Turlough O'Carolan Country
Near Carrick-on-Shannon, three places are closely associated with the last and most famous Irish bard Turlough O'Carolan (1674–1738). Having spent most of his life in Mohill, the bard lies buried in Kilronan Church, whilst Keadue celebrates the O'Carolan Harp Festival every year in early August in his honour. To get to Mohill, take the N4 towards Dublin from Carrick-on-Shannon and turn off east just past Drumsna, taking the R201. To get to Kilronan Church, take the R280 northwards, turning west in Leitrim on the R284 to Keadue and from there head west in the direction of Sligo.

A good 15km/9 miles southeast of Carrick-on-Shannon stretches Lough Rinn; on the lake's northeastern shore, an attractive park surrounds the 19th-century **Lough Rinn House**. The interior of the building, erected by the third Earl of Leitrim, is worth seeing. (Opening times May–Sept daily 10am–7pm.)

Carrick-on-Suir (Carrarig na Siúire)

D 4

Republic of Ireland, province: Munster	**County:** Tipperary
Population: 5,200	**Information:** Tel. (0 51) 4 07 26 (June–Aug.)

Thanks to its brewery and wool production, the market town of Carrick-on-Suir, 20km/12 east of Clonmel, rose to prominence in the Middle Ages. The town lies near the Irish southern coast on the River Suir, which marks the county border between Tipperary and Waterford.

After Henry VIII in 1541 took on the title of King of Ireland, England (under Elizabeth I in particular) tried to claim Ireland once and for all through the settlement of English estate owners. Thanks to their construction activity during the course of the 16th and 17th centuries, Tudor castles appeared, the most important example being Ormond Castle in Carrick-on-Suir.

History

Today's Ormond Castle, the former seat of Earl Butler of Ormond, consists of a fortification dating from 1450 and a manor house, added on in 1568. That house was erected for Queen Elizabeth I of England, but she probably never stayed there. The manor house gives an idea of what an Elizabethan »mansion« looked like: broad, gabled on the outside, with on the inside a long hall and gallery containing stucco portraits. Climb the castle tower for a great view. (Opening times: mid-June–mid Sept daily 9.30am–6.30pm.)

Ormond Castle

Around Carrick-on-Suir

North of Carrick-on-Suir, on the border between the counties of Kilkenny and Tipperary, two places with important High Crossesare Kilkeeran (8km/5 miles) and Ahenny (10 km/6.2 miles). Of the three crosses in the churchyard of Kilkeeran, the western cross, dating from the 9th century, is worth seeing. Its base shows eight horsemen, with interlacing geometric motifs. The lower part of the cross shaft, for instance, shows intertwined goose-like animals.

★ High Crosses in Kilkeeran and Ahenny

In Ahenny, also in a churchyard, stand two especially impressive crosses. These feature figurative carvings on the bases only; on the northern cross, for instance, cross-bearing monks and a pony carrying a headless man can be seen. Both crosses are covered in skilfully carved geometric patterns such as spirals, braiding and rosettes. In their style, the carvings so resemble those of the »Book of Kells« that they can be dated to around the 8th century.

Cashel (Caiseal Mumhan)

D 4

Republic of Ireland, province: Munster
Population: 2,500

County: Tipperary

The small town of Cashel, which emerged during the course of the construction of the Cathedral, seems to be completely in the shadow of the magnificent Rock of Cashel. Apart from this impressive structure, visible from afar, the Folk Village is also worth a visit.

There is more to Cashel than the Rock, with its many pubs, restaurants and shops. Very interesting is a visit to the Cashel Folk Village

The Rock village
◄ Folk Village

ROCK OF CASHEL

★ The mighty 12th-century cathedral on the Rock of Cashel appears lifted heavenwards and still imbued with the dignity and power of a medieval diocesan church. A stone fort stood at this site as early as the 5th century, and Brian Boru was crowned High King here in 977. Squatting in the shadow of the cathedral, Cormac's Chapel, constructed in 1127–1134, is considered by many to be the most interesting Norman church in Ireland.

🕐 Opening times:
daily 9am–7.30pm, in winter to 4.30/5pm

① **Entrance hall**
Visitors enter the cathedral through the entrance hall.

② **Tower house**
This bulky turreted building, erected in the 15th century as a residence for an archbishop, has more the appearance of a castle.

③ **Spiral staircase**
The two towers on either side of the nave and the side aisles feature sets of stairs.

④ **Crossing Tower**
The crossing tower was constructed as one of the last parts of the cathedral; the choir (dating from around 1230) is the oldest part, followed by the transepts, nave and crossing.

⑤ **Round Tower**
At a height of just under 28m/92ft, this round tower was erected around the same time as Cormac's Chapel.

⑥ **Cormac's Chapel**
A masterpiece of Norman sacred architecture. Note the two square towers finished in two different styles, allegedly modelled on St Jacob's Church in Regensburg, Germany. The chapel has no side aisles, and its roof has a conspicuously steep pitch.

⑦ **Hall of the Vicars Choral**
Visitors enter the walled enclosure here. The 15th-century former residential building has been converted into a museum, housing St Patrick's Cross. The wooden ceiling is painted.

Rock of Cashel Plan

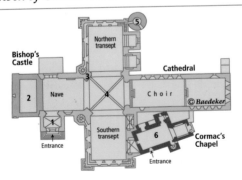

Bishop's Castle

Northern transept

Cathedral

Nave

Choir

©Baedeker

Southern transept

Cormac's Chapel

Entrance

Entrance

1 Entrance Hall
2 Tower House
3 Spiral staircases
4 Crossing tower
5 Round tower
6 Cormac's chapel

10 m
33 ft

The cathedral's northern transept is joined to a nearly 28m/92ft-high round tower dating from the time of Cormac's Chapel. The entrance of the tower is 3.6m/12ft above ground.

◄ Round tower

Of particular interest is Cormac's Chapel (1127–1132). Architecture and sculptural works show the influence of German and English master builders, without losing its Irish character, still evident, for instance, in the pitched stone roof. The transepts resemble towers, and three-dimensional motifs liven up the walls. The former main entrance (north doorway) has an ornate sectionalized design; its features include a fine tympanum showing a centaur hunting a lion with bow and arrow. Inside, look for the impressive, beautiful sarcophagus from the 12th century, ornately decorated with Scandinavian ornaments.

◄ Cormac's Chapel

✔	DON'T MISS

- Cormac's Chapel is considered the most interesting Romanesque church in the whole of Ireland!

A short walk leads from the foot of the rock to the nearby ruins of the former Benedictine Hore Abbey with its bulky crossing tower. The archbishop of the time handed it over in 1272 to the Cistercians of Mellifont, as he had been told in a dream that the Benedictines were out to kill him.

Other sights
◄ Hore Abbey

 VISITING CASHEL

INFORMATION

Town Hall
Tel. (062) 61333
Open: April–Sept

WHERE TO STAY

► **Mid-range**
Cashel Palace
Main Street
Tel. (062) 62707
Fax (062) 61521
www.cashel-palace.ie
In the 18th century, Cashel Palace (23 rooms) served as episcopal see; some of the trees in the park were planted for the coronation of Queen Anne. That much tradition comes at a price!

► **Budget**
Baileys of Cashel
Main Street
Tel. (062) 61937, fax (062) 62038
www.baileys-ireland.com
This Georgian town house (8 rooms), built in 1709, stands in the centre of Cashel; its restaurant serves traditional Irish cuisine.

WHERE TO EAT

► **Expensive**
Chez Hans
Rockside
Tel. and fax (062) 61177
Located in a converted 19th-century church, the »Chez Hans« restaurant is particularly famous for its outstanding seafood creations.

Brú Ború ▶ At the carpark for Cashel Rock, the Brú Ború arts centre offers traditional Irish dance, song, storytelling and theatre. A restaurant, exhibition space and a craft shop complete the picture.

Bolton Library St John's Cathedral (1750–1783) on John Street was built as a replacement for the crumbling cathedral on the Rock. The collection of early manuscripts and valuable early prints of the Bolton Library, including »the smallest book in the world« can be admired May–Sept daily between 10am and 4pm (Tel. (062) 61944).

Castlebar (Caisleán an Bharraigh)

C 2

Republic of Ireland, province: **County:** Mayo
Connaught
Population: 6,400

Castlebar, in the northwest of Ireland, is the capital of County Mayo and boasts a small airport. Mainly anglers come here, drawn by the lake paradise south of Castlebar: Lough Mallard, Castlebar Lough and Islanddeady Lough.

Castlebar Races The centre of today's market town with small industries is the Mall, a pretty square planted with lime trees. In 1798, an English unit took flight in Castlebar when Irish and French forces landed there – an event that has entered the annals of history as Castlebar Races.

Around Castlebar

✶
Strade Take the N5 northeast, in the direction of Foxford, to reach Strade. The ruined church of a former abbey boasts fine sculptures and tombs. One tomb carved around 1475 is considered the most splendid example of the flamboyant style in Ireland. For reasons unknown, the saints are represented engaged in hearty laughter. A small
Michael Davitt museum commemorates the Fenian and founding member of the
Memorial Irish National Land League, Michael Davitt (1846–1906), who is bu-
Museum ▶ ried in Strade .(Opening times: April–Oct Tues–Sat 2–6pm.)

Knock Take the N60 to Claremorris, and from there carry on northeast on the N17, to reach the village of Knock (pop. 440), a place of pilgrimage that is visited by a million pilgrims every year. The fame of Knock stems from an apparition of the Virgin Mary in 1879, when the Mother of God, accompanied by Saint Joseph and John the Evangelist, allegedly appeared to 15 locals

? DID YOU KNOW ...?

■ In order to make the trip a comfortable experience for pilgrims, an airport was inaugurated in Knock in 1986 that can even accommodate jumbo jets.

at the back of the old parish church. The basilica erected in the immediate vicinity holds a congregation of 12,000.

Not that far from here, the **Folk Museum** is dedicated to 19th-century Irish rural life. The main attraction is the »museum within a Museum«: a fully furnished thatched cottage. (Opening times: May–Oct daily 10am–6pm, July and Aug till 7pm.)

Take the N84 south to reach Ballintubber Abbey (►Lough Corrib, Lough Mask), situated on the northern shore of Lough Carra.

Ballintubber Abbey

CASTLEBAR

INFORMATION

Linenhall Street
Tel. (094) 2 1207
open: April–Sept

★ Causeway Coast

A 5

Northern Ireland, province: Ulster   **Counties:** Antrim and Derry

The Causeway Coast is arguably the most beautiful and interesting stretch of coast in Northern Ireland. 40,000 basalt pillars form the famous Giant's Causeway, whilst splendid beaches, romantic castles and a whiskey distillery ensure a varied trip.

In 1774, the eccentric Bishop of Derry and 4th Earl of Bristol, Frederick Augus Hervey, had a mighty castle built at Downhill, of which only the outer walls survive. The real attraction in the grounds is the small Mussenden Temple, standing close to the cliff edge. One theory says that Hervey had the structure built in 1783 after the death of his cousin Mrs Mussenden, to whom he was very close. Others claim the clergyman used the temple as a library. In any case, in the summer, Mussenden Temple forms a romantic backdrop for classical concerts and readings. Walks in the surrounding countryside yield wonderful views of the coast. Directly below Mussenden Temple, Downhill Strand used to be the setting for horse races organized by the bishop, with lucrative parishes the coveted »prize money« for participating clergy. (Opening times: July–Aug daily noon–6pm; April–June and Sept Sat, Sun / bank holidays noon–6pm.)

★
Downhill & Mussenden Temple

Wishing Arch near Portrush

Portstewart and Portrush Drive on for some 10km/6 miles (16km/10 miles) to reach the popular holiday resorts of Portstewart and Portrush. Their Victorian charm has faded, but west of Portrush stretches a 5km/3-mile sandy beach; look out for the Wishing Arch. Portrush itself also offers good opportunities for swimming.

Coleraine A little inland follows Coleraine; the lively town on the River Bann used to be known mainly for its salmon, distilleries and linen production. Today, with North West 200, the fastest motorcycle racecourse in the world (between Portstewart, Coleridge and Portrush), it has added another string to its bow.

✶
Dunluce Castle On the way to Giant's Causeway, don't miss Dunluce Castle, a romantically ruined castle, built in the 14th century on a rocky ledge and subsequently altered several times. In 1584 it was conquered by the MacDonnells, the lords of Antrim, and restored six years later. The money for this came from the gold treasure salvaged from the Spanish galleon »Girona«, shipwrecked in 1588 off the coast. Parts of the treasure can be seen in the Ulster Museum in ►Belfast. The castle occupies a relatively exposed position on a high cliff; the kitchen

Walk the Carrick-a-rede Rope Bridge near Ballintoy, one of the attractions on the Causeway Coast.

! Baedeker TIP

Take advantage of the Distillery Reserve!
Here, as well as in other Irish distillery shops, distillery reserve whiskeys are available that are not for sale anywhere else. Visitors looking for something special should take advantage! For those curious about how the Scottish product (spelled without the »e«) compares to this, Bushmills can oblige: the Scotch House Tavern on Main Street has a large selection of Scottish whiskies!

crashed into the sea during a storm in 1693. (Opening times: April–Sept: Mon–Sat 10am–6pm, Sun 2–6pm; Oct–March Tues–Sat 10am–4pm, Sun 2–4pm.)

Bushmills boasts the oldest licensed whiskey distillery in the world. Irish monks are said to have produced the »water of life« here as early as the 13th century, and in 1608 the distillery was granted a licence by James I. During a visit, a film tells visitors that apart from the spelling, there are two significant differences in the production of Bushmills malt whiskey and Scottish malt whisky. In Scotland, the malted barley is dried over a turf fire, which lends the whisky a smoky note. Conversely, Bushmill's product is characterized by a milder, honeyed flavour. Here, the malted barley is dried in sealed ovens, without being exposed to smoke. At Bushmills, the whiskey is distilled three times, in Scotland usually only twice. Visitors can see the working distillery and afterwards sample a whiskey at the bar, have a bite to eat or browse in one of the shops. (Opening times: April–Oct Mon–Sat 9.30am–5.30pm, Sun noon–5.30pm; Nov–March Mon–Fri 10am–5pm.)

★
**Bushmills
Distillery**

Take the historic narrow gauge railway, which is in service again between Bushmills and the Giant's Causeway. A return trip takes around 45 minutes.

**Bushmills
Railway**

After some 13km/8 miles, the spectacular Giant's Causeway (footpath), a formation of around 40,000 basalt pillars, awaits. The basalt pillars of different heights and diameter are volcanic in origin. Following a subterranean eruption around 60 million years ago, the cooling lava formed into the prismatic shapes tourists admire today. Some of the conspicuous rock formations have names, for instance the Camel, the Granny, the Wishing Chair, the Chimney Tops, the Giant's Boot and the Organ.
According to one legend, the Causeway was the work of Finn McCool, Ulster warlord and commander-in-chief of the King of Ireland's army. All the outrageous stories involving Finn McCool make

★ ★
**Giant's
Causeway**

▶ VISITING CAUSEWAY COAST

WHERE TO STAY

▶ **Mid-range**

Bushmills Inn
9 Dunluce Road, Bushmills
Co. Antrim BT57 8QG
Tel. (0 28) 20 73 30 00
www.bushmillsinn.com

This feelgood hotel – and the restaurant, with its open turf fire and gas light – offers a very special atmosphere! Close by: the famous whiskey distillery and the unique Giant's Causeway.

him a giant. The story goes that he fell in love with a giantess living on the Hebridean island of Staffa and started the construction of a path to safely bring his lover across to Ulster.

Visitor centre ▶ The Giant's Causeway Visitor Centre features a small museum and an audiovisual room. By the way, the parking fees at the Visitor Centre are steep; so far, it is still possible to park for free at the Causeway terminus of the Bushmills Railway. (Opening times: July/Aug daily 10am–7pm; Sept–June 10am–5pm.) From here, a 10-minute walk on a tarmacked path leads to the most impressive clusters of pillars; the shuttle bus is of course faster and more comfortable. To take a different way back, there are two options: either pass the basalt pillars and take the first path going uphill, which after some 30 minutes leads back to the visitor centre. Alternatively, carry on along the coast, admiring more interesting rock formations as you go, and return to the visitor centre after a round trip of 7km/4.5 miles.

Dunseverick Castle
The remains of Dunseverick Castle are accessible by road or a hiking trail starting at the Causeway. However, there is nothing to remind the visitor of the former importance of Dunseverick; when it was the capital of the Kingdom of Dalriada, one of the royal roads from Tara, seat of the Kings of Ireland, ended here.

Ballintoy & Whitepark Bay
With its wonderful beach and a youth hostel in a fantastic location, Whitepark Bay mainly draws backpackers. From the bay, a narrow road leads to the tiny but incredibly scenic harbour of Ballintoy. In summer, there are boat trips all around Sheep Island, a rocky island with a colony of cormorants.

Carrick-a-rede Rope Bridge
For anybody who has always wanted to play at being Indiana Jones, the Carrick-a-rede Rope Bridge provides a suitable challenge. From mid-March to September, an 18m/19.6-yard rope bridge spans a 24m/80ft chasm east of the village. The bridge gives salmon fishers access to the fish grounds, but crossing the swaying contraption has

The impressive basalt pillar of the Giant's Causeway ➔

now become a popular dare with tourists. Starting from the car park at the Larrybane Visitor Centre, it takes 15 minutes to reach the bridge on foot.

Carry on now, from the last stop on the Causeway Coast to the picturesque port of Ballycastle (►Antrim Coast & Glens).

Cavan (An Cabhán)

C 4

Republic of Ireland, province: Ulster **County:** Cavan
Population: 3,500

Nestling amidst hills and lakes, the county capital of Cavan is not far from the southern border of Northern Ireland. Traditionally, Cavan's main importance lay in crystal manufacture – until the factory burned down in 2003. Horses are also important here; nearly every weekend there are showjumping events, whilst several times a year, auctions take place here. Megalithic tombs, ruined churches and sizeable pikes are the main attractions of the surrounding countryside.

Around Cavan

Kilmore Cathedral
Northwest of Cavan, some 5km/3 miles west of the R198 leading from Crossdoney to Killykeen Forest Park, have a look at the 19th-century Kilmore Cathedral , the remarkable late-Romanesque doorway in particular, originally from a monastery on Trinity Island (Lough Oughter). In the churchyard lies the tomb of the famous English bishop William Bedell (1571–1642), who was the first to translate the Bible into Irish. A copy is on display in the chancel. Further northwest, the winding bays of Lough Oughter snake their way into the countryside; the Lough is traversed by the Erne River and resembles a water maze. The forest and lake area has been declared **Killykeen Forest Park** , offering fine hiking trails, a chance to go kayaking, angling and horse-riding. A typically Irish round tower castle is the 13th-century ruined Clough Oughter.

Take the R201 from Killeshandra towards Belturbet to reach, 1km/ 0.5 miles south of Milltown, the beautifully scenic ruins of the

! Baedeker TIP

Sparkling Crystal

Instead of the old crystal factory, a brand-new showroom was set up after the fire, exhibiting the famous crystal and other fine crafts. Opening times are Mon–Fri 9.30am–6pm, Sat 10am–5pm and Sun noon–5pm.
The Cavan Crystal Showroom is situated in the Cavan Crystal Hotel some 2km/1.2 miles northeast of the town centre on the N3 (Dublin Road, Tel. 433 18 00, www.cavancrystaldesign.com).

Drumlane: a round tower and a church, nestling picturesquely between two lakes. The church dates from the 13th and 15th century, the tower – still 14m/46ft high and featuring heavily weathered bird reliefs – from the 12th century.

It is only a 5km/3-mile drive east to **Belturbet**, near the border with Northern Ireland. Belturbet is a departure point for cabin cruisers on the Erne River, with its plentiful fish. The Shannon-Erne Waterway (►Carrick-on-Shannon) connects with the Shannon.

CAVAN

INFORMATION
Farnham Street
Tel. (049) 4 33 19 42
Open: April–Sept
irelandnorthwest@eircom.net

Excursions into County Cavan

On the R192 leading southeast from Cootehill to Sherock, after 5km/ 3 miles, look out for Cohaw and the mound of a megalithic grave with five chambers and a dual court. Lough Sillan near Shercock, which has a campsite, is well-known for the large pikes caught there. Another 13km/8 miles south, in the most easterly corner of the province, lies the little town of Kingscourt. In the parish church of St Mary's, don't miss the colourful stained-glass windows designed by Evie Hone in the 1940s. To the northwest stretches the Dún an Rí Forest Park, offering good walking trails, picnic sites and a wishing well.

Via Cootehill t Kingscourt

Take the N3 running south to reach, after around 30km/20 miles, the town of Virginia. Situated on the wooded slopes of Lough Ramor, this pleasant town offers varied leisure pursuits, including a 9-hole golf course, angling, a swimming beach, and boat hire. In **Cuilcagh House**, a few miles northeast of Virginia, Jonathan Swift worked on his novel »Gulliver's Travels«.

Virginia

Follow the R200 via the Iron Mountains and the Bellavally Pass down to Glangevlin, on the foot of **Cuilcagh Mountain** (630m/ 2,067ft). It is in this untouched area that the Shannon rises, in the Shannon Pot. The mountains here are good climbing terrain.

Dowra lies on the upper reaches of the Shannon; between the river and Mt Slievenakilla (545m/ 1,788ft), a 5km/3-mile section of the mysterious **Black Pig's Dyke**, an ancient earth wall guarding the borders of Ulster, winds its way. The 17km/10.5-mile Cavan Way

 Baedeker TIP

»Good luck and tight lines!« on Lough Sheelin

Another day trip from Cavan, some 24km/15 miles south on the R194, is Lough Sheelin, well-known as a paradise for anglers, who can base themselves at Mount Nugent. The heavily indented Lough Gowna (some 20km/12 miles further west) has good fishing too.

hiking trail runs between Dowra and Blacklion, situated 10km/6 miles northeast. Blacklion is also the final stop on the Ulster Way.

★ ★ Cliffs of Moher (Aillte an Mhothair)

D 2

Republic of Ireland, province: Munster

County: Clare

Even shrouded in mist or whipped by storms, the Cliffs of Moher in the west of Ireland, south of Galway Bay, count among the most spectacular sights in the country. At the southern tip of the cliff wall, the sheer cliffs jut 120m/394ft out of the sea, and a breathtaking 200m/656ft at O'Brien's Tower further north.

Magnificent cliffs
The spectacular cliffs stretch for a good 8km/5 miles. Seagulls, guillemots and other sea birds nest here, the ocean calls from down below with a thundering voice, while rocky stags rise from the water. A visit to the Cliffs of Moher is easily combined with a drive around the ► Burren.

O'Brien's Tower
From the car park at the visitor centre and café, a path leads to a nearby sandstone plateau at the cliff's edge and to O'Brien's Tower, which on clear days in particular yields a magnificent view across the sea to the Aran Islands. The viewing tower was erected in 1835 by Sir Cornelius O'Brien, who set up a small tearoom in the tower. (Opening times: tower and visitor centre March–Oct daily 10am–6pm.)

A walk to Hag's Head
Whilst the fantastic view from O'Brien's Tower usually has to be shared with many other sightseers, visitors walking to Hag's Head at the southern end of the Cliffs of Moher will encounter few people.

Around the Cliffs of Moher

Lahinch
East of the cliffs, via the fishing village of Liscannor, past the ruined 15th-century Kilmacreehy Church and along Liscannor Bay, with its good sandy beach, the road leads to the popular holiday resort of Lahinch (pop 550). With its white cube-like houses and the Promenade, it appears almost Mediterranean. There are two 18-hole golf links, as well as a sports and leisure centre.

Ennistymon
Some 4km/2.5 miles east of Lahinch lies the holiday resort of Ennistymon (pop. 1050). The rocky Cullenagh River, which runs through the town, has plentifulriver trout.

The Cliffs of Moher – worth seeing at any time

Take the N67 south from Lahinch to reach, after 12km/7.5 miles on a road branching off Spanish Point, a promontory lined by cliffs. In 1588, many of the dead crew of the Spanish Armada were washed ashore here, hence the name. There is a nine-hole golf links near the point, as well as a wonderful sandy beach.

Spanish Point

Clonakilty (Cloich na Coillte)

Republic of Ireland, province: Munster

County: Cork

Population: 2,500

Holidaymakers appreciate the area around Clonakilty in the south of Ireland for its attractive sandy beaches and opportunities for water sports and deep-sea angling. The peninsula of Inchadoney forms the border of the inner part of Clonakilty Bay.

Clonakilty was founded in 1614 by the first Earl of Cork as a planned town for English settlers. Today, Clonakilty and its surroundings are heavily rural. There is a small heritage museum and a fine park, Kennedy Gardens.

History

Around Clonakilty

Lisnagun Ring Fort
Some 30,000 ring forts are strewn all over Ireland; northeast of Clonakilty near the Mount Carmel Hospital, reached on the N71, stands the only reconstruction. The Lisnagun Ring Fort, a fortified settlement with a souterrain and a small farmhouse, aims to bring the 10th century to life for visitors.

Some 10km/6 miles east of Clonakilty, reached via the N71 and R600, lies **Timoleague** (pop. 310) with its abbey, founded in 1240. As a joint foundation of a Gaelic noblewoman and a Norman nobleman, the monastery accepted both Irish and English monks. Today, all that remains of this important ecclesiastical site are ruins from later centuries: the church with its side aisle and transept, the tower and remains of monastic buildings. Also worth a visit in Timoleague are the Castle Gardens, a small park with huge rhododendron shrubs and various types of palm trees.

Timoleague

Rosscarbery
In a picturesque position on an elevation by the sea lies the small town of Rosscarbery (pop. 450), which once had a monastery of great teaching fame going back to the 6th century. Remains of the monastery can be found near the old restored cathedral. Horse-riding trips into the surrounding countryside are available from here.

Coppinger's Court
Around 3km/1.8 miles west of Clonakilty, Coppinger's Court is a ruined manor house with picturesque turrets, gables and chimneys. Nearby, visit the birthplace of Michael Collins (1890–1922); the house where he spent his childhood and youth was burned down, but the Memorial Centre gives an insight into the life and work of the Irish politician and erstwhile rival of de Valera.

On the road leading to Glandore (R597), on an elevation along a side road, stands the impressive Drombeg Stone Circle, erected around the beginning of the Christian Era. In the middle of the circle, made up of 17 standing stones, the cremated remains of a human skeleton have been found. A few metres/yards further west, parts of

▶ CLONAKILTY

INFORMATION
25 Ashe Street
Tel. (0 23) 3 32 26

WHERE TO STAY
▶ **Mid-range**
Dunmore House
Muckross
Tel. (0 23) 3 33 52
Fax (0 23) 3 46 86
All rooms have a splendid sea view.

two round huts have been excavated, dating from the 2nd–4th centuries AD. The next stop is Glandore, a holiday resort in a pretty location, blessed with a mild climate and opportunities for angling and swimming.

◄ Glandore

Clonmacnoise (Cluain Mhic Nóis)

C 4

Republic of Ireland, province: Leinster
County: Offaly
Information: Tel. (0905) 7 41 34

With its many tombs strewn between ruined buildings, and High Crosses from early Christian and medieval times, the walled enclosure of Clonmacnoise appears like a large, desolate cemetery. The old monastic settlement in the heart of Ireland occupies a secure position on an elevation on the eastern shore where the Shannon describes a sweeping arc.

Every year on 9 September, St Ciaran's feast day, a pilgrimage to Clonmacnoise takes place, with mass said at a covered open-air altar. Tradition says that St Ciaran founded the monastery in January 545 BC, only to die the same year. The monastery developed into one of the most important ecclesiastical sites in Ireland, soon enjoying the prestige of a university. In the scriptoria, monks produced valuable

Unique monastic settlement on the Shannon

Clonmacnoise Plan

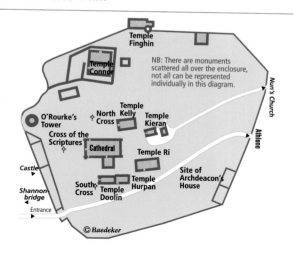

NB: There are monuments scattered all over the enclosure, not all can be represented individually in this diagram.

Temple Finghin

Temple Connor

O'Rourke's Tower

North Cross

Temple Kelly

Temple Kieran

Nun's Church

Cross of the Scriptures

Cathedral

Temple Ri

Athlone

Castle

South Cross

Temple Doolin

Temple Hurpan

Site of Archdeacon's House

Shannon bridge

Entrance

© Baedeker

manuscripts, such as the 11th-century »Annals of Tighernach« and the 12th-century »Book of the Dun Cow«. In their workshops, they manufactured croziers, reliquaries and other liturgical items. It was not least for these precious objects that the monastic town was plundered several times between 834 and 1204, initially by the Vikings, then by the Normans, who in 1179 burned down over 100 houses. But it was only once English soldiers from Athlone had stolen all that they could grab hold of in 1552, and the enclosure had again been devastated a hundred years later under Cromwell, that the monastery fell into ruin for good.

> ! **Baedeker TIP**
>
> **Boat trip to Clonmacnoise**
> For the most impressive view, approach Clonmacnoise by boat. Visitors with a bit of time should come from the direction of ►Athlone.

At the entrance, a visitor centre is sheltering some tombs and crosses from the effects of the weather. (Opening times: mid-March–mid-Sept daily 9am–6pm, mid-Sept–mid-March daily 10am–5pm.) Clonmacnoise gives a good idea of what a typical Irish monastic enclosure would have looked like; in contrast to monasteries on the continent, several small churches (11th–13th centuries) are scattered across the enclosure. Countless wattle-and-daub huts would have filled the gaps between them. To the left of the entrance, look for around 200 early Christian (8th–12th century) tombs, some of which feature Ogham inscriptions. The frequently carved phrase »OR DO ...« with an Irish name after it means »a prayer for ...«. Some of the slabs and stones are of exquisite beauty and high artistic quality.

★★ Monastic enclosure ☐

In front of the cathedral rises one of the finest High Crosses in Ireland, the »Cross of the Scriptures« or »Flann's Cross«, after the High King Flann (877–915), to whom it is dedicated, according to an inscription hardly legible now. The cross, over 4m/13ft high, was sculpted in the early 10th century from soft sandstone. Its west side features the Soldiers Guarding the Tomb of Christ, the Arrest of Christ, the Betrayal of Judas, and above, Christ on the Cross. The lower part of the east face shows King Dermot helping St Ciaran put in one of the cornerstones of the church; at the very top, look for the Last Judgment. The south face depicts a bishop, and David with Harp. On the north face can be made out a bishop, a man with pan pipes and a falconer; then, at the base, look for horsemen, chariots and hunters as well as various animal figures.

★ Cross of the Scriptures

North of the cross stands a fragment of a cross with figurative and ornamental decorations. To the south of the Cross of the Scriptures, look for a third High Cross, dating from the 9th century, with a Crucifixion scene on its west face.

← *Ornate stone portal in the monastic settlement of Clonmacnoise*

Cathedral The Cathedral at the centre of the cluster of buildings comprises parts dating from the 10th–15th centuries. The medieval carvings of St Patrick as well as two other saints above the north entrance are worth seeing.

Round towers In the north of the monastic enclosure, the 11th-century Temple Connor and the 12th-century Temple Finian (also called Temple Finghin), which has a 17m/56-ft round tower attached to its chancel in the manner of a belltower, merit attention. Nearly all photos of the monastic grounds show this picturesque building. A second round tower, O'Rourke's Tower, 18m/59ft high, stands separately close to the bank of the Shannon.

View of one of the monastic settlement's round towers

East of the cathedral stands the cell-like Oratory of St Ciaran, a small 9th-century church containing presumably the tomb of the founder of the monastery. Near the southwestern corner of the temple, look out for an old grindstone, once used for preparing medicines for the monastery. Today, rain water collected here is said to cure warts. ◀ Temples

To the east of the walled monastic enclosure lies the ruined Nun's Church, accessed by a footpath from Temple Kieran. The church has two well-preserved parts: the entrance and the chancel arch, both featuring rich decorations; particularly fine are the patterns on the chancel arch capitals. ◀ Other buildings

At nearby Shannonbridge, a different kind of guided tour is on offer: a trip on the Bog Railway across the boggy plain. **Drive across the bog**

Clonmel (Cluain Meala)

D 4

Republic of Ireland, province: Munster
Population: 16,000

County: Tipperary

Thanks to the cider produced here, the fame of the county capital of Tipperary has spread far beyond its confines. Clonmel's Irish name Cluain Meala roughly translating as »honey meadow«, it is also considered one of the most beautiful towns in Ireland.

Clonmel lies on the northern bank of the River Suir in a picturesque river landscape. The market town is the administrative capital of the county and at the centre of a region with a long history of horse and dog breeding. Laurence Sterne, the author of »Tristram Shandy«, was born here in 1713. In 1815, Clonmel became the first town in Ireland to have a regular passenger service with another town. An Italian immigrant, Charles Bianconi, who started out framing pictures and went on to be voted mayor, first established a horse-carriage service between Clonmel and Cahir, then extended his system of »Bianconi Cars« all over southern Ireland. **Four legs make history**

The Protestant St Mary's Church is located close to sections of the former fortification walls with their three towers. The church with octagonal tower was redesigned in 1857. Note the tracery at the east window, as well as various tombs from the 16th/17th century. A few metres/yards away, West Gate, a former city gate, stands at the end of O'Connell Street. At the other end of the street, the old Main **St Mary's Church**

 CLONMEL

INFORMATION
Community Office, Town Centre
Tel. (052) 22960

Guard, said to have been built after designs by Christopher Wren, is decorated with the coat-of-arms of Clonmel and that of the Earls of Ormonde who once had their family seat here. Opposite, across from the town hall on Parnell Street, the library houses an art collection and a local heritage museum.

Around Clonmel

Fethard Heading north, the R688 leads to the quaint little town of Fethard (pop. 980). Fethard's only signposted sight is the small Folk Museum in the former railway station. Here, there are various agricultural tools to admire and, on Sundays, a market to visit. Good propositions for mountain hikes are Slievenamon (710m/2,329ft) northeast of Clonmel and the Comeragh Mountains south of the town – at 743m/2,437ft, Knockamaffrin is the highest peak here.

Cong (Conga)

C 2

Republic of Ireland, province: **County:** Mayo
Connaught
Population: 300

A visit to this beautiful village in the West of Ireland means walking in the footsteps of John Wayne and Maureen O'Hara. This is where in 1198, after spending fifteen years in seclusion, Roderick O'Conor died, the last of the Irish High Kings.

✳
Cong Abbey

Between Lakes of Lough Mask and ► Lough Corrib , teeming with fish, lies the pretty, tranquil village of Cong. At the village entrance stand the ruins of Cong Abbey, an Augustinian monastery built in the 12th century. The skilfully carved entrance and various capitals of the cloister (dating from the early 13th century) are good examples of Irish Romanesque. Don't miss the restored Monk's Fishing House on the river. An opening in the ground allowed the monks to fish from the comfort of their cottage. This is where the Cong Cross was made, a masterpiece of precious metals and enamel work commissioned by King Turlough O'Conor around 1123 and today kept in the National Museum in Dublin.

Cloister of Cong Abbey

Situated near the monastery, in a park on Lough Corrib, Ashford Castle acquired its current aspect in the 19th century, when a member of the Guinness family lived here. Today, it is considered one of the best hotels in the country.

Ashford Castle

In 1951, John Wayne and Maureen O'Hara spent some time in Cong, where the Hollywood classic »The Quiet Man« was filmed. The Quiet Man Heritage Cottage on Abbey Street attempts to be an exact recreation of John Ford's location. The small house also holds an archaeological and historical exhibition on the history of the town.

Hollywood stars
in Cong

Around Cong

The limestone soil of the landscape between ► Lough Corrib and Lough Mask holds numerous caves. The most interesting are Kelly's Cave – probably established as a burial site in the Bronze Age – and the Pigeon Hole. Pick up the key to Kelly's Cave from Cong's Quiet Man Coffee Shop. Both caves are situated at approx. 1.5km/1 miles from Cong and easily accessible on foot. Near the Pigeon Hole and the Ballymaglancy Cave (3km/1.8 miles east of Cong), the Giant's Cave, a megalithic burial chamber, is open to the public.

Caves
& Co.

✴ Connemara   <small>(Conamara)</small>

C 1/2

Republic of Ireland, province: Connaught   **County:** Galway

The landscape of Connemara is one of the prime sights in the country, with its jagged mountain ranges, barren lone peaks, valleys enfolding dark lakes and a coast where rocky and sandy beaches alternate.

The wild romantic landscape stretches along the heavily indented west coast of Ireland, north of Galway Bay. Sports fans get their money's worth here, as well as holidaymakers looking for peace and quiet. The population of Connemara remain attached to their traditions, and large parts of the area are still Irish-speaking, evident in Irish-only road signs.

Gaeltacht

Clifden, a small market town (pop. 1,800) out west, is the main town of Connemara. It is situated at the end of Clifden Bay, one of the many narrow inlets that rise eastwards towards the Twelve Bens. In August, the famous Connemara Pony Show, with its diverse folkloric contests, attracts many visitors.Below the town, the Owenglin flows down to the valley in beautiful cascades. In the right season, at Weir Bridge, situated at the southern end of Clifden, watch shoals of sal-

Clifden

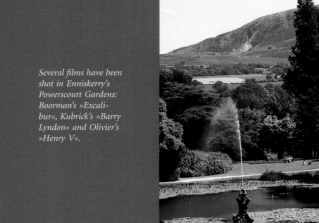

Several films have been shot in Enniskerry's Powerscourt Gardens: Boorman's »Excali-bur«, Kubrick's »Barry Lyndon« and Olivier's »Henry V«.

BITTERSWEET

The Emerald Isle has little truck with movie glamour – but films are another story! Outside Hollywood, Ireland is American companies' second-favourite location for shooting a movie; both Moby Dick and James Bond fought for their lives on Irish locations. The new Irish cinema, however, offers more than just a scenic backdrop, it shows daily life, in all its bittersweet glory.

James Joyce himself inaugurated Dublin's first cinema in 1909, and the Irish discovered a new passion. They have remained passionate moviegoers ever since. The classic *Man of Aran* by **Robert Flaherty** was awarded the Golden Lion in Venice 1934. As early as 1901, **Sidney Olcott** had started visiting nearly every year to stage stories from the olden days. Olcott's films, such as *Ireland the Oppressed* delighted the Irish emigrants in particular. To this day, the Emerald Isle continues to attract directors revelling in Ireland's landscapes and colours, which are familiar to cinema audiences worldwide.

Whales and »Doppelgangers«

Between 1954 and 1956, **John Huston** was shooting *Moby Dick* on the Irish coast, falling in love with the country and the people. For several years, he lived near Galway, developing a passionate interest in Irish literature. James Joyce was a particular favourite, and Huston championed the establishment of a Joyce museum at the Martello Tower near Dublin, the original setting of the first chapter of *Ulysses*. Huston's last film is also a homage to Joyce, but whilst *The Dead* was an opulent production, the director had old Dublin Town rebuilt in California.

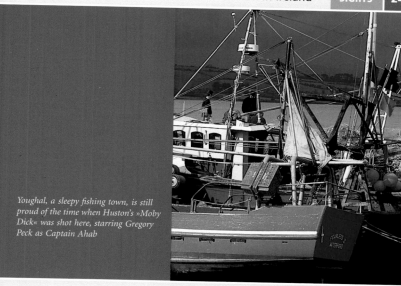

Youghal, a sleepy fishing town, is still proud of the time when Huston's »Moby Dick« was shot here, starring Gregory Peck as Captain Ahab

The Neighbours Come to Visit

Carol Reed, David Lean and Stanley Kubrick came over from England. Reed's collaboration with Graham Greene started in 1947, and *Odd Man Out* was one of Reed's films based on a Graham Greene novel: the portrait of an underground fighter fleeing through the Belfast night after an assassination.In 1970, David Lean, a master of big emotions on the big screen, directed *Ryan's Daughter*. In this tragic love story set in 1916, the love of a married Irishwoman (Sarah Miles) to a British officer (Robert Mitchum) is defeated by the historic situation and social conventions. The Dingle Peninsula and the village of Dunquin were given a great boost by the film. To this day, many film buffs make the pilgrimage to the original locations. For *Barry Lyndon*, Stanley Kubrick tried to reconstruct the period around 1800 in minute detail, using hundreds of candles to stage night-time banquets and filming the scene with his special lens. In the film, its settings carefully composed like paintings, the erring and wanderings of the Irish rogue take three hours.

Up for an Oscar

Irish directors Neil Jordan and Jim Sheridan have not shied away from tricky subjects, taking political and social issues to the big screen in impressive features from the early 1980s onwards. The two Sheridan films *The Boxer* and *In the Name of the Father* show IRA fighters, court debates and daily life in prison. For his 1983 film on the IRA, *The Crying Game*, Jordan was awarded an Oscar, and the *Michael Collins* biopic received the Golden Lion in 1996. The foundation of the National Film Board boosted the Irish film industry between 1981 and 1987. Its dissolution after six years of existence had a negative artistic impact, but it was

All together now:
»The Commitments« (1991)

revived in 1993 and the film business is booming today, with more films being shot in Ireland than ever.

Commitments & Co.

The suburbs of Dublin, inhabited by families that argue the hell out of each other but stick together in adversity, their daily grind made bearable by Guinness and humour: this is a common image projected by recent Irish films. *The Commitments* marked the start of a new era. In 1991, **Alan Parker** filmed this first part of Roddy Doyle's trilogy, **Stephen Frears** the next two, *The Snapper* and *Fish & Chips*. Using a sharp critical eye for the social scene and good music, the films give authentic insights into contemporary Irish society. Also based on works of literature are Sheridan's *My Left Foot*, which tells the story of a handicapped boy, and *Angela's Ashes*. Films such as *Hear My Song*, on the unintentional comeback of a singer, and *Waking Ned Devine* draw much on the wit of their characters. In the latter film, a whole village joins forces to pocket the lottery winnings of one villager who suffers a fatal cardiac arrest on hearing the happy news. Like other Irish films of recent years, this unspectacular but well-made comedy delights through its fast pace, wit, music and spectacular landscapes. One thing is for certain: the films coming out of Ireland are great »craic«!

mon working against the current. A bit further south, look for the remains of the first transatlantic transmitting station set up by Guglielmo Marconi (1874–1937), an Italian radio pioneer who moved to England in 1896. Heading west, outside Clifden, don't miss a very special tour – on foot or by bike: the 12km/7.5 miles long Sky Road leads through a wonderfully rugged coastal landscape.

A Drive through Connemara

From Clifden, the main access road for the northern coast of Connemara is the N59. Past the quarries of Streamstown, a road turns off left to the fishing village of Cleggan, whose livelihood depends on lobster fishing. The top of Cleggan Hill, with a ruined watchtower, offers a breathtaking view. From Cleggan, boats go to Inishbofin (pop. 200). A visit to Inishbofin is worthwhile for its sandy beaches and attractive cliffs alone – not to mention the possibilities for sailing, deep-sea angling and birdwatching. The island is also home to old coastal defences, stone cottages and the remains of a barracks from the time of Cromwell, who established a kind of penitentiary camp there for priests and monks.

Cleggan

◄ Insihbofin

Continue on the N59 via Moyard to Letterfrack. Thanks to the mild climate, in some places fuchsia hedges grow to great heights in this area. Here is also the visitor centre and thus the main access to the Connemara National Park. The centre has information on flora, fauna and the settlement history of this 2,000ha/5,000-acre area, which may be explored on two shorter well-marked trails or on a day trip. (Opening times: park all year round; visitor centre May–Sept daily 10am–6pm.)
North of Letterfrack, turn left onto a small road leading to Tully Cross and Renvyle. At the tip of the scenic peninsula, look for the remains of a castle and a church, as well as a dolmen.

Letterfrack

★

◄ Connemara National Park

◄ Detour north

From Letterfrack, the N59 runs through the valley of Dawros River to the lakes at Kylemore, nestling between mountains. When the rhododendron and fuchsia blossom, this area displays an overwhelming beauty. To the left, beyond the first lake, rises the castle-like Kylemore Abbey, built in the 19th century by a wealthy merchant as a country home and today owned by Irish Benedictines. A part of the building is open to the public; there is also a restaurant and a crafts centre. (Opening times: March–Oct daily 9am–5pm; Nov–Feb daily 10am–4pm.)

Kylemore Abbey

Moorings at Killary Harbour

Through the Lough Inagh Valley A recommended shortcut for getting to Recess is offered by the narrow 16km/10-mile road along Lough Inagh, which lies between the Twelve Bens (east of Clifden) and the Maamturk Mountains. At 718m/2,355ft, Benbaun is the highest of the Twelve Bens, whilst the others are not much lower. Lichen and moss, the red of the heather and the white of the quartzite give colour to their steep slopes. At the southern shore of Ballynahinch Lough stands the hotel of the same name, a castle that was built in the 18th century by the Martin family, who during the Great Famine (1845–1849) gave away large parts of their estate to help the poor.

▶ VISITING CONNEMARA

WHERE TO STAY

▶ Luxury

Abbeyglen Castle
Sky Road, Clifden
Tel. (0 95) 2 12 01
Fax (0 95) 2 17 97
www.abbeyglen.ie
This stately castle stands amidst a romantic park with a waterfall and a panoramic view of Clifden town.

▶ Mid-range

Ardagh Hotel & Restaurant
Ballyconneely Road, Clifden
Tel. (0 95) 2 13 84, fax (0 95) 2 13 14
www.ardaghhotel.com

Quiet hotel, located some 2km/1.2 miles outside Clifden, with a good restaurant (speciality: lobster and other seafood).

▶ Budget

Roundstone House Hotel
Roundstone
Tel. (0 95) 3 58 64
Fax (0 95) 3 59 44
diar@eircom.net
Pleasant hotel in the picturesque coastal village of Roundstone, which has a lot to offer holidaymakers: water sports and angling, hiking, golfing and pony-trekking.

Follow the road as it winds its way past Kylemore Lough and Lough Fee through a hollow to Killary Harbour, a fjord stretching inland for 16km/10 miles, which once served as a base for the British Navy. **Killary Harbour**

In the north, beyond the bay between the Mweelrea Mountains and the peak of Bengorm (700m/2,296ft) there is a view into the Valley of Delphi, a rocky valley of impressive beauty. It was given its name by Lord Sligo, who called his fishing cottage there »Delphi«.

The road leads along the southern shore of the fjord to Leenane (pop. 50), a handy base for anglers and hillwalkers. The Leenane Cultural Centre is dedicated to wool production and processing, which are important for the regional economy. The visitor centre comprises a

Maam Cross sheep fair

bit of land where several breeds of sheep are kept. There are good walking trails in the surrounding countryside, one of them leading to the Ashleag Waterfall at the eastern tip of Killary Harbour.

Take the R336 south from Leenane to the road junction of Maam Cross. The road follows the course of the Joyce River, which marks the boundary of the charming Joyce's Country (►Cong). **Onwards via Maam Cross**

◀ Pearse's Cottage

From here, the road leads south through a maze of small lakes, until reaching, after 9km/5.5 miles, Screeb and a narrow inlet, which would hardly seem different from the lakes and rivers around it if it was not for the tides leaving their traces at the shores. Here too, patches of soil artificially made fertile with seaweed and sand can be found between irregular dry-stone walls. Near Gortmore, 5km/3 miles west of Screeb on the R340, stands the small cottage used by Patrick Pearse (1879–1916) as a summer house. An exhibition commemorates the leader of the 1916 rising. From here, the road carries on along the coast of Kilkieran Bay to Carna. The inlet is a good place to catch sea trout, the lakes around it have river trout.

Roundstone

Further west, hit the coast road again and follow it to Roundstone (pop. 280), a village founded in the early 19th century for Scottish fishermen. Today, this holiday resort is mainly visited by artists and natural scientists; the village – as well as the surrounding countryside – captivating the visitor through fine shell beaches.

Roundstone Musical Instruments is without a doubt one of the most interesting shops in Roundstone, as it is here that the »bodhráns«, tambourine-style hand drums covered with goatskin, are made and sold. Bodhráns are as much a part of traditional Irish music as flutes, harps and fiddles. Workshops are available too.

Ballyconneely Bay

At Ballyconneely Bay, the coast road (here called R341) turns inland in the direction of Clifden, passing on the way the ruined Bunowen Castle and the wonderful white sandy beach of Trá Mhóir.

Roundstone – one of the prettiest places on the Connemara coast

✶ Cork (Corcaigh)

E 3

Republic of Ireland, province: Munster
Population: 180,000

County: Cork

Some consider the university city on the southern coast a »Paris of Ireland«, others detect Dutch flair in Cork. This is due to the many bridges spanning the river and the old canals. The third-largest city in Ireland only became prosperous in the 19th century thanks to the establishment of an international market for butter. In 2005, the vibrant metropolis had a successful stint as European Capital of Culture.

Today still, the River Lee dominates the cityscape. Many canals have been filled in, but the two arms of the river (North Channel and South Channel) enclose the city centre like an island, spanned by bridges. Along the Quays with their limestone walls, the channels are often lined by trees. However, visitors may miss the historical ambience, as numerous wars have not left many old buildings. There are only a few notable 18th-century buildings; the Old Town's character around the North Channel and South Channel is dominated mainly by churches from the early 19th century. The main shopping drag is St Patrick's Street with its side streets.

City of bridges

Cork has an international airport and counts among the largest industrial centres of the republic. The port, used for exports, plays a major role in the economic prominence of the city. Cork is also considered the spiritual centre of southern Ireland; several cultural asso-

Seat of economic power

Highlights Cork

Around Grand Parade and St Patrick's Street
Charming heart of the city

English Market
The huge selection of seafood is a feast for the eyes for fish lovers

Crawford Municipal Art Gallery
Extraordinary collection of Irish painting and stained-glass

St Finbarr's Cathedral
Today, a neo-Gothic cathedral occupies the site of the former monastery

St Ann's Shandon
Sublime views from the town landmark

Cork Public Museum
Exhibitions on the history of the region in a magnificent Georgian house.

ciations have their headquarters here, amongst them the Cork Literary and Scientific Society, founded in 1820, a college of the National University of Ireland, as well as cathedrals of both religions.

Festivals Major events in Cork are the popular international jazz festival (taking place on the last two weekends of October) and the film festival in early October. Also of interest are the International Choral Festival (May) and the folk festival (September).

History

around 650	St Finbarr founds a monastery on the Lee
12th–17th centuries	The city is at the centre of bitter fighting between English and Irish
18th century	Cork prospers as trading centre for Irish butter
1920	During the War of Independence, the Black and Tans burn down the city centre, two mayors are assassinated

Around 650, St Finbarr founded a **monastery** in the marshland of the Lee – the Irish name of Corcaigh (»swamp«) makes reference to this geographical feature. Today, St Finbarr's Cathedral occupies this

Cork Plan

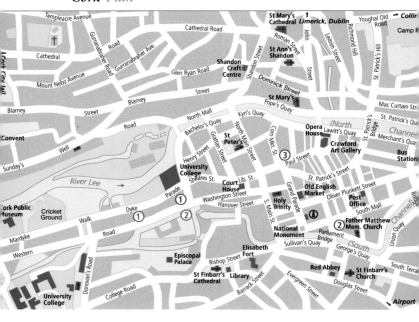

position. Between the 12th and 17th centuries, the city was conquered, lost again and re-conquered several times by the English or the Irish. It gained its city charter from King John in 1185 and had a mayor from 1318. During the 18th century, the city was known as an important commercial centre with its huge **Buttermarket**. During the Great Famine, many citizens left the city. Nearby, Cobh (or »Queenstown«) became an important embarkation point for the emigration to America: over 3 million Irish are thought to have emigrated from here between 1815 and 1970. The city also played an important role during the **War of Independence**; in 1920, two mayors were murdered, large parts of the city suffered fire damage, and the politician Michael Collins was assassinated in the nearby countryside.

Sights in Cork

The city centre of Cork lies on a river island. Once, the centre was criss-crossed by canals and bordered by warehouses and residences built by wealthy merchants. Picturesque bridges and quays continue to lend the place a Dutch aura, although today most waterways have been filled in; only the irregular course of many streets points to what lies beneath.

City on the river island

One such street is Grand Parade, today forming the centre of Cork.
At its southern end, the National Monument commemorates the Irish patriots who, in the period of 1798–1867, died for their country. To the east, in Bishop Lucey Park, remains of the old city wall and the entrance of the old grain market survive. Between Grand Parade and St Patrick Street, have a good look at the English Market, a covered fruit and vegetable market (main entrance via Princess Street). The decorations, arches, wells and galleries are as interesting as the extensive selection of merchandise, seafood in particular. Stroll through St Patrick's Street and its little side streets, exploring the many shops, or stop at one of the restaurants and pubs. At the end of St Patrick's Street,

Grand Parade

◄ National Monument

Where to stay
① Achill House
② Lancaster Lodge
③ Jurys Cork

Where to eat
① Cafe Paradiso
② Jacobs on the Mall
③ Gingerbread House

200 m
660 ft

Car Ferry Terminal

Summer Hill
Glanmire Road
Kent Station
Organs Quay
Custom House
River Lee
Victoria Road
Albert Road
The Marina
Gas Works
Blackrock Road

© Baedeker

The enclosed Cork City Market has French flair.

Father Matthew Statue ▶

near St Patrick's Bridge, the founder of the abstinence movement, Father Matthew (1790–1861), has been honoured by a statue. He preached south of South Mall at Holy Trinity Church (also called Father Matthew Memorial Church).

Corn Market Street & Paul Street

The continuations of Grand Parade, Corn Market Street and Paul Street are also good for a leisurely window-shop or stroll. Markets, nice bars, local as well as exotic restaurants and boutiques vie for business.

In the Huguenot Quarter at Rory Gallagher Square (corner of Paul Street/ Careys Lane), an unusual sculpture commemorates the late rock musician (1949–1995), who used to live only a few doors down from here. The sculpture features a bent electric guitar, surrounded by flowing notes and lines from Gallagher's lyrics.

Crawford Municipal Art Gallery

One block further west, at Emmet Place, stands the largest art gallery in Cork. Built in 1724 in limestone and red brick, the building first served as customs office and art college. Today, the Crawford Municipal Art Gallery presents an extraordinary collection of Irish painting, amongst them works by Jack Yeats (1871–1957). Don't miss the exhibition of international artists as well, such as Miró and Rouault. (Opening times: Mon–Sat 10am–5pm.) Visitors who have worked up an appetite should rest their museum legs in the restaurant, which can be recommended whole-heartedly.

✔ DON'T MISS

- The Crawford Municipal Art Gallery shows three windows by Ireland's most famous stained-glass artist, Dublin-born Harry Clarke (1889–1931).

On the northern shore of the River Lee stands the landmark of the city of Cork, St Anne's Church. Crossing the Christy Ring Bridge to Pope's Quay, the portico with Ionic columns belonging to the Dominican church of St Mary's (1832–1839) catches the eye. Also remarkable is the 14th-century Flemish ivory statue of Our Lady of the Graces on the main altar. To the northwest, take Dominick Street to get to the Butter Exchange, the former centre of the butter trade, today housing the Shandon Crafts Centre. Here, watch artists and craftspeople at work.

Shandon

◄ *St Mary's*

◄ *Butter Exchange*

In the immediate vicinity stands St Ann's Shandon (1722), with a fine tower made of natural stone in various colours. Locally, the tower, appearing like a three-fold extended telescope is called »pepperpot«. It is said that the monks chose the shape of a salmon for the 3m/10ft weather vane to display their right to fish in the river. The church has some letters written by the English poet and clergyman John Donne (1572–1631), as well as a small collection of Bibles. (Opening times: Mon–Sat 10am–5pm.)

★
◄ *St Ann's
Shandon*

🕐

On the other side of the city centre, south of the river, the neo-Gothic St Finbarr's Cathedral (1865–1880) occupies a dominating position on the site of an earlier monastery. It was built in 1878 after designs by William Burges in honour of the founder and patron saint of Cork. Extraordinary features are the vaulted ceiling, decorated with paintings and gold leaf and showing Christ surrounded by angels, as well as the fine mosaics and stained-glass windows.

*St Finbarr's
Cathedral*

! *Baedeker* TIP

Ring the Bell

If you have you always wanted to ring the chimes, this is your chance. For a small fee, ring the »Bells of Shandon« – the selection of tunes stretches from »Ave Maria« to »Danny Boy«, »When Irish Eyes are Smiling« and other Irish evergreens. Don't be afraid to get it wrong, instructions are provided! Also, the top of the tower offers a fine sweeping view over the city.

Cork Public Museum West of the city centre, Fitzgerald Park houses the former prison, the University College Park, as well as the Cork Public Museum. Located in a splendid Georgian house, the latter offers an overview of the history of the region from its early Christian beginnings to today. Find out about the role of the city in the Irish liberation movements, and admire the silver and glassware on display, as well as the crochet and lace work that Cork was once famous for. (Opening times: Mon–Fri 11am–1pm and 2.15–5pm, Sun 3–5pm.)

University College South of here, beyond Western Road and the South Channel, University College (founded in 1845), is a branch of the National University, teaching some 4,000 students. The university has some very interesting collections of Ogham stones, for example, or early publications from Cork (viewing can be arranged on request). In the Honan Chapel, look out for Goal Gate (1818) and the stained-glass by Sarah Purser and Harry Clarke.

Idyllic atmosphere – University Park

In **Cork City Jail** on Convent Avenue, guided tours of the former prison are available. In the National Radio Museum on the upper floor, admire a fine collection of old radios. (Opening times: March–Oct daily 9.30am–6pm; Nov–Feb daily 10am–5pm.)

The **Cork Heritage Park** is located in the grounds of the former estate of the Pike family in Bessberro, 5km/3 miles east of Cork. Small exhibitions highlight the role of the family and the Quaker heritage, as well as the story of the shore area, including an ecological analysis of its flora and fauna. The Garden of Reflection, by the way, features a petting zoo for children. (Opening times: April–Sept daily 10.30am till 5.30pm.)

Around Cork

Blarney and Lee Valley Without a doubt the most-visited sight near Cork is ▶Blarney, 9km/5.5 miles northwest of Cork. Off the beaten track, take a hiking trip west of Blarney, to the Lee Valley.

Riverstown House Around 7km/4.5 miles northeast of town, Riverstown House lies near the N8. The pretty Georgian country house took on its current aspect in the mid-18th century, when the bishop of Cork was residing here. The Francini brothers, famous Italian stucco artists, created extraordinary playful stucco features for the dining hall. (Opening times: mid-May–mid-Sept Wed–Sat 2–6pm, otherwise by appointment.)

Fota Island

Small Fota Island, east of Cork and connected to the mainland by a bridge, offers several attractions. In Fota Wildlife Park, waterfowl, giraffes, zebras, antelopes, monkeys and many other animals populate the grounds, attracting children in particular. (Opening times: mid-March–Oct Mon–Sat 10am–6pm, Sun 11am–6pm.)
Not interested in animals? Fota House and its adjacent park (Fota Arboretum) are open to the public. A famous art collection is scheduled to go on display here in the future In the early 19th century Fota House was converted from a hunting lodge into a fine residence.

Cobh

24km/15 miles south of Cork, on Great Island, the port of Cobh (pop 6250, formerly called »Queenstown«) used to be the point of departure for thousands of Irish families emigrating to America. The relatively modern town was an important port of call for cruise liners. The area around the harbour, dominated by a richly decorated neo-Gothic church, offers some picturesque scenery. Also attractive is the Cobh Heritage Centre in the former railway station (1862). The visitor centre documents the town's eventful history (The Queenstown Story), for instance its role during the Great Famine. Moreover, Queenstown was the last port of call of the »Titanic« before its sinking. In front of the Cobh Heritage Centre, a monument has been erected commemorating Annie Moore and her two brothers. Annie Moore was the first immigrant entering the US via Ellis Island – a similar sculpture commemorates her there also. (Opening times: daily 10am–6pm.)

Annie Moore Monument in front of Cobh Heritage Centre

Cork Harbour

Dotted around the bay of Cork Harbour lie fortifications dating from various periods, with small holiday resorts in-between, popular due to their mild climate.

Crosshaven

The R609 and R612 lead to Crosshaven (pop. 1350), a favourite holiday resort at the mouth of the Owenboy River.

▶ VISITING CORK

INFORMATION

Cork City,
Grand Parade
Tel. (021) 4273251
Fax (021) 4273504

WHERE TO EAT

► Expensive

② *Jacobs on the Mall*
30A South Mall
Tel. (021) 4251530
kingsley@eircom.net
Former Turkish bath showing contemporary Irish art. Modern dishes show a taste for daring, innovative food combinations.

► Mid-range

① *Cafe Paradiso*
16 Lancaster Quay, Western Road
Tel. (021) 4277939
Fax (021) 4274973
www.cafeparadiso.ie

A real treat for vegetarians is Cafe Paradiso near Jurys Hotel. The oven-baked crêpes come particularly recommended.

► Inexpensive

③ *Gingerbread House*
10 Paul Street
Tel. (021) 4276411
Unpretentious coffees, sandwiches, soups and pizzas in a friendly atmosphere. Open daily 9am–10pm.

PUB

Hibernian Bar
Oliver Plunkett Street
Tel. (022) 21588
This genuine pub above a pharmacy is a great place to have a quiet chat and to soak up the atmosphere.

WHERE TO STAY

Baedeker recommendation

► Luxury

③ *Jurys Cork*
Western Road
Tel. (021) 6070000
Fax (021) 6316999
www.jurysdoyle.com
Enjoy the view over the River Lee in a relaxed atmosphere or head out for a stro to the nearby South Mall, Grand Parade St Patrick's Street.

► Mid-range

② *Lancaster Lodge*
Lancaster Quay, Western Road
Tel. (021) 4251125
Fax (021) 4251126
www.lancasterlodge.com
Only a few minutes from the city centre, with comfortable rooms and suites, good service, and substantial breakfast.

► Budget

① *Achill House*
Western Road
Tel. (021) 4279447
www.achillhouse.com
Nice guesthouse with a warm and relaxed atmosphere and pretty rooms.

The drive along Lake Allua is beautiful: in spring, gorse in bloom adorns the shore, in summer, white water lilies catch the eye

In 1794, the Royal Gunpowder Mills were founded in the village of Ballincollig, 8km/5 miles west of Cork on the N22 to Killarney, producing gunpowder for the British Army until 1903. Guided tours explain the history of the factory and the manufacture of gunpowder. (Opening times: April–Sept daily 10am–6pm.)

25km/16 miles away, Macroom (also on the N22), is fairly unremarkable but owes its fame to its proximity to the place (at Beal-na-Blath) where on 22 August 1922 the Irish politician Michael Collins was shot dead. Collins was a leader of the rebellion of 1916 and later organised Irish resistance. In the civil war of 1922, he tried to defend the Free State born out of the 1921 peace with England against the radical position of de Valera (▶ Famous People). Travelling through west Cork, he was ambushed at a site marked by a memorial stone. To get to the site, turn off the N22 between Cork and Macroom onto the R590 to Crookstown and take a right onto the R585 in the direction of Beal-na-Blath and the Michael Collins Ambush Site (4km/2.5 miles away).

The roads around Macroom are well-known scenic routes: the R618, for instance, winds its way past Carrighadrohid Castle (on an island) to Dripsey, famous for its woollen mills. The R584 leads west to Inehigeelagh, a holiday resort for anglers and artists in a picturesque location on the eastern tip of long Lough Allua with its white water lilies. From here, the road leads up via the hamlet of Ballingeary to the famous Pass of Keimaneigh. The mountain pass runs for over 112km/70 miles between steep rocky scenery full of ferns and flowering plants. Just before the summit, a little road branches off to the right towards the forest park and Lough Gougane Barra.

Macroom and around

◀ Michael Collins Ambush Site

◀ Tips for day trips

★ Derry (Doire)

A/B 4

Northern Ireland, province: Ulster   **District:** Derry
Population: 72,500

As the scene of »Bloody Sunday« in 1972, the second-largest city in Northern Ireland entered the history books for its part in the bloody fighting between the British government and the IRA. However, Derry (called Londonderry before 1984) has a lot going for it, not least its attractive location on the River Foyle and an old town with charming alleyways and old-fashioned pubs that have been sensitively redeveloped.

City in a state of emergency
A good example of the reconstruction work in the old town is the Craft Village, a gallery of shops recreating a turn-of-the-century alleyway. In Shipquay Street, Magazine Street and Bishop Street in particular, a number of Georgian houses are left.

However, the Troubles (► Baedeker Special p.46) have continued to leave their mark on the city up to this day, with Protestant and Catholic inhabitants living on clearly segregated estates. The Protestants vehemently protect their traditional neighbourhoods mainly in the parts of the city east of the River Foyle, whilst the majority of the Catholic population lives in the recently redeveloped Bogside and on the Creggan Estates. Since the partition of Ireland in 1921, Derry had been cut off from a large part of its hinterland, but the extremely porous border allowed for a lively economic exchange.

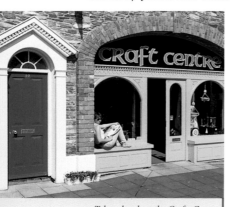
Take a break at the Crafts Centre

Many Irish living in the north of the Republic of Ireland take advantage of the lower prices here. Derry's economic prominence is built on the harbour and industries such as textiles (Du Pont), mechanical engineering, chemicals and ceramics.

History
In 546, St Columba (Colmcille) founded a monastery on the estuary of the Foyle (Lough Foyle) that he called Doire (»oak forest«). Later, the monastery was repeatedly attacked and destroyed along with the surrounding settlements. During the course of the colonization of Ulster by James I, who sent predominantly Protestant settlers from England and Scotland to Derry under the leadership of wealthy com-

mercial guilds from London, city and county were declared a »branch of London« in 1613 and renamed Londonderry. The great city wall dates from this time. In 1689 they withstood a 105-day siege, an event commemorated in the annual march of the Apprentice Boys. The partition of Ireland in 1921 made Londonderry a border city. In the recent past, the city gained notoriety as one of the focal points in the violent conflict between Catholics and Protestants. The Bloody Sunday Memorial commemorates the worst day: On 30 January 1972, British soldiers opened fire on civil rights' demonstrators without warning, killing 13 people. When in 1984 the Nationalists took the town hall, Derry was renamed, but on road signs and in Unionist Protestant parlance, the city continues to be called Londonderry.

◄ Bloody Sunday

Derry Map

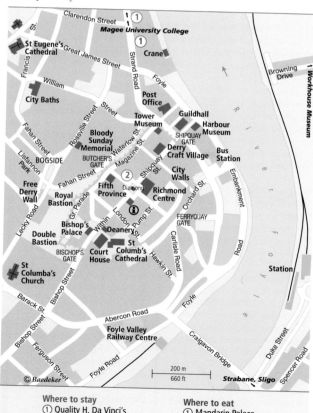

© Baedeker

200 m
660 ft

Strabane, Sligo

Where to stay
① Quality H. Da Vinci's
② Tower Hotel

Where to eat
① Mandarin Palace

Sights in Derry

★
City walls
The city wall surrounding Derry's old town is said to be the best-preserved in the United Kingdom. With the exception of three gates added later, it still looks the way it did in 1618. The wall forms a nice promenade; for the best view over the city head for the Walker Monument on the Royal Bastion. Four old gates lead into the city: Butcher's Gate, Shipquay Gate, Ferryquay Gate and, the most beautiful, Bishop's Gate.

Tower Museum
The exhibition in the Tower Museum tells the story of Derry and the region from the Stone Age to today in a modern, engaging way. The museum has already received several awards for its considered presentation of the history of the city. Amongst the exhibits, look for a well-preserved boat said to date back to the time of St Columba (around 520), as well as a photograph from the year 1932 showing Amelia Earhart crossing the Atlantic by plane on her own – the world-famous pilot confused Derry with Paris and landed in the area by mistake. (Opening times: July–Aug Mon–Sat 10am–5pm, Sun 2–5pm; Sept–June Tues–Sat 10am–5pm.)

Derry Craft Village
Close by, look out for the Derry Craft Village, a »village« set up between Shipquay and Magazine Street to showcase life in Derry from the 16th to the 19th centuries. The windows are all designed in the style of a different period. Craftspeople exhibit their wares in small shops for visitors to buy; there are also workshops available. Or just have a quiet drink at the Craft Village, watch a chess match on the huge chess board or have a go yourself.

The Fifth Province
Using a multitude of dramatic effects and audiovisual techniques, the Fifth Province in the Calgach Centre introduces the visitor to the history and culture of the Celts. Some parts are a little over the top, but the section with the stories centred around the warrior Calgach, for instance, is nicely done. (Opening times: May–Sept daily 10am–6pm.)

St Columb's Cathedral
Abutting Court House to the east, is St Columb's Cathedral. Built between 1618 and 1633, this is the first post-Reformation cathedral to have been newly built in in Ireland, or Great Britain, for that matter. During the 19th century, it was redesigned in a Gothic revival style. Look out for some interesting details: the heads of 16 bishops of the city carry the ceiling as corbelled stones, and worked into the bishop's throne is the armchair of Bishop Bramhall, who consecrated the church in 1633. The chapter house shows documents and exhibits from the time of the Siege of Derry (1688/89), such as the cannon ball that James II had fired into the city, as an exhortation to surrender. (Opening times: April–Oct Mon–Sat 9am–5pm; Nov–May Mon–Sat 9am–4pm.)

▶ VISITING DERRY

INFORMATION

44 Foyle Strret
Tel. (0 28) 71 26 72 84
www.derryvisitor.com

WHERE TO EAT

► Moderate

① *Mandarin Palace*

Ground Floor, Queens Court
Lower Clarendon Street
Tel. (0 28) 71 37 36 56
stanlee@mandarinpalace.fsnet.co.uk
Oriental restaurant, with a nice view
of the Foyle River and Bridge. Attentive and efficient staff serve good
Chinese cuisine with excellent-value
set meals.

PUB

Peadar O'Donnell

63 Waterloo Street
Tel. (0 28 71) 37 23 18
Daily traditional music in the pub
named after an Irish union activist.

WHERE TO STAY

► Mid-range

② *Tower Hotel*

Butcher Street
Tel. (0 28) 71 37 10 00
Fax (0 28) 71 37 12 34
www.towerhotelgroup.com
The only hotel within the city walls,
with a modern lobby and elegant,
light rooms. The ground floor has a
bistro with modern art on the walls.

► Budget

① *Da Vinci's*

15 Culmore Road
Tel. (0 28) 71 27 91 11
Fax (0 28) 71 27 92 22
www.davincishotel.com
Modern hotel on the northern tip of
the city shore road near the main
roads. The large, well appointed
rooms are complemented by the
modern lobby, an atmospheric bar
and a restaurant with an elegant
ambience.

In the south-western corner of the walled city, the neo-Gothic St Columb's Cathedral (Church of Ireland) was built in the 19th century
on the site of an earlier church; nearby, look for St Columb's Stone,
traditionally considered to be the prayer stone of St Columba.

St Columb's Cathedral

Scenes from the history of the city are depicted on the famous
stained-glass windows of the Guildhall, the town hall of Derry, designed in 1890 in the neo-Gothic style. The Guildhall is also located
outside the city walls, and easily accessed via Shipquay Street.

Guildhall

The small old-fashioned Harbour Museum is housed in two rooms
of the former harbour commissioner's office in Guildhall Street. On
display are some ship models and the prow of the »Minnehaha«.
(Opening times: Mon–Fri 10am–1pm and 2–4.30pm.)

Harbour Museum
🕑

For a good insight into contemporary Irish and international art,
head for the city's art galleries. Worth a mention here are the Or-

Art Galleries

chard Gallery (Orchard Street), the Context Gallery (5 Artillery Street) and the McGilloway Gallery (6 Shipquay Street).

Foyle Valley Railway Centre

Near the imposing, two-storey Craigavon Bridge (1933), on the western bank of the River Foyle, the Foyle Valley Railway Centre documents the railway history of the region. Visitors can even take a short trip on a diesel locomotive built in 1934. (Opening times: Tue–Sat 10am–4.30pm.)

Bogside & the Free Derry Monument

The road beyond Butcher's Gate is very busy. The concrete wall on the central reservation bears the famous slogan »You are now entering Free Derry«, marking the entrance to the Bogside neighbourhood, where the Catholics live. There are some political murals around here, such as the one on the gable wall opposite the Bogside Inn, showing the faces of the 13 demonstrators shot dead by British soldiers on »Bloody Sunday« in Derry in 1972. Today, the victims of this tragic event are commemorated by the Bloody Sunday Memorial a few paces up the hill.

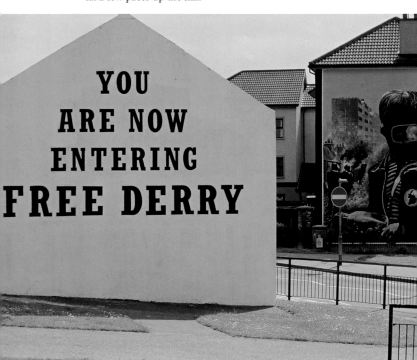

The Bogside is famous for its political murals.

On the other side of the river, the Workhouse Museum (23 Glender-mott Rd) was established in the former poor house of the city in 1998. Between 1840 and 1946, it sheltered up to 800 people. By means of an exact reconstruction of the appalling conditions, the museum aims to introduce the visitor to the reality of life in an institution like this: poverty, hunger, as well as very patchy medical care. In the basement, an exhibition explains the role of Derry in the Second World War.

Workhouse Museum

Around Derry

From the eastern bank of the River Foyle, the A2 leads via two charming villages, Eglington and Ballykelly, to Limavady in the Roe Valley (29km/18 miles). Here, a plaque (51 Main Street) and a mural celebrate one of the most famous Irish songs: in the mid-19th century, Jane Ross was listening to a busker playing »Londonderry Air«. She copied the folk melody, and this became the first step towards the worldwide spread of the »Danny Boy« air, which is still played today on St Patrick's Day (► Baedeker Special p.34) and at funerals.

Limavady

The well-known Irish song »Danny Boy« was written in Limavady.

Less than 2km/1.2 miles south of town stretches Roe Valley Country Park, good for walking, hiring a canoe, fishing, or visiting old water-mills, formerly used in linen production. For further information, head for the Visitor Centre. (Opening times: daily 9am–5pm; the park is always accessible.)

Roe Valley Country Park

Around the market town of Dungiven (25km/16 miles southeast of Derry on the A6) a sign on the road leading to Antrim points to the 12th-century Dungiven Priory. There was a ceremonial site here in pre-Norman times; the Augustinian monastery was built later – eventually becoming part of the manor house – and today is a romantic ruin with a wonderful view of the River Roe. The chancel of the church became the burial site of the O'Cahans, featuring an extraordinary and fairly well-preserved tomb dating from the 15th century: the sculpture of an armed man, an O'Cahan chieftain who died in 1385 who seems to be lying beneath a canopy. Below him six nooks are visible, holding small figures wearing kilts, probably Scottish mercenaries.

★ **Dungiven Priory**

The way to Maghera (►Lough Neagh, Around) leads via the A6 over Glenshane Pass (alt 555m/1,820ft), offering fine views of the ►Sperrin Mountains.

Maghera

✱ Dingle Peninsula

D 1/2

Rep. of Ireland, province: Munster   **County:** Kerry

Dingle seems to signal the end of the world. This barren but magnificent peninsula attracts artists, photographers and many holidaymakers. Depending on the weather and the season, the landscape is subject to an ongoing change of colour and mood, which has inspired many filmmakers too.

Peninsula of stone monuments

On Dingle, the northernmost peninsula in County Kerry, nearly 1,500 stone monuments stand along the coast road, including beehive huts, Ogham stones and early churches, as well as several fortifications dating back to the Iron Age. In the west of the peninsula lies one of the seven Irish-language Gaeltacht areas, those parts of Ireland where Irish is the majority language. Old traditions, customs and crafts remain alive here.

The peninsula is traversed by a mountain range, with its highest elevation Brandon Mountain (approx. 940m/3,084ft). At Brandon Head, the mountain range descends from a height of 750m/2,460ft in a near sheer drop down to the sea. To the west, the countryside is hilly and dotted with typically Irish farms and hamlets. Dandlion-yellow cornfields, scarlet-red fuchsia hedges, pale green fern and black moss dominate the colour scheme. The impressive landscape has often served as a backdrop for films, such as »Ryan's Daughter« (1970) or »Far and Away« (1992) with Tom Cruise and Nicole Kidman.

Drive around Dingle Peninsula

Caherconree Promontery Fort

Drive west from ► Tralee along Tralee Bay, to reach Camp. To the southeast of the village rises Caherconree mountain (813m/2,667ft). Below the summit stands a mighty promontory fort, accessible via a signposted path starting at a car park on the road between Camp and Aughills.

Magnificent beach at Inch

In Camp, the R559 turns off southwest, winding its way through hilly terrain; after 8km/5 miles, a minor road leads south towards Inch, a holiday resort in a sheltered location. Here, the Inch Peninsula, a 5km/3-mile dune ridge with a dream of a sandy beach, stretches out to sea.

✱ Dingle

Dingle (pop. 1,270), the main town on the peninsula of the same name, lies on a protected bay with fine beaches. Alongside opportunities for deep-sea angling, boating and mini golf, the port with its numerous colourful little houses makes a suitable base to explore the

The steep coast line of the Dingle Peninsula offers spectacular views. →

! **Baedeker TIP**

Fungie, the tame dolphin
In the winter of 1984, the fishermen in the bay noticed a dolphin following their boats and performing jumps. As »Fungie«, as the animal has come to be called, continues to enjoy being here, there are now »Swimming with the Dolphin« tours on offer. The one-hour boat trips start from the pier.

antiquities on the western side of the peninsula. If Fungie doesn't turn up, or the weather is bad, a visit to Dingle Oceanworld, an aquarium on the harbour displaying fish and other sea-dwelling creatures, is a good idea. Of particular interest are an underwater glass tunnel, a sharp pool and »touch pools«. (Opening times: July–Aug 9am–9pm, Sept–June daily 9am–5pm.)

Dunbeg Fort & Beehive Huts

The road leads west via Milltown and Ventry, where the sea pounds a wild shore scenery. From Ventry, the road leads along the rocky south coast. To the left, at Fahan (approx. 200m/220yd south of the road), immediately above the sea lies the fine promontory fort of Dunbeg, consisting of four defensive ramparts and a strong stone wall. Inside, look for the remains of a house, laid out round on the outside and square on the inside. A subterranean passage leads to the outer buildings. A few miles further to the west, at Glanfahan, stand groups of beehive huts, all in all 417 buildings, erected in dry-stone, plus 19 souterrains and 18 standing stones.

Slea Head

Slea Head is the name of the southwestern point of the peninsula; there is a spectacular view from the small road at the foot of Mount Eagle.

From the small fishing port of Dunquin, take a trip to the Blasket Isles. Basic information on the islands can be picked up from the Blasket Centre at Dunquin. (Opening times: Easter–Sept daily 10am–6/7pm.)

The main island, declared part of the National Historic Park, Great Blasket was populated until 1953. It has been said that the people were, in their settled way of life, »the happiest in the world«. At the centre of the island stand the ruins of a church. From the ridge (285m/935ft), look across Blasket Sound towards the rugged coast of Kerry. This is the strait where in 1588 the »Santa Maria de la Rosa« of the Spanish Armada ran aground.

Slea Head on Dingle Peninsula

On Inishtooskert, the island situated about 6km/3.5 miles northwest of the peninsula, look out for the ruins of a small church, a well-preserved beehive hut and three crosses.

Dún an Óir Fort & Riasc Monastic Settlement

Leaving Dunquin in a northerly direction, visit the commendable Louis Mulcahy Pottery on the way. After approx. 3km/2 miles, a small road turns off to the left, at a beach and a hotel. Behind the hotel, keep on the left, taking a right at the next crossroads to finally reach the site where the old Dún an Óir (»gold fort«) castle used to stand; today, the only reminder is a nearby sculpture. In 1580, 600 Spanish and Irish soldiers surrendered here, but were still slaughtered by the English.

The main road leads on to Ballyferriter and Riasc. Between the remains of a hermitage, discover a remarkable pillar stone from Early Christian times, decorated with a cross and spiral decorations.

★ Gallarus Oratory

Next stop is Gallarus Oratory, looking like a boat laid upside down onto the ground (Gallarus = possibly »shelter for foreigners«). The walls, over 1m/3ft thick and erected practically without mortar, vault over the 3 x 4.5m(10 x 15ft) floor space; the stones were chosen with such care and laid on top of each other with such precision that the building, despite its advanced age of probably 1,200 years, remains dry. A local legend holds that anyone who leaves the oratory through the window is purified of sin. However, the window is only 12cm/5in wide. Visiting the chapel is free; the Visitor Centre charges an entrance fee, but has a tearoom.

From the slightly elevated position of the chapel, you can make out the ruins of the 16th century Gallarus Castle some 1km/0.5 miles to the west: a four-storey tower, with vaulted rooms.

Gallarus Oratory – a place for contemplation

Kilmalkedar Church

At the crossroads above Gallarus, bear hard left to reach Kilmalkedar Church, one of the most important sacred sites on the peninsula. A monastery was founded here in the 7th century, but all that survives is a 12th-century Romanesque church with interesting sculptures on the tympanum of the main entrance and on the chancel arch. The whole church shows the influence of Cormac's Chapel in ►Cashel. In the church stands an alphabet stone showing both Ogham markings and Latin letters. In the churchyard, look for an old sundial, amongst other things, whilst less than 150m/492ft away stands a medieval building, St Brendan's House, and nearby St Brendan's Oratory.

▶ VISITING DINGLE PENINSULA

INFORMATION
Tel. (066) 9 15 11 88
open: May–Oct

PUB

O'Flaherty's
Bridge Street
Tel. (066) 9 15 19 83
The best amongst Dingle's many pubs
offering good traditional music.

WHERE TO STAY
► **Luxury**
Benners Hotel
Main Street, Dingle
Tel. (066) 9 15 16 38
Fax (066) 9 15 14 12
www.bennershotel.com
No expense was spared in moderniz-
ing this 300-year-old hotel, which
offers a high level of comfort (antique
furnishings, TV, etc.). The hotel
restaurant is famous for its fish dishes.

Off the beaten track
On Brandon Mountain , the remains of St Brendan's Oratory and
some stone cottages survive. The climb, on well-marked paths from
Cloghane, Faha or from the west, is worth doing because of the magnificent view from up there.

Connor Pass ►
From Dingle, take a drive northeast across the Connor Pass, a splendid route with rewarding views. Whilst the imposing Beenoskee
mountain rises 826m/2,709ft to the right of the road, to the left, a
Rough Point ►
promontory runs northwards far out to sea. From Castlegregory, a
quiet holiday resort between Tralee Bay and Lough Gill, the road
leads after 7km/4.5 miles to the point of the narrow peninsula,
Rough Point, in front of which a group of islets spread out.

Donegal (Dún na nGall)

B 3

Republic of Ireland, province: Ulster   **County:** Donegal
Population: 3,000

**The Irish name Donegal (Dún na nGall = »castle of the strangers«)
recalls the Vikings, who in the 9th century established a fortification here. The lively town owes its current appearance to the British, who in the 17th century laid out the diamond-shaped market
square. Today still, »The Diamond« is the focal point for numerous
pubs, hotels and shops.**

Three days of dancing and singing
In Donegal, the River Eske flows into Donegal Bay. The town is the
administrative seat of County Donegal. The obelisk on the market
square was erected in honour of the Four Masters (see Donegal Abbey). Every year, at the end of June/early July, the three-day Donegal

Town Summer Festival takes place, celebrated with songs, dances and storytelling, but also leaving space for the arts and crafts.

Donegal Castle

Donegal Castle stands as impressive ruins a few paces away from the market square, on a rock on the shore of the River Eske. The castle used to be the seat of the Kings of Tir Chonaill from the O'Donnell family, an Irish dynasty. There may originally have been a Viking castle here, of which no trace now remains. In 1607, the estate fell into English hands. At that time, the exterior of the large square tower (1505) was altered by fitting windows; on the main floor, a splendid fireplace was built, with relief escutcheons. In 1610, a manor house was added. (Opening times: March –Oct daily 9.30am–6.30pm.)

The remains of the 15th-century Franciscan **Donegal Abbey** occupy a picturesque position on the mouth of the River Eske (reached by taking a little road at the village entrance, coming from Ballyshannon). Here, the Four Masters, Michael O'Clery and his three assistants wrote their famous »Annals of the Four Masters«, a monumental work of historiography.

Find out more about the history of the **steam engine**, which up to 1959 was serving Ballyshannon and Derry, at the Donegal Railway Heritage Centre in the northeast of the town.

 DONEGAL

INFORMATION

The Quay
Tel. (073) 2 11 48
Open: April–Oct

WHERE TO STAY

► **Mid-range**
Harvey's Point Country Hotel
Lough Eske
Tel. (074) 9 72 22 08
Fax (074) 9 72 23 52
This hotel lies approx. 5km/3 miles outside Donegal, in pretty scenery on Lough Eske. Good French-Swiss cuisine.

Donegal Craft Village

The area around Donegal is famous for its tweed fabrics and knitwear. Coming from the direction of Ballyshannon, at the entrance of the town, the Donegal Craft Village attracts many visitors. Clustering around a yard are the workshops of artists and craftspeople. A good selection of tweed fabrics can be found at »Magee's« on the Diamond in Donegal town. Here, the fabrics are still produced on the labour-intensive hand loom.

Around Donegal

Lough Eske and the Blue Stack Mountains

Around 8km/5 miles northeast of town, Lough Eske offers good fishing opportunities. Driving around the lake, take a detour to a waterfall, 3km/2 miles further north. The valley carries on into the Blue Stack Mountains, where a pretty small lake, Lough Belshade, is hemmed in by high rock walls.

Pure relaxation at Lough Eske

Lough Derg   The R232 and R233, southeast of Donegal, lead to Lough Derg. At Station Island lies a cave that in pagan times was considered the entrance to the underworld; in the Middle Ages, the place came to fame as St Patrick's Purgatory, after a knight errant reported glimpsing purgatory there. Every year, the cave is at the centre of an important pilgrimage, undertaken nearly exclusively by Irish faithful. During their three-day stay, the pilgrims on the »toughest pilgrimage in Christendom« submit themselves to numerous acts of penitence, vigils and fasting. From 1135 the site was in the charge of Augustinian Canons, from 1497 of Franciscans from Donegal. The pilgrimage was known across Europe, but was suppressed by order of the Privy Council for Ireland in 1632 and remained forbidden in the 18th century. However, in 1813 the three-day order of exercises was established, and the number of participants swelled to its peak of 30,000 in 1846, just before the Great Famine.

Rossnowlagh   On the Atlantic, 20km/12.5 miles south of Donegal, lies Rossnowlagh, a holiday resort with a fine sandy beach. The modern Franciscan monastery houses the Donegal Historical Society Museum, showing objects from the Stone and Bronze Age, amongst them an exquisitely wrought sword, found during construction works in nearby Ballyshannon. (Opening times: daily 9am–6.30pm.)

Downpatrick (Dún Pádraig)

B 6

Northern Ireland, province: Ulster   **County:** Down
Population: 10,300

The county town of Downpatrick is closely associated with the national saint of Ireland, St Patrick, who in 432 chose this spot to start converting the Irish. Around Downpatrick, a picturesque landscape opens up.

St Patrick's activity was the beginning of the Christianization of the island. (► Baedeker Special p.34) After studying Christian doctrine in France, the saint sailed to Ireland, landing at the village of Saul, situated 3km/2 miles north of Downpatrick. This is where St Patrick built the first church on Irish soil; he is said to have died in this area on 17 March 471.

In 1177 Downpatrick, in Irish Dún Pádraig (»Patrick's fort«), was conquered by the Norman John de Courcy, who heavily promoted the cult of St Patrick, in order to endow the place with more significance. Distrusting the Augustinians, settled here in 1136 by St Malachy, he replaced them with English Benedictines, for whom he had an abbey church built on the cathedral hill.

All about St Patrick in Downpatrick

Started in 1790, today's Down Cathedral was built on the ruins of an earlier church; individual capitals and the baptismal font are parts of the original building. Excavations had revealed the presumed mortal remains of the three great Irish patron saints Patrick, Brigid and Columcille; in reaction to this, de Courcy transferred the seat of his diocese from Bangor to Downpatrick and arranged for the construction of the first cathedral.

★
Down Cathedral

After its destruction by English soldiers in 1538, it stood empty for over 250 years. Whilst it is unlikely that the actual mortal remains of the three saints are buried here, a granite stone in the churchyard bearing the inscription »Patric« is said to mark the grave of St Patrick. Every year, for St Patrick's Day (17th March), the site turns into a place of pilgrimage.

Down County Museum	The Down County Museum, housed in the former 18th-century prison, tells the story of the county, with a St Patrick's Heritage Centre in the gate house dedicated to the saint's life and works, and, at the far end of the compound, 18th-century cells with life-like puppets. From the museum, a signposted path branches off to the Norman castle of Mound of Down. (Opening times: mid-June–mid-Sept Mon–Fri 11am–5pm, Sat/Sun 2–5pm; mid-Sept–mid-June Tues–Fri 10am–5pm, Sat 11am–5pm.)
St Patrick's Centre	Directly opposite Down County Museum, the brand-new St Patrick's Centre is the place to get multimedia information on Ireland's national hero and the country's Christianization. (Opening times: June–Aug Mon–Sat 9.30am–6pm, Sun 10am–6pm; April, May and Sept Mon–Sat 9.30am–5.30pm, Sun 1–5.30pm, Oct–March Mon–Sat 10am–5pm.)
Quoile Countryside Centre	From Strangford Road, take a turn off to the Quoile Countryside Centre, with information on the animals and plants of the region.
Inch Abbey	In a very idyllic position, on a former marshy island on the Quoyle River, lies Inch Abbey. The Cistercian abbey was founded by de Courcey around 1180, as a penance for the destruction of the monastery at Erenagh. (Opening times: April–Sept Tues–Sat 10am 7pm, Sun 2–7pm; Oct–March Tues–Sat 10am –4pm, Sun 2–4pm.)
In the footsteps of St Patrick	There are more sites associated with St Patrick nearby. A narrow road behind the hospital leads after 2km/1.2 miles to what probably used to be a pagan sacrificial site where the saint was active. It is said the water from the local springs is able to cure various ailments. The site seems to have been particularly popular in the 17th century, when separate bath houses for men and women were erected. Near Saul (3km/2 miles north-east of Downpatrick off the A2), St Patrick is said to have landed in 432. To the west of the village is the site where St Patrick founded the first monastery on Irish soil, commemorated by a small memorial church.

Around Downpatrick

Strangford	From Saul, a coastal road leads east to Strangford (16km/10 miles north-east of Downpatrick). This old Viking settlement is situated in a picturesque location on the southern tip of Strangford Lough, dominated by a 16th-century tower house, Strangford Castle. Some 3km/2 miles west of Strangford, Castleward House manor was built in 1760. The façade shows both classical and Gothic features – it is said that the couple who built it, Lord and Lady Bangor, were not able to agree on a style. The estate also includes fine parks, a fortified tower house, a laundry, a theatre, a saw mill and a mill, as well as a restaurant and a shop. The park is open all year round. Every

summer, events are held in these idyllic surroundings, such as the Ulster Summer Festival of Opera. (Opening times: May–Aug Fri– Wed 1–6pm; April, May and Sept weekends only.)

A few miles further north the holiday resort of Killyleagh on Strangford Lough is the birthplace of Sir Hans Sloane, the founder of the British Museum in London. The surroundings are very picturesque, with the ► Mourne Mountains looming to the south-west.

Killyleagh

Only 4km/2.5 miles south of Strangford, 15th-century Kilclief Castle rises above the strait. No fewer than seven castles used to guard the fishing village of Ardglass 9km/4.8 miles further south, at the time when Ardglass was an important harbour. One of those, Jordan's Castle, is still partly preserved. West of Killough, situated beyond the bay, look out for a very nice beach. Near St John's Point is the start of probably the most beautiful coastal drive in Northern Ireland, leading to Newry (62.5km/39 miles). Via Dundrum Bay, which at low tide is partly exposed, the road carries on in the direction of Newcastle.

Dundrum, 4km/2.5 miles south of Clough, is a picturesque fishing village with fine sandy bays and a tower surrounded by a moat which used to belong to a castle. At this site, De Courcy had begun building a fortification in 1177 in order to better guard the road between Drogheda and Downpatrick. In 1210, King John I had the castle confiscated and a tower added, but in 1652, Cromwell's army razed the castle.

Towards Dundrum

> ! **Baedeker TIP**
>
> **Butterfly House**
>
> Seaforde Tropical Butterfly House, 2km/1.2 miles north of Clough on the A24 near Seaforde, is worth a detour: hundreds of tropical butterflies flap around a glasshouse in the middle of the park. The many exotic insects and reptiles are safely kept behind glass. (Opening times: Easter–Sept Mon–Sat 10am–5pm, Sun 2–6pm.)

Following the road 6km/3.5 miles further south, the seaside resort of Newcastle offers many amenities, amongst them a golf links. Newcastle is situated on the western tip of Dundrum Bay and on the foot of Slieve Donard, at 836m/2,743ft the highest peak in the ► Mourne Mountains. Climbing Slieve Donard takes some 2 hours; the summit offers a spectacular view all the way to the coast of Scotland.

Newcastle

West of Slieve Croob (532m/1,745ft, approx. 20km/12.5 miles west of Downpatrick) stands what is probably the best-known Stone Age monument in Ulster: the 2.5m/8-ft Legananny Dolmen. Against the backdrop of the Mourne Mountains, it appears fairly impressive, but not as bulky as other dolmens, as it seems to stand on three »feet«, like a tripod. The site is reached by signposted byroads, but the last part (a narrow gravel path) is better done on foot.

★ Legananny Dolmen

Drogheda (Droichead Átha)

C 5

Republic of Ireland, province:
Leinster
Population: 25,000

County: Louth
Information: Tel. (041) 3 70 70
(June–Aug)

Thanks to its port, cement and steel works, and breweries, Droghe-da, Droichead Átha (»bridge over the ford«) in Irish, is an important industrial town. There are few sights though.

Chequered history

Drogheda lies north of Dublin on the mouth of the River Boyne. In 911, Vikings expanded the town into a base for their raids. Later, the Anglo-Normans erected a bridge and fortified the town on both banks of the Boyne. In the 14th and 15th centuries, Drogheda was one of the four capitals of Ireland; the town had its own mint, and a university was established in 1465. Parliament met here several times well into the 17th century, but in 1649, Cromwell took the town, and in 1690, after the Battle of the Boyne, Drogheda surrendered to the army of King William III of Orange.

St Peter's Church (Catholic)

On the right-hand side of West Street, the Catholic St Peter's Church was built (in the neo-Gothic style) to commemorate the canonized archbishop of Armagh, Oliver Plunkett, executed in 1681 in Tyburn (near London). Plunkett's embalmed head is kept as a relic in a shrine in this church.

St Lawrence's Gate

Of the original ten gates the town had, only St Lawrence's Gate on St Lawrence's Street is left. Its two mighty round towers enclose a sturdy passage.

Millmount Fort & Museum

On the southern side of the river – behind the bridge following Shop Street – lies Millmount Fort. Originally a passage tomb such as New-grange in the ►Boyne Valley, it was fortified in the 12th century and used until 1800 as a fortification. Today, the fort houses a museum with exhibits on the history of the town. There is a nice view of Drogheda from the fort. (Opening times: Mon–Sat 10am–6pm, Sun 2.30–5.30pm.)

St Peter's Church

At the corner of Peter's Street and William Street, look for the pretty St Peter's Church (Church of Ireland), built in 1748 on the ruins of an earlier church destroyed by Cromwell. The rococo stucco work inside is worth seeing.

Magdalene Tower

The 14th-century Magdalene Tower above the town used to be the bell tower of a Dominican priory. Here, in 1395, the English king Richard II held an assembly in the church of Mary Magdalene at which four Irish chieftains pledged allegiance to him.

Around Drogheda

Northwards

5km/3 miles east of Drogheda, the road leads past the impressive Beaulieu House (mid-17th century), to reach, at Baltray, an 18-hole golf course/links and a 5km/3 mile sandy swimming beach. Some 3km/2 miles further north lies Termonfeckin, where a 15th century tower house features a pretty spiral staircase as well as an unusual vaulted roof constructed in the same way as the vault of Newgrange, 4,000 years older. In the graveyard of St Feckin's Church stands a 10th-century High Cross: the east face has a representation of the Crucifixion, the west face Christ in Glory; the other sides are covered with geometrical patterns and interlacing motifs. Clogherhead has good sandy beaches, especially near Port Oriel harbour.

◄ Termonfeckin

◄ Clogherhead

Southwards

South of Drogheda, already in County Meath, the seaside spa resorts of Bettystown, which has a golf links, and Laytown, both boast beaches nearly 10km/6 miles long. Outside Laytown, in the direction of Julianstown, the Sonairte National Ecological Centre has a nice nature garden and exhibitions looking at the use of renewable energies: wind, water and solar power. Take the road inland – between the R108 and the R152 – to reach the important burial site of Fourknocks (1800–1500 BC) with a large passage tomb and two smaller burial mounds. Some 8km/4.5 miles southwest of Drogheda, on the Nanny River lies **Duleek** (pop 1730). In the grounds of the priory stand the ruins of a church and a High Cross (probably 10th century). The church contains a number of fine monuments, amongst them a tomb with carved figures of saints, angels and coats-of-arms.

★
Mellifont

From Drogheda, take the R168 in the direction of Collon; after 4km/ 2.5 miles, at Tullyallan, take the turn for Mellifont. Here on the Mattoch River, stand the ruins of a once significant Cistercian monastery: Mellifont Abbey, founded in 1142 and built with the help of French monks. By 1272, Mellifont had become the mother house of 24 other monasteries. After its dissolution (1539), the monastery was converted into a fortified manor house. Today, very little remains of the original building: to the north a castle-like gatehouse with a bulky tower, the remarkable crypt of the church, parts of the two-storey, octagonal »lavabo« or washing house adjoining the cloister (with reconstructed arcades) and the vaulted 14th-century chapterhouse, now housing various architectural fragments. Parts of the floor feature glazed tiles from the church. Wall stumps and marks on the ground suggest that the monastery

Mellifont Abbey

⊙   was laid out using Clairvaux as a model. (Opening times: May–mid-June and mid-Sept–Oct daily 10am – 5pm; mid-June–mid-Sept daily 9.30am – 6.30pm.)

✶ ✶ Dublin (Baile Átha Cliath or Dubhlinn)

C 5

Republic of Ireland, province: Leinster   **County:** Dublin
Population: 1.1 million (with suburbs)

The vibrant metropolis of Dublin is more than just the capital city, it is the cultural and economic heart of Ireland, situated in a beautiful position around a wide bay that opens onto the Irish Sea. Visitors experience the expanding city as open, likeable, even Mediterranean in character.

Capital of the Republic of Ireland

Nearly a third of all Irish live in Dublin which, since 1990, has experienced rapid growth. New buildings and construction sites show how the city is changing. Entire districts are being redeveloped: for example Temple Bar, more recently the area around Smithfield Market, and currently the Docks. As in all big cities, Dublin has its share of social contrasts: the classy residential quarters and shopping malls on the southern shore of the Liffey stand in stark contrast with the often desolate northern working-class quarters, where the number of unemployed and young drug addicts is relatively high, and it it not uncommon to see beggars.

Highlights Dublin

Trinity College with Old Library
The famous Book of Kells is on display in this temple of books.
► page 286

Powerscourt House
Elegant department store with shops and galleries, with the Civic Museum nearby
► page 289

National Museum
Ireland's rich treasure chest
► page 290

Merrion Square
Linger awhile amongst elegant Georgian buildings and a nice park
► page 291

National Gallery
On display are important Irish artists, as well as German and Spanish masters
► page 294

Temple Bar District
Colourful pub and artists' quarter south of the Liffey
► page 295

Dublin Castle
Lavishly furnished state apartments
► page 296

St Patrick's Cathedral
Largest church in Ireland, impressive interior
► page 298

History

448	St Patrick converts Baile Atha Cliath to Christianity.
840	Danes raid the town and fortify it.
988	Irish King Mael Sechnaill II conquers the city.
1014	Victory of Irish High King Brian Boru over the Danes.
1172	Irish chieftains pledge loyalty to King Henry II. Dublin becomes seat of government for »the Pale« region.
1649	Cromwell takes the city.
1916	Easter Rising. Large parts of the city are destroyed.
1919	First independent parliament, supported by the Sinn Féin political movement.
1988	Millennium celebrations (though the exact founding date is not known with absolute certainty).
1991	Dublin becomes »European Capital of Culture«.

During the wars of the 15th and 16th centuries, Dubliners mostly sided with the opponents of the English king. After 1730 the city grew to be the largest metropolis in the British Empire. Architecture and the arts flourished, and the Wide Street Commission oversaw the emergence of one of the most spacious and magnificent cities in Europe. With the **Act of Union** in 1801, Ireland's political union with Great Britain, this short period of freedom came to an end. In the following years, resistance against British rule grew; in 1844, Lord Mayor Daniel O'Connell was incarcerated »for incitement of discontent«. A secret brotherhood was carrying out political murders, and separatist activities increased.

During the quashing of the **Easter Rising** and in the ensuing civil war, large parts of the city centre were destroyed. Even after the ratification of the treaty in 1922 which made Ireland a Free State, in fact up to 1927, Dublin still saw internecine fighting, and most public buildings were not restored until 1931. During **World War II** the country remained neutral.

Over subsequent decades, relatively little was done for the city, and there was even some ill-considered demolition of fine Georgian terraces. It was only when Dublin was nominated »European Capital of Culture« in 1991 that a wave of reconstruction and restoration started, improving Dublin's image enormously. Today, the city looks beautiful, with many restored historic buildings, and the authorities are taking the conservation of Dublin's heritage very seriously.

? DID YOU KNOW ...?

■ In Irish, Dubhlinn means »dark pool«. The oldest Irish name and the one that is most used today »Baile Átha Cliath« is inspired by its location: »settlement of the hurdle ford«.

Dublin City centre

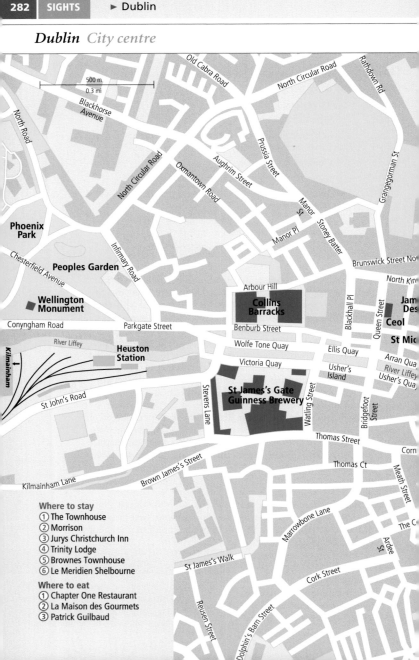

500 m
0.3 mi

North Road

Old Cabra Road

North Circular Road

Rathdown Rd

Blackhorse Avenue

Prussia Street

Oxmantown Road

Aughrim Street

Grangegorman St

North Circular Road

Manor St

Stoney Batter

Phoenix Park

Infirmary Road

Manor Pl

Brunswick Street No

Peoples Garden

Chesterfield Avenue

Arbour Hill

North Kin

Wellington Monument

Collins Barracks

Blackhall Pl

Queen Street

Jam Des

Conyngham Road

Parkgate Street

Benburb Street

Ceol

River Liffey

Heuston Station

Wolfe Tone Quay

Ellis Quay

St Mic

Kilmainham

Victoria Quay

Usher's Island

Arran Qua

River Liffey

Usher's Qua

St John's Road

Stevens Lane

St James's Gate Guinness Brewery

Watling Street

Bridgefoot Street

Thomas Street

Corn

Kilmainham Lane

Brown James's Street

Thomas Ct

Meath Street

The C

Marrowbone Lane

Corn Street

Ardee St

St James's Walk

Cork Street

Reuben Street

Dolphin's Barn Street

Where to stay
① The Townhouse
② Morrison
③ Jurys Christchurch Inn
④ Trinity Lodge
⑤ Brownes Townhouse
⑥ Le Meridien Shelbourne

Where to eat
① Chapter One Restaurant
② La Maison des Gourmets
③ Patrick Guilbaud

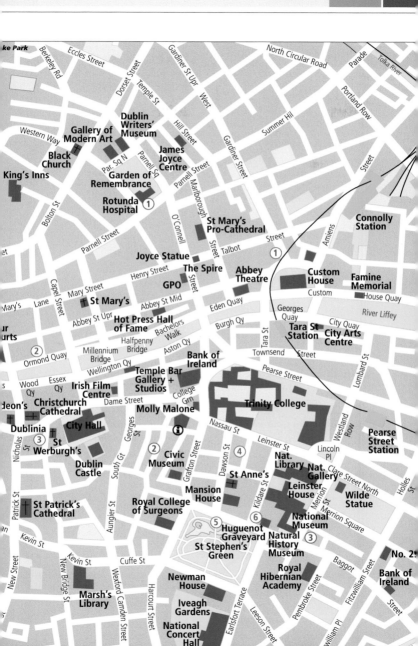

● VISITING DUBLIN

INFORMATION
www.visitdublin.com
Suffolk Street
Tel. (01) 8 50 23 03 30
Baggot Street Bridge
Tel. (01) 2 84 47 68

WHERE TO EAT

► Expensive
③ *Patrick Guilbaud*
21–24 Upper Merrion Street
Dublin 2
Tel. (01) 6 76 41 92
One of the most exclusive restaurants in Dublin, tastefully decorated with original works by Irish artists. Imaginative – often innovative – French cuisine.

► Moderate
① *Chapter One Restaurant*
18/19 Parnell Square North
Tel. (01) 8 73 22 66
Fine restaurant sharing the historic ambience of the Dublin Writers' Museum. The excellent »pre-theatre menus« are good value.

► Inexpensive
② *La Maison des Gourmets*
15 Castle Street
Dublin 2
Tel. (01) 6 72 72 58
This gem serves delicacies from the French patisserie and deli below.

PUBS

The Brazen Head
Bridge Street, Dublin 8
This cozy pub, the oldest in Dublin, has been going since the 13th century.

Davy Byrne's
Duke Street, Dublin 2
Famous Dublin pub, which also features in James Joyce's novel *Ulysses* (►Baedeker Special p.292).

Temple Bar Pub
This traditional meeting place in the trendy Temple Bar quarter is particularly popular with tourists.

WHERE TO STAY

► Luxury
⑥ *Le Meridien Shelbourne*
27 St Stephen's Green
Dublin 2
Tel. (01) 6 63 45 00
Fax (01) 6 61 60 06
www.shelbourne.ie
The most upmarket hotel in Dublin. From this central base, explore a wealth of sights on foot, go on a shopping expedition or kick off a night on the town. The hotel facilities are top-of-the-range: the restaurants, bars, and tea lounge, as well as the Shelbourne Club with pool, sauna, steam bath, and more.

② *Morrison*
Ormond Quay
Dublin 1
Tel. (01) 8 87 24 00
Fax (01) 8 78 31 85
www.morrisonhotel.ie
One of the most luxurious hotels in Europe and an architectural masterpiece, featuring comfortable rooms and suites with modern furnishings, a restaurant and various bars.

The new Millennium Bridge

⑤ *Brownes Townhouse*
22 St Stephens Green
Dublin 2
Tel. (01) 6 38 39 39
Fax (01) 6 38 39 00
www.brownesdublin.com
This lovingly restored Georgian period townhouse has a long history and can boast many illustrious guests. The stylish brasserie serves delicious Continental cuisine.

▶ **Mid-range**
④ *Trinity Lodge*
12 South Frederick Street
Dublin 2
Tel. (01) 6 17 09 00
Fine Georgian townhouse in the heart of Dublin.

③ *Jurys Christchurch Inn*
Christchurch Place
Tel. (01) 4 54 00 00
Fax (01) 4 54 00 12
christchurch_inn@jurysdoyle.com
Central location near Temple Bar, and good value for money.

▶ **Budget**
① *The Townhouse*
47–48 Lower Gardiner Street
Dublin 1
Tel. (01) 8 78 88 08
Fax (01) 8 78 87 87
www.townhouseofdublin.com
The writers Dion Boucicault and Lafcadio Hearn once lived in this Georgian townhouse, a good base in the city centre.

✳ Cityscape

The River Liffey divides the city into a northern and a southern part. The two parts are connected by bridges, the most important being **O'Connell Bridge**. Further upstream, **Father Matthew Bridge** marks the spot where the Liffey used to be crossed originally.

Apart from the two cathedrals, few buildings in Dublin are pre-18th century. The cityscape is dominated by numerous public buildings from the 18th and early 19th centuries. Their classical façades and domes are evidence of the skill of architects such as Sir Edward Lovett Pearce, Richard Cassels and Thomas Cooley or James Gandon and Francis Johnston, but there are also many private buildings with a simple, noble appearance lending an architectural unity to entire blocks. Unfortunately, many of these have been torn down and replaced with modern office blocks. Thankfully, in recent years, actions by citizens' groups were able to stop most of this happening.

! Baedeker TIP

Literary Pub Crawl

During the Literary Pub Crawl, actors lead visitors through pubs and other places associated with literature. They act out scenes and recite extracts from books and sing songs, whilst the audience partakes of the odd pint. Book through Tourist Information or the Duke pub in Duke Street. Music lovers can go on a Musical Pub Crawl.

Explore on your own In the city centre, look for Tourist Trails (signposted sightseeing trails); pick up a brochure in the Tourist Information Offices, where they also have information on festivals and special events such as Bloomsday (►Baedeker Special p.292).

College Green • Trinity College

College Green was already a meeting place in Viking times, and later Ireland's centre of power, until the Act of Union. Today, it is the seat of the most prestigious university, Trinity College. Opposite, note the classical façade of the Bank of Ireland – this is the building where in the 18th century the country's parliament convened.

✳ *Trinity College* The buildings of this university are spread out over a large public park. Founded in 1592 by Elizabeth I, Trinity College was exclusively reserved for Protestants up to 1793. Catholics have only been able to study for a degree and apply for scholarships here since 1873 – women had to wait until 1903. TCD's most famous students include Samuel Beckett, Edmund Burke, Robert Emmet, Oliver Goldsmith, Jonathan Swift, John Millington Synge and Oscar Wilde. Currently, some 6,000 students are enrolled here.

In front of the 90m/100-yd classical façade are statues of poet and playwright Oliver Goldsmith and philosopher Edmand Burke (1863/

Trinity College Dublin Plan

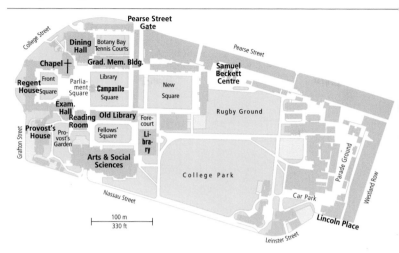

1865). In the first courtyard, to the left, stands the **Chapel**, to the right, the **Examination Hall** (1779–1791, formerly a theatre), both designed by Sir William Chambers. In the **Dining Hall**, built in 1743 by Richard Cassels behind the chapel, hang paintings of members of the university. In the centre of the square, the **Campanile** (1853) immediately draws attention; nearby, look for a sculpture by Henry Moore.

✷✷
Old Library

The most interesting building on campus is the Old Library, built between 1712 and 1732. Since 1801, the library has been a copyright library, i.e. it is entitled to receive a copy of every book printed in Great Britain and Ireland. Around 5,000 manuscripts and nearly 3 million printed books are held here. Its treasures include manuscripts, incunabula and early prints.

On the ground floor, the »Colonnades« of the Old Library, the famous 8th-century *Book of Kells* is on display. The book containing the four Gospels has 680 exquisitely illustrated pages, of which a different one is shown every day; the beginnings of the Gospels and the individual chapters are particularly beautifully designed. Further valuable manuscripts are the *Book of Durrow*, the *Book of Dimma* and the *Book of Armagh* (7th–9th century).

From the ground floor, a pretty set of stairs leads up to the Long Room, a beautiful library 60m/200ft in length lined with books and the busts of writers and philosophers. Look out for two of the oldest Irish harps. (Opening times: Mon–Sat 9.30am–5pm, Sun ☺ noon–4.30pm, in peak season, turn up early!)

The Old Library is Trinity College's treasure house.

Another tourist attraction on the university campus is the »Dublin Experience«, a multimedia show on the history of the city in the Arts Building. (Showings are on the hour May–Sept daily between 10am and 5pm).

Douglas Hyde Gallery ▶
The same building holds the Douglas Hyde Gallery, which shows contemporary Irish art in changing exhibitions. (Opening times: Mon–Wed and Fri 11am–6pm, Thu 11am–7pm, Sat 11am–4.45pm).

Bank of Ireland
Opposite, the Bank of Ireland was built in 1729 as a parliament building following a design by Sir Edward Lovett, but sold in 1802 – after the Act of Union – to the Bank of Ireland. Architecturally, the façade, with its various pillar arrangements and groups of statues (the result of several alterations), is considered one of the most successful in Dublin. The former House of Commons is now the main banking hall and may be visited during opening hours. The former House of Lords, featuring a coffered ceiling and chandeliers, is also open to the public.

Between Grafton Street and the National Museum

Grafton Street
Grafton Street, one of the main shopping streets in Dublin (pedestrianized), runs south of College Green.

On Grafton Street

Next to Bewley's Café, a narrow street leads to the imposing Powerscourt Town House. Built in the 1770s, originally as a town house for the Viscount of Powerscourt, it now houses elegant offices and department stores, cafés, exclusive shops and galleries. A few doors further down, the Civic Museum shows a wealth of exhibits alongside old city maps and models of historic Dublin. (Opening times: Tues–Sat 10am–6pm, Sun 11am–2pm). At the corner of Suffolk Street, look for the bronze statue of cockle and mussel seller Molly Malone.

Also on Grafton Street stands the National Wax Museum, showing wax figures of Irish politicians (Charles Stewart Parnell, Douglas Hyde, Eamon de Valera), actors and writers (James Joyce), as well as replicas of famous personalities from around the world, such as Madonna or Pope John Paul II. (Opening times: Mon–Sat 10am–6pm, Sun noon–6pm.)

In Dawson Street, east of Grafton Street, stands **Mansion House** (1705), which has served as the seat of the Lord Mayor of Dublin and the Royal Irish Academy since 1715. It contains an important library holding manuscripts dating from the 6th to 17th century, amongst them the *Cathach* Psalter, written by St Columba. Both institutions are difficult to gain access to; it is best to enquire at Tourist Information.

★
Powerscourt House and Civic Museum
🕐

World of Wax

🕐

Dawson Street

Leinster House Further east stretches the part of Dublin called »Georgian City«. Monumental **Kildare Street** boasts Leinster House – the parliament building, seat of the Dáil Éireann (parliament) and Seanad Éireann (senate). Originally, this solid, somewhat sober building (1745, Richard Cassels) was the townhouse of the Dukes of Leinster. Outside parliamentary sessions, there are guided tours. (Guided tours: Sat 10.30am – 3.30pm).

Seat of the Dáil Éireann

Every Irish writer since James Joyce has spent time in the **National Library**. The episode of Stephen Daedalus' literary debate in Joyce's novel *Ulysses* also makes a direct reference to this reading room. The library holds collections of first editions, especially 17th-century Irish literature, old maps and topographical works. (Opening times: Mon 10am – 9pm, Tue/Wed 2pm – 9pm, Thu/Fri 10am till 5pm, Sat 10am – 9pm.)

★★
National Museum

In Ireland, outstanding works of art are collected centrally, making the National Museum a veritable treasure trove for Irish antiquities from prehistory to the late Middle Ages. The Great Hall shows Irish gold artefacts from different periods.

Particularly valuable exhibits are kept in the Treasury next door, amongst them the silver 8th-century Ardagh Chalice, with gilded decorations. One of the most precious artefacts is the 8th-century **Tara Brooch**. Its intricate decorations are said to have influenced the artists who created the Book of Kells (► Baedeker Special p.64). Gilded bronze features inlay patterns made from silver, copper and enamel. Equally impressive is the 12th-century **Cross of Cong**, a procession cross made of oak, with silver and gilded bronze plates in the shape of animals. The most beautiful amongst the reliquary shrines is the 12th-century **Shrine of St Patrick's Bell**, decorated with gilded silver, gold filigree and precious stones. Containing a bell, it is attributed to St Patrick. (Opening times: Tue–Sat 10am – 5pm, Sun 2 – 5pm.)

 DON'T MISS

- Tara Brooch im Treasury
- Bell Shrine of St Patrick's

A branch of the National Museum in the former Collins Barracks is devoted to applied art.

Around St Stephen's Green

Follow Kildare Street on to **St Stephen's Green**, a 9ha/22-acre park established and paid for by Arthur Guinness in 1880, that has remained popular ever since. In July and August, there are lunchtime concerts with Irish music. Very beautiful are the various gardens, ponds and monuments for famous Irish people. Hiding behind an ornate Victorian façade is the **St Stephen's Green Shopping Centre**. In the 18th and 19th centuries, everybody who was anybody went for a stroll on the northern side of the park, Beaux Walk, and still today, visitors can reside in style at the Shelbourne Hotel (1867). Next to the hotel, in a shady garden, lies the old Huguenot graveyard dating from 1693. Many French Huguenots who came to Ireland fleeing persecution from Louis XIV are buried here. The building on the southern side of St Stephen's Green, with the house numbers 85 and 86 is called **Newman House**, in memory of John Henry Newman, the first rector of the Catholic University, the predecessor of University College. Belonging to University College Dublin, it has been lavishly restored and is worth a visit for its elaborate stucco works. No. 85 was built in 1738 for Captain Hugh Montgomery, whilst house no. 86 was begun in 1765 after designs by Robert West. (Opening times: June–Sept: Mon–Fri noon–4pm, Sat 2pm–4pm, Sun 11am–1pm.)

Next to Newman House stands the neo-Byzantine Catholic University Church or Newman Chapel. When it was being built in the middle of the 19th century, the lavishly designed interior was very controversial. Today, many couples hold their weddings here.

◄ Catholic University Church

In Harcourt Street, branching off from the southwestern corner of St Stephen's Green, there is a good large bar called **»Odeon«**, which, between 1859 and 1958, used to be the terminus of the train line between Dublin and Bray. Bram Stoker, the author of *Dracula*, lived here (at no. 16) as did George Bernard Shaw (no. 61).

◄ Harcourt Street & Shaw's birthplace

Take Harrington Street to reach Synge Street. No. 33 was the birthplace of George Bernard Shaw in 1856. After extensive restoration it now appears again as it did when the Shaw family lived here. (Opening times: May–Oct: Mon–Sat 10am–1pm and 2–5pm.)

◄ Shaw House

Merrion Square • Georgian Dublin

Merrion Square, with its pretty Archbishop Ryan Park and elegant buildings, was built around 1762. Doors in all the colours of the rainbow greet visitors here, with decorated doorknobs and foot mats adorning the typical Georgian entrances.

★ **Merrion Square**

Baedeker TIP

Iveagh Gardens

A veritable jewel in the heart of Dublin are the Iveagh Gardens, surrounded by a mighty wall and hidden behind Newman House. The entrance is reached via Earlsfort Terrace or Clonmel Street, off Harcourt Street. Relax and leave the stress and strain of the metropolis behind you.

A silent prayer – Paddy Dignam's funeral at Glasnevin Cemetery

»ULYSSES« – A LITERARY BAEDEKER

In Dublin, 16 June is not any old day – it's Bloomsday! Every year, hundreds of people wander through the city centre, on their own or in groups, come to a halt at the odd crossroads or building, open a book and look around them. The 800-page work is their guide to the city. It is not a conventional travel guide, however, but a novel: the literary masterpiece of the Irish writer James Joyce (1882–1941).

Ulysses describes the course of one day: 16 June 1904, from eight in the morning to the next morning around 3am, in the life of three inhabitants of Dublin: advertising agent **Leopold Bloom, his wife Molly** and the teacher and writer **Stephen Dedalus**. Joyce described the steps taken by Bloom and Dedalus through the Irish capital so faithfully, that even today it is possible to use the novel as a guide for a literary pilgrimage through the city centre. *Ulysses* is, in the words of writer Frank Delaney, a »literary Baedeker«. Whilst Joyce was writing his major work, he told a friend: »I want to give a picture of Dublin so complete that if the city one day suddenly disappeared from the earth it could be reconstructed out of my book.«Since 16 June 1954, »Bloomsday« has started to become a hit with the tourists: on that day, four Dubliners celebrated the day that Leopold Bloom had crossed Dublin for the

first time. During their literary tour, Joyceans mainly use the 8th episode of the novel, which begins in Middle Abbey Street and ends in Kildare Street. Bronze plaques in the pavement show the way and point to the relevant page numbers of the standard English edition. (For more information, pick up a copy of the *Ulysses Map of Dublin* published by the tourist office.)

The Novel

Ulysses consists of 18 episodes. The focus of the first three is Stephen Dedalus, whilst Leopold Bloom, a modern Everyman, appears in the fourth episode. After breakfast with his wife Molly, Bloom starts his daily odyssey through Dublin: post office, mass, public baths, cemetery (to attend a funeral), publishing house, pub, restaurant, and library. Later, Leopold's path crosses that of Stephen Dedalus'. They first make a detour to

a coaching inn before continuing on to Bloom's flat at 7 Eccles Street. When Dedalus goes home, Bloom lies down next to Molly to sleep.

The 18 episodes of the novel correspond to the 24 cantos of **Homer's Odyssey.** As Odysseus travels through the Greek islands, Bloom travels the streets of Dublin. Part of Joyce's genius lies in the way he challenges traditional narrative structures, with the plot losing its central role. *Ulysses* is one of the first novels to take up the psychoanalytical insights of Sigmund Freud. 20 hours or so in the daily life of three inhabitants of Dublin are portrayed: their actions, their encounters with other citizens of their home town, their thoughts, desires and dreams. The main narrative devices are interior monologue, chains of association, changing points of view, a fragmented chronology and ungrammatical syntax. An easy read this ain't! With new forms of expression, in particular the »«stream of consciousness« narrative technique that he developed further, James Joyce was of decisive influence on the art of the 20th-century novel.

Changing Dublin

In recent decades, Dublin, which so far has largely been spared wars and natural disasters, has experienced radical change. Many streets and lanes were redesigned, and houses torn down. Only the large boulevards have survived, if not always in the shape Joyce knew them. Even Bloom's house is no longer there...Along with many other locations from the novel, »Barney Kieran's« and »Burke's« pubs have disappeared, as has the coaching inn, but at many corners, something of the old Dublin is still there. For instance, the place where the novel kicks off: the **Martello Tower,** in the Dun Laoghaire suburb, today houses the Joyce Museum. **Glasnevin** cemetery is well worth visiting as well as »Bailey's«, today one of Dublin's classiest pubs. Opposite lies »Davy Byrne's« pub, were a hungry Bloom had a gorgonzola sandwich – today only on offer on Bloomsday. To purchase a small and cheap souvenir, head for »Sweeney's« on Lincoln Place, where Joyceans come to buy a piece of lemon soap, just as Leopold Bloom did on 16 June 1904.

Monument to Oscar Wilde

An unusual monument in the northwestern corner of the square shows Wilde lounging on a rock. At no. 1, **Oscar Wilde** spent his childhood; he was born, however, in 1854 in nearby 21 Westland Row. Also living here at Merrion Square at one time were politician Daniel O'Connell (no. 58), W B Yeats (no. 82), the Austrian Nobel Prize winner for physics in 1933, Erwin Schrödinger (no. 65), and the writer Joseph Sheridan Le Fanu (no. 70). This part of town still preserves an aura of splendour and tranquility despite the many offices surrounding the square now. Some weekends, performers and street vendors come to the park.

★
National Gallery

Head for Merrion Street to discover the treasures of the National Gallery , which was inaugurated in 1864. The gallery is divided into four main departments: Milltown Wing, Dargan Wing, North Wing and the Millenium Wing for international exhibitions in Clare Street.

Milltown Wing ▶

It is best to start in the Milltown Wing, where works by **Irish artists** are on display; the most famous here is *The Conjuror* by Nathaniel Hone the Elder, believed to show the former president of the Royal Academy, Joshua Reynolds. Many paintings show a romanticized representation of the poor rural population, for instance Augustus Burke's *Connemara Girl*. Irish 20th-century art can be found in Rooms 5 and 6; look out for the landscape paintings by Paul Henry and the portrait of Lady Lavery by her husband John Lavery in particular.

Dargan Wing ▶

Yeats Room in the Dargan Wing is mainly dedicated to the painter Jack B Yeats, brother of the writer W B Yeats. Carry on into the impressive **Shaw Room** with its magnificent Waterford Crystal chandeliers.

In the North Wing, Room 32 is the most interesting, showing the famous portraits of James Joyce (by Jacques Blanche) and Sean O'Casey (by Augustus John). Works by British artists are displayed in Rooms 33–36; for instance, works by **J M W Turner**. On the second floor of the northern wing (Rooms 23 and 24), admire some interesting altar paintings and early Renaissance paintings, amongst them a work by **Fra Angelico**. Rooms 26 to 30 show German, Flemish and Dutch art. Of particular interest is the Spanish collection (Room 31) with works by **El Greco**, Goya, Velázquez and Picasso. Room 24 houses Italian masters such as Titian and Tintoretto; the definite highlight here, however, is **Caravaggio's** *The Taking*

▶ DON'T MISS

■ Caravaggio's *The Taking of Christ* (Room 24)
■ Works by Irish artists in the Milltown Wing
■ Tired? Head for the excellent Fitzer's restaurant

of Christ, which for over 60 years hung unnoticed in a Jesuit building in Leeson Street. (Opening times: Mon–Wed, Fri and Sat 9.30am–5.30pm, Thu 9.30am to 8.30pm, Sun noon–5.30pm.)

On the opposite side of Merrion Square, one of the magnificent Georgian residences has been converted into a museum: no. 29 in **Lower Fitzwilliam Street**. The late 18th-century building has been furnished to look exactly as it did when it was built and the widowed merchant's wife Olivia Beatty moved in here with her three children. (Opening times: Tue–Sat 10am–5, Sun 2–5pm.)

Laid out between 1791 and 1825, **Fitzwilliam Square** is arguably the best-preserved square in the Georgian style; the buildings here draw the eye with their beautifully wrought doors and fan lights.

Burke's »Connemara Girl«

Temple Bar

Stretching between the southern banks of the Liffey and Dame Street, the Temple Bar quarter used to be inhabited by workmen, tradespeople, painters and writers. With its 200-year old houses and cobblestone pavements, it was originally destined to make way for a central bus station. However, it was then decided to redevelop this part of the old town, preserving its historic character. Numerous houses in the narrow alleys (some of them pedestrianized) have already been restored. Many of those now house small shops, studios, pubs, nightclubs and restaurants, the area around Temple Bar turning into a kind of artists' quarter. Head for the Temple Bar Information Centre in Eustache Street to pick up the *Temple Bar Guide* with a good street map or the *In Dublin* brochure; they make finding your way a lot easier. (Opening times: Mon–Fri 9am–6pm, Sat 11am–4pm; June–Aug also Sun noon–4pm.)

◄ Information Centre

To the north of this part of the Old Town, Halfpenny Bridge spans the River Liffey. This elegant metal construction was erected in 1816 and financed through a toll fee – hence the name (its official name is Liffey Bridge). It is one of the oldest cast-iron bridges in the world, and was the only pedestrian bridge across the Liffey until 2000.

Halfpenny Bridge

Dublin Castle and Surroundings

✳ **Dublin Castle**

Behind City Hall rises Dublin Castle. This hill already had a Celtic and later a Danish fortification before King John (1204–1226) had a castle built here, of which, however, hardly anything remains. Most of today's buildings date from the 18th and 19th centuries. From the time of Elizabeth I, to the creation of the Free State in 1921, the castle was the seat of the viceroys and the British administration.

On the eastern short side of Upper Yard is an entrance to Lower Yard. To the right is Record Tower, one of the four old corner towers, well preserved, with walls nearly 5m/17ft thick giving an idea of what the medieval castle looked like. The **Chapel Royal** (Church of the Most Holy Trinity) is a neo-Gothic building (1807–1814); its exterior is remarkable because of its bizarre decoration: over a hundred carved limestone heads of famous Irishmen.

The former State Apartments at Dublin Castle

The State Apartments are shown to visitors during a half-hour guided tour, unless they are being used for a function (access is opposite the entrance from the street, Cork Hill, in Upper Yard). Look out for the colourful Donegal and Killybegs carpets, as well as the Waterford Crystal chandeliers and the green Connemara marble floor at the entrance. A guided tour includes **St Patrick's Hall** with its painted ceiling (1778), the Throne Room, lavishly decorated with gold (1740) and a 200-year-old throne, and the State Drawing Room, furnished with original pieces. After the tour of the State Apartments, visitors are shown the remnants of the medieval castle (entrance at the Powder Tower). (Opening times Mon–Fri 10am– 12.15pm and 2pm–5pm, Sat, Sun 2pm–5pm.)

◄ State Apartments

⏲

The grounds of Dublin Castle also hold the unique collection of the American Chester Beatty . This carefully put together exhibition, which received the European Museum of the Year Award in 2002, enchants visitors with its variety, wealth and delight in colours. The exquisite exhibits include manuscripts, early prints and modern art prints, icons, miniatures from Europe, Africa, the Middle East and Asia – not to mention Egyptian papyrus texts, beautifully decorated editions of the Koran and the Bible, Japanese colour woodcuts and Buddhist images. (Opening times: Mon–Fri 10am–5pm, Sat 11am–5pm, Sun 1pm– 5pm; Oct–April Mon closed.)

★

◄ Chester Beatty Library

⏲

Right in front of the castle, on Lord Edward Street stands the town hall, originally built by Thomas Cooley between 1769 and 1779 as a Royal Exchange, and today serving as the seat of the municipal authorities. The entrance hall of the imposing domed building is decorated with statues of local celebrities. (Opening times: Mon–Sat 10am–5pm, Sun 2–5pm.)

City Hall

⏲

West of Dublin Castle runs Werburgh Street, where Dublin's first theatre used to stand. It is also said that the first church in Dublin was erected on the site of the small St Werburgh's Church. In 1754, the building burned down, apart from the tower and the façade. It was, however, rebuilt only a few years later. The interior, with its Gothic pulpit, is worth seeing.

St Werburgh's Church

> ! **Baedeker** TIP
>
> **The world's best fish & chips**
> In Werburgh Street, Leo Burdock's allegedly serve the best fish & chips (in the world!).

Cathedrals

The oldest part of Dublin lies to the west of Dublin Castle; this is where the Vikings first founded a city. This is also the site of the original Four Courts. Today, modern buildings dominate the district, but Christchurch and St Patrick's, two cathedrals dating from the 12th century, have weathered the times. Both belong to the Church of Ireland.

Around Christchurch Cathedral

Opening times:
April–Sept: daily
10am–5pm

Christchurch Cathedral owes its current aspect to extensive reconstruction between 1871 and 1878. Apart from the crypt running the length of the entire nave, only a portal at the southern transept and possibly parts of the transepts still date from the 13th-century building. However, there is enough left to get an idea of the former glory of this church. The **crypt** holds numerous interesting fragments from various periods, as well as 17th-century statues of Charles II and James II. In the nave, look for an austere-looking tomb showing a reclining knight. It is called »Strongbow's Grave« after the Norman who destroyed the church, only to have it rebuilt in 1172.

The former Synod Hall, connected with Christchurch Cathedral by a bridge, shows the »Dublinia« exhibition, looking at the history of Dublin from the arrival of the Normans in 1170 to the dissolution of the monasteries in 1540, using videos and many exhibits, amongst them a to-scale model of the city, tools and crafts. (Opening times: April–Sept: daily 10am–5pm; Feb and March: Mon–Sat 10am to 4.30pm.)

Christchurch Cathedral – the oldest stone building in Dublin

Close by rises **St Audoen's Church**, the only church in Dublin that has remained unaltered from the Middle Ages. Of the original building, the 13th-century nave, where Mass is still held today, the choir, the southern transept (both roofless) and two chapels are still standing. (Opening times: June–Sept: daily 9.30am–5.30pm.)

St Patrick's Cathedral

Opening times:
Mon–Fri 9am–6pm,
Sat 9am–5pm;
Nov–March also
Sun 10am–4.30pm

Over the centuries, Christchurch Cathedral has played a leading role in Irish history, even though it was St Patrick's Church that was elevated to cathedral status in the 13th century. When it was founded in the 11th century, the church stood on marshy land outside the city walls. In common with Christchurch Cathedral, the aspect of the church today – at a length of 93m/102yd, the largest in Ireland – owes most to all too rigorous rebuilding (1864–1869). The bulky tower on the northwestern corner was erected at the end of the 14th century, its cap dates from 1739. The lofty interior, in sober Early English style, is also impressive.

*The choir stalls of St Patrick's →
with a magnificent lectern in the fore ground*

The cathedral has several tombs and numerous monuments. At the second pillar, to the right of the entrance, the graves of **Jonathan Swift** (1667–1745) and Esther Johnson (1681–1728) are marked by bronze plaques. Of the tombs, the following are worth a closer look: to the right of the baptismal chapel (with an old baptismal font), the Boyle Monument of the Earl of Cork (1631) with several figures, of which the child probably represents Robert Boyle, who went on to become a famous physicist; and on the northern wall, opposite the entrance, a monument for **Turlough O'Carolan,** the last of the Irish Bards (1670–1738, ►Carrick-on-Shannon). The choir, which served as a chapel for the Knights of the Order of St Patrick from 1783 to 1869, features their banners, swords and helmets above the stalls. Take a literary walk in the small park of St Patrick's Cathedral: Irish writers are honoured by twelve commemorative plaques set in the wall.

Marsh's Library
⏲
Opening times:
Mon, Wed–Fri
10am–12.45pm
and 2pm–5pm,
Sat 10.30am–
12.45pm

To the right of St Patrick's, a narrow alleyway swings round to Marsh's Library, the oldest public library in the city, founded by archbishop Marsh and built in 1701 by Sir William Robinson. The library holds 25,000 volumes printed between the 16th and 18th century, maps, many kinds of manuscripts, and some incunabula, i.e. books printed before 1500. The most beautiful and oldest edition in the collection is Cicero's *Letters to Friends* from Milan (1472). During the 1916 Easter Rising the library was shelled. However, its pleasant reading room has remained practically unaltered, including the three »cages«, inside which users wishing to consult valuable books had to work under the watchful eye of the guard.

The Liberties, Guinness Brewery and Kilmainham

The Liberties

West of St Audoen's, Thomas Street turns into James Street, leading into an area known as the Liberties, as French Hugenots fleeing religious persecution settled here – outside the jurisdiction of the city.

Guinness Brewery & Hop Store

Along James Street stretches the large compound of St James's Gate Brewery, better known as Guinness Brewery. This is where around 60% of all beer drunk in Ireland is brewed (► Baedeker Special p.96). The brewery was founded in 1759 by Arthur Guinness. In the 19th century, despite rival beers being imported from England and various economic crises, it became the most important brewery in Ireland. Around 1870, it even became the biggest in the world, with exports rising. In 1936, the brewery founded its first branch abroad in London. Today the company also brews in Nigeria, Ghana, Cameroon and Malaysia. 40% of all beer produced here at the company headquarters is for export. The brewery itself cannot be visited, but the visitor centre (Guinness Hop Store, Crane Street) tells you everything about the art of brewing beer, followed, of course, by a tasting session. (Opening times: daily 9.30am–5pm, July–Aug to 10pm.)

Nearby, the Royal Hospital today houses the Irish Museum of Modern Art. The building, erected between 1680 and 1687 after designs by Sir William Robinson, was intended for invalids and war veterans. No expense or effort was spared during the 1980s restoration of this classical building in the French-Dutch style (the tower dates from 1701). Today, the Great Hall is used for concerts, banquets and conferences. In the chapel, look out for the wooden carvings and the Baroque stucco ceiling. Parts of the building were extended to create exhibition space for the Irish Museum of Modern Art. Since 1991, Irish and international 20th-century art, as well as contemporary art, has been presented in fitting surroundings.

Royal Hospital Kilmainham & Irish Museum of Modern Art
🕐
Opening times:
Tue–Sat
10am–5.30pm,
Sun noon–5.30pm

Follow the Naas Road into town and cross the Grand Canal to reach the district of **Kilmainham**. Situated between Emmet Road and Inchicore Road, Kilmainham Jail, built in 1792, was used until 1924 to incarcerate countless Irish patriots, of whom many were executed. The restored compound today houses a museum which keeps their memory alive. Visitors can see the cells, and numerous exhibits give an insight into the darker aspects of Irish history. (Opening times: May–Sept: daily 10am–6pm; Oct–April: Wed–Fri 1pm to 4pm, Sun 1pm–6pm.)

Kilmainham Jail: from prison to museum

North Dublin: Around O'Connell Street

O'Connell Street, on the northern bank of the Liffey, is one of the most important thoroughfares in Dublin. To get to the famous Abbey Theatre or the elegant Custom House, follow Eden Quay in an easterly direction. The Abbey Theatre on the corner of Marlborough and Lower Abbey Street opened in 1904. The Irish national theatre, whose first directors were W B Yeats and Lady Gregory, quickly became famous internationally, but many of their performances were controversial to say the least: for instance the first nights of J M Synge's *The Playboy of the Western World* (1907) or Sean O'Casey's *The Plough and the Stars* (1926). In 1951, the theatre burnt down, and it took 15 years for the Abbey Theatre to reopen. More experimental drama is staged in the smaller Peacock Theatre.

❓ DID YOU KNOW ...?

■ After a 55-year wait, Dublin has had a tram again since 2004: LUAS, which in Irish means something like »fast«. The Green Line connects St Stephen's Green with the southern suburb of Sandyford (journey time 22 min), the Red Line takes 45 minutes from Connolly Station via O'Connell Street and Abbey Street, past the Four Courts, down to the southern suburb of Tallaght.

Custom House

The former customs building is thought to be the masterpiece of the English architect of Hugenot descent James Gandon (1743–1823), who was very active in Dublin. In 1921, during the War of Independence, the Custom House burnt out completely, but the damage to the exterior was repaired following original designs. The best view of the long frontage, with its Doric portico and 38m/125ft domed tower above, can be had from opposite the building.

Rowan Gillespie's »Famine Memorial«

Some 200m/220yd east of the Custom House, President Mary Robinson, in 1997, unveiled the **Famine Memorial** honouring all those who died or were forced to emigrate during the time of the Great Famine (1845–1849). The memorial represents seven life-size, emaciated figures who seem to be dragging themselves along the Quay in the direction of the harbour. The impressive monument was donated by Norma Smurfit, the well-known divorced wife of a rich Irish entrepreneur.

O'Connell Street

Originally, O'Connell Street was laid out as a wide well-to-do residential street, but it has lost many of its old buildings through the civil wars. Today, the main artery of the city, completely altered in recent years, is a turbulent commercial street with cinemas, restaurants, pubs, snack food joints and amusement arcades. The central reservation boasts statues of Irish patriots, amongst them Daniel O'Connell (near O'Connell Bridge) and Charles Stewart Parnell (both ► Famous People), as well as temperance activist Father Matthew. Following the street, note the imposing building of the General Post Office) on the left-hand side. Opened in 1817, it turned into the nerve centre of the 1916 rebellion led by Patrick Pearse and James Connolly. A monument in the Great Hall (*Death of Cú Chulainn*) preserves the memory of the Irish freedom fighters.

The *Spire* replaced the sculpture of Joyce's Anna Livia, thought to symbolise the Liffey. Sharp Irish tongues gave the river goddess the nickname »the floozy in the jacuzzi«. By the end of 2007, the statue was installed in her new home in the Croppy Memorial Gardens facing Collins Barracks. A life-like bronze statue of James Joyce stands at the corner of O'Connell St / East Street North, near the GPO.

? DID YOU KNOW ...?

■ Rising up in the middle of O'Connell Street is the 120-metre/394-ft *Millenium Spire*. This new Dublin landmark had been intended to be up for the Millenium celebrations but was only completed in January 2003. Weighing 126 tons and costing four million euros, the steel needle measures three metres/3.3yd at its base and 15cm/9.7 inches at its top. *The Spike* or *The Stiletto in the Ghetto*, as some Dubliners jokingly call it, stands on the site of Nelson's Column, blasted by the IRA in 1966, and is illuminated at night.

For fans of Irish pop and rock music, the Hot Press Irish Music Hall of Fame is a must. The entrance fee is somewhat steep, but the audiovisual tour is informative and the exhibits well displayed, showing contemporary music's roots in traditional music. The focus is on singers and bands such as Van Morrison, Gary Moore, U2 and Boyzone. Visitors can admire various memorabilia, for instance the T-shirt worn by Bob Geldof during the Live Aid concert, or Sinéad O'Connor's photo album. (Opening times: daily 10am–5pm.)

★
◄ Hot Press Irish
Music Hall of Fam

West of the GPO, St Henry Street leads to Moore Street, with its market boasting colourful fruit and veg stalls.

◄ Moore Street
Market

East of O'Connell Street, at the corner of Marlborough and Cathedral Street, stands Dublin's most important Catholic church, St Mary's Pro-Cathedral. Inspired by the Theseus temple in Athens, it was consecrated in 1825. Every Sunday at 11am, the well-known Palestina Choir performs here.

◄ St Mary's
Pro-Cathedral

From Parnell Square to Mountjoy Square

At the end of O'Connell Street , in Parnell Street, stands the Rotunda Maternity Hospital, founded as early as 1757 as Ireland's first maternity ward to combat the high rate of infant mortality. To pay for the hospital's construction, Dr Bartholomew Mosse collected funds at balls, song recital evenings and concerts held especially for this purpose. The main building with its columned halls is crowned by a domed tower; an ornate stucco ceiling adorns the chapel. The Rotunda itself houses the Ambassador Cinema. In one part of the building, children are delivered still, and the Gate Theatre has had its home in the Assembly Rooms since 1929.

Rotunda
Maternity
Hospital

Behind the Rotunda lies a park, bordering Parnell Square. In 1966, the Garden of Remembrance was laid out here, with the sculpture *Children of Lir* by Oisin Kelly (1970) dedicated to all who gave their lives for Ireland's freedom.

◄ Garden of
Remembrance

Since 1927, Charlemont House, built on Parnell Square North by the English architect Sir William Chambers in 1762, has been housing the Hugh Lane Municipal Gallery of Modern Art. The gallery, founded in 1908, takes its name from Hugh Lane, an important member of the Irish artists' and literary scene at the beginning of the 20th century. As an art collector, Lane took an early interest in the Impressionists and subsequent art movements. He acquired an outstanding collection, including, amongst others, Camille Corot, Edgar Degas, Juan Gris, Edouard Manet, Claude Monet, Pablo Picasso, Camille Pissaro and Auguste Renoir. When Lane died, he had just loaned his collection to the Tate Gallery in London; in his will, however, he had bequeathed it to the city of Dublin. Following a lengthy legal battle, the collection was split, with the two halves now rotating every five years between the two museums. In 1998 Francis Bacon's studio, left as it was at the artist's death, was installed in the gallery.

Municipal
Gallery of
Modern Art
◷
Opening times:
Tues–Thu
9.30am–6pm, Fri/
Sat 9.30am–5pm,
Sun 11am–5pm

Celebrating literature in style – the Writers' Museum is housed in two 18th century villas.

Dublin Writers' Museum

Opening times:
Mon– Sat
10am–5pm, Sun
11am–5pm

Next to the art gallery, the Dublin Writers' Museum) occupies two 18th-century houses. Whilst no. 18 honours the great Irish writers such as Jonathan Swift, Oscar Wilde, W B Yeats, Bernhard Shaw and James Joyce, as well as their work, with displays of manuscripts, first editions, letters, photos and the tools of their literary trade, no. 19 serves as a meeting point and showcase for contemporary writers and their new work. Attend a reading, raid the bookshop or have a snack at the museum café to complete the visit.

Mountjoy Square

East of Parnell Square, Denmark Street leads to Mountjoy Square. Legend has it that in 1014, at the Battle of Clontarf, Brian Boru pitched his tent here. As a child, James Joyce lived nearby, in 14 Fitzgibbon St, attending Belvedere College (Great Denmark Street), which he went on to describe in *A Portrait of the Artist as a Young Man*. Sean O'Casey sets the action of *The Shadow of a Gunman* on Mountjoy Square, calling it »Hilljoy Square« in the piece; and Brandan Behan grew up nearby (14 Russell St).

Croke Park GAA Museum

Some 2km/1.2 miles east of Mountjoy Square, past the Royal Canal, stands Ireland's most important sports stadium. Croke Park is supposed to host Gaelic sports (hurling, Gaelic football) only, but in recent years it has increasingly been used as a venue for pop and rock concerts. Here, the political situation in Ireland is never far away – read up on it at the on-site museum. (Opening times: May–Sept: daily 9.30am–5pm; Oct–April: Tue–Sat 10am–5pm, Sun noon–5pm.)

King's Inns, St Michan's & the Four Courts

Upper Dorset Street (the main arterial road towards the airport) and Bolton Street lead to Henrietta Street, a somewhat neglected dead-end, at the end of which rises the King's Inns on Constitution Hill (designed in 1795 by James Gandon; the two wings on the western façade are later additions). The King's Inns is the headquarters of the supreme Irish jurists' association. During the day, take a stroll through the inner courtyard to Inns Garden, from where there is a very good view of the building. On its western side, take the exit to Constitution Hill, from which St Patrick is said to have looked down on the city.

King's Inns

From Constitution Hill , Church Street leads to St Michan's Church, the oldest building north of the Liffey. After several restorations, not much is left of the original church, built as early as 1095: only the tower and some fragments. The church owes its grisly fame to the fact that some mummified bodies are on display in the crypt – due to the tannic acid in the air the corpses do not decompose. The crypt also holds the death mask of Wolfe Tone, one of the leaders of the United Irishmen, as well as the remains of two of his companions. Another extraordinary feature is the carving on the gallery, representing seventeen musical instruments and made from one piece.

St Michan's Church
🕐
Opening times: Mon–Fri 10am–12.45pm and 2–4.45pm, Sa 10am–12.45pm

Near the banks of the Liffey, on Inns Quay, the Four Courts, seat of the Irish supreme court, are architect James Gandon's masterpiece. Gandon built the courts between 1786 and 1802, using an older

★
Four Courts

Ireland's supreme court of law: the Four Courts

building (1776–1784, by Thomas Cooley). Suffering heavy shelling during the 1922 civil war, by 1931 the building had been restored with few alterations. The river front, 139m/152yd long, with a Corinthian portico, is dwarfed by a domed round structure. In the past, the central hall below gave access to the original four courtrooms giving the building its name: Exchequer (financial matters), Common Pleas (private actions), King's Bench (penal law) and Chancery. The judges still wear black robes and white wigs today.

Around Smithfield

Head west from the Four Courts to reach cobblestoned Smithfield, an area famous for its horse fairs, held here for the past 300 years, which still take place on every first Sunday of the month. The recently revitalized Smithfield Village, which includes the large Chief O'Neill's Hotel, the Old Jameson's Distillery, the Ceol Irish Traditional Music Centre, and the Jameson Chimney Observation Tower, projects a very contemporary image.

Ceol Irish Traditional Music Centre In the Ceol Irish Traditional Music Centre learn everything about traditional Irish music, beginning with instruments such as the Uilleann Pipes (the bagpipes exclusively found in Ireland), all the way

Blacksmith at the Smithfield Horse Fair

to dance and its traditions. In the Children's Room, children and whoever feels young enough is encouraged to follow dance steps listening to a tune. The cinema shows an interesting film, and the Ceol shop sells books, videos, DVDs and CDs. (Opening times: Mon–Sat 9.30am–6pm, Sun 10.30am–6pm.)

Old Jameson's Distillery

In 1966, the Jameson Distillery closed its doors, merged with other whiskey producers under the name »Irish Distillers« and has been blending ever since in huge ultra-modern facilities in Midleton (County Cork). In the warehouse of the former distillery, the »Whiskey Corner« has been set up: a film tells the 1000-year story of the Irish »water of life« which may be sampled afterwards. (Opening times: May–Oct daily 10am–5.30pm).

Jameson Chimney Observation Tower

Enjoy sweeping views over Dublin from the top of the 150m/492-ft chimney of the former distillery, directly in front of the Chief O'Neill's Hotel. Buy your tickets for the Jameson Chimney Observation Tower at reception or at the entrance to the Ceol shop. (Opening times: Mon–Sat 9.30am–6pm, Sun 10.30am–6pm.)

Collins Barracks

A few streets further west, the extensive 18th-century barracks compound of Collins Barracks is today **part of the National Museum**. Its collection includes furniture, glass ware, silver, ceramics and weapons. In the Curator's Choice Room, curators from across Ireland show the 25 most extraordinary and strange objects from their collections. (Opening times: Tues–Sat 10am–5pm, Sun 2–5pm.)

Ballsbridge

Royal Dublin Society

In the southeast of the city, seperated by the River Dodder, lies the Ballsbridge district of Dublin. To the right, the Royal Dublin Society Showgrounds occupy a large compound on Merrion Road. Well-kept lawns, low white fences, and pretty buildings form the background to the Horse Show, organized annually by the Royal Dublin Society in August. This huge horse fair is said to be the largest for Irish thoroughbreds, attracting many overseas buyers. Races, tournaments, trials, award ceremonies and auctions add to the fun. This is also an important social event, with the big hotels organizing various balls. The Spring Show in early May is dedicated to livestock, agricultural produce and machinery.

◄ Dublin Horse Show

Northern Suburbs

★ Phoenix Park

From Collins Barracks, Parkgate Street leads west to 808ha/1,997-acre Phoenix Park. This public park also contains the residence of the President of Ireland, formerly for the Viceroy (1751–1754, by Nathaniel Clements) and the Apostolic Nunciature. To the left of Main Road stands the 60m/197ft obelisk of the *Wellington Monument*

Greater Dublin Plan

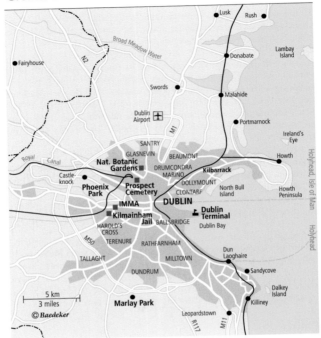

(1817, by Sir Robert Smirke), an eye-catcher for visitors coming from the city centre; then follow sports fields, the residence of the US ambassador and, over to the west, the Ordnance Survey. At the northern end lies the Phoenix Park Race Course, and to the right of Main Road, the People's Garden and the Zoological Gardens noted for their successful lion breeding programme. (Opening times: Mon–Sat 9.30am–6pm, Sun 11am–6pm.)

Prospect Cemetery   Leave Phoenix Park through Cabra Gate or Ashtown Gate and take the Navan Road and Cabra Road, then a left via Phibsborough Road to the Glasnevin or Prospect Cemetery, where David O'Connell, Charles Stewart Parnell and Sir Roger Casement (all ►Famous People) lie buried alongside many other Irish freedom fighters.

Botanic Gardens   To the northeast, the 20ha/49-acre Botanic Gardens are well worth a visit. The cast-iron Palm House was erected in 1842–1850 by Richard Turner. (Opening times summer: Mon–Sat 9am–6pm, Sun 11am–6pm; winter: Mon–Sat 10am–4.30pm, Sun 11am–4.30pm.)

Some 5km/3.1 miles out of the city centre, in the suburb of Marino, lies Casino Marino (1765–1771, by William Chambers), a summer house for the Earl of Charlemont. The magnificently furnished rooms are only open to visitors as part of a guided tour. (Opening times: June–Sept: daily 10am–6pm; May, Oct: daily 10am–5pm; Nov–March: Sun, Thu noon–4pm; April: Sun, Thu noon–5pm.)

Casino Marino

🕓

Clontarf Road follows the northern bank of the harbour towards Howth, stretching up the picturesque slopes of rocky (quartzite and shale) foothills. The old part of town lies to the northwest of the peninsula, around the big fisheries' harbour and marina. From here, take a trip to **Ireland's Eye**, an island 2km/1.2 miles offshore (worth seeing are a small church and a Martello tower). Rising above Howth Harbour, the ruin of the Collegiate church **St Mary's Church** (National Monument, 14th/15th century) has two naves of different lengths; in the southern nave, look for the fine tomb (approx. 1470) of the Lawrence family.

★
Howth

The picturesque harbour town of Howth is famous for its good fish restaurants

To the west stands **Howth Castle**, a crenellated building dating from the 15th century, which has an uneven aspect due to several restorations. Only the park of the castle is accessible, featuring an 18th-century French garden, bordered by 9m/29-ft hornbeam hedges and glorious rhododendrons. Also in the grounds is the **National Transport Museum**, with historic transport on display (tractors, double-decker buses, trams, etc.).

Ben of Howth ▶ The highest point, best reached from the part of town called The Summit to the east of the peninsula, is the Ben of Howth (173m/567 ft), on top of which lies a burial mound, with a beautiful 360° view.

! **Baedeker** TIP

Along the cliffs
On the eastern and southern side of the peninsula, a scenic Cliff Walk runs along the cliffs. Take a detour to Baily Lighthouse, dating from 1814, at the southeasterly tip, and past the chapel of St Fintan's, which probably dates back to the 9th century.

North of Dublin

On the outskirts of Dublin, the N1 leads through **Santry**. In St Papan's Church (1709), look for a 14th-century baptismal font, a retable from 1709, and a pulpit.

Drive on another 6km/3.5 miles to reach **Swords**. Surrounded by walls on five sides, Swords Castle (13th–15th century) was the seat of the archbishops of Dublin. A chapel, the gate lodge and towers are still preserved; also a 22.5m/74ft round tower (the entrance and roof are modern), as well as the 14th-century church tower of an old monastery.

Newbridge House Drive north on the N1; after 3km/2 miles, a right-hand turn (R126) leads to Donabate. Here, a museum opened in Newbridge House in 1992, shows rural life in 18th-century Ireland. Visitors can see Newbridge House, as well as various workshops, workers' quarters, and a farm with animals and tools used in the 18th century. (Opening times: Tue–Fri 11am–5pm, Sat 11am–6pm, Sun 2pm–6pm).

Lambay Island Heading back back onto the N1, the R127 branches off towards Lusk. To the east, on the coast, the village of **Rush** is famous for its flower bulbs. From Rush Pier there are boats to Lambay Island. In the 8th century, the island saw one of the first Viking raids in the country. The defensive installations you see date from the time around 1550. Today, the rocky (porphyry) island, 130m/426ft in elevation, is a bird reserve and may only be visited with permission from the owner, Lord Revelstoke.

Ardgillan Demesne North of Skerries, the Ardgillan estate lies on the road to Balbriggan (R127). The manor house, surrounded by a large park, has been restored and may be visited. (Opening times park: daily 10am–dusk; manor house April–Oct Tues–Sun 2.30pm–5.30pm; Nov–March Sun only)

Balbriggan itself, on the River Delvin, is a quiet holiday resort with nice sandy beaches and a nine-hole golf links.

Balbriggan

Northeast of Dublin

From the northeastern suburbs or from Howth, via the R106, head for the 3km/12-mile Velvet Strand at Portmarnock. This small holiday resort has a championship golf course.

Portmarnock

Some 2km/1.2 miles west of town stands the 13th-century St Doulagh's Church, with its original stone roof, a chapel and a crenellated 15th-century tower. Attic rooms in the tower, above the chapel and in the crypt point to a hermit's church. Some 100m/110yd northeast of the church, in a field, look for a well covered by an octagonal cover with stone roof.

✴
**St Doulagh's
Church**

Some 10km/6 miles north of Dublin lies the small popular seaside resort of Malahide. On the southwestern edge of town, surrounded by beautiful gardens, stands Malahide Castle. The building features medieval, Georgian and modern elements. Inside, the remarkable

Malahide

✴
◄ Malahide Castle

Malahide Castle

Great Hall with its oak-wood fittings is the only one in Ireland to have preserved its medieval aspect and to have served its original purpose up to 1975. Today, the castle houses the National Portrait Gallery, which forms part of the National Gallery in Dublin. The portraits in this collection are worth seeing, either because of who painted them (William Hogarth, Sir Joshua Reynolds, amongst others) or because of who sat for them (Anne Boleyn, Robert Dudley, James Gandon, Jonathan Swift, Daniel O'Connell, amongst others). (Opening times June–Oct Mon–Fri 10am–5pm, Sat 11am–6pm, Sun 2–6pm; Nov–May Sat, Sun 2–5pm.)

Fry Model Railway ▶
Another attraction in the park of Malahide Castle is the Fry Model Railway. It took Irishman Cyril Fry decades of work to create a model railway to a scale of 1:43, which is unrivalled in its originality and detail. (Opening times: April–Oct Mon–Thu 10am–5pm, Sat 11am–6pm, Sun 2pm–6pm.)

Skerries
From Lusk, the R127 leads past the ruins of a 15th-century church and castle in Baldongan, to Skerries (good sandy beach and golf links). There are three small islands just off the shore: St Patrick's Island, with the ruins of an old church, and Colt Island, also Shenick's Island, with a Martello Tower, which at low tide may be reached on foot.

West of Dublin

Clondalkin
Take the R113; 4km/2.5 miles northwest of Tallaght, look for Clondalkin, founded by St Mochuas in the 7th century. Today, only a 25.5m/84-ft round tower is left; there are also two granite crosses and a baptismal font in the Church of Ireland graveyard opposite.

Lucan
Up the River Liffey, the N4 leads via the suburb of Chapelizod to Lucan, once a popular spa resort, adjoining on its western side the extensive estate of Lucan House (1776); the interior has fine decorations by James Wyatt, Michael Stapleton and Angelika Kauffmann.

Finglas
On the N2 leading northwest, still on the outskirts of Dublin, Finglas has the ruins of a medieval church, with a 12th-century High Cross in the churchyard. 3km/2 miles to the west, slightly elevated, lies Dunsink Observatory, which between 1782 and 1921 was the observatory of Trinity College.

★ Dunsoghly Castle
Approx. 5km/3 miles north of Finglas, to the right of the N2, stands a castle that has preserved its original oak-wood roof – very rare in Ireland: 15th-century Dunsoghly Castle, a square tower with small rectangular corner turrets. There is a magnificent view from the connecting galleries. The roof structure was to serve as the model for the reconstruction of Bunratty Castle (▶Ennis). South of the Castle lie the remains of a small chapel (1573).

Dundalk (Dún Dealgan)

B 5

Republic of Ireland, province: Leinster
Population: 26,000

County: Louth

Half-way between Dublin and Belfast, Dundalk is a nice, lively but modest town, 35km/22 miles north of Drogheda, near the border with Northern Ireland.

Dundalk has little of interest to offer the visitor but appears a busy and prosperous town thanks to various industries establishing themselves here. As early as the 10th century, Dundalk saw fights at sea between the Irish and Vikings. The town was fortified in 1185, but burnt down in 1253 and 1315. After that, the town was for 300 years the corner stone of the »English Pale«, as the eastern part of Ireland under English jurisdiction was called, and as such heavily fought over. In 1690 King William III of Orange conquered Dundalk. The fortification was razed in 1724.

Industrial town on the east coast

In the centre of town, on Crowe Street, lie the pretty Court House and the Town Hall (both dating from the 19th century). In Seatown Place stands a mighty seven-storey old wind mill, and on the main road going north rises the 18th-century Catholic church of St Nicholas (the tower itself is older). St Patrick's Cathedral was built in 1848, taking King's College Chapel in Cambridge, England, as its model. The County Museum, housed in the former warehouse of a tobacco factory, is worth a visit; the exhibition telling the history of the local tobacco industry is particularly interesting.

Sights in Dundalk

! *Baedeker* TIP

Pub culture
Don't miss a visit to the art-nouveau Century pub!

Around Dundalk

From Dundalk, the border crossing to Northern Ireland is only 13km/8 miles away. There are no longer guards, and the high-tech surveillance facilities are being dismantled. Changing money is no problem north of the border. Getting to Derry (Londonderry) is easiest on the N53 going west; for Belfast stay on the N1. Walkers, bikers or drivers wanting to go directly to the Mourne Mountains can take a ferry that runs (June–Sept) from Omeath to Warrenpoint (Co. Down).

To Northern Ireland

Towards the Cooley Peninsula

Faughart ►

Northeast of town, the pleasant hilly Cooley Peninsula stretches between Dundalk Bay and Carlingford Lough. Follow the N1 to Faughart (Foichard), the birthplace of St Brigid. The second patron saint of Ireland (alongside St Patrick) is commemorated here with a grotto and a church (St Brigid's Shrine). There is a nice view from the hill with the Old Graveyard; Irish King Edward Bruce (died 1318) lies buried at its western end. The fabled hero Cu Chulainn is said to have been born nearby.

Proleek Dolmen

Continue on the N1. At Ballymascanlon, in the grounds of the Ballymascanlon Hotel, look for the Proleek Dolmen. Its capstone, weighing some 40 tons, rests on only three legs. Legend has it that if you manage to throw a pebble onto the top of the capstone so that it stays there, a wish will be granted.

Carlingford

On the northeastern side of the peninsula lies the small old town of Carlingford (pop. 650), dominated by the bulky 13th-century King John's Castle, occupying a commanding position on a rock above the harbour. Nearby stands a former fortification tower (Tholsel) which served as meeting place for the elders of the town. Just off the Square in the centre of town, a narrow street brings you to The Mint, a former mint in a fortified town tower house. Taffee's Castle, opposite the railway station, is a large rectangular tower house with a pretty spiral staircase. To the west of town, Carlingford Forest is a good place for a stroll; the viewpoint there offers splendid panoramic views of Carlingford and the coast.

▶ DUNDALK

INFORMATION

Jocelyn Street
Tel. (042) 9 33 54 84
Fax (042) 9 33 80 70

The southern coast

South of Dundalk, the small holiday resort of Blackrock has an 18-hole golf links, tennis courts and opportunities for watersports. Anglers will find plenty of salmon and trout in the River Fane. Another 5km/3 miles south (near the N1), the churchyard of Dromiskin has a round tower and a High Cross, and there are several well-preserved castles in the area. Some 2km/1.2 miles south of Dromiskin, in Castlebellingham, Bellingham Castle, today a hotel, is located in picturesque scenery.

Castlebellingham ►

Ardee

Southwest of Dundalk, the town of Ardee (pop. 3450) boasts two town castles: Hatch's Castle and turreted Ardee Castle, which houses a small museum. St Mary's (Church of Ireland) was built using parts of an older church, featuring a nicely sculpted baptismal font. Around 3km/2 miles southeast, look out for the remains of the Jumping Church of Kildemock. The locals claim that the church

Jumping Church of Kildemock ►

walls moved in 1715 to exclude the grave of an excommunicated member of the parish.

The town of Louth, north of Ardee, used to be so significant that it gave its name to the county. St Mochta's House is a 12th-century two-storey oratory with a vault and stone roof.

Louth

To the east, on the N53, almost within the town limits of Dundalk still, an earth mound rises over 18m/60ft high. This is said to be the birthplace of the fabled hero Cu Chulainn. Today, there is a nice view from the ruins on top.
Nearby Castletown Castle, a four-storey building with flanking towers, dates from the 15th century.

Castletown Castle

The ruins of 13th-century Castle Castleroche stand some 7km/4.5 miles northwest of Dundalk. This triangular building with bastions appears particularly impressive seen from the plains.

Castleroche

King John »Lackland« is said to have drafted the first pages of the Magna Carta, the first English »constitution«, at Carlingford Castle.

Dungarvan (Dún Garbhán)

D 4

Republic of Ireland, province: Munster
Population: 7,200

County: Waterford

Dungarvan is a lively coastal town in the centre of the south coast of Ireland. Situated around 40km/25 miles southwest of Waterford, Dungarvan is framed by the Comeragh and Knockmealdon Mountains.

Ideal base
The town offers visitors fine sandy beaches as well as a range of accommodation options and makes an excellent base for day trips.

The parts of town on either side of the Colligan River are connected by a bridge erected in 1815, spanning the water with a 22.5m/74ft arch. On the right-hand river bank stand the ruins of King John's Castle (1185), and the top floor of the nearby 17th-century Old Market House now houses a small municipal museum.

▶ DUNGARVAN

INFORMATION
Town Centre, The Square
Tel. (058) 4 17 41

Look out for a bizarre structure in the churchyard of St Mary's: the Old Gable Wall, with round openings, the purpose of which is still a matter of speculation.

The Augustinian abbey on the left-hand river bank was established around 1290; its tower, however, was only added in the 15th century. East of Dungarvan, **Clonea** is a popular small resort with a fine sandy beach and a golf links.

Cunnigar Peninsula
Pleasant beaches can also be found to the south of Dungarvan town, on the Cunnigar Peninsula, accessible by ferry. Take a hike via the Ring Gaeltacht (An Rinn), famous for its Irish language school, and the old-fashioned fishing village of Ballynagaul, to the foothills of Helvick Head (R674). The walk offers many delightful views of Dungarvan Harbour and the mountains to the north. The area to the south of Dungarvan Harbour, between the N25 and the sea, is the only area on the east coast where Irish is still the majority language.

Some 15km/9.5 miles north of Dungarvan (R672), at **Touraneena Heritage Centre**, a farmhouse furnished in the style of the late 19th century may be visited, as well as a smithy.

? DID YOU KNOW ...?

■ Heading west from Dungarvan, the N72 leads past a monument to a feted greyhound. Master McGrath won the prestigious Waterloo Cup three years on the trot, and in 37 races was only beaten once.

Dun Laoghaire

C 5

Republic of Ireland, province: Leinster
Population: 55,000

County: Dublin

At the beginning of the last century, Dun Laoghaire was still a small fishing village. Today, the town is a pretty suburb of Dublin, appreciated by the capital's wealthy inhabitants as a pleasant place to live.

Dun Laoghaire (pronounced »Dun Leery«), after a visit of King George IV temporarily named »Kingstown«, had to wait until 1921 to get its old name back. This is the most important passenger port and marina in Dublin Bay. Whilst the town's fashionable residential quarters stretch east into the hills, commercial life takes place in the streets near the harbour.

Most important harbour of Dublin Bay

At the time of its establishment (1817–1821), the large harbour was a major feat of engineering. The eastern pier is popular for a stroll, whilst anglers congregate on the quieter western pier.

Harbour

The National Maritime Museum was set up in a former seamen's church. An extensive collection of model ships, paintings, photographs, documents and much more highlights Ireland's seafaring traditions. (Opening times: May–Sept Tues–Sun 1–5pm.)

National Maritime Museum ⏲

Two sculptures catch the eye: directly on the shore, an obelisk rising out of four stone balls was erected in honour of King George IV; one of the balls has since been damaged by an IRA bomb. On the other side of Queen's Road, the *Christ the King* sculpture, erected in 1926, serves as a monument for the soldiers fallen in the First World War. The Dominican monastery in Lower George's Street is worth a look, not least for the Celtic symbols in the oratory.

Sculptures and symbols

❓ DID YOU KNOW …?

■ At the foot of Joyce's Tower lies the Forty Foot Pool, where mostly elderly men take to the water in all weathers. This custom goes back to the end of the first chapter of *Ulysses*, where Buck Mulligan sets out to have his morning swim here. Today, women are also allowed to use the Forty Foot Pool. Everybody has to keep their clothes on though – skinny dipping is prohibited!

▶ VISITING DUN LAOGHAIRE

INFORMATION

Ferry Terminal Building
Tel. (01) 6 02 40 00

WHERE TO STAY

▶ **Mid-range**

Royal Marine Hotel
Marine Road
Tel. (01) 2 80 19 11
Fax (01) 2 80 10 89
www.ryan-hotels.com
Set in a magnificent park, this comfortable hotel (104 rooms) has views of Dublin Bay and the picturesque harbour of Dun Laoghaire.

▶ **Budget**

Kingston Hotel
Adelaide St (off Georges St)
Tel. (01) 2 80 18 10, fax (01) 280 12 37
The 30 rooms of the Kingston Hotel offer sweeping views over Dublin Bay.

WHERE TO EAT

▶ **Moderate**

Brasserie na Mara
Dun Laoghaire Harbour
Tel. (01) 2 80 67 87
This good restaurant in the former railway station specializes in seafood.

Joyce's Tower

From the harbour, a minor road runs along the swimming beach in the direction of Joyce's Tower. This rocky outcrop offers a sweeping view of Dublin Bay. Martello towers such as these were built to guard against a potential invasion by Napoleonic troops. James Joyce, who in 1904 lived in the tower for a while, describes it in his novel *Ulysses*. Today, Joyce's Tower holds a library with original manuscripts and rare editions of his works, as well as some of the writer's personal belongings. (Opening times: April–Oct Mon–Sat 10am–1pm and 2–5pm, Sun 2–6pm; in winter contact the Tourist Office.)

Around Dun Laoghaire

Dalkey

To the south, merging with Dun Laoghaire, lies the little town of Dalkey, today one of the most popular (and expensive) residential areas around Dublin. In the main street, two fortified houses of the medieval fortification still survive: 16th-century Archbold's Castle and what is today the town hall.

! *Baedeker* TIP

Climbing

The old granite quarries are well suited for rock climbing!

On **Dalkey Island**, close to the coast, look out for the remains of an old church and a Martello tower. The short crossing by boat from the tiny Coliemore harbour takes only five minutes. Sorrento Terrace and Sorrento Park, on the town's southern beach, offer attractive views.

South from Sorrento Point stretches Killiney Bay, with a beach and resort of the same name. The garden villas on the slopes exude a distinct Mediterranean flair. Beyond the railway line, which here follows the shore, lies a rocky beach, whilst Killiney Hill Park is a good place for a stroll.

◄ Killiney

To the west of town, near the R117, occupying a most impressive position atop a hill near Kilternan, stands the 4,000-year-old Kilternan Dolmen, with its 1.80m/6ft-thick capstone resting on ten orthostats.

◄ Kilternan Dolmen

The privately-owned lie to the north of Kilternan on the R117. The gardens have wonderful old trees, and the rockery and water garden are worth seeing. (Opening times: March–Nov Tue, Sat and bank holidays 11am–5pm, Sat 2–6pm.)

◄ Fernhill Gardens

⌚

Ennis (Inis)

D 3

Republic of Ireland, province: Munster
Population: 18,000

County: Clare

Ennis, the administrative centre of County Clare, is an important hub in the west of Ireland. Railway lines as well as main roads meet here, and international Shannon Airport is also only 25km/16 miles away.

The surrounding area and local small-scale industries make Ennis a lively market town and commercial centre, which has preserved an olde-worlde appearance thanks to its narrow and winding streets. The River Fergus winds its way through the town in wide sweeps.

✱
Important hub

Standing at the end of Abbey Street, the Franciscan Ennis Friary, was founded in 1241. The church, which dates from the time of the friary's founding, was continually extended in subsequent centuries. It features particularly fine statues, amongst them a representation of St Francis with the Stigmata (on the southwestern side of the tower), the McMahon tomb (around 1475, on the southern wall), a royal tomb showing on several panels the Passion of Christ, and a small representation of the Flagellation, complete with a cockerel in the cooking pot (for an explanation of the legend, see ► Kilkenny, St Canice's Cathedral). In the 14th century, 375 monks and 600 students lived and studied in the monastery, which continued to be inhabited by Franciscan monks until the early 17th century. (Opening times: end of May–Sept daily 9.30am–6.30pm.)

✱
Ennis Friary

⌚

Nearby, in Harmony Row, the De Valera Museum and Library holds documents on Ennis and the region and the history of Ireland, as well as the fountain pen used in 1938 by Eamon de Valera (►Famous

De Valera Museum and Library

▶ VISITING ENNIS

INFORMATION
Arthur's Row
Tel. (065) 6 82 83 66

WHERE TO STAY

► **Mid-range**
Old Ground
O'Connell Street
Tel. (065) 6 82 81 27
This ivy-clad hotel combines tradition
with modern amenities.

► **Budget**
Fountain Court
Northwest
Tel. (065) 6 82 98 45
Fax (065) 6 84 50 30
Kyran@fountain-court.com
By car, it is only a 4-minute drive
from Ennis to Fountain Court – still,
this hotel is located in quiet rural
surroundings. The guesthouse, situ-
ated on a hill, is very well appointed
and has various leisure facilities.

PUBS

Cruise's
Abbey Street
Tel. (065) 4 18 00
Turf fire and live music
every evening.

People) and Neville Chamberlain to sign the treaty ordering the return of the occupied Irish ports by the British. (Opening times: Mon,
Wed and Thu 10am–5.30pm, Tue and Fri 10am–8pm, Sat 10am–
2pm.)

Around Ennis

Quin Abbey

10km/6 miles southeast of Ennis, on the R469 near Quin, impressive
Quin Abbey consists of the well-preserved ruins of a Franciscan friary, erected in 1402 on the foundations of a castle that burned down
in 1286. Its bastions are still visible today. The tombs in the church
date from the 15th to 19th centuries. The cloister is also well preserved. On the other side of the small river stands the 13th-century
St Finghin's Church.

**Knappogue
Castle**

Follow the R469 to reach, after 4km/2.5 miles, Knappogue Castle.
The tower house, originally built in 1467 by the MacNamara clan
and in their possession, with a brief interruption in Cromwell's time,
until 1800, has been restored preserving its original style and, aided
by antique furniture, exudes a medieval flair. In the summer, »Medieval Banquets« (► Practicalities) are held in an annex. (Opening
times: May–Oct daily 9.30am–5pm.)

After another 2km/1.2 miles, a little road branches off to the left, leading to the Craggaunowen Project . The art collector John Hunt purchased the grounds in the mid-1960s and restored the 16th-century Craggaunowen Castle. The castle holds a small collection of medieval religious art from the Hunt Collection (► Limerick: National Institute for Higher Education). The gatekeeper's lodge to the left of the castle entrance has been converted into a chapel. Look out for the 15th-century bronze cross. Hunt has created an interesting open-air museum, reconstructing the daily life of Bronze Age man, with a Crannóg (Bronze Age lake dwelling) and a stone ring fort, both with huts and tools from that period. The leather boat used by young explorers to retrace the medieval voyage of St Brendan (►Famous People) under 6th-century conditions is on display in a glass house. (Opening times: mid-March–Oct daily 10am–6pm.)

Craggaunowen Project

Reconstruction of the »curragh« leather boat used by St Brendan

The R462 leads south to Sixmilebridge, a pretty village with the »Georgian dollhouse« Mount Ievers House (1736). A byroad leads southwest from here to the village of Bunratty.

Sixmilebridge

This is one of the main tourist attractions in Ireland: Bunratty Castle and Folk Park. Following a chequered history of destruction and reconstruction, the castle, erected in the 15th century, was purchased by Lord Gort in 1954 and beautifully restored. Today, Bunratty Castle and its grounds are managed as a charitable foundation. The entrance hall and banqueting hall, as well as the chapel and living quarters are furnished with exquisite furniture from the late Middle Ages and Early Renaissance. Visitors can attend medieval banquets (► Practicalities) and there is a shop on the lower floor.
Stretching behind the castle, Bunratty Folk Park has an interesting open-air museum. Numerous little houses, workshops and shops, as well as a complete village street, show life as it would have been in late 19th-century Ireland. (Opening times: daily 9.30am–4.30pm, park June–Aug accessible to 6.30pm.)

Bunratty Castle and Folk Park

A few kilometres/miles east of Bunratty, Cratloe Woods House, in the village of Cratloe, is a 17th-century manor. It is an example of a traditional long house, but was considerably extended in the 19th century. (Opening times: June–mid-Sept Mon–Sat 2–6pm.)

Cratloe

Ballycasey Workshops ⏲ In the Ballycasey Workshops on the access road to Shannon Airport, visitors are welcome to watch craftspeople at work and purchase their leatherware, jewellery, woollens, ceramics and much more. (Opening times: Mon–Fri 10am–6pm.)

Shannon International Airport Situated so close to Shannon International Airport, Bunratty is often overrun with tourists. Since this airport became redundant as a refuelling stop for US flights, various industries have been established here. Bunratty itself has 7,000 inhabitants.

Newmarket on Fergus From Shannon Airport, the N18 leads north back to Ennis, passing Newmarket on Fergus, a small market town and commercial centre. A bit further north, Dromoland Castle (around 1830), today a luxury hotel with golf course, lies resplendent in extensive parklands. The fine gardens are open to everybody. Carrying on in the direction of Ennis, the village of Clarecastle shares a name with a destroyed castle of the same name in the River Fergus.

Bunratty Castle houses many a popular medieval banquet.

Take the N85 northwest from Ennis, and the R476 at Fountain Cross, reaching after some 6km/3.6 miles the grounds of Dysert O'Dea. The castle, built in 1480, has been restored at great expense and houses an archaeological museum.

★
Dysert O'Dea

From the castle, a 6km/3.5-mile History Trail leads to 25 archaeological sites, all within a radius of 3km/2 miles. The church of the monastery took on its current aspect towards the end of the 17th century, following the model of the original 12th/13th-century building. The Romanesque archway, with fine geometric patterns, foliage and almost Far Eastern human masks is worth seeing. Near the northwestern corner of the church, the 12m/40ft stump of a round tower is still visible; to the east, look for a High Cross in a meadow. Unusual is the fully clothed figure of Christ on the Cross, on the east face. The other sides are divided into panels with geometrical designs, human figures and animal interlacing. (Opening times: museum: May– Sept daily 10am–6pm.)

Enniscorthy (Inis Coirthaidh)

D 5

Republic of Ireland, province: Leinster
Population: 3,800

County: Wexford

Tranquil Enniscorthy is a small hilly town in the southeast corner of Ireland. The town developed around a Norman castle, which is also its main attraction.

The town lies on the western bank of the River Slaney, rising steeply on both sides, on the main Dublin–Wexford road. The river, navigable up to here, sees much boat traffic with Wexford, some 25km/16 miles further south.

Town on the river

In 1798, one of the bloodiest battles against English rule was fought to the east of Enniscorthy.

A market and commercial hub has developed around **Enniscorthy Castle**. Cromwell conquered the castle in 1649, and the rebels who controlled the town in 1798 used it as a prison. Today, the **Wexford County Museum** shows finds from the Stone Age to the present day, as well as information on the local crafts. (Opening times: June–Sept Mon–Sat 10am–1pm and 2–6pm, Sun 2–5.30pm; Oct–Nov and Feb– May daily 2–5.30pm.)

▶ ENNISCORTHY

INFORMATION
Castle Hill
Tel. (054) 3 46 99
open: mid-June–mid Aug

United Irishmen

The award-winning National 1798 Visitor Centre documents the battle of the United Irishmen against the British on 21 June 1798 on Vinegar Hill. A multimedia presentation takes the visitor back through time, placing the event in the context of today's democracy, explaining weapons and flags, describing the course of battles and introducing the leaders. Songs and ballads recall the uprising, and the many courageous women who took part in the battle are not forgotten either. (Opening times: Mon–Sat 9.30am–6pm, Sun 11am–6pm.)

Ceramics has a long tradition in and around Enniscorthy. Hillview Pottery, Charley's Bridge Pottery (founded in 1654) and Badger's Hill Pottery offer a warm welcome even if you just want to browse. All three potteries lie on the road leading to New Ross. There is another one, Kiltrea Bridge Pottery, to the northwest of the town centre.

Around Enniscorthy

Around 13km/8 miles north of Enniscorthy, on the N11, lies **Ferns** (pop. 920), once episcopal see of the county. Three churches and other buildings occupy the grounds of the former monastery, cut in two by the road. The churchyard of the Protestant church has several High Crosses. Ferns Castle (around 1200) is a large rectangular keep, reinforced by round towers.

Gorey, Courtown

Further northeast on the N11 lies Gorey, once an important cattle market. Drive along the coast via the R742 to reach Courtown, a popular family holiday resort with an 18-hole golf links and fine sandy beaches.

Enniskerry (Ath na Scairbhe)

C 5

Republic of Ireland, province: Leinster
Population: 1,280

County: Wicklow

Enniskerry is considered one of the prettiest villages in Ireland and makes a good base for hikes into the mountains.

✶ ✶
Powerscourt House and Gardens

Enniskerry, founded by the Powerscourt family in the 18th century, lies southwest of Dublin in a hollow in the foothills of the Wicklow Mountains. The entrance to the domain of Powerscourt, with gardens and landscaped park counting amongst the most beautiful in the country, is situated around 800m/0.5 miles south of the village, with a mile-long avenue leading into the estate. The manor house (1731, designed by Richard Cassels) forms the centre of the estate. It burned out completely in 1974 but was rebuilt and reopened in 1997. The entrance hall features an exhibition about the the rich of the estate. From the manor house the partly terraced gardens stretch up the slopes, filled with statues, mosaic floors and cast-iron lattice-work. Other marvels are the artificial pond, small woods with exotic trees, plantations of rhododendron and other flowering shrubs, an Italian and a Japanese garden as well as a red deer park. Several spots offer a wonderful view of the surrounding mountains: Great Sugarloaf and Kippure. (Opening times: March–Oct daily 9.30am to 5.30pm.) Several films have been shot in the parts of the park left in a more natural state, e.g. John Boorman's *Excalibur* (1980), Stanley Kubrick's *Barry Lyndon* (1975) and Lawrence Olivier's *Henry V* (1943).

Take an hour's hike to the famous **Powerscourt Waterfall**, at 120m/ 394ft the highest waterfall in Ireland. Here, the waters of the Dargle plunge down in magnificent cascades, especially after heavy rains. (Opening times: summer daily 10.30am – 7pm; winter to dusk)

Some 3km/2 miles above, the **Glencree River** flows into the Dargle, on its course through a scenic valley from Glendoo Mountain. At the end of a rewarding drive up the valley, the road reaches a cluster of houses called St Kevin's, formerly English barracks protecting the Military Road. Nearby, in a hollow, lies a **German war cemetery**. It never seems totally abandoned, as people visit, praying the Irish way in front of the crosses, or reading the English, Irish and German inscriptions on the memorial stone: »... But War sent me to sleep in Glencree.«

Famous Powerscourt Waterfall

Around Enniskerry

The Scalp   Some 3km/2 miles north of Enniskerry, the main Dublin road cuts through a rocky pass. Between the steep slopes of the Scalp, the glaciers of the last Ice Age cut a deep drainage channel, depositing massive granite blocks. The pass is not only impressive to look at, it is also popular with climbers, offering an ideal terrain with great routes!

Fanad Peninsula

A 4

Republic of Ireland, province: Ulster   **County:** Donegal

This peninsula jutting far out into the Atlantic is famous for its impressive cliffs, hiding a surprising wealth of unspoilt habitats.

Fascinating peninsula   The Fanad peninsula, in the northernmost part of Ireland and County Donegal, stretches to a length of 20km/12 miles between the narrow Mulroy Bay in the west and the broad estuary of Lough Swilly in the east, to Fanad Head to the north.

Drive around Fanad Peninsula

Milford, Carrowkeel   Drive north from ▶Letterkenny on the N56, to reach Milford, situated at the southern tip of Mulroy Bay, with the »Grey Mare's Tail« waterfall nearby. Lough Fern and other smaller lakes make Milford popular with anglers.

Arch of Doagh Beg

Here, the R246 branches off north, leading along the fjord-like bay. Look out for a dolmen with a massive 2 x 4 m(6.5 x 13ft) capstone just before Carrowkeel (Kerrykeel), situated at the foot of the Knockalla Mountains.

Keep on the R246 and its continuation to reach the northern tip of the peninsula, Fanad Head, which offers stunning views. Driving further south, along the west coast of Lough Swilly via Portsalon, is the way to get to the unique cliff tunnels: most famous are the Seven Arches (up to 90m/300ft long) and the Great Arch of Doagh Beg. The village itself has a pretty harbour and an 18-hole golf links. The Knockalla Mountains that the road heads towards slope down steeply to the lake. The gun battery was erected to guard against the advance of the French.

Fanad Head

The R247 leads to Rathmullan (pop. 530), an attractive holiday resort with a sandy beach. The ruins of a 15th-century Carmelite friary hold a church converted into a residence by a 17th century bishop. Near the port, The Battery Visitor Centre was established in a gun battery erected in the early 19th century. The exhibition is mainly dedicated to the »Flight of the Earls«: following the failed uprising against the English in 1607, the local earls O'Donnell and O'Neill fled to France from Rathmullan. Their extensive estates were confiscated and handed over to English and Scottish settlers (►History). (Opening times: May–Sept Mon–Sat 10am–6pm, Sun 12.30–6pm.)

Rathmullan

Fermanagh Lakeland

B 3/4

Northern Ireland, province: Ulster   **County:** Fermanagh

A third of County Fermanagh in the west of Northern Ireland is covered by water. At the heart of the region, the lively holiday resort of Enniskillen is situated exactly between Lower and Upper Lough Erne.

Lough Erne, a maze of waterways, inlets and islands around 32km/20 miles long and up to 9.5km/6 miles wide, is considered the most beautiful lake in Ireland and a paradise for water sports and angling. In the summer, it is popular with motorboats. The lake's southern part, Upper Lough Erne, is dotted with a multitude of islets and more rugged than Lower Lough Erne to the north. The western shore runs near the border with the Republic of Ireland.

Lake scenery with countless islets

Explore the area by land, on foot, by bike and by car along the roads winding their way along the shore. Or hire a boat in Belleek and cruise in peace and quiet between the over 200 islands. Since the

Rowing and hiking

opening of the 61km/38-mile Shannon-Erne-Waterway (between Lough Erne and Shannon), the 360km/224 miles between Belleek and Killaloe may be covered in comfort on inland waters.

Enniskillen The county town of Enniskillen is a pleasant lively place (pop. 11,450). The centre of town is situated on an islet, with the River Erne here connecting both parts of the lake. Portora Royal School, founded by James I in the early 17th century, counts both Oscar Wilde and Samuel Beckett amongst its pupils. Enniskillen has a Catholic majority. Many people remember the name of Enniskillen for the IRA bomb attack of 1987, when eleven people died at a Remembrance Day religious service.

Enniskillen Castle ▶ Enniskillen Castle houses the Fermanagh History Heritage Centre, as well as the museum of the Royal Enniskillen Fusiliers, which has interesting displays on the early history of Fermanagh and some reproductions of the stone statues on White Island. The military museum ⊙ shows uniforms, weapons and medals. (Opening times: May–Sept Mon, Sat, Sun 2–5pm, Tues–Fri 10am–5pm; Oct–April Mon 2–5pm, Tues–Fri 10am–1pm and 2–5pm.)

Cole's Monument ▶ Standing on a small hill amidst a Victorian-style park, Cole's Monument is a tall Doric column erected in honour of Galbraith Lowry Cole (1772–1842), who was born here and served as general under Wellington. Climb up to the top of the monument for some nice ⊙ views. (Opening times: May–Sept daily 2–6pm.)

✶ ✶ Drive around Lower Lough Erne

✶ Devenish Island At the southern tip of Lower Lough Erne, not far from Enniskillen, lies Devenish Island. The island has the ruins of a monastery founded in the 6th century by St Molaise, including a completely preserved round tower. Some original parts of the 12th-century St Mary's Abbey and Great Church are still standing; particularly impressive is a cross of nearly 2m/6.5ft height. In the summer, there are several ferries to and from Trory, 5km/3 miles north of Enniskillen. (Opening times: April–Sept Tues–Sat 10am–6.30pm, Sun 2–7pm)

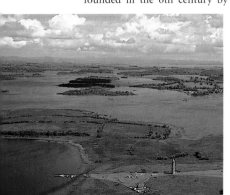

Lough Erne – lakes as far as the eye can see

In the old **Killadeas Churchyard**, look out for hewn stones dating back to the 7th/8th century – considered evidence of the transition from the pagan to the Christian worldview. One of them, the Bishop's Stone, shows on one side a clergyman with cross and bell, on the other a grotesque **moonface** (see photo). Take the B82 along the river in the direction of Kesh to reach Killadeas Churchyard, following the sign for the Manor House Country Hotel and carrying on for 6km/3.7 miles to Killadeas. The churchyard is located past the entrance to the village, after approx. 1km/0.6 miles, on the left-hand side.

Turn left from the A35 onto the B82, leading to Castle Archdale Marina. From April to September there are daily crossings to **White Island**. On the island, a path from the pier leads to a ruined 12th-century church. Looking through the late-Romanesque doorway, mysterious stone figures come into view. Probably erected in the 7th and 9th centuries, they predate the church by a few hundred years. From left to right, there are: a Sheela-na-gig (woman with crossed legs in a provocative pose), an abbot and abbess with a priest's bell and crozier, a clergyman scratching his chin, a man holding a pair of griffins by the scruff of their necks, warriors with sword and shield, and one incomplete figure. To this day, it has not been ascertained whether these are pagan representations or the incarnation of the seven deadly sins, or indeed whether the eighth figure – a face reminiscent of a death mask – really belongs to the series.

Detour to Drumskinny Stone Circle

Kesh (A35), northeast of ►Omagh is well worth a detour. The town is an ideal base for angling, as well as for hikes into the ►Sperrin Mountains. On the A32, after a few kilometres, the road branches off towards the Bronze Age Drumskinny Stone Circle (7km/4.5 miles northeast of Kesh). This circle, comprised of 39 stones, also includes a small stone cairn and a row built from twelve other stones.

Boa Island

At the northern tip of Lower Lough Erne, narrow Boa Island may be approached from both directions by a bridge connected with the shore. Stone figures, nearly 2,000 years old, lend the Christian graveyard of Caldragh a pagan air. The 73cm/29-inch Caldragh Idol, two figures back to back with large mouths and narrow-set eyes, are reminiscent of representations of Janus. Their long hair interlaces, with the crossed arms and the belt only hinted at. There are various interpretations of the slightly smaller Lusty Man on the neighbouring island of Lustymore, with one theory claiming it as an Iron Age goddess.

Castle Caldwell Forest Park

Some 5km/3 miles west of Boa Island, on the A47, lies Castle Caldwell Forest Park. The Fiddler's Stone at its entrance is a memorial to a drowned musician. Of the castle, only some ruins are left. Today, the park, with its pleasant walking trail, is a bird sanctuary.

Belleek

The village of Belleek (pop. 550), on the border between Northern Ireland and the Republic of Ireland, has been famous since 1857 for its porcelain manufacture, established by a landowner who inherited the estate and wished to improve its condition and provide employment. On weekdays there are guided tours (9am–4.30pm, Fri 9am–3.30pm); there is also a small museum, a showroom and shop, as well as a café. (Opening times: April–Oct daily, Nov–March Mon–Fri only.) The Explore Erne Exhibition gives a good overview of the region's history. (Opening times: mid-March–Oct daily 10am–6pm.)

Lough Navar Forest Drive

After a few kilometres'/miles' drive through Lough Navar Forest (back on the road leading south on the western shore), a viewpoint high up on the Cliffs of Magho offers a wonderful view over the lake. Many hiking trails lead through the conifer forest. Comprising a few small lakes, the forest also forms part of the Ulster Way running all the way around Northern Ireland.

Tully Castle

Some 5km/3 miles further on, take a detour to Tully Castle, a fortified Plantation House with a well-preserved protective wall. The gardens, laid out in the style of the 17th century, are exquisite, the herb garden in particular. (Opening times: April–Sept Tue–Sat 10am–7pm, Sun 2–7pm.)

Monea Castle

Monea Castle, the best-preserved Plantation Castle in Ireland, stands a little apart from the lake on a rock. Built in 1618 by Protestant immigrants, its style (the towers, in particular) is reminiscent of Scottish castles.

✴ Drive around Upper Lough Erne

Sheelin Antique Lace Museum

Heading southwest from Enniskillen, a 8km/5-mile drive leads to the popular holiday resort of Bellanaleck. Lacemaking has a long tradition in Fermanagh; the local museum has a fine collection from the period between 1850 and 1900. Lace, linen and oil lamps can be purchased here.

West of the A32 (heading for Swanlibar), a byroad leads to **Florence Court**. Dating from the 18th century, this is one of the finest manor houses in the region. The exquisite rococo stucco above the stairs and the collection of Meissen porcelain and copperplate engravings are particularly worth seeing. In the park, look for the original Florence Court Oak, said to be the ancestor of all Irish oak trees. (Opening times: May–Aug Wed–Mon 1pm–6pm, April, Sept and Easter Sat, Sun and bank holidays 1–6pm.)

> ! **Baedeker** TIP
>
> **Food & Drink**
> Take a break in the nearby Sheelin Restaurant – it's 200 years old!

Continuing on the byroad, visit the **Marble Arch Caves**, situated on the northern flank of the Cuticagh Mountains: a cave system with lakes and waterfalls, 700m/2,300ft of which have been made accessible to visitors. The guided tour starts with a subterranean boat trip past impressive stalactites and stalagmites. (Opening times: mid-March–Sept daily 10.30am–4.30pm.)

Back on the A509, cross the Upper Lough Erne at Derrylin. To the south stretches the 760ha/1,878-acre **Crom Estate**, with woods, parks and marshland. Of the castle, only some ruins are left, but the area is excellent for hiking, boating, biking or camping. (Opening times: April–Sept Mon–Sat ⊙ 10am–6pm, Sun noon–6pm.)

Fermoy (Mainistir Fhear Muighe)

D 3

Republic of Ireland, province: Munster
Population: 2,300

County: Cork

Amongst sports anglers, Fermoy is considered the most important fishing centre in the south of Ireland. Regular championships are held in and around Fermoy.

The Blackwater river flowing through Fermoy is particularly rich in salmon. This is the only Irish river to have roach, and its tributaries are good for river trout fishing. Otherwise, the small market town, situated a little inland from the southern coast of Ireland between the foothills of the Knockmealdown and Nagles mountains does not have that much to offer.

Angling centre in the south

Around Fermoy

Technically already in County Tipperary, a good 25km/16 miles north-east of Fermoy, Mitchelstown Caves is an extensive system of stalagmites and stalactites, including Desmond's Cave, named after one 16th-century Earl of Desmond who had a high price on his head and used the cave as a hiding place. New Cave, also boasting fine sta-

Mitchelstown Caves

lactite and stalagmite formations, was only discovered in 1833. At 120m/130yd long and 12m/39ft high, New Cave can claim to be the largest cave in the British Isles. (Opening times: daily 10am–6pm.)

Towards Mallow and Kanturk

To reach Anne's Grove Gardens, leave Fermoy on the N72 going west and turn off north in Castletownroche to reach, after 2km/1.2 miles, this beautiful park with many exotic trees and flowers on the shores of the Awbeg. (Opening times: April–Sept Mon–Sat 10am–5pm, Sun 1–6pm.)

Continuing on, pass the village of Killavullen and, to the west on a cliff above the River Blackwater, the home of the Hennessy family, whose cognac distilled in France is world-famous today.

The town of Mallow, 30km/18.6 miles west of Fermoy, in the wooded valley of the River Blackwater (good fishing), has an important sugar industry and was a popular spa in the 18th and 19th centuries. Alongside the Courthouse and the Market House, look out for a picturesque bell tower, 18th-century residential houses and reminders of the town's heyday: the old Spa House, the race course and »Spa Glen«, with three bubbling wells on Fermoy Road. At the southeastern end of town, next to a small museum, the turreted ruins of Mallow Castle date from the 16th century.

The market town of Kanturk, around 20km/12 miles west of Mallow, has a 17th-century fortress belonging to the MacCarthys which was never completed.

✴ **Galway** (Gaillimh)

C 2

Republic of Ireland, province: Connaught
Population: 57,000

County: Galway

In the summer, holidaymakers from all over the world join the Irish in the largest city in the west of Ireland. Galway is the seat of a bilingual university, contributing to the city's young atmosphere. Over half of »Galwegians« are between 14 and 44 years old.

Gateway to the wild west of Ireland

In the past 30 years, Galway has experienced a big economic boom and substantial increase in population (over 40%) rivalled by few other European cities. At the same time, the cultural importance of the city has increased, and tourism is booming too. Situated in a picturesque location on the northeastern tip of Galway Bay, where the plentiful waters of the River Corrib empty into the Atlantic, the capital of the county of the same name is an episcopal see; at the university (part of the National University of Ireland), most lectures are held in Irish. The Taebhdhearc na Gaillimhe theatre also keeps Gaelic culture and language alive. From Rossaveal, 1½ hour drive west on

Sunny lane in Galway's Old Town

the R336 from Galway, there are regular ferry services to the ►Aran Islands. Flight connections to the islands leave from Connemara Regional Airport at Inverin, on hour's drive to the west, also via the R336. Whilst the city itself has few sights, it is a suitable base from which to explore ►Connemara.

There has been a settlement at this site since prehistoric times. The building of the castle (1124) and its conquest by Richard de Burgo (1232) marked the fast rise of Galway to a booming Anglo-Norman town. Fourteen families of noble merchants (»Tribes«) turned Galway into a kind of city-state, loyal to England despite several attacks by the Irish – who were not allowed into the town.

History

In 1473, a big fire destroyed the town, rebuilt subsequently. Trade with western European countries, including Spain, made Galway wealthy. In the 16th and 17th centuries a Free School famous for its scholarship is said to have had 1,200 pupils, but as the town sided with the Irish, large parts were razed by Cromwell's army. During its conquest by the forces of King William (1691) Galway suffered further damage.

Numerous festivals and fairs are held, e.g. a jazz festival (February), the Festival of Literature (April) and a film festival (early July). The Galway Arts Festival lasts for two weeks (end of July / early August),

Festivals

Galway Plan

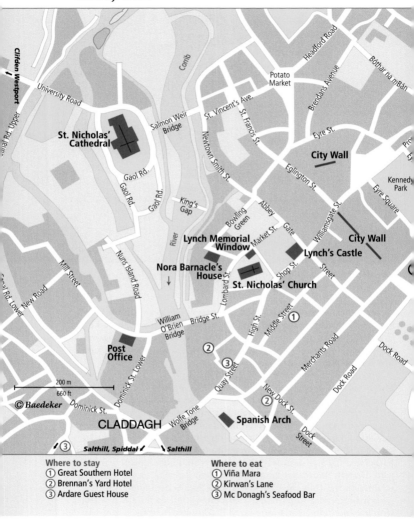

Clifden Westport

University Road

Gaol Rd. Upper

Corrib

Potato Market

Headford Road

Bóthar na mBan

Brendan's Avenue

St. Nicholas' Cathedral

Salmon Weir Bridge

St. Vincent's Ave.

St. Francis St.

Newtown-Smith St.

Eglington St.

Eyre St.

City Wall

Kennedy Park

Eyre Square

Gaol Rd.

Gaol Rd.

King's Gap

River

Bowling Green

Abbey

Market St.

Gate

Williamsgate St.

City Wall

Eyre St.

Lynch Memorial Window

Lynch's Castle

Mill Street

Nuns Island Road

New Road

Canal Rd. Lower

Nora Barnacle's House ↓

Lombard St.

St. Nicholas' Church

Shop St.

Street

William O'Brien Bridge

Bridge St.

High St.

Middle Street

①

Merchants Road

Dock Road

Dock Road

Post Office

Dominick St. Lower

②

③

Quay Street

New Dock St.

②

Dock Street

200 m
660 ft

© Baedeker

Dominick St.

Wolfe Tone Bridge

Spanish Arch

CLADDAGH

③ Salthill, Spiddal ／ ＼ Salthill

Where to stay	Where to eat
① Great Southern Hotel	① Viña Mara
② Brennan's Yard Hotel	② Kirwan's Lane
③ Ardare Guest House	③ Mc Donagh's Seafood Bar

with theatre, art and music events, as well as a parade. At the end of July, Galway Race Week involves a typically Irish popular festival at the race course in Ballybrit (3km/2 miles to the east). The highlight of the year however is the Galway International Oyster Festival in late September, with the World Oyster Eating championships.

► VISITING GALWAY

INFORMATION

Galway City Aras Failte
Forster Street
Tel. (0 91) 53 77 00
info@irelandwest.ie

Salthill Promenade
Tel. (0 91) 52 05 00
Open: May–Aug

WHERE TO EAT

► Expensive
① **Viña Mara**
19 Middle Street
Tel. (0 91) 56 16 10
info@vinamara.com
Spacious restaurant, chic but relaxed, with attentive service. The dishes are Mediterranean, with Irish and other influences.

► Moderate
② **Kirwan's Lane**
Kirwan's Lane
Tel. (0 91) 56 82 66
Modern restaurant with adventurous dishes in a friendly atmosphere.

► Inexpensive
③ **McDonagh's Seafood Bar**
22 Quay Street
Tel. (0 91) 56 50 01
Old-fashioned place specializing in seafood. Very popular with the locals.

PUB

Tigh Neaachtain
17 Cross Street
Tel. (0 91) 56 88 20
The legendary sessions are for sale – on CD.

WHERE TO STAY

► Luxury
① **Great Southern**
Eyre Square
Tel. (0 91) 56 40 41
Fax (0 91) 56 67 04
www.greatsouthernhotelgalway.com
Imposing Victorian hotel in the city centre, elegantly furnished, with conference rooms and a rooftop swimming pool.

► Mid-range
② **Brennan's Yard**
Lower Merchants Road
Tel. (0 91) 56 81 66
Fax (0 91) 56 82 62
info@brennansyardhotel.com
This old converted stone building is located in the heart of Galway, near the Spanish Arch. The rooms are nicely furnished with antique pine. Try the lively Spanish Bar for evening entertainment.

► Budget
③ **Ardare Guest House**
9 Father Griffin Place
Tel. (0 91) 58 26 38
Fax (0 91) 58 39 63
ardare@iol.ie
Functionally appointed family-run guesthouse.

Sights in Galway

Eyre Square

In memory of the US president with Irish ancestors, the centre of Eyre Square was redesigned as a John F Kennedy Memorial Park. On the northwestern side of the park stands Browne's Gateway, the rebuilt main entrance of a patrician house from Galway's heyday. Drawing the eye is the monument to the Gaelic-language poet Pádraic O'Conaire (1882–1923), portrayed sitting on a boulder.

To the west of Eyre Square stands the modern Shopping Centre of the same name which, thanks to its cafés, is now a popular meeting place. Part of the old city walls were restored and have been incorporated into the mall.

★
Lynch's Castle

From Eyre Square, Williamsgate Street, one of the city's main shopping streets, leads to 16th-century Lynch's Castle. The grey building, decorated with coats-of-arms is today the headquarters of a bank. It was much altered during restoration works in the 1960s. The castle was once the residence of the Lynchs, a noble family that provided several mayors (see photo below).

Lynch's Window

The execution of Lynch's son by the hand of his own father was commemorated by a black marble plaque on the wall of the old prison. The site of Lynch's Window on Market Street is said to be the place where the execution took place.

★
St Nicholas Church

St Nicholas Church (Collegiate Church of St Nicholas of Myra), also on Market Street, was built in the 14th century. Altered several times, it still looks like a medieval parish church. Look out for the three-gabled western façade, the gargoyles (rare in Ireland), as well as tombs and a lectern inside. The noticeable feature of the church clock is that it only has three clock faces. The northern side is empty.

Nora Barnacle birthplace

The birthplace of Nora Barnacle, the wife of James Joyce, is a few steps from the church (no. 8 Bowling Green), there are literary evenings on Wednesdays. (May–Sept daily 10am to 5pm.)

? DID YOU KNOW ...?

■ When James Lynch, an incorruptible man only thinking of the greater good, was mayor, he condemned his own son to death for murdering a young Spanish sailor. Lynch had to execute him personally as nobody else could be found to do it, and retreated to a monastery afterwards. The expression »to lynch somebody« is said to have its roots in this story.

On Kirwan's Lane there are still many traces of the 16th and 17th centuries to discover. Fourteen Norman merchant families, the Tribes of Galway, shared all commerce in Galway between themselves. The fourteen medieval lanes that bear their names form the core of the old town. After its redevelopment, the quarter is now buzzing with life, many cafés, good restaurants and shops.

Kirwan's Lane

Built in 1594, the Spanish Arch city gate, on the left-hand side of the Corrib, is all that remains of the bastion that was part of the city walls, designed to protect the ships of the mostly Spanish merchants from looting. The small Galway City Museum next door is dedicated to the history of the city and displays arms found in Galway Bay. (Opening times: Mon–Sat 10am–1pm and 2–5pm.) ⏱

Spanish Arch

On the other side of the Wolfe Tone Bridge lies the old fishing village of Claddagh. For centuries, it harboured an independent cooperative of fishermen, until it had to make way for modern buildings. Claddagh was immortalized in the song *Galway Bay* and its Claddagh Ring.

Claddagh

Further north, **Salmon Weir Bridge**, built in 1818, spans the River Corrib. In the spring, this is a good spot to watch thousands of salmon congregating on the river bed before starting their trek up-river. From the sea to ► Lough Corrib they only have to clear 6km/3.5 miles.

The **Cathedral of St Nicholas** on the right bank of the river was consecrated in 1965. Its dimensions – 100m/328ft long and 47m/154ft wide – make it one of the largest churches in Ireland. The cathedral stands on the site of a former prison for Irish patriots, which was almost exclusively built with money donated by the faithful. Look out for the mosaics in the side chapels.

> **! Baedeker TIP**
>
> **Claddagh Ring**
>
> The Claddagh Ring may be seen not only here, but all over the world where there is an Irish influence/community. It shows a heart held by two hands topped by a crown, and stands for friendship, loyalty and love. If the tip of the heart points towards the hand, the wearer's heart is taken; if it points to the fingertips, the wearer's heart is still free. The ring has been worn since the middle of the 18th century. Today, it is more popular than ever, mostly bought as a souvenir.

The beach of Salthill can be reached on foot from the city centre. In the summer it is often overrun with tourists. If the beach is too busy, or the weather bad, try Leisure World, with various pools and a giant slide, or go for a nice walk on the sea promenade: across a broad sandy beach, there are views of the mountains of Clare with the ► Burren, as well as the ► Aran Islands. Northeast of the city, on the N17, lies the village of Claregalway with the ruins of a Franciscan friary founded in 1290. In the church, a tomb features the representation of a primitive plough.

Salthill, Claregalway

Around Galway

Clarinbridge

Driving south from Carnmore via Oranmore on the N18 brings the visitor to Clarinbridge, a pretty little village famous for its excellent oysters and mussels. Some 2km/1.2 miles further on, in **Kilcolgan**, the N67 turns off to the right. Around 1km/0.6 miles west of the main road lie the ruins of Drumacoo Church, with fine sculptures on window and portal walls. Also look out for the impressive holy well associated with St Surney.

Dunguaire Castle

Drive southwest for 10km/6 miles on the N67 to reach . This is a fortified 16th-century tower house, fully furnished and open to the public. In the evening, medieval banquets are held in the hall.

Spiddal

Follow the R336 along the coast, past Barna to Spiddal (pop 300), a pretty holiday resort with good fishing grounds. At Spiddal Craft Centre, visitors can watch Irish arts and crafts being made and purchase the products. (Opening times: May–Oct Mon–Sat 9am–5.30pm, Sun 1–6pm.)

Galway's highlight of the year: International Oyster Festival

Glencolumbkille (Gleann Cholm Cille)

B 3

Republic of Ireland, province: Ulster   **County:** Donegal
Population: 260

Glencolumbkille, Irish Gleann Cholm Cille (»St Columcille's Valley«), is a picturesque holiday resort in the north of Ireland. It is situated at the most westerly point of County Donegal in a valley that opens up towards the Atlantic into Glen Bay.

The area boasts a sandy bay and splendid sections of cliff, reached via a boggy treeless upland valley, following the dark-brown Owen-wee River.

The area around Glencolumbkille is one of the Irish-speaking parts of Donegal. St Columba lived and meditated at this lonely spot. According to a legend, Bonnie Prince Charlie, the last Stuart pretender to the throne, spent time here whilst fleeing from the English. When Glencolumbkille was threatened in the mid-20th century by the lack

Picturesque holiday resort

Step into a traditional cottage in Glencolumbkille's open-air museum.

of industries, Father James McDyer founded a cooperative in order to optimize agricultural production. Successfully harnessing the locals' craftmaking skills, McDyer was able to create better markets for their produce. Thatched cottages were built for holidaymakers, whilst the Folk Museum attracts daytrippers.

Folk Village & Museum
This open-air museum can claim to be one of the best folk village museums in the country. Situated at the western end of the village, it consists of four thatched houses with furnishings and equipment that represent different periods of Irish life between 1700 and 1900, as well as a school building. The museum shop has local produce for sale and the tea shop offers tasty home-made snacks. All thanks to Father James McDyer! (Opening times: April–Sept Mon–-Sat 10am– 6pm, Sun noon– 6pm)

Every year, on 9 June (St Columcille's feast day), a **pilgrimage** takes place, with the pilgrims obliged to walk around the 15 stations in the valley three or seven times (by sunrise). They also lay down a pebble at the foot of the standing stones and pray.

Baedeker TIP

Summer courses
In order to preserve the cultural heritage of the region, the Ulster Cultural Foundation (Foras Cultúir Uladh) offers various courses between March and October, teaching Irish, the dances of Donegal or the fiddle, harp or bodhrán drum, tapestry weaving or painting (the shoreline and seascapes). On offer are also group hikes and archaeological workshops (for more information, call 0 73 / 3 02 48 or email oifig@oideas-gael.com).

Malinmore
Southwest of Glencolumbkille, Malinmore is a pretty holiday resort around a bay lined by picturesque cliffs, offering diving, snorkelling and fishing. At Cloghanmore, look for a approx. 3,500 year-old court cairn.

Rathlin O'Birne ▶
The coastal waters around the island of Rathlin O'Birne offer rich fishing. The island has some antiquities as well as a lighthouse.

★★ Glendalough (Gleann dá Loch)

C 5

Republic of Ireland, province: Leinster **County:** Wicklow

Nestling in a romantic valley with two lakes, the famous monastic settlement of Glendalough has retained its magic to this day.

Splendid location
This once very important holy site, founded by St Kevin in the 6th century, lies inland from the east coast of Ireland, just under 40km/ 25 miles south of Dublin. On the main R755 road leading south from Bray, through the mountains to Arklow, a wooded valley opens

Glendalough's well-preserved 10th-century round tower

up to the west at Laragh. After passing it, a further 2km/1.2-mile-drive brings you to the village famous both for its architectural monuments and its beautiful scenery: the ruins of the monastic town of Glendalough (Gleann dá Loch = »valley of the two lakes«). In the summer months at weekends, many daytrippers come to visit; it is quieter during the week. The valley belongs to the Glendalough Forest Park, part of the ▶Wicklow Mountains, offering many opportunities for hiking, hillwalking and climbing.

St Kevin started out living here as a hermit, but his pious erudition attracted so many students that he founded a monastery. When the saint died at a very old age, in 618, the monastery was just beginning to flourish. Later, over a thousand pupils are said to have lived there. The annals report Viking attacks and several fires in the 12th century, whilst in 1163, Abbot Laurence O'Toole was anointed archbishop of Dublin. In 1214, the Normans assigned the monastery to the episcopal see, and another fire in 1398 marked the beginning of a slow but definite decline. The buildings were only restored in 1875–1880; since then, their architectural fabric has been well preserved.

History

Glendalough *Plan*

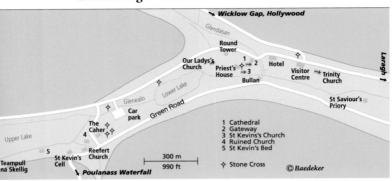

Visitor Centre

⏲

The monastic site is open at any time (visitor centre: daily 9.30am–6pm). Parking is available at the visitor centre as well as between Upper and Lower Lake. The best thing to do is to begin with the informative video in the visitor centre and then to start the tour through the grounds from Upper Lake, where the nucleus of the site was located. The pretty Green Road path leads from Upper Lake to the remains of the monastic settlement: alongside a model of the monastery, there are various tomb slabs, capitals and other finds from the monastic site. Look out for a 12th-century High Cross (Market Cross), showing a Crucifixion, an abbot, and interlacing ornaments. This cross probably used to stand on the pilgrimage route to Glendalough.

Upper Lake

Teampull na Skellig ▸

St Kevin's Cell ▸

Reefert Church ▸

The small rectangular Teampull na Skellig church, built on a rock, is only accessible by boat. The oldest parts of the partly restored church date back to the late 7th century. Steep steps carved into the rock lead to a small cave known as St Kevin's Bed. In the Bronze Age, this rock cave probably served as a burial site. Of easier access is St Kevin's Cell – a beehive hut where the saint is said to have lived. Near a small bridge stands the 11th-century Reefert Church, with a choir and nave. To the right of the car park, between the Upper and Lower Lakes, the remains of an ancient stone fort (the Caher) as well as three stone crosses are visible. They probably served as boundary markers and were later used as stations on the pilgrimage route.

Lower Lake

St Mary's Church ▸

The main cluster of monastic buildings stands downriver, near the visitor centre. They date from the time of the monastery's heyday and were accessed through the Gateway. The nearby round tower, with a height of 31m/102ft and a diameter of 5m/16ft, is preserved in its original state, apart from the top of its cap, restored using old stones. Its entrance is situated over 3m/10ft above ground. Next door, at St Mary's Church, erected in the 10th century from granite blocks, the faithful worshipped at the tomb of St Kevin well into the 18th century. Priest's House is a 12th-century Hiberno-Romanesque building, with a much older lintel relief above the entrance door. The largest church in the grounds of Glendalough is the cathedral, with choir, central nave and sacristy (11th and 12th century). It lost its cathedral status in the early 13th century.

◄ Priest's House
◄ Cathedral

A most remarkable architectural monument in Glendalough is St Kevin's Church, erroneously called »Kitchen« because of its chimney-like bell tower. St Kevin's was built in the 11th/12th century, of hard mica schist, with a pitched roof. The interior still holds a few stone masonry finds from the region.

◄ St Kevin's Church

On the right-hand side of the road leading to Laragh stands the 11/12th-century Trinity Church, which preserves its original granite chancel arch.

◄ Trinity Church

To the east, beyond the river, the most recent cluster of buildings, the 12th-century St Saviour's Priory, was restored around 1875. There are some very good examples of Romanesque stonemasonry on the chancel arch and windows, as well as some outbuildings.

◄ St Saviour's Priory

Gort (Gort Jase Guaire)

C 3

Republic of Ireland, province: Connaught
Population: 1,100

County: Galway

The little market town of Gort lies far out to the west of Ireland, south of Galway Bay – an ideal base for exploring the sights of the area!

The broad through road of this pleasant town is lined by 18th-century houses. Typical for an Irish provincial town are the tall chimneys, the grey, unadorned façades and large market square.

Typical provincial town

Around Gort

To the north of town, west of the N18, lies Coole Park. Many Irish writers used to visit this manor house (destroyed in 1941), which was the residence of writer Lady Gregory (1852–1932) a friend of W B Yeats and supporter of the Irish literary revival. What has remained is a magnificent cedar-lined avenue and the Autograph Tree, a copper beech with a trunk that shows the carved initials of writers, amongst them George Bernard Shaw, W B Yeats and Sean O'Casey. The Coole Park Interpretative Centre has information on the flora and fauna of the park and a portrait collection of Lady Gregory and her literary friends. (Opening times: mid-June–Aug daily 9.30am–6.30pm; mid-April–mid-June and Sept Tue–Sat 10am–5pm.)

Coole Park

Thoor Ballylee Amidst picturesque river scenery, 7km/4.5 miles north of Gort, stands Thoor Ballylee, a 16th-century four-storey keep. The poet William Butler Yeats (▶ Famous People) bought and restored the tower, living there from 1921 to 1929, as shown by a stone plaque with his verses. The tower houses a museum with Yeats memorabilia and first editions of his works. (Opening times: Easter–Sept daily 10am–6pm.)

Southwest of Gort, on the R460, the ruins of the former monastic site of **Kilmacduagh** nestle in green pastures on a lake, with the Burren as a backdrop. The round tower is 34m/112ft high and stands at a 60cm/2ft angle (like the »Leaning Tower of Pisa«). Its entrance, at a height of 7.80m/26ft, can only be reached via a staircase. Next to the tower stands the Cathedral (12th/15th century) with nave, choir and transepts. In the northern transept, look out for some interesting traditional representations of the Crucifixion. To the right of the Cathedral stands St John's Church. Of all the other smaller churches,

Medieval tower house Thoor Ballylee

O'Heyne's Church in the northwestern corner is the most beautiful: animal and plant motifs adorn the pillars of its chancel arch. Across the road, opposite the Cathedral, rises St Mary's Church.

Grand & Royal Canals

C 3–4

Republic of Ireland, Central South

The Grand Canal is an important recreation area popular with amateur skippers. On the canal banks, mingle with anglers and people out for a walk.

Grand Canal The 130km/80-mile canal leads right through the province of Leinster, connecting Dublin Bay with the ▶ Shannon and Barrow rivers. It was built between 1756 and 1804; further branches were added in the 19th century. Barges with heavy loads used the canal up to 1960, when commercial transport on the linking canals was ended. The differences in elevation are overcome by 52 locks in total. (Boats must not be over 18.5m/60.7ft long, 3.9m/12.5ft wide, have a draught over 1.2m/4ft or a height above water level over 2.75m/9ft). Every boat coming through the canal has to have a name or number, and the highest permissible speed is 8mph/5kmh. Keep to the right and overtake on the left; the locks may only be passed in daylight. Boats can be hired at several towns along the canal. To obtain a guide with descriptions of the canal, ring (01) 677 75 10.

Royal Canal

Like the Grand Canal, the Royal Canal starts its 146km/91-mile journey in ► Dublin and also connects Dublin Bay with the ► Shannon and Barrow rivers. It runs further north than the Grand Canal, meeting the river above Lough Ree. There are 47 locks.

After a planning and preparatory period of over 30 years, building work on the Royal Canal began in 1792. In 1817, the link with the Shannon was established, as well as canals connecting nearby towns, which resulted in a significant increase in cargo and passenger transport. However, towards the end of the 19th century, there was an inexorable decline in the amount of cargo and number of passengers and, in 1961, the Royal Canal was officially closed to commercial shipping. Today, the Royal Canal Amenity Group strives to preserve the canal as a cultural monument and recreation area.

Boats and anglers

The Royal Canal is rewarding for amateur skippers. The dimensions of the boats are prescribed by the smallest of the lock chambers: 22.9m/75ft long and 4m/13ft wide, permitting a draught of 1.4m/4.5 ft. The lowest bridge has a height of 3.05m/10ft. In the Royal Canal, passionate anglers can hope for bream, roach, red-eye, tench, pike and the occasional trout.

Horn Head (Corrán Binne)

A 4

Republic of Ireland, province: Ulster   **County:** Donegal

Horn Head is the name of the point of a peninsula jutting out into the Atlantic in the far north of the country. A scenic highlight!

Birders' paradise with a view

The N56 leads to the small holiday resort of Dunfanaghy, which is a good base for trips to Horn Head and the surrounding area. Dunfanaghy has a harbour (Port-na-Blagh), an 18-hole golf links and fine sandy beaches.

A hike along the western coast of the peninsula to the actual **Horn Head** is especially recommended: The point falls steeply 180m/590ft down to sea, with the ocean stretching into infinity beyond small islands and promontories, whilst the view inland offers mountain

ranges, with Mount Muckish and Mount Errigal in the background. Horn Head is also famous for its seabirds. Driving straight across the peninsula towards the point, the best views of the cliffs can be had from the east (Traghlisk Point).

Southeast of Marble Hill, **Ards Peninsula** has a Capuchin monastery. The grounds and park may be visited by appointment with the Fathers. The area of the peninsula jutting into Sheep Haven Bay is a wild bird sanctuary and stretches across the northern coast of the ▶ Ards Peninsula.

South of the monastery, on another peninsula, the ruined **Doe Castle**, a four-storey building within a turreted yard, dates back to the 16th century. The churchyard

Scenery at Horn Head, with Doe Castle

holds the graves of many leading Donegal families.

Creeslough ▶ Some 10km/6 miles south of Dunfanaghy lies Creeslough, with picturesque Duntally Bridge and a waterfall. Look out for the modern church of St Michael's.

✶ Inishowen Peninsula (Inis Eoghain)

A 4/5

Republic of Ireland, province: Ulster   **County:** Donegal

The largest peninsula in Donegal is also the northernmost part of Ireland: Inishowen Peninsula, in Irish Inis Eoghain (»Eoghan's island«). Alongside its furthest point at Malin Head, the peninsula offers ruined castles, churches and prehistoric relics.

Largest of Donegal's northern peninsulas
On its western side, the inlet of Lough Swilly leads far inland, whilst to the east, the bay of Lough Foyle forms the border with Northern Ireland as an inland lake. To the north, the open ocean embraces the coastline of Malin Head. A signposted route (Inis Eoghain 100) leads 160km/100 miles around the peninsula, though this may be shortened by cutting through inland.

Buncrana
The main town in the region, with 3,200 inhabitants, is Buncrana. This is a pleasant holiday resort which owes its popularity mainly to

the almost 5km/3-mile Lisfannon Beach on the eastern shores of Lough Swilly. In order to please the mainly Northern Irish holiday-makers, the leisure and entertainment facilities have been greatly expanded over the last years. An industry with a long tradition in and around Buncrana was textile production. Until its closure, the US-American company »Fruit of the Loom« employed some 2,000 people here. Production was moved to cheaper Morocco in 2006.

The well-preserved **O'Doherty's Keep** (14th/17th century) is an architecturally simple structure in a pretty location on the water. Beyond the bridge, the manor house of Buncrana Castle is unfortunately

Five Finger Strand, west of Inishowen Peninsula

increasingly falling into disrepair. The nearby Vintage Car & Carriage Museum shows a collection of vintage cars, carriages and Victorian bicycles.

Also of interest is the restored Tullyarvan Mill on the edge of Buncrana (heading for Dunree Head), housing an art exhibition, a textile museum, a small arts and crafts shop and a café. Find out about the history of the place, its flora and fauna as well as the mill and the linen industry. Exhibitions are held here, and, on summer evenings, cultural events with traditional Irish music take place. (Opening times: April–Sept Mon–Sat 10am–6pm, Sun noon–6pm.) ◄ Tullyarvan Mill

On Lough Swilly, 6km/3.5 miles south of here, lies the village of Fahan. In the churchyard of the former monastery, look for an early cross slab dating back to the 8th century: two standing figures can be seen on the side of the cross shaft, the cross itself is covered in exquisite interlacing. On one of the short sides (the northern one), look for a Greek inscription – rare in Early Christian Ireland. **Sights south of Buncrana** ◄ Fahan

Some 3km/2 miles further on, the path branches off towards Inch Island, connected with the mainland and famous for the many bird species living here. The way south passes Grianán of Aileách. ◄ Inch Island

From Buncrana, take the byroad going northwest to Dunree Head; at Fort Dunree, 6km/3.5 miles down the road, consider a visit to the military museum. Videos explain the history of the fort and the region, including the landing of Wolfe Tone on this coast during the rebellion of 1798. (Opening times: April–Sept Tues–Sat 10am–6pm, Sun noon–6pm.) **Drive around Inishowen Peninsula** ◄ Dunree Head

Gap of Mamore ► Carry on via the breathtakingly steep Gap of Mamore pass (with a gradient of up to 30%!). Its strange beauty is best appreciated by driving it from south to north. At the end of the pass, Dunaff Head is waiting, with a stunning view.

Ballyliffin ► Carry on, via Clonmany to Ballyliffin, popular with visitors because of its 3km/2-mile Pollan Strand. Jutting up at the northern tip of the Doagh Peninsula, the scenic ruins of Carrickabrahey Castle lie right by the sea, near a rock that spurts water from a fissure at high tide.

Carndonagh ► Next stop Carndonagh (pop 1,600), a little town with a (threatened) tradition of shirt manufacture and breweries. Opposite the church stand three Early Christian monuments, amongst them the 7th-century St Patrick's Cross, one of the earliest in Ireland. The cross shape is still only suggested, the lower part shows a human figure with outstretched arms, and smaller figures standing at its side. The back of the cross is decorated with interlacing and another figure. To the right and the left of the cross, look out for standing stones adorned with reliefs, showing David with the Harp and a bird and a man with two bells, amongst others. Further monuments can be found in the churchyard.

Baedeker TIP

Climbing
Dunaff Head to the north offers magnificent cliffs for climbing!

Malin Head ► Drive north for another 5km/3 miles. The road passes Malin, from where the R242 leads past the pretty country house of Malin Hall (1758) towards Malin Head, with a splendid view of the neighbouring cliffs! A short walk (1km/0.5 miles) leads west to Hell's Hole, a narrow and deep rock cavern offering a great natural spectacle at high tide.

Southeast from Malin Head towards Glengad Head, cliffs stretch for many kilometres/miles – rising up to 240m/787ft above the sea. The angling centre of Culdaff lies south of these cliffs.

Clonca ► After another 3km/2 miles, in Clonca, look out for a ruined church with a remarkable if badly weathered High Cross (with representations of the Miracle of the Loaves and Fishes and Peter Fishing) and a finely carved gravestone. There are further historical remains in the area: the Bocan Stone Circle to the east and a group of High Crosses in Carrowmore, to the southwest.

Moville ► The R238 leads to Moville, a popular holiday resort on Lough Foyle, once a port on the transatlantic route.

Greencastle ► Approx. 4km/2.5 miles to the northwest, Greencastle, has the ruins of a large castle, built in 1305. Nearby stands a Martello tower, erected in 1810 (today a hotel).

Inishowen Head ► Drive northeast on the R241 to reach Inishowen Head. From here, another splendid stretch of cliffs stretches northwest, with views across to Northern Ireland. These, and the attractive valley of Glenagiveny, make the area popular with tourists.

Some 0.5km/500yd north of Muff a path turns off to the left towards the fine Ardmore Gallan, a heavily decorated Bronze Age stone.

◄ Muff & St Aengus Church

At the junction of the R238 and the N13, the modern St Aengus Church is a round structure with a strip of windows and curved tent roof topped by a glass pyramid. This conspicuous building is said to be influenced by the shape of the Grianán of Aileach, rising only 4km/2.5 miles further south.

The Grianán of Aileach (Grianán means »palace of the sun«) is a round stone fort dating back to Early Christian times. It commands an elevated position, surrounded by three concentric earth walls. The fort's windowless wall, built without the use of mortar, is 5m/16.4ft high and, at its foot, 4m/13ft thick. It encloses a grassy space accessed via a low passage. Small chambers were laid out inside the wall. It is not known when this site was built; between the 5th and the 12th centuries however, it was the seat of the Kings of Ulster. Razed in the 12th century, the fort was restored at the end of the 19th century.

★
Grianán of Aileach

The walls of the ring fort offer panoramic views across the green, undulating hillscape, from the Lough Swilly fjord to the Fanad Peninsula.

★
◄ View

★ Kells (Ceanannus Mór)

C 5

Republic of Ireland, province: Leinster

County: Meath

Population: 2,200

Kells was once an important centre of Early Christian culture. Today, the town still holds some remnants of medieval times.

Hearing the name of the town, most people think first of all of the famous *Book of Kells*, a jewel of Irish book illumination. The Gospel manuscript, stolen in 1006, is today kept in the library of Trinity College in ► Dublin (► Baedeker Special p.64). Visitors can at least see a facsimile edition of the *Book of Kells* on site, in the modern St Columba's Church.

Small town with important monastery

As early as the 6th century, St Columba had founded an ecclesiastical site here. In the 9th century, monks from Iona (Scotland) fleeing the Vikings came here. In subsequent centuries, the monastery was plundered and re-established several times. The town, fortified by the Normans, hung on to its position up to the dissolution of the monastery in 1551. Of the once mighty fortifications, nothing is left today. The ruins of the monastery consist of the round tower, three High Crosses and St Columba's House.

Round Tower & South Cross

The former monastery churchyard is located in the centre of town. It is easy to find; look out for its 30m/100ft 10th-century round tower with five windows. Next to it, the South Cross (probably dating back to the 9th century) is dedicated to St Patrick and St Columba. It boasts rich decorations: at the base, a procession of chariots, animal-like creatures and interlacing can be made out. The southern side shows the Fall, Cain and Abel, the Three Young Men in the Furnace, above them Daniel in the Lion's Den, the Sacrifice of Isaac (left), Paul and Anthony in the desert (right) and David with the Harp, as well as the Miracle of the Loaves and Fishes (top). The western side has representations of the Crucifixion and Christ in Judgment, David Killing the Lion and the Bear, as well as a number of panels with scrollwork and mythical beasts.

The round tower of Kells

Some 30m/33yd away, the preserved rump of a very large cross features biblical scenes, some of them of ambiguous iconography. The **Market Cross** in the centre of town was made much later. An inscription says that it was erected in 1688 following a 9th-century model, in the tradition of medieval High Crosses.

St Columba's House

Northwest of the South Cross, outside the churchyard walls, stands Columba's House. Stay left on leaving the churchyard to visit the oratory (possibly dating back to the 10th century), with its steeply vaulted stone roof. The thick, sloping walls meet at the ridge; a steep ladder leads to the wall of a chamber supporting the roof. The entrance was originally 2m/6.5ft above ground.

Around Kells

Loughcrew Cairns

Heading west from Kells for some 20km/12 miles, the R168 and R154 run through the range of hills of Slieve na Calliagh (»mountain of the witch«). On the road between Drumone and Millbrook, the burial ground of Loughcrew is well worth visiting. Around 30 passage graves lie on two neighbouring elevations, only some of them featuring discernible burial chambers. Of particular interest is Cairn T in the eastern group. Measuring 36m/118ft in diameter, it houses a large chamber with side chambers, as well as decorated stone blocks. From up here, there is a wonderful sweeping view over the fertile plains of Meath.

Carry on northwest, in the direction of Virginia (►Cavan, Around); to the left of the road, look for a tower on the Hill of Lloyd, offering an attractive view. Inside the ruins of St Ciarán's church, on the banks of the Blackwater River, stand three simple High Crosses, an Early Christian tombstone and a holy well.

Hill of Lloyd

◄ Ciarán's Church

Kenmare

►Ring of Kerry

Kildare (Cill Dara)

C 5

Republic of Ireland, province: Leinster
Population: 4,300

County: Kildare

Brigida of Kildare (453–521), revered as Ireland's second patron saint alongside St Patrick, founded her famous double monastery for both monks and nuns here, under the shared supervision of an abbot and a nun.

The eternal flame that was kept burning by the nuns only went out at the dissolution of the monastery. Today, Kildare is the centre of Irish horse-breeding and associated economic sectors.

Famous monastery

A reminder of the glorious past of the town is St Brigid's Cathedral. Dating from 1223, the cathedral was restored several times, most recently in 1875–1896. Of the medieval tombs inside, the most interesting is the tomb of Fitzgerald of Lackagh (died 1575). The fine round tower in the churchyard is probably fairly recent. Topped with a modern cap, it is 32m/105ft high and easily climbed.

St Brigid's Cathedral

Tully, on the southeastern edge of Kildare, is the home of the Irish National Stud). Starting from the visitor centre, the tour begins in the Japanese Gardens, laid out at the beginning of the 20th century by Japanese gardeners, using plants imported specially for the purpose. The 20 stations of »Life of Man« were designed by the landscape gardener to symbolize life's path from the cradle to the grave. Leave through the »Gateway to Eternity«. (Opening times: mid-Feb–mid-Nov daily 9.30am – 6pm.)
Don't miss a guided tour of the National Stud – many famous race horses were born here. The stud was founded around 1900 by the Scotsman William Hall-Walker, who used fairly eccentric breeding methods: stallions and mares were mated according to their star

★ ★
Irish National Stud

signs, and every foal was given its own horoscope. If this did not please the manager, the foal would be put up for sale. Even so, Hall-Walker became a successful horse breeder. In 1915, he gave his stud to the English government, and in 1943 it finally passed over to the Irish state.

Walking around the grounds, look out for some of the valuable breeding stallions, and in the spring and early summer, the breeding mares enjoying the pastures with their foals. Watch a saddle-maker and a blacksmith at work, or visit the Irish Horse Museum, documenting the history of the horse from the Bronze Age to the present day. One of the exhibits on display is the skeleton of Arkle, one of the most famous Irish racehorses.

The Curragh To the east of the stud, in the plain of the same name, lies the world-famous race course of the Curragh, where every year in late June/early July the Irish Derby is held. All five Irish classic races are held here, the Derby since 1866.

Around Kildare

Hill of Allen The top of the Hill of Allen, 8km/5 miles north of town on the R415 used to be the site of a castle belonging to the Kings of Leinster. Now, a tower offers a commanding view of the surrounding countryside.

Old Kilcullen To the east, on the River Liffey – the bridge dates back to 1319 – lies the small town of Kilcullen. 3km/2 miles to the south, in Old Kilcullen, the remains of a monastery founded by St Patrick are still

Dun Ailinne ▶ visible: fragments of a High Cross and a round tower. Between Kilcullen and Old Kilcullen, to the west of the N78, lies Dun Ailinne hill fort, once the residence of the Kings of Leinster.

Kilkee (Cill Chaoi)

D 2

Republic of Ireland, province: Munster
Population: 1,300

County: Clare

Kilkee is a pleasant family resort in the west of Ireland, which rose to fame as a diving centre.

Pretty coastal town Lying on a semi-circular bay with a long sandy beach, Kilkee is shielded against the Atlantic Ocean by the Duggerna Rocks. Head west along the beach to pass some impressive rock formations – dominated by the 60m/200-ft Lookout Hill. On a clear day, there are good views from here, but take care at the edge of the cliffs!

Around Kilkee

South-east of Kilkee lies the market town and port of Kilrush (pop. 2,750). Kilrush Creek Marina, 3km/2 miles south from here, on the mouth of the River Shannon, has good moorings and is a useful supply stop for yachts, which may be chartered here too. Pack a picnic and take a walk under the old trees of Kilrush Wood, east of town. The motto of the Heritage Centre in the town hall is »Kilrush in Landlord Times«. (Opening times: Mon–Sat 10am–6pm, Sun 2–6pm.)

Kilrush

⏱

From Kilrush, a ferry goes across to Scattery Island; pick up some information from the Scattery Island Centre on Merchants Quay. Until 1978, the island, with a surface of just under 1 sq km/0.4 sq miles was inhabited; today, the village is in ruins. However, the island can look back on an important ecclesiastical past, starting with St Senan's founding of a monastery in the 6th century. The monastery's heyday was in the 14th and 15th century; it was destroyed during the reign of Elizabeth I. The round tower, with a height of 35m/115ft one of the highest in Ireland, can be seen from afar. An unusual feature is the entrance door at ground level. To the east stands a cathedral, to the north a 12th-century Romanesque church, and to the southeast, an Early Christian church with medieval extensions. The traditional custom was that new boats on their first outing would start by sailing once around the island »following the sun«, in a gesture of deference. In order to guard against shipwreck, seamen would take beach pebbles with them.

Scattery Island

 KILKEE

INFORMATION

O'Connell Square
Tel. (0 65) 9 05 61 12
tourisminfo@shannon-dev.ie
Open: June–early Sept

The N67 ends at Killimer, from where you can take a car ferry over the mouth of the Shannon to Tarbert (near ►Ballybunion). Operating in a north-south direction, the ferry saves a detour around the mouth of the River Fergus and the Shannon of about 90km/56 miles.

Killimer

A recommended drive starts from Kilkee on a minor road southwest along the coast, past Fooagh to Fooagh Point, with its holy well and spectacular rock scenery of tunnels, caves and cliffs. Via the peninsula, the road leads to Carrigaholt, where the ruins of a tall, slender 15th century tower house standing above the harbour are worth seeing. The castle yard is well preserved too. The village has a language college teaching Irish. Drive west along a scenic route to Loop Head, with its lighthouse and stunning views. The cliffs just offshore are Diarmaid's and Grainne's Rock.

From Kilkee to Loop Head

◄ Carrigaholt

◄ Loop Head

★ ★ Kilkenny (Cill Chainnigh)

D 4

Republic of Ireland, province:
Leinster
Population: 18,700

County: Kilkenny

Kilkenny, without a doubt the most beautiful inland city, is also called »Marble City«. Indeed, polished Kilkenny limestone is everywhere, looking like the blackest marble.

Medieval inland city

The city lies in the southeast of Ireland on the banks of the peat-brown River Nore. Winding streets and lanes lend Kilkenny a special charm, rows of pretty Georgian houses add elegance. Over the last centuries, extensive restoration works have been carried out on the historic fabric, so that today, the overall impression is of a medieval city. Since times immemorial, Kilkenny has been divided into three districts: Irishtown, with the cathedral as a landmark, High Town, dominated by Kilkenny Castle, and, on the other side of the River Nore, the eastern district, with St John's Priory.

Picturesque houses lining the River Nore

Kilkenny *Map*

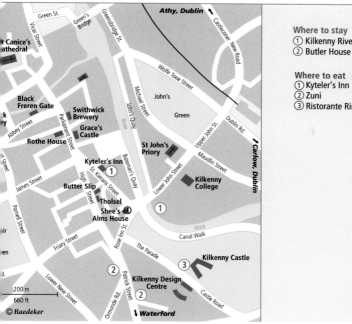

Where to stay
① Kilkenny River Court
② Butler House

Where to eat
① Kyteler's Inn
② Zuni
③ Ristorante Rinuccini

Economic prosperity came to Kilkenny with the settlement of various small industries, turning the city into a trading centre for the region's agricultural produce and an attractive tourist destination. The Kilkenny Design Centre enjoys an excellent reputation all over Ireland and has in recent years been highly influential, setting new trends in high-end Irish produce and packaging design. Many of the craftspeople and artists living in the city try to benefit from the prestige of this institution.

It was St Canisius/St Canice who built a church here in the 6th century. In pre-Norman times, Kilkenny was the seat of the Kings of Ossory, later falling to the Ormondes. In the 14th century, »parliaments« convened here several times. The infamous Parliament of 1366 issued by decree the Statutes of Kilkenny: no Anglo-Norman (i.e. the settled English) was allowed to marry an Irishwoman, take on Irish customs, speak Irish or wear Irish clothing. The Irish, on the other hand, were not allowed to live in a walled town. Though rigidly implemented, the laws were not able to stop the mixing of Anglo-Normans and Irish. From 1642 to 1648, the city was the seat of the Confederation of Kilkenny, an association of Old Irish and

History

▶ VISITING KILKENNY

INFORMATION
Shee Alms House
Tel. (0 56) 5 15 00

WHERE TO EAT
▶ Expensive
③ **Ristorante Rinuccini**
1 The Parade
Tel. (0 56) 7 76 15 75
info@rinuccini.com
Named after the 17th-century arch-bishop, a »bon vivant« and ambassa-dor of the Holy See in Ireland, this is a family-run restaurant with classic Italian cuisine.

▶ Moderate
② **Zuni**
26 Patrick Street
Tel. (0 56) 7 72 39 99
www.zuni.ie
The chic modern design in leather and dark wood draws the rich and beautiful into this former theatre. Daring, generous and varied dishes are served with a smile.

▶ Inexpensive
① **Kyteler's Inn**
Kieran Street
Tel. (0 56) 772 10 64
This historic pub serves international dishes, with an emphasis on fresh produce. Worth seeing!

WHERE TO STAY
▶ Luxury
② **Butler House**
16 Patrick Street
Tel. (0 56) 7 76 57 07
Fax (0 56) 7 76 56 26
www.butler.ie
This Georgian building, once the residence of the Earls of Ormond, has been refurbished to a contemporary style and equipped with all modern amenities.

▶ Mid-range
① **Kilkenny River Court**
The Bridge, John Street
Tel. (0 56) 772 33 88
Fax (0 56) 772 33 89; krch@iol.ie
Modern rooms with traditional col-our schemes, fine views of the River.

Anglo-Irish Catholics as an independent parliament. However, this assembly split, and the Anglo-Irish came to an agreement with the English. In 1650, Cromwell took the city, granting the besieged an honourable withdrawal.

Sights in Kilkenny

✱
Kilkenny Castle

The Norman fortress occupies a commanding position above the River Nore amidst the flowerbeds of a large park and is one of the most famous castles in the country. William de Marshal started building the castle on this site, which already had a wooden tower, in the 13th century. From 1391 to 1931, the property, which was re-peatedly altered over the course of the centuries, was the residence of the Butler family. Some of the former formal reception rooms have

Medieval: Kilkenny Castle

been restored. Most attractive is the Long Gallery, with a fine tapestry and a splendid vault painted with Celtic and pre-Raphaelite motifs. The gallery has been extended to show portraits of some members of the Butler family. The Butler Gallery is considered one of the most important Irish art galleries outside Dublin. (Opening times: June–Sept daily 10am–7pm; April and May daily 10.30am–5pm; Oct–March Tue–Sun 11am–12.45pm and 2–5pm.)

From President Street, Irishtown Bridge and St Canice's Steps (1614) lead to one of the most beautiful cathedrals in Ireland, St Canice's Cathedral. The church seen today was begun around 1251 on the foundations of an earlier building and completed in 1280. The low, sturdy 14th-century tower and the walls of the side aisles, transept and clerestory are crenellated. The interior has kept its spacious light-filled character despite various restorations (most recently in 1863–1864).

★
St Canice's Cathedral

Numerous fine tombs survive, amongst them in the northern side aisle that of Henry de Ponto (the oldest, dating back to 1285) and Edmund Purcell (1549). The latter is remarkable because of the **representation of a living cockerel in the cook pot**, an image sometimes found on Irish sculptures.

In the choir, look for the tombs of the Bishop of Ledrede (1360) and Bishop Rothe, in the southern transept the tomb of the eighth Earl of Ormonde and his wife

? DID YOU KNOW ...?

■ An old Irish folk legend says that when Jesus was risen from the grave, one servant brought the news to the kitchen of the High Priest. With a mocking laugh, the cook said this was as impossible as for the cockerel boiling in the pot to become alive again, whereupon the cockerel flew up from the pot and started crowing down from its rim.

! Baedeker TIP

Kyteler's Inn

To meet nice people and eat well in the process, head for the popular Kyteler's Inn (Kieran Street). This house however, has a dark past: in the 14th century, a certain Alice Kyteler is said to have lived here, drawing suspicion by outliving four husbands. Mrs Kyteler was able to escape being convicted as a witch by fleeing the town. Consequently, it was her old maidservant who ended up being burnt as a scapegoat at the stake.

(1539) and, in the southern side aisle, those of Viscount Mountgarrett in knight's armour, Bishop Walsh (1585), as well as one with a lady wearing a traditional Irish garment. The black-marble St Ciaráns Chair in the northern transept and a 12th-century baptismal font in the nave are worth seeing.

Near the southern transept, in the grounds of an Early Christian cemetery, stands a round tower of around 30m/100ft height, built between 700 and 1000. The tower offers fine views of the city and surroundings, but the staircase is very narrow and steep!

Black Abbey

Black Abbey was formerly part of a Dominican monastery founded in 1225, so it was not the stones that gave the monastery its name, but the monks' black habits. The southern transept and the tower date mainly from the 14th/15th century. Inside, look out for the medieval alabaster sculpture of the Holy Trinity and a roughly carved oak wooden figure of St Dominic.

★
Rothe House

Rothe House (1594–1610) in Parliament Street is a merchant's house built in the Elizabethan style, with two inner courtyards. In the hall, antique oak furniture, paintings and items of clothing are on display. Also on show are a large kitchen, a bakery and a brewery. ⊙ The building houses the City and County Museum. (Opening times: April–Oct Mon–Sat 10.30am–5pm, Sun 3–5pm; Nov–March Sat, Sun 3–5pm.)

Smithwick's Brewery

Heading south from Parliament Street, cross the small Bregagh River, the border between Irishtown and High Town. Directly to the left, in the grounds of Smithwick's Brewery, the remains of St Francis' Friary (founded around 1232) are still visible. It was around that time that the fine seven-light east window was made. Smithwick's is the oldest brewery in Ireland – even without considering the friary, where beer was probably made centuries ago. Beer lovers may take part in a ⊙ guided tour of the brewery, with a tasting session afterwards (summer Mon–Fri 3pm).

To the right, on Abbey Street, stands a gate of the old town fortifications, Black Freren Gate. To the left, on Parliament Street, look out for the Courthouse, erected on the ruins of 13th-century Grace's Castle. At the corner of Bateman's Quay and St Kieran's Street, a monument commemorates the Confederation Hall, where the parliament convened 1642–1649. St Kieran's Street leads to the oldest house in Kilkenny, Kyteler's Inn.

Black Freren Gate

Some 70m/80yd further on, a narrow lane connects St Kieran's with High Street. The Butter Slip owes its name to the butter stalls that used to be set up here. The town's insignia and annals reaching back to the year 1230 are kept in the Tholsel (1761) on High Street, today's town hall. The Tourist Information is located in the former Shee Alms House in Rose Inn Street, founded in 1582 by Sir Richard Shee as a hospital for the poor and in use up to 1895. Opposite Kilkenny Castle (Castle Ward), the Kilkenny Design Centre studios are housed in the former stables, offering a broad range of high-quality crafts (textiles, jewellery, glass, ceramics, etc). Take the opportunity to watch the craftspeople, whose work is sold all over Ireland, at work.

From Butter Slip to Jonathan Swift

On the other side of the river, Kilkenny College is the successor of St John's College, founded in 1666, which was attended by Jonathan Swift and George Berkeley. Today, it serves as County Hall. Nearby stand the ruins of the 13th century St John's Priory. The arrival of Cromwell's army spelt disaster for its famous fine windows.

◄ Kilkenny College

Around Kilkenny

A byroad leads to Dunmore Cave, situated 10km/6 miles north of Kilkenny. The visitor centre above the entrance to the cave shows the finds unearthed there during excavations: bones, coins, and simple tools, amongst other things. Many of the exhibits date back to the 10th century. In 928, some 40 people hiding from the Vikings in Dunmore Cave were discovered and brutally slaughtered. One of the most impressive formations in the limestone cave is a stalagmite measuring over 6m/19ft called Market Cross.
(Opening times: mid-March–mid-June Tues–Sun 10am–5pm; mid-June–mid-Sept daily 10am–7pm; mid-Sept–mid-March Sat, Sun 10am–5pm.)

★ **Dunmore Cave**

Some 7km/4.5 miles east of Kilkenny, a small road branching left off the N10 leads to the privately-owned 15th-century Clara Castle, a well-preserved tower house with six storeys. After 2km/1.2 miles, the R702 turns off to the right towards Gowran (pop 480) with its interesting parish church (c1275); its tower has been incorporated into the modern 19th-century church. Inside, look for fine lancet arches and pillars of black marble, as well as some exquisitely wrought sculptures and tombs (14th–17th century).

Towards Gowran

Via Kilfane to Thomastown

Carry on south on the N9, passing the lovely park and waterfall of Kilfane Glen, to reach, after another 2km/1.2 miles, the village of Kilfane. It is worth getting out of the car at the church and visit the over life-size effigy of the knight Thomas de Cantwell on his 13th-century tomb.

Detour to Duiske Abbey ►

Take the byroad to the R703 leading to Graiguenamanagh on the Barrow River. In the town, look out for the former Duiske Cistercian Abbey. The churchyard south of the choir has two small granite High Crosses with representations of biblical themes as well as ornaments.

Follow the N9 south from Kilfane for 4km/2.5 miles to Thomastown. Worth seeing here are a ruined 13th-century church, as well as the high altar in the Catholic parish church, which originally stood in the former abbey church of Jerpoint (see below).

★ Inistioge

Picturesque Inistioge (pop. 270) lies on the wooded shores of the River Nore, spanned here by a pretty 18th-century bridge. The village has been used as a backdrop for Hollywood films such as *Widow's Peak* (1993). Of the Augustinian abbey, founded in 1210, only a few remains survive, but there is a lovely hike from the village up to Brandon Hill (511m/1,676ft), with a cairn and a stone circle at the summit, rewarded by a magnificent view over the valleys of the Barrow and Nore Rivers.

Another nice idea for a trip is Woodstock Park on Mt Alto, 1km/0.5 miles south of Inistioge, a wonderful area for strolls and picnics. At the foot of the mountain, look out for a small pottery selling beautiful ceramics in pastel shades.

★ ★ Jerpoint Abbey

The monastic ruins of Jerpoint Abbey, some 3km/2 miles southwest of Thomastown, are amongst the most beautiful in Ireland. Founded in 1158, Jerpoint Abbey was Cistercian from 1180 up to its dissolution in 1540. The Cistercian influence is visible: the three-aisled church with transept and apse is joined to the south by the cloister and, to its side, the monastic buildings, of which only the sacristy and chapter house on the eastern side survive. In compliance with the rules of the Cistercian order, the imposing 15th-century tower stands above the crossing. As the tower is in danger of collapsing, it is no longer possible to climb it. The nave is divided into rooms for brothers and lay brothers. The church has fine tombs, e.g. of Bishop O'Dulany of Ossory (died 1202), with striking rows of carved Weepers on their plinths. In the cloister, look out for the impressive figurative relief sculptures standing be-

The Weepers – a group of six saints

tween the twin columns in the arcading. These were carved by master stone mason Rory O'Tunney,
probably between 1501 and 1552.
Allegedly, the church of St Nicholas west of the abbey holds the
grave of St Nicholas. It is said that
after the crusades, the knights of
Jerpoint brought his body from
Myra, in what is today Turkey, to
bury it here. The saint's grave is
marked by a broken stone slab
with the engraved image of a
monk. (Opening times: mid-June–Sept daily 9.30am–6.30pm;
May–mid-June and first half of Oct
Tues–Sun 10am–5pm.)

Jerpoint Abbey Plan

Kells, not to be confused with the
former monastery of the same
name in the north of the Republic,
preserves the extensive ruins of a
fortified Augustine monastery
founded in 1193. Dating from the
14th and 15th century, they form a
most impressive group of medieval
buildings. The church with nave, transept, choir and Lady Chapel
has a crossing tower as well as two other towers, one of which probably served as the prior's residence. To the south, the remains of the
convent buildings abut a courtyard guarded by walls and two towers.
The extensive area to the south of the courtyard is similarly fortified
by five towers.

Kilree, a 3km/2-mile drive south from Kells via a small byroad, also
preserves the remains of a monastery: a 29m/95-ft round tower
(without a cap) and a badly weathered High Cross, possibly dating
from the 9th century. The cross is here to mark the grave of the Irish
High King Niall Caille, who is supposed to have drowned nearby. As
he was not a Christian, his last resting place is outside the church
boundaries.

◄ Round Tower
& High Cross

Some 10km/6 miles west of Kilree, on the N76, lies the market town
of Callan. Before reaching the town, the road passes the Callan Famine Graveyard, commemorating the victims of the Great Famine in
Ireland, but also of the famines in Bangladesh (1974) and Angola
(1994). Callan still preserves some historic buildings, amongst them
the remains of a 15th-century Augustinian friary and the 16th-cen-
tury St Mary's Church. The carefully restored Rice House gives an
idea of what a typical late 18th-century farm house would have
looked like.

◄ Callan

Jerpoint Abbey

Killamery ▶ Drive south from Callan for 8km/5 miles to reach Killamery. Here, the heavily weathered decoration of a 9th-century High Cross shows a line of chariots, a hunting scene, David with the Harp and other biblical scenes, as well as numerous geometrical patterns and animal-like creatures.

West of Kilkenny Northwest of Kilkenny, the R693 leads to Freshford. The western gable of the local church (1730) comprises the fine Romanesque doorway of an earlier church. Beyond the boundary, already in County Tipperary, lie the ruins of Kilcooly Abbey, founded in 1182 as a

✳
Kilcooly Abbey ▶ daughter house of the Cistercian abbey of Jerpoint. The entrance is on the western side of the estate. The church was built between 1445 and 1470 on the site of the previous building and contains numerous sculptures. Between the southern transept and the sacristy, look out for the choir screens decorated with carved relief figures: there is the Crucifixion, St Christopher and a bishop, a mermaid holding a mirror, followed by two fish, as well as the arms of the Butler family. Of the tombs in the choir, the most interesting is the reclining figure of Knight Piers Fitz Oge Butler. The sarcophagus shows reliefs of saints and Early Church Fathers carved as Weepers. Master stone mason Rory O'Tunney created these figures and tombs around 1526. Also look out for the two seats on the crossing piers at the end of the nave, as well as the tomb of Abbot Philip (died 1463) in front of the altar. Amongst the ruins of the monastery, the circular vaulted dovecote stands out.

Killaloe (Cill Dalua)

Republic of Ireland, province: Munster
County: Clare
Population: 1,050

Killaloe is a water sports centre and also a meeting point for numerous cabin-cruise skippers. Restaurants, pubs and shops have joined the many boat hire companies.

Town between the waters

This small town lies at the spot where the Shannon leaves long Lough Derg to make its way through the Arra Mountains and Slieve Bernagh towards the plain of Limerick.

A walk through time

Killaloe's St Flannan's Cathedral was built in 1185 on the site of an older church, incorporating its Romanesque doorway. Next to it stands an extraordinary stone, with an inscription in both Viking runes and Ogham inscriptions: »Pray for Thorgrim, who made this stone.« In the cathedral grounds, 12th-century St Flannan's Oratory is a small Romanesque church with a fine doorway and a well-preserved stone roof.

Also of interest is St Molua's Oratory near the Catholic parish church. Dating from the 9th/10th-century, it was transferred here in 1929 from an island in the Shannon when the planned raising of the water level to serve local power stations threatened to flood it.

▶ KILLALOE

INFORMATION
The Bridge
Tel. (0 61) 37 68 66
open: May–Sept

The Killaloe Heritage Centre, housed in the Tourist Information building, has information on the history of the area.

Around Killaloe

Lough Derg

Stretching out to the north of the town, Lough Derg is the largest of the Shannon lakes, with 67 islets. The boundary between the counties Clare and Tipperary runs right through the lake. A scenic road (R463) follows its western shore, past the scant remains of the once large fort of Beal Boru that gave its name to the famous King Brian Boru.

Tuamgraney

On the western bank of the lake, the church of Tuamgraney is said to be the oldest Irish church still in use – parts of the building date back to the 10th/11th century. The small head high up on the east gable represents St Cronan, founder of the first monastery here (around AD 550). To obtain information on the region's history, head for the East Clare Heritage Centre, which also organizes trips to Holy Island.

Holy Island The fastest way to get to Holy Island (also called Inishcealtra) is from the angling centre of Mountshannon. In the 7th century, St Caimin founded a monastery on the island, and pilgrims and penitents came here up until the end of the 17th century. Today, Holy Island is a lonely spot with five churches, a round tower, an anchorite cell and churchyard.

Killarney (Cill Airne)

D 2

Republic of Ireland, province: Munster
Population: 7,300

County: Kerry

Blessed with magnificent lakes stretching to the south and east, known as Killarney Area, the town is a very popular holiday destination.

Long tradition of tourism As early as 1750, Lord Kenmare initiated a tourist infrastructure in the town; by the 19th century, Killarney was an essential destination, for wealthy English travellers in particular.

St Mary's Cathedral The Catholic St Mary's Cathedral, near the entrance to Killarney National Park, was built in the mid-19th century in the neo-Gothic Early English Style after plans by the architect of the Houses of Parliament in London, A W Pugin. During the Famine, the church served as a refuge for many of the local poor; today still, a huge tree marks a mass grave where women and children were laid to rest. The cathedral has a spire 85m/280ft in height, fine screens of Caen stone in the choir and the vault of the Kenmare family, benefactors of this church, in the Lady Chapel.

> ❗ *Baedeker* TIP
>
> **Angling**
> The area has many good fishing grounds, e.g. the Flesk and Laune rivers, the lakes in Killarney National Park for trout and salmon, as well as the ponds to the south towards Kenmare, with rainbow trout, amongst others.

National Museum of Irish Transport The museum can be found on East Avenue Road, leading towards a bus station. Alongside the collection of vintage cars, antique bicycles and motorbikes, a fully equipped workshop from the 1930s is also on display. Worth seeing are the *Silver Stream*, designed by an Irishman and built in 1907, as well as a *Wolseley Siddeley* (1910), which W B Yeats used to get about! (Opening times: April–Oct daily 10am–6pm.)

Killarney Area Plan

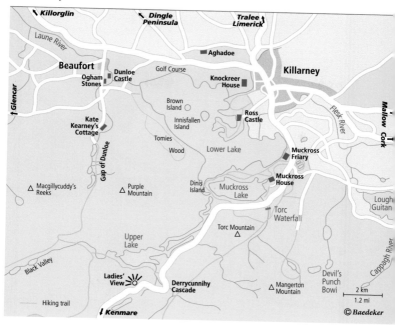

✳ Killarney Area

Famous for its beautiful scenery, this area is one of the biggest tourist attractions in Ireland. In an area rich in scenic ruins, the three lakes of Killarney National Park are the main draw: Lower Lake (Lough Leane), immediately southeast of Killarney is the largest lake, separated by a promontory from Muckross Lake (Middle Lake). A narrow waterway connects both with Upper Lake, the smallest of the three. The lake scenery framed by mountains and hills enchants through its ever-changing display of light and colour. Thanks to the mild climate, the shores feature a dense cover of luxuriant forest, with oak, arbutus, bamboo, and giant ferns, amongst many others. In the early summer, high foxglove shrubs line the roads, and colourful rhododendrons, as tall as trees, cover the slopes.

Tours

There are several ways to explore the lakes, either on your own or using a local tour operator. Most visitors take advantage of the offers for a package with a jaunting car (open carriage), pony and boat. Here is one idea for a tour: take a jaunting car from Killarney around the northern shore of the Lower Lake to Kate Kearney's Cottage; from there, take a pony, jaunting car or your own two feet through

Waiting for a fare outside Muckross House

the Gap of Dunloe to Upper Lake; from the lake's southern tip, take the boat across Muckross Lake to Ross Castle, and after that, take the car back to town. Visitors not in the mood for an expensive jaunting car may prefer to explore the area by bike (there are several bike hire companies in Killarney).

Killarney National Park Killarney National Park covers an area of 10,000 ha/25,000 acres. The nature reserve encompasses Lower Lake, Muckross Lake und Upper Lake including the shore line. The centrepiece is the Bourne Vincent Memorial Park around Muckross House, given to the nation by the family in 1932. Various signposted walking trails lead through the park, famous for its oak woods and red deer.

Knockreer House & Gardens ► Located west of the centre of Killarney, in a garden a few minutes' walk from the cathedral, Knockreer House is worth a visit.

Ross Castle ► Situated on a promontory in Lough Leane, Ross Castle is a late 15th-century fortress, preserving the tower with rounded turrets at the centre of the fortification. A prophecy said that the castle could only be conquered through an attack by water. In 1652, Cromwell's general Ludlow had a large boat brought over and set up in the lower lake in order to bombard the castle from there. The defenders, thinking the prophecy was coming true, surrendered. (Opening times: April daily 11am–6pm; May and Sept daily 10am–6pm; June–Aug daily 9am–6.30pm; Oct daily 10am–5pm.)

From the pier at Ross Castle, row across to quiet Innisfallen Island, to visit the remains of a monastery. This is the site where, in the early 13th century, the *Annals of Innisfallen* were written, today kept in the Bodleian Library in Oxford, England. The small 12th-century church on the northeastern shore was built from red sandstone. With its cover of mountain ash, ash, yew and holly trees, the island is a good example of the local forest.

◄ Innisfallen Island

At the heart of the national park stands Muckross House (1843), a beautiful Victorian villa and one of the most important stately homes in Ireland. The elegantly furnished rooms are a reflection of the life-style of the landed gentry. In the basement of the building, various workshops for traditional craftspeople have been established: a smithy, a weaver's, a pottery and a saddle-maker's. The gardens around Muckross House are famous for their beauty and the splendour of their flowers, in particular the azaleas and rhododendron bushes, as well as for the extensive water garden and rockery. (Opening times: Nov–mid-March daily 9am–5.30pm; mid-March–June daily 9am–6pm; July and Aug daily 9am–7pm; Sept and Oct 9am–6pm.)

★
◄ Muckross House & Gardens

To the east of the manor house, these three traditional farms, run according to the old ways of working the land, offer a trip back in time. Have a chat with the farmer and his wife whilst they go about their daily chores in the house, in the field or tending the animals. (Opening times: May daily 1–6pm; June–Oct daily 10am–7pm.)

Muckross Traditional Farms

From Muckross House, a path leads around the northern shore of Muckross Lake to the Meeting of the Waters (see below).

Splendidly situated in a green setting, ruined 15th-century Muckross Abbey is said to be one of the best-preserved Franciscan abbeys in the country. The only Franciscan tower in Ireland has the same width as the nave of the church; it was only added after the church was built. The cloister, with an old yew tree at its centre, as well as the adjacent buildings survive complete. There is a splendid view of the lake from the upper parts of the monastery. The monks were driven out by Cromwell's supporters in 1652.

★
◄ Muckross Abbey

A hike through the , to the west of Lower Lake, guarantees attractive scenery. This rocky defile separates the Macgillycuddy's Reeks (► Ring of Kerry) from Purple Mountain (822m/2,697ft), rising up to the east, and its northern foothills. By car, the best way to get to the valley is via the R562, leading around the Lower Lake. There is parking at Kate Kearney's Cottage. Visitors who prefer not to hike through the valley (it is a walk of around 4km/2.5 miles up to the top) may hire a pony or a jaunting car.

★
Gap of Dunloe

Plenty of natural beauty: the Gap of Dunloe with its small lakes

Five small lakes are fed by a fast-flowing small river. According to legend, St Patrick banished all snakes into the uppermost one, Serpent Lake. The bulky rocks on either side of the valley make for good echoes. From the top (239m/784ft), there is a splendid view of mountains, valleys and lakes in all shades of green, the yellow and brown of the plants and the red of the sandstone.

Other sights
Dinis Island, Meeting of the Waters ►

Continue walking on the northern shore of Muckross Lough with its strange limestone rocks, and cross Brickeen Bridge over to Dinis Island for the best view of the Meeting of the Waters, where Upper Lake, Muckross Lake and Lough Leane converge. Boat hire companies advertise trips on all three lakes. The road leads around the lake to the N71, running through the park between the shore and Torc Mountain (530m/1,739ft).

Torc Waterfall ►
Mangerton Mountain ►

On the eastern side of the mountain, the Torc River's attractive Torc Waterfall plunges down over an 18m/59ft sandstone precipice. The locals call the lake where the river rises the »Devil's Punch Bowl«.

VISITING KILLARNEY

INFORMATION

Beech Road
Tel. (0 64) 3 16 33
user@cktourism.ie

WHERE TO EAT

► Expensive

Gaby's Seafood Restaurant
27 High Street
Tel. (0 64) 3 25 19
A pleasant ambience and excellent
seafood dishes (lobster and salmon in
particular) make Gaby's Seafood Restaurant very popular. Advance booking is recommended!

► Moderate

The Celtic Cauldron
Plunkett Street
Tel. (0 64) 3 68 21
Nice pub restaurant, serving dishes
from Ireland, Wales and Scotland –
haggis, anyone?

WHERE TO STAY

► Luxury

Aghadoe Heights Hotel
Northwest, Aghadoe
Tel. (0 64) 3 17 66, fax (0 64) 3 13 45

info@aghadoeheights.com
Luxury hotel with the level of comfort
you would expect.

► Mid-range

Gleann Fia Country House
Deerpark
Tel. (0 64) 3 50 35, fax (0 64) 3 50 00
www.gleannfia.com
Centrally located hotel with restau-
rant in a quiet side street.

► Budget

Ross Castle Lodge
Ross Road
Tel. (0 64) 3 69 42, fax (0 64) 3 69 42
rosscastlelodge@eircom.net
Surrounded by alder woods, this
pleasant guesthouse is in a convenient
location right opposite the entrance to
the National Park and a 20-min walk
into town.

The path up Mangerton Mountain (827m/2,713ft) also leads past
here. From its summit, enjoy a breathtaking view over mountains
near and far, lakes, valleys and inlets – at its most impressive with
clouds casting big shadows and squalls of rain drifting across the
countryside.

Further up, on the Kenmare road, make sure to stop at Ladies' View,
which owes its name to the fact that Queen Victoria took a break
here with her ladies-in-waiting some 100 years ago to admire the
unique panorama. Continue on towards Kenmare, passing Molly's
Gap, a pass reaching a height of 275m/902ft.

✱
◄ Ladies' View

Enjoy another extraordinary view from the Aghadoe Heights, to the
north of Lower Lake on a little hill to the right of the R562. In Agha-

✱
◄ Aghadoe Heights

doe, the ruined monastery (open to the public) has an Ogham stone incorporated into the southern wall of the church. To the southwest of the church stand the remains of a round 13th-century castle. The hill above offers a sweeping view over the lakes and hills: from the Paps (685m/2,247ft) in the southeast to Mangerton Mountain (840m/2,756ft), and all the way to Carrantuohill (1040m/3,412ft) in the southwest.

Tomies Wood A nice idea is to take a walk through Tomies Wood (circular trail: approx. 7km/4.5 miles). Walkers will meet few other people here on the western side of the Lower Lake, whilst the view over the lake scenery is spectacular.

Killybegs (Na Cealla Beaga)

B 3

Republic of Ireland, province: Ulster   **County:** Donegal
Population: 1,630

Alongside Greencastle and Inishowen, Killybegs, on the southern coast of Donegal, is one of the most important fishing ports in the country. Here, Donegal Bay forms a natural harbour, cutting deep inland.

Important fishing port This small town is home to both the fish-processing and the sail-making industry. Don't miss the arrival of the fishing trawlers and the unloading of the catch. It is possible to arrange a ride on a trawler. The town also has a carpet-maker, which exports its famous products to places like Buckingham Palace and the Cunard Line steamers. The workshops can be visited.

Around Killybegs

Dunkineely Some 8km/5 miles east of Killybegs, Dunkineely is the start of a road 8km/5 miles out to sea to St John's Point, leading past a ruined castle on a narrow promontory, with excellent fishing grounds and good beaches.

Kilcar The picturesque village of Kilcar, west of Killybegs, is famous for the tweed hand-spun at several local mills. The cliffs and caves south of here, at Muckross Head, are accessible at low tide.

★
Slieve League Another 4km/2.5 miles inland lies Carrick, above the spot where the Glen River flows into scenic Teelin Bay. It is well worth taking a detour to Slieve League. To reach the highest sea cliffs in Europe, with a height of 590m/1,936ft, take the car to Teelin. From there, the narrow road carries on to Bunglass Point (3km/2 miles to the south-

west), ending at a car park a few paces below the cliffs. The question now of course is: are you happy with a nice view, or do you want to take a hike? Bunglass Point is the beginning of the **One Man's Path**, which is only recommended for sure-footed walkers with a good head for heights. The ridge leads some 4km/2.5 miles past steep slopes up to the summit of Slieve League. The path is not marked, but can be made out fairly easily. Less experienced hikers should take the **Old Man's Path**, signposted from Teelin village. The time needed is approx. 1.5 to 2 hours for both paths, with a height differential of just under 400m/1,312 ft. Both paths require more or less the same degree of fitness and sturdy shoes.

The highest sea cliffs in Europe

★ Kinsale (Ceann Saile)

E 3

Republic of Ireland, province: Munster
Population: 1,800

County: Cork

To this day, Kinsale has preserved some of its 18th-century charm. Narrow lanes with colourful houses and the picturesque harbour give the town an almost Mediterranean flair.

This popular day-trip and holiday destination lies above the broad estuary of the Bandon River. Its harbour is today only used for fishing (mackerel) and the well-equipped marina. In order to serve its international sailing clientele, numerous good restaurants and wine bars have established themselves in Kinsale. The best view of the town can be had from Compass Hill (southwest of the town centre) or from the road leading to Charles Fort.

Gourmet capital on the south-western coast of Ireland

From 1602 onwards, Kinsale was an English town, the Irish were not allowed to live here until the end of the 18th century. The harbour used to be an important naval port: in 1601, a Spanish fleet brought several thousands of men here to join the Irish in fighting the English. They had to surrender, however. A consequence of this decisive victory of the English was the »Flight of the Earls« to central Europe, sealing Ireland's dependence on Britain. According to legend, a certain Alexander Selkirk sailed from this harbour in the early 18th century, only to be shipwrecked and stranded on a desert island. Sel-

History

kirk's fate allegedly gave Daniel Defoe the idea for his novel *Robinson Crusoe*. William Penn, founder of the US state of Pennsylvania, was also born in Kinsale.

St Multose Church

St Multose Church is the most remarkable building in town. Built in the 12th century and altered several times, it serves today as parish church. The tower with its Romanesque door is on the northwestern side. The statue above the western door shows St Multose, who is credited with founding the monastery that once stood on this site. Inside the church there is an interesting collection of 17th-century tombs and a medieval baptismal font.

French Prison

In Cork Street stands a well-preserved tower house called French Prison or Desmond Castle, dating back to the 15th/16th century. Used in the early 19th century as a prison for French soldiers, the tower today houses a small wine museum. (Opening times: mid- June–mid-Sept. daily 9.30am – 4.30pm.)

Kinsale Museum

The municipal museum, located in the pretty Court House (1706), preserves some of the traditional long black hooded cloaks that used to be worn by local women. (Opening times: Mon–Fri 11am – 1pm and 3 – 5pm.)

Picturesque Kinsale Harbour

⏵ VISITING KINSALE

INFORMATION
Pier Road
Tel. (021) 4 77 22 34
Open: March–Nov
user@cktourism.ie

WHERE TO EAT
► **Moderate**
Crackpots
3 Cork Street
Tel. (0 21) 4 77 28 47
This bistro restaurant does not only offer good and imaginative cuisine, but also displays artworks and ceramics.

WHERE TO STAY
► **Mid-range**
Actons
Pier Road
Tel. (0 21) 4 77 99 00
Fax (0 21) 4 77 22 31
info@actonshotelkinsale.com
Situated above the harbour, this hotel is famed for its special atmosphere and cuisine.

► **Budget**
Kieran's Folkhouse Inn
Guardwell
Tel. (0 21) 4 77 23 82
Fax (0 21) 4 77 40 85
folkhse@indigo.ie
Pleasant guesthouse, with live music every night in the bar.

Head for Summer Cove, 3km/2 miles south of town, on the eastern side of the harbour, to visit Charles Fort (1677). The outer defences of the star-shaped well-preserved fort are 12m/39ft high. On the southwestern corner stands a lighthouse, and the enclosure holds the ruins of 19th-century barracks. Take a guided tour, but be careful walking on the parapets! On the opposite side of the harbour a similar structure catches the eye: James Fort.

Charles Fort

Around Kinsale

Take the R600 southwest from Kinsale to the village of Ballinspittle, dominated by the Ballycateen Ring Fort with its three deep ditches and an overall diameter of 120m/130yd. The name Ballinspittle refers to a long-lost medieval hospital, which was probably a foundation of the Knights Templar.
Further south, the Old Head of Kinsale juts far out into the sea: a ruined castle and a lighthouse, set in spectacular cliff scenery.

Ballinspittle

◄ Old Head of Kinsale

From Kilbrittain (pop. 1,950), the R603 leads to Bandon, where there is good trout fishing. The town was founded in 1608 for English settlers. Not least because of this, Bandon's parish church, Kilbrogan Church, built in 1610, was one of the first Protestant churches in Ireland.

Bandon

Letterkenny (Leitir Ceanainn)

B 4

Republic of Ireland, province: Ulster   **County:** Donegal
Population: 10,000   **Information:** Tel. (0 74) 2 11 60

Letterkenny, in the furthest northwest of Ireland, is the main town in County Donegal and an ideal base for exploring northern Donegal. The town lies on the banks of the river Swilly, from where you can see the spot where the river flows into Lough Swilly.

St Eunan's Cathedral, County Museum

The symbol of the town, stretching alongside the O'Cannons hills, is the tower of St Eunan's Cathedral (1901), with Celtic-style carvings and stained glass. The County Museum was established in a building that was originally used as a poorhouse, and later by the local authorities. The exhibits highlight the history, archaeology and geology of Donegal, as well as the county's past inhabitants' way of life. (Opening times: Tue–Sat 11am–12.30pm and 1–4.30pm, Sun 1pm–4.30pm.)

Around Letterkenny

Rathmelton

Further northwest, Rathmelton (or Ramelton, pop. 920) is a meeting place for anglers. Particularly pretty is the harbour, framed by Georgian houses. The 17th-century Old Meeting House today serves as a genealogical research centre. Don't miss the ruins of Tullyaughnish Church, with Romanesque carvings on the eastern wall.

Newmills Corn & Flax Mills

In the village of Newmills, 6km/3.5 miles southwest of Letterkenny, the Newmills Corn & Flax Mills visitor centre has information on the processing of corn and flax. (Opening times: mid-June–Sept daily 10am–6.30pm). A stroll along the river leads to the former cottage of a flax thresher and a village blacksmith.

Colmcille Heritage Centre

The Colmcille Heritage Centre in Gartan, 17km/11 miles to the northwest of Letterkenny, is dedicated to the life, work and times of St Columba the Elder (Colm Cille). On the way to the Heritage Centre, signposts lead to the ruins of Colmcille Abbey and the saint's birthplace. (Opening times: May–early Oct Mon–Sat 10.30am–6.30pm, Sun 1–6.30pm.)

Glebe House

In 1953, the English painter and art collector Derek Hill bought splendid Glebe House on the shore of Lough Gartan. Glebe House used to be a rectory, and later a hotel. Today, it is Hill's remarkable art collection that attracts most visitors. The focus of the 300 paintings and drawings is on modern painting (Degas, Renoir, Picasso, Yeats, Kokoschka, amongst others), but the works by »naive« Tory painters promoted by Hill are worth seeing too.

The converted stables display changing exhibitions, and the bistro shows a video about Derek Hill and his lovely residence. (Opening times: Easter and mid-May–late Sept Sat–Thu 11am–6.30pm.)

West of Lough Gartan stretches Glenveagh National Park. The entrance and visitor centre are situated on the northern shore of Lough Beagh and can be accessed via the R251. With a surface area of 100 sq km/39 sq miles, the national park was founded in 1986. At its centre, Lough Beagh is surrounded by impressive mountain and bog scenery. From the visitor centre, there is a shuttle bus to Glenveagh Castle, 3km/2 miles away, private cars being banned from the national park. The castle, built in the year 1870 in neo-Gothic style, stands in magnificent, mediterranean-looking parkland. Don't miss the herb garden. (Opening times: Easter–Oct Sat–Thu 10am–6.30pm.)

Glenveagh National Park

11km/7 miles north of Letterkenny lies Kilmacrenan. Situated near the bridge, Lurgyvale Thatched Cottage is worth a visit. The kitchen offers tea and scones with home-made jam. On Thursday evenings, there is traditional music with singing and dancing, and in the summer, visitors can have an introduction to traditional crafts. (Opening times: Easter–Sept daily 10am–7pm.)

Kilmacrenan
◄ Lurgyvale Thatched Cottage

Drive some 3km/2 miles further west to see the Rock of Doon, a remarkable flattened rock that was once the coronation site of the O'Donnell kings. The climb is rewarded with panoramic views across bog scenery. Pilgrims also visit the »Holy Well« for its curative powers.

◄ Rock of Doon, Doon Well

Limerick (Luimneach)

D 3

Republic of Ireland, province: Munster
Population: 79,000

County: Limerick

Abroad, the name »Limerick« is mainly associated with the famous five-line humourous verse (and more recently, with Frank Mc Court's best-selling memoirs »Angela's Ashes«), hardly ever with the third-largest Irish city, in the southwest of the country.

Several main throughroads and railway lines meet here, Shannon Airport is only 24km/15 miles away, and Limerick also has a fairly busy if not very large port. Over the past decades, the establishment of modern branches of industry (optical, electronic, and medical technology) has raised Limerick's profile as the home of major industries. There are also corn mills and tobacco-processing companies, as well as factories producing textiles, cement and steel cable.

Junction at the mouth of the Shannon

Despite this, unemployment is relatively high and the overall standard of living low. Enormous efforts are being made to promote tourism in this area.

Parts of the older quarter in the north (English Town), especially where the Shannon and Abbey rivers meet, don't exactly appear inviting to visitors. Just to the south however, you will find the medieval core of the city (Irish Town) and Newtown Pery, laid out in the 18th century, with a much more wealthy aspect – Newton Pery is the commercial and banking district. In the area around O'Connell Street and Mallow Street, handsome Georgian residences can still be found.

History   In the 9th century, the Vikings established a base at the »bare place«, as the translation of the city's Irish name suggests. From here, they undertook their marauding raids inland and were only driven out by the famous king Brian Boru. Later, Anglo-Normans and Irish alternated as rulers of Limerick. In 1210, King John had a castle and a bridge built. Over the following centuries the city became more powerful and sided with the English. In the 17th century, Limerick was besieged and captured several times, for the last time in 1691, the year of the »Broken Treaty«. At the time, 10,000 Irish soldiers, as well as the Irish nobility were granted an honourable retreat after bravely defending Limerick, by a treaty signed by King William III himself. However, the English parliament refused to ratify the treaty, not recognizing the religious freedom enshrined in the treaty. The soldiers went to France and joined Louis XIV's army. Over the course of the following decades, tens of thousands of Irish soldiers were to join the army in France and Spain, whilst the broken Treaty of Limerick became a symbol for English occupation in Ireland.

»Limerick«   The origins of the five-liner are uncertain, in all probability it actually came from England. Sometimes the name »Limerick« is also traced back to an Irish 19th-century song, describing in various stanzas the adventures of the inhabitants of various Irish cities. The following verse may give a flavour of what a »Limerick« is:

English Limerick

There was a young lady of Wilts,
Who walked up to Scotland on stilts;
When they said it was shocking
To show so much stocking,
She answered »Well, what about kilts?«

American Limerick

A wonderful bird is the pelican,
His bill can hold more than his belican,
He can take in his beak,
Food enough for a week,
But I'm damned if I see how the helican.

Sights in Limerick

Limerick's main sights are to be found in English Town. The Protestant St Mary's Cathedral, near Matthew Bridge, was built at the end of the 12th century, under Donal Mór O'Brien, last king of Munster. The western doorway dates from this time. The main parts of the church however, are 15th century. The magnificent oak choir stalls were carved in 1489; its 23 misericords (support ledges for choristers), decorated with imaginatively wrought creatures, make the choir unique in Ireland. Also look out for the tombs, and climb the tower (36m/118ft) for a wonderful view.

St Mary's Cathedral

Situated on the river banks, impressive 13th-century King John's Castle rises above the Shannon. No expense was spared in the recent restoration of the pentagonal fortress consisting of a main block, three round corner towers, a bastion and a twin-towered gatehouse marred by later additions.

King John's Castle

Today, parts of the site are used for exhibitions, with recreated scenes bringing to life the history of Ireland and the city. There is also an audiovisual presentation, as well as excavations of pre-Norman houses, defenses and siege tunnels. (Opening times: mid-April–Oct daily 9.30am – 5.30pm.)

The best view of the imposing castle is to be had from the other side of the river, the site of the Treaty Stone where the Treaty of Limerick is said to have been signed in 1691 – it was, however, never complied with. Pass the 18th-century Bishop's Palace and the old tollgate before crossing the river via Thomond Bridge.

Limerick Castle: completed in 1202 for King John »Lackland«

The former Custom House today houses the excellent collection of art historian John Hurt. The founder of the Craggaunowen Project (► Craggaunowen Castle, Ennis) collected nearly 2,000 pieces, mainly medieval liturgical artefacts from the European mainland, but also Irish finds from the Bronze Age and early Christian times. In their significance for medieval Irish art, the Hunt Museum exhibits are second only to the National Museum in Dublin. (Opening times: Tue– Sat 10am – 5pm, Sun 2 – 5pm.)

✱

Hunt Museum

⊙

Limerick *Plan*

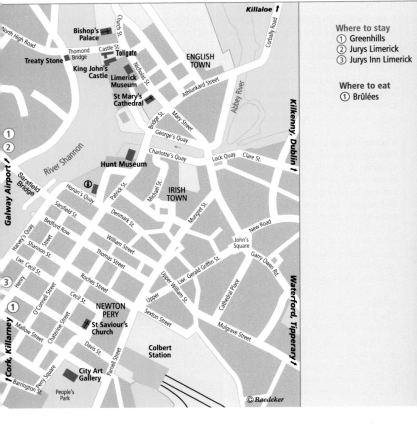

Killaloe †

Where to stay
① Greenhills
② Jurys Limerick
③ Jurys Inn Limerick

Where to eat
① Brûlées

© Baedeker

Sarsfield Bridge Sarsfield Bridge (1824–1835) over the Shannon is a copy of Pont Neuilly in Paris. Sarsfield Street leads to the part of town called Newtown Pery.

Newtown Pery Southwest of Irish Town stretch the districts of the more recent expansion of the city. Today, the heart of the city is O'Connell Street, with the Daniel O'Connell Monument rising up at its end. In 1829, O'Connell successfully fought for religious freedom for Catholics in Ireland. Spot some particularly splendid Georgian houses with their colourful doors in Mallow Street, with People's Park at its eastern end. In St Saviour's Dominican Church, the statue of Our Lady and the surprisingly modern-looking stained-glass windows are worth seeing. It is said that the statue was gifted to the Dominicans in 1640

St Saviour's
Dominican
Church ►

by a Limerick man. Limerick's art gallery only recently moved into ◄ Art Gallery
the People's Park. On display are works by international and Irish artists, such as Jack Butler Yeats and Sean Keating. (Opening times: ⊕
Mon–Fri 10am–1pm and 2–6pm, Sat 10am–1pm.)

Around Limerick

Some 20km/12 miles east of Limerick, at the foot of the Slievefelim   Moroe
Mountains, lies Moroe village, with the Benedictine monastery of
Glenstal Abbey, founded in 1927 amidst extensive parkland.

At Holycross, 25km/16 miles south of Limerick, don't miss this most   ★
interesting site of prehistoric excavations. In the last century, during   Lough Gur
drainage works on the lake it was discovered that its banks had been   Stone Age
inhabited as far back as Neolithic times. Several finds are on display   Centre
at the visitor centre on the lake, whilst models, graphics and audiovisuals in the Lough Gur Stone Age Centre give background information about the site. (Opening times: mid-May–Sept daily 10am– ⊕
6pm.)

❯ VISITING LIMERICK

INFORMATION
Arthur's Quay
Tel. (061) 317522
limericktouristoffice@shannondev.ie

WHERE TO EAT
► **Expensive**
① *Brûlées*
Corner Mallow/Henry Street
Tel. (061) 319931
brulees@eircom.net
This restaurant, on the ground floor
of a Georgian building, serves classic
Irish cuisine with a modern twist.

WHERE TO STAY
► **Luxury**
② *Jurys Limerick*
Ennis Road
Tel. (061) 327777
Fax (061) 326400
limerick@jurysdoyle.com
The hotel has a garden behind the
house and generous rooms.

► **Mid-range**
① *Greenhills*
Ennis Road, Northwest
Tel. (061) 453033
Fax (061) 453307
info@greenhillsgroup.com
Modern hotel, with all amenities. The
restaurant's speciality is lamb (reared
at the hotel's farm).

► **Budget**
③ *Jurys Inn Limerick*
Lower Mallow Street
Tel. (061) 207000
Fax (061) 400966
jurysinnlimerick@jurysdoyle.com
Purpose-built hotel with rooms furnished in light wood, some with a
view of the Shannon. Central location
and value-for-money, with an informal restaurant and cozy pub.

Walking around the extensive area, the monuments you see include: no. 4 – a wedge-shaped passage tomb (approx. 2000 BC); no. 7 – an 8th-century stone fort; no. 8 – an Early Christian oval stone fort; no.

Wedge tomb

12 – a Stone Age burial site, a double wall with a standing stone (menhir) at its centre; no. 16 – a burial mound with a circle of standing stones (approx. 1500 BC); no. 17 – a fine double stone circle (which has not been dated with certainty), with an earth wall and ditch; no. 22 – a small stone circle with large blocks; no. 23 – a crannóg, originally an artificial island, now connected to the shore; no. 28 – an impressive stone circle (approx. 2000 BC), a place of worship with an almost monumental entrance.

In the area, also look for the medieval Bourchier's Castle (16th century), Black Castle (14th century) as well as the ruins of the 17th-century New Church.

Kilmallock, 34 km/21 miles south of Limerick on the R512, is a long-established rural town. Parts of the 15th-century Collegiate Church of Saints Peter und Paul date from the 13th century (round tower), and there are some handsome headstones. The 14th-century King's Castle and Blossom's Gate in Emmet Street bear witness to the significance of the town in the Middle Ages. The town museum shows a model of Kilmallock as it would have looked in 1600, and a small collection of exhibits shows what life was like in this region in the 19th and 20th centuries. (Opening times: daily except Sat 1.30–5pm). To the north stand the ruins of a Dominican priory (13–15th century) with a church displaying good samples of stone masonry. The five-light east window, as well as tombs in the chancel, are worth seeing. The tower (27m/89ft) is supported by narrow bays.

Detour to Kilfinane Motte and Castle Oliver ►

Approx. 10km/6 miles to the southeast, Kilfinane lies at the foot of the Ballyhoura Mountains. Kilfinane has a particularly large motte, from the top of which you have a splendid view of the countryside around. In the scenic southwest side valley of Glenosheen, two avenues lead past unusual gatekeeper's lodges to 19th-century Castle Oliver, complete with crenellations, towers and bastions. This is the alleged birthplace of Marie Gilbert, also known as Lola Montez, the famous mistress of King Ludwig I of Bavaria.

From Kilmallock, the R518 and R520 lead west to the lively market town of Newcastle West (32km/20 miles southwest of Limerick). The ruins of a castle founded by the Order of the Knights Templar in the centre of town date from the 12th century. 8km/5 miles south of Newcastle West, you will come across Glenquin Castle, a well-preserved tower house, dating from the 15th century, with six storeys.

Newcastle West

Drive west from Limerick on the N69 past some ruins, reaching, after 4km/2.5 miles, Mungret Abbey, a monastery school of some prominence at the time, and 6km/3.5 miles further on, 15/16th-century Carrigogunnell Castle, built on a rock. From here, enjoy a beautiful view of the Shannon and the surrounding area. Kildimo has the remains of a small 13th-century Knights Templar church as well as a parish church, dating from 1705. Carrying on, 12th century Killulta Church appears on top of a hill; look for the triangular window.

Towards Askeaton

From Kilcornan village, you can go forwalks in Coillte Forest Park (Curraghchase Forest Park), for instance to what remains of 18th-century Curraghchase House. Celtic Park & Gardens features copies of important Irish monuments and has a rose garden. Children in particular will appreciate the horses, sheep, deer, and poultry. (Opening times: May–Oct daily 9am–7pm.)

◄ Coillte Forest Park

In Askeaton, on the River Deel, the ruins of 15th-century Desmond Castle rise on a rocky islet in the river near the bridge. The castle features a tower house and a banqueting hall (9x27m/30x89ft), with pretty windows, blind arcades and a vault. On the eastern bank of the river, the 15th-century Franciscan friary still has a few well-preserved buildings. The church has some beautiful windows and a fine cloister with twelve marble lancet arches, containing a representation of St Francis. The refectory and other rooms also survive.

Askeaton

Drive on for 11km/7 miles to reach the sea harbour of Foynes, situated in a scenic position, on the mouth of the Shannon. During the Second World War, Foynes was a focal point for the entire North Atlantic passenger air traffic. The Foynes Flying Boat Museum takes visitors back to this time, with the original terminal building, the radio and weather room as well as photographs showing the first flying boats used on the Atlantic route. One of them is on display outside the museum. (Opening times: April–Oct daily 10am–6pm.)

On to Foynes & Glin

13km/8 miles further west, 19th-century Hamilton's Tower rises above Glin harbour. Outside the village, Glin Castle has been in the possession of the Knights of Glin for 700 years, and they have been living here in an unbroken line for the same length of time. The rooms inside the castle, built in Georgian neo-Gothic style, are worth seeing, with elegant stucco ceilings (staircase, hall, library), as well as Irish furniture from the 18th century, and family portraits (18th–20th century). Guided tours are available, and visitors can also stay here in style.

Lismore (Lios Mór)

D 4

Republic of Ireland, province:
Munster
Population: 650

County: Waterford
Information: Tel. (0 58) 5 48 55

Lismore is a village near the southern coast of Ireland. Situated on the broad River Blackwater, Lismore hugs the foot of the Knockmealdown Mountains.

A place of scholarship

There was a monastery on this site as early as the 7th century; its school was famed for its scholarship. The 9th-century English king Alfred is also said to have studied here.

Lismore Castle

Lismore Castle, perched magnificently on a high rock, was probably built in the 12th century, on the site of a monastery, by the later King John. It was a bishop's residence for four centuries and was later briefly leased to Sir Walter Raleigh. In 1602, the castle passed into the hands of Richard Boyle, later Earl of Cork. His son Robert Boyle (1627–1691), a famous natural scientist (Boyle/Marriotte Law), was born here. Today, the castle belongs to the Duke of Devonshire. It was expanded several times during the 19th century, and it was during those works that significant finds were made: the 15th-century »Book of Lismore«, as well as the Lismore Cross; today, both may be admired in the National Museum in Dublin.

Lismore Castle is not open to the public, but may be rented from time to time by interested parties with the necessary funds. The gardens, however, are open to visitors. (Opening times: mid-May–mid-Sept Mon–Fri 1.45–4.45pm.)

St Carthage's Cathedral

St Carthage's Cathedral was built in the 17th century by Richard Boyle, using parts of a 13th-century church (the chancel arch and the window in the southern transept). Look out for the tomb of the MacGrath family (1557), with representations of the Crucifixion, an Ecce Homo scene, several saints and apostles, as well as ancient headstones in the western wall of the nave.

Lismore Heritage Centre

An audiovisual show in the Lismore Heritage Centre brings to life the history of the town and its surroundings.

Around Lismore

Cappoquin

East of Lismore, where the River Blackwater turns southwards, lies the scenic fishing town of Cappoquin. The tides reach all the way to here. Worth a trip out of town is Glenshelane Park. A few kilometres further north, in the hills, the Trappist Mount Melleray Abbey was built in 1833. Accommodation can be had in the guest quarters.

At Affane, 2km/1 mile south of Cappoquin, look for a large Georgian manor house where Sir Walter Raleigh (1552–1618) planted the first cherry trees in the British Isles. Sir Walter was also the first to cultivate potatoes and tobacco in Ireland. Near Villierstown (south of Affane), Dromana Gate is a curious gatehouse in a style reminiscent of Indian architecture.

Affane

Londonderry

►Derry

Longford (An Longfort)

C 4

Republic of Ireland, province: Leinster
County: Longford
Population: 4,000

Longford, to the north-east of Lough Ree in the centre of Ireland, is a busy hub, with interesting places to visit around the town.

The main town of Longford County offers plenty of leisure activities: golf, tennis, fishing and hunting; horse and greyhound races are held here too.

Sports centre

Around Longford

Heading north-east from Longford on the R194, after 6km/3.5 miles look out for Carriglass Manor. This private manor house was built in 1837 by Thomas Lefroy, said to have been a friend of Jane Austen's in her youth. Allegedly, Lefroy was the model for Mr Darcy, one of the main characters in *Pride and Prejudice*. The house has furniture and paintings from the 18th century, and the former stables now house a costume museum. (Opening times: mid-June–early Sept Mon, Thu–Sat 1–5.30pm, Sun 2–6pm.) ⏲

Carriglass Manor

The next stop is the angling town of **Granard**. Don't miss what is possibly the largest motte in Ireland (12th century) near this small town. Some 4km/2.5 miles to the east, starting at Lough Kinale and running 10km/6 miles northwest to Lough Gowna, stretches a part of Black Pig's Dyke. This defensive

 LONGFORD

INFORMATION
Market Square
Tel. (0 43) 4 65 66
Open: May–Sept

structure consists of a series of earthwork walls for the protection of the connecting roads and runs straight through the north of Ireland (►Cavan, Around). The individual sections were built between 300 BC and AD 300. Here, the wall is up to 6m/20ft high, and at its base 9m/30ft strong, with a ditch to each side.

Corlea Trackway

The Corlea Trackway Visitor Centre (15km/9 miles from Longford, 3km/2 miles from Kenagh) is dedicated to the Bog Road, a road of wooden planks from the Iron Age. The trackway was built into the boggy landscape near the Shannon in 148 BC and is said to be the longest of its kind in Europe. In recent years, a stretch of 18m/60ft length has been excavated and is now on display in a climatized room. An exhibition explains the conditions at the time when the Bog Road was built and the work of the archeologists; there is an interesting film too. (Opening times: April/May daily 10am–5pm; June–Sept 9.30am–6.30pm)

Towards Ballymahon

South of Longford, Edgeworthstown boasts the manor house where the novelist Maria Edgeworth (1767–1849) was born. Famous colleagues such as Walter Scott and William Wordsworth came to stay here. On the way to Ballymahon, take a short detour off to the right to Ardagh, with small St Mel's Church, allegedly founded by St Patrick. Ballymahon, with a scenic location on the River Inny, has good fishing.

Lough Ree

Take the R392 again in a northwesterly direction to Lanesborough on the Shannon, which flows into Lough Ree here. Both the river and the lake have great fishing (trout). Lanesborough is also a popular stop for boat trips on the ►Shannon. The power station near the town, on the eastern shore, runs on peat.

Inchcleraun ►

The island of Inchcleraun in Lough Ree preserves the ruins of an ancient monastery.

Lough Corrib • Lough Mask

C 2

Republic of Ireland, province: Connaught

County: Galway, Mayo

At over 45km/28 miles long, Lough Corrib in the west of Ireland, north of Galway Bay, is the largest lake in the Republic; in some places, however, it is only a few hundred yards.

★ Lough Corrib

The scenery around the lake is very varied: plains to the east, hills to the west, and to the north, the mountains of Connemara can be spied on the horizon. The green banks with occasional clumps of trees and pastures form hundreds of small bays, promontories and

Flowering trees on the shore of Lough Corrib

peninsulas that seem to blend into rows of tiny islands. The region is ideal for boating and a paradise for fish and fishermen. Many water-birds live here, such as pochards, coots and gulls. To the north, sub-terranean rivers connect Lough Corrib with Lough Mask; the former emptying into the sea via the River Corrib. From ►Galway, pleasure boats leave in the summer for ►Cong.

Sights around the lakes

It is possible to go around the lake, but mostly the road runs at a certain distance from the shore; the only roads leading down to it are cul-de-sacs.

Heading northwest from ►Galway, the road leads first to Moycullen, a good fishing base, and, past Ross Lake, soon reaches Aughnanure Castle (1500), jutting up from a rocky island. The six-storey tower house features two corner oriels of the type typical for the Western Irish and Scottish defensive style. Each of the two courtyards is flanked by a round tower. (Opening times: mid-June–mid-Sept daily 9.30am–6.30pm.)

Aughnanure Castle

⏱

After a few kilometres, the road reaches Oughterard. The town, often called »Gateway to Connemara«, lies snugly in a green setting on the shore of the Owenriff River (plenty of fish here), and is well-known in fishing circles. On the other hand, the numerous accommodation options and restaurants also attract tourists looking for a different kind of relaxation.

Oughterard

Inchagoill From Oughterard or ►Cong, hire a boat to go across to picturesque Inchagoill island, to see the remains of two churches. The smaller one dates from the 5th century, the larger structure, dating from the 12th century, is considered a good example of Hiberno-Romanesque style. A 75cm/30in obelisk nearby marks a burial site. Its inscription »Lie Luguaedon macci Menueh« (stone of Luguaedon, son of Menueh) is taken to refer to the nephew and helmsman of the Irish apostle.

Cornamona The narrow road along the northern shore ofis a dead end. To drive around the lake, use the N59. From the road intersection at Maam Cross (► Connemara), take the R336 north to Maam Bridge. From there, the L101 running east leads to the scenic fishing village of Cornamona. From here, visit Castle Kirke with 12th-century Hen's Castle. An island in Lough Nafooey is nearly completely occupied by the ruins of a massive tower.

> ! **Baedeker TIP**
>
> **Hill walking and mountain climbing**
> Cornamona also makes a good base for hikers and mountain climbers. The mountains to the west (Joyce's Country) offer good walking routes.

Clonbur After a drive of 8-km/5-mile in parts hugging the lake, stop at Clonbur, on the isthmus between Lough Mask und Lough Corrib. There is a fantastic view from Mount Gable to the west of the village. To just drive around Lough Corrib, follow the road east and drive via ► Cong to Ballinrobe.

Lough Nafooey As the road sweeps around Lough Mask, drive on the pretty side road from Clonbur to the village of Tuar Mhic Éadaigh (Toormakeady), past the atmospheric mountain lake which appears, depending on the weather, either sombre or brightly luminous. From here onwards, the road is signposted as »Lough Mask Drive«.

★ **Ballintubber Abbey** North of Partry, on the isthmus between Lough Mask and Lough Carra, off the N84, stands Ballintubber Abbey. The abbey was founded in 1216 by the king of Connaught near the site where St Patrick had founded a church as early as 441, coming down from Croagh Patrick (►Westport). Despite the havoc wrought by Cromwell's army, mass has been said here regularly to this day. Look for a skilfully wrought tomb in a chapel in the sacristy of the cruciform church. The church and cloister were restored in the 1960s. This church is the starting point for the 35km/22-mile pilgrimage up Ireland's holy mountain Croagh Patrick, which can be seen rising up in the distance through the arcades of the cloister.

Lough Carra The road from Ballintubber to Ballinrobe runs across the isthmus between Lough Mask and Lough Carra. Both lakes are connected by a subterranean river. A cairn on a small island in the emerald-green

Lough Carra marks the grave of the poet and novelist George Moore (1852 – 1933, »The Lake«).

Only 11km/7 miles away, **Ballinrobe**, on the Robe River, is also called the »fishing capital of the West« because of the many fishing opportunities around the town.

Some 10km/6 miles south of Ballinrobe, a little side road near the eastern shore of Lough Mask leads to the park of **Lough Mask Estate**. Separated only by a narrow channel from the park lies the island of **Inishmaine**, on which with the ruins of a small 13th-century Augustinian abbey still stand; its cruciform church features remarkable stone masonry work depicting animals and foliage.

Continuing closer to the shore, the R346 and R334 lead to Ross Abbey via ► Cong. At Headford, a signposted road branches off. The Franciscan abbey also known as Ross Errilly has extensive ruins that are worth seeing. Founded in 1351, the friary stayed in the possession of the monks till 1753. Most of the parts that still survive today, such as the tower and the southern transept with a double aisle, date from the 16th century. To the north of the cloister with its magnificent arcades lies a second courtyard, around which are arranged several utility rooms: a kitchen with water tank for fish, an oven in the mill room, as well as a refectory with recesses for Bible readings. All in all, this is arguably one of the best-preserved ruins of a Franciscan friary in Ireland.

✳
Ross Abbey

From Headford, make a detour to the market town of **Tuam**, only a few kilometres further east. Tuam is a good fishing centre and was, for a long time, a place of great significance for the church. Today

Ross Abbey *Plan*

© Baedeker

Kitchen
Mill room
Pantry
Courtyard
Refectory
Cloister
Sacristy
Chancel
Nave
Transept   Transept   Chapel

50 m
165 ft

still, it is the seat of a Catholic archbishop as well as an Irish-Anglican bishop. The 19th-century Protestant St Mary's Cathedral on Galway Road has a barrel-vault choir with nice sculptures on the chancel arch and east window; both belonged to the original church (12th–14th century). Also worth seeing are the exquisitely carved shaft of a 12th-century High Cross and the Baroque choir stalls in the southern aisle. A little to the northeast lies Dunmore, an ancient settlement with the ruins of a castle and an abbey. From Tuam, take the R347 and the N63 (direction of Roscommon) to the ruins of the former Cistercian abbey of Knockmoy (founded in 1190), picturesquely situated on a small lake. On the northern wall of the choir, look out for some medieval frescoes (c1400), which are rare in Ireland. Only the black contours are left, showing Christ in the act of blessing, the Martyrdom of St Sebastian and a scene from the legend of the Three Dead and Three Living Kings. Below the three dead kings, the inscription reads: »We have been as you are, you shall be as we are.«

Dunmore ▶

Knockmoy ▶

Annaghdown

Some 8km/5 miles south of Headford, a little road turns off right towards Annaghdown, which has some interesting monastic ruins. Parts of Annaghdown Abbey date from the 12th century, the main church and the monastery building were only built 300 years later.

Lough Erne

▶ Fermanagh Lakeland

Lough Neagh (Loch nEathach)

B 5

Northern Ireland, province: Ulster   **Counties:** Antrim, Derry and Armagh

With a surface area of 388 sq km/150 sq miles, a length of 32km/20 miles and a width of up to 16km/10 miles, Lough Neagh is the largest inland lake in the British Isles. The borders of the counties Antrim, Derry and Armagh run right through it.

Birds and fish

Six rivers flow into this lake, situated approx. 20km/12 miles west of Belfast. The banks of Lough Neagh have been settled since prehistoric times, and with the lake being so rich in fish, the surrounding area is one of the most important habitats for many different species of birds in Western Europe. Around 100,000 wild birds come here to spend the winter. The lake is known most of all for its eels; up to 10 tons are caught here every year. Although there is some fish-processing industry here, a large part of the catch is exported to the Netherlands and Germany. There is no road around the island, nor a decent footpath. The banks are low, covered in vegetation and marshy in places. Leisure facilities, such as the yacht harbours at Oxford Island and Ballyronan, are only gradually being set up.

Sights around Lough Neagh

The Lough Neagh Discovery Centre on Oxford Island (Co. Armagh) uses videos and an exhibition to introduce visitors to the history of the lake, placing special emphasis on the indigenous flora and fauna. There are some nice hiking trails, as well as boat tours to the islands in Lough Neagh. (Opening times: April–Sept daily 10am–5pm, Oct–March Wed–Sun 10am to 5pm.)

Lough Neagh Discovery Centre

> **? DID YOU KNOW …?**
>
> ■ Legend has it that Lough Neagh was created by Finn MacCool, as was Giant's Causeway. One day Finn MacCool, pursuing a Scottish giant, grabbed a lump of soil and tossed it at him. Unfortunately, the Scot managed to escape, but the hole that stayed behind where MacCool had lifted the lump filled up with water, creating Lough Neagh, whilst the lump fell into the sea, creating the Isle of Man.

Antrim (pop. 20,000), which gave the county its name, lies at the mouth of Six Mile Water. Burned down in 1649 by General Monro, in 1798 the town successfully resisted an attack by the United Irishmen. Few old buildings remain, amongst them the court, built in 1762. The airport of ►Belfast (Belfast International Airport) is only 6km/3.5 miles away. Over the centuries, Antrim Castle (1622) was burned down and rebuilt several times. Now all that is left are the castle gardens, laid out by Le Nôtre, creator of the gardens in Versailles, France. One mile northeast of the town, in Steeple Park, look for a mighty and particularly well-preserved round tower, over 27m/88ft high.

From Antrim, drive north to Ballymena, a predominantly Protestant town – and home ground of Unionist firebrand Reverend Ian Paisley. Actor Liam Neeson, who shot to worldwide fame with his title role in »Schindler's List« (1992), was born here. Neeson went on to star in »Michael Collins« 1996, »Star Wars – Episode I« 1999 and »Love Actually« (2003).

Ballymena

Protestants from Moravia (in today's Czech Republic) settled in the area around Gracehill (pop. 680), 2km/1.2 miles west, in the mid-18th century, where they continued to live according to their faith, following the strict principles that had made them the target of persecution in their home country. Two entrances lead into their church, one for men and one for women. The cemetery is also segregated by gender.

Gracehill

Near Cullybacky, 6km/3.5 miles west of Ballymena, stood the home of the ancestors of Chester Alan Arthur, 21st President of the United

◄ Arthur's Cottage

States of America. The former family home can be visited and, in the summer months, actors in period costume explain how bread was baked and quilts sown in the olden days.

Hillsborough In the small town of Hillsborough (pop. 24,000), southwest of Belfast, at the end of Main Street, impressive Hillsborough Castle catches the eye. In the years 1923–1973, this used to be the residence of the governor of Northern Ireland, today it is the residence of the British Secretary of State for Northern Ireland. At the foot of the hill, the neo-Gothic St Malachy's Church with its two 18th-century organs is worth a visit.

Banbridge South of Lough Neagh, the small town of Banbridge was established at the time of the Industrial Revolution. This is the start of **Brontë Interpretative Centre** ► the Brontë Homeland Drive, stretching along the valley River Bann valley toward Rathfriland, 16km/10 miles further south. The father of the two famous writers, Patrick Brontë, was born here, teaching for a long time at the local school. The locals are convinced that the gloomy atmosphere described in Emily Brontë's *Wuthering Heights* was inspired by her father's tales. In any case, the neighbouring village of Drumballyroney is now home to Northern Ireland's Brontë Homeland Interpretative Centre, with an exhibition on this family of ⏱ writers. (Opening times: March–Oct Tues–Fri 11am–5pm, Sat/Sun 2–6pm.)

Around Dungannon Take the M1 towards Dungannon, driving around Lough Neagh along its southern bank. From there, good detours could lead to The **Peatlands Park** ► Argory, Ardress House (both ►Armagh) or Peatlands Park, which is particularly popular with children and adolescents. Here, young visitors can learn about peat and the bog garden, with its typical plants, such as the sundew, one of two indigenous carniverous plants. Riding a little open train used in the past to transport peat, they can then take a 15-min tour of the place, past two lakes, a small forest ⏱ and an orchard. (Opening times: Easter–late Sept Sat/Sun 2–6pm; July and Aug daily.)

! *Baedeker* TIP

Irish Linen Tour

In Banbridge, book a place on the Irish Linen Tour, including the Irish Linen Centre in Lisburn (see photo), a flax farm in Dromore and a working linen mill. If you don't want to do the whole tour, pick up some information from the long-established Ferguson Linen Centre on Scarva Road, west of town.

Dungannon (pop. 9400), a market town with various industries used to be the seat of the O'Neills from the 13th to the early 17th century. Visit Tyrone Crystal Ltd in Killbrackey on the northeastern edge of town; the company was founded in the early 1970s by a Catholic priest involved in the community to fight the enormously high unemployment in the region. Today, a guided tour shows what is involved in producing well-crafted glass objects, available for purchase on site. (Opening times: April–Oct Mon–Sat 9.30am–3.30pm, Nov–March Mon–Fri 9.30am–3.30pm.)

◄ Tyrone Crystal

Follow the A4 west of town, then take a signposted road towards Castlecaulfield (approx. 6km/3.5 miles). Reached after another mile, Parkanaur Forest Park used to be the residence of the Burgess family; the Victorian building has now been converted into a training centre for adults with special needs. Visitors are free to walk around the grounds at leisure. The fallow deer grazing here are said to make up the oldest herd in Ireland and have their origins in a present by Queen Elizabeth I, in 1595.

◄ Parkanaur Forest Park

Only a few miles further north, at the village of Donaghmore, look for Donaghmore High Cross, put together from two individual pieces. The biblical scenes depicted here are similar to the ones seen on the Ardboe Cross (see below).

◄ Donaghmore High Cross

Following the road around Lough Neagh, the A29 leads to Cookstown where, until recently, Catholic and Protestant areas were strictly segregated and guarded. For a look at Tullaghoge Fort first, take a right turn onto the B520 just before reaching Cookstown. The fort used to be the burial place of the O'Hagans and the 11th-century coronation site of the kings of Ulster.

Cookstown

East of Cookstown, on the shore of Lough Neagh, look for the 4m/13ft Ardboe Cross on the site of a 6th-century monastery. Despite its weathered state, this is considered one of the most beautiful High Crosses in Ulster. Its 22 panels show on the eastern side scenes from the Old Testament (Adam and Eve, the Sacrifice of Isaac, etc.) and on the northern side, scenes from the New Testament (the Adoration of the Magi, Jesus' Entrance into Jerusalem, the Crucifixion, etc.). It is believed to be the earliest High Cross in Ulster. Here are also ruins of a church and abbey founded in 590 by St Coleman. Close by, visit Coyle's Cottage, a 300-year-old fisherman's hut.

◄ Ardboe Cross

6km/3.5 miles west of Cookstown off the A505, right past Kildress Church, Wellbrook Beetling Mill lies in a pretty wooded valley on the bank of the Ballinderry. In the mill, the last part of the process of linen manufacturing is explained. »Beetling« is how the lustrous sheen is achieved, the hard fabric being hammered and passed through (heated) rollers. Between the 18th and the 20th century, linen manufacture was the most important industry in Ulster. Wellbrook alone had six mills; its wooden hammers were powered by water. (Opening times: July–Aug Wed–Mon 2–6pm; April–June and Sept Sat/Sun and bank holidays 2–6pm.)

◄ Wellbrook Beetling Mill

Springhill House

Also impressive is Springhill House (1795), an estate some 8km/5 miles northeast of Cookstown. There is beautiful antique oak furniture, but the library, the armoury and the large costume collection are equally fascinating. Not one but two ghosts are said to haunt the premises at night. Don't miss the gardens and park! (Opening times: April and June–Sept Sat/Sun 2–6pm; July–Aug Fri–Wed 2–6pm.)

Heading north, don't leave without visiting Maghera Old Church. There was a monastery here as early as the 6th century, but it was raided by the Vikings in 832. The most interesting features of the ruined church (10th/12th century) are the motifs on the door jambs and the Crucifixion scene on the lintel. You can't miss the stone pillar in the churchyard. Decorated with a carved cross, this is said to mark the grave of St Lurach, the original founder of the monastery.

! **Baedeker TIP**

Day trips
Visit the Sperrin Mountains, for instance the Beaghmore Stone Circle nearby (see picture).

Loughrea (Baile Locha Riach)

C 3

Republic of Ireland, province: Connaught
Population: 3,400

County: Galway

Up-and-coming Loughrea got its Irish name Baile Locha Riach (»town on the grey lake«) from the small lake southeast of town.

St Brenda's Cathedral

The most interesting building in town is St Brenda's Cathedral, with some very fine windows showing the development of Irish stained glass in the 20th century. In addition, there are further good examples of modern art, such as a cycle showing the Stations of the Cross.

Around Loughrea

✷ Turoe Stone

Some 6km/3.5 miles north of town, on the R350 near Bullaun, look for the 3rd century Turoe Stone, an oval block of granite, some 90cm/3ft high, with a smooth lower quarter and a meander pattern above. The rounded upper half is decorated with a curvilinear relief ornament typical of the Celtic La Tène period. Originally, the stone stood beside a prehistoric ring fort, and was used for ritual purposes.

From Loughrea, drive southeast along Lough Rea and take a half left turn at Carrowkeel, to get (via Duniry) to Pallas. The imposing 16th century castle, which has hardly suffered any damage over the centuries, is open to visitors. Around 30km/20 miles southeast of Loughrea, at the northern end of Lough Derg and at the mouth of the Shannon, lies Portumna, a good base for golfing, fishing, sailing and rowing (there is a new marina). In the state-owned Portumna Forest Park just out of town visit Portumna Castle, a large structure dating from 1618 and fortified by corner towers, and the Dominican friary, the ruins of a monastery, consisting of a church with beautiful eastern window and monastic buildings.

Towards Portumna

Taking the R349 or R348 northwest to Athenry, the scenery gradually becomes more rocky and bare. Until the late 16th century, the little town of Athenry was fairly important; it still preserves many medieval buildings. Athenry Castle (1235–1250) consists of a ruined gabled tower standing within the remains of outer walls with two corner turrets. Of a Dominican friary, founded in 1241 and much altered and destroyed many times, only the ruined church remains, containing a number of funerary monuments. Of the Market Cross, only the base and the top part survive, showing figurative carvings of the Crucifixion and the Virgin with Child. The remains of the medieval fortifications, probably dating from the early 14th century, mark the boundaries of the old town; the tower-like north gate is well-preserved.

Athenry

Monaghan (Muineachán)

B 5

Republic of Ireland, province: Ulster   **County:** Monaghan
Population: 5,700

Only 8km/5 miles from the border with Northern Ireland, Monaghan is the administrative and agricultural centre of the county of the same name.

The Ulster Canal, connecting Belfast with the western coast of Ireland, runs right through the town. Today however, the canal is a fairly neglected waterway. There was a settlement here as early as the 9th century, whilst today's Monaghan dates from the 18th and 19th century.

A town with history

Near the neo-Gothic parish church of St Patrick's look for the pretty Courthouse (1829) containing the excellent County Museum and a small art gallery. On Market Place, the small elegant structure of the Market House catches the eye, built in 1792 in the classical style. On Old Cross Square stands the slightly earlier Old Infirmary Building

Sights

of 1768, and not far from there, the Market Cross (1714). Its slender spire makes the neo-Gothic St Macartan's Cathedral a local landmark in the south of Monaghan. Convent Lake, with its Crannóg, lies at the end of Park Street on the other side of the canal. The St Louis Convent Heritage Centre has information on the convent, the Crannóg and the history of the town.

Around Monaghan

Take the R185 north out of Monaghan for 11km/7 miles to the picturesque village of **Glaslough.** At the edge of the village begins the extensive park of Leslie Castle, built in the second half of the 19th century. Join a guided tour to visit the castle, still in the hands of the Leslie family. It is possible to stay overnight in one of the rooms or to just have dinner here.

Lough Muckno To the southeast of Monaghan lies **Castleblayney.** Beside it, Lough Muckno, the largest and most beautiful of the Monaghan lakes, offers good fishing. 20km/12 miles further south, a cooperative in Carrickmacross produces high-quality lace, sold at the local Lace Gallery on the Square.

Clones West of Monaghan, directly on the border with Northern Ireland Clones (pop. 1,920) was founded by St Tigernach. The famous crochet lace of Clones is still made by hand today, examples are shown in the Clones Lace Gallery in the Canals Stores. (Opening times: Tue–Sat 10am–6pm.) On the main square (The Diamond), a 4.5m/15ft High Cross dating from the 10th century is decorated with scenes from the Bible. The cemetery has a round tower (23m/75ft) and a house-shaped shrine with remarkable finials. Not far from there, in another churchyard, stands the 12th-century ruined abbey church. The abbey was originally founded by St Tigernach in the early 6th century. Both cemeteries have several interesting headstones from the 17th and 18th centuries.

MONAGHAN

INFORMATION

Market House
Tel. (0 47) 8 11 22
Open: April–Oct

WHERE TO STAY

▶ **Luxury**
Four Seasons
Coolshannagh
Tel. (0 47) 8 18 88, Fax (0 47) 8 31 31
info@4seasonshotel.ie
Relax in style at the fireplace in the bar, in the restaurant with a good dinner, in the pool, or in the hotel sauna.

✳ Monasterboice (Mainistir Bhuithe)

C 5

Republic of Ireland, province: Leinster

County: Louth

Its extraordinary High Crosses make Monasterboice one of the most important sights in Ireland. The monastery was founded in the 5th century by St Buite, a pupil of St Patrick's.

Happily, the ruins of the medieval monastic enclosure may be visited in peace and quiet; there is no visitor centre, nor that many tourists. The ruins lie right within a cemetery on the east coast of Ireland, reached via the R168.

In 1097, valuable manuscripts perished when the round tower burned out. The old cemetery preserves two churches, a round tower, three High Crosses, two early tomb slabs and a working sundial of uncertain age. The entrance of the round tower (33m/108ft), which is missing its cap, lies 1.8m/6ft above ground. For security reasons, it is no longer accessible.

Medieval monastery

The most impressive High Cross is Muireadach's Cross (Southern Cross), standing near the entrance. This is one of the most beautiful in Ireland and was named after the donor whose name is inscribed on the western side of the cross. Until recently, it was assumed that this was Muireadach II, who died in 922. New research has shown that the cross was made as early as the first half of the 9th century, which would refer to the first abbot, who died at Monasterboice in 844.

✳ ✳ Muireadach's Cross

The 5.1m/17ft monolithic cross is adorned on all sides by detailed and skilfully carved reliefs. The scenes, mostly depicted on square panels, are to be read from the bottom up. On the eastern side, look for Adam and Eve, Cain and Abel, David and Goliath, Moses Striking the Rock, the Adoration of the Magi, Christ in Judgment and Archangel Michael Weighing the Souls. The top, carved in the shape of a shrine, depicts the meeting of the hermit saints Paul and Anthony in the desert. The western side shows the Capture of Christ, Doubting Thomas, Christ with SS Peter and Paul, the Crucifixion, and a scene that experts have not been able to interpret. The northern side shows again Paul and Anthony, the Flagellation, the Hand of God and interlacing motifs. The southern side depicts the Flight to Egypt, Pilate, and more interlacing, whilst the base shows hunters and animals, interlacing and fretwork.

Unusually high at 6.4m/21ft, and also richly carved, is the Tall Cross (or Western Cross). Of the overall 22 panels, only a few can be made out properly. On the eastern side, look for representations of David Killing the Lion, the Sacrifice of Isaac, the Three Young Men in the

✳ Tall Cross

Furnace, the Capture of Christ, the Ascension, and St Michael with the Devil. The western side depicts Soldiers Guarding the Tomb of Christ, the Baptism, the Mocking of Christ, the Kiss of Judas, and the Crucifixion.

Of the northern cross at the edge of the churchyard only the top and a piece of the shaft are preserved.

North Cross

✶ Mourne Mountains

B 5/6

Northern Ireland, province: Ulster   **County:** Down

»Where the Mountains o' Mourne sweep down to the sea« – this well-known folk song has made the Mourne Mountains the most famous in Ireland. The Mournes are traversed by a single road, the B27 from Kilkeel to Hilltown.

They cover a surface area of 24km/15 miles in length and 13km/8 miles in width. The mountain range owes its characteristic shape to its 12 rounded peaks, rising to the east to a height of up to 610m/ 2001ft. A popular but difficult hiking trail leads from Newcastle to Slieve Donard, passing the Mourne Wall, erected in the early 20th century to protect the two reservoirs in Silent Valley.

Soft hill scenery in Northern Ireland

Some 35km/22 miles north of Newcastle, still in the Mourne Mountains, look for the Legananny Dolmen (►Around Downpatrick) rising up; this is one of the most beautiful and most photographed sights in the country.

Legananny Dolmen

Newcastle (pop. 7,200) has beena popular holiday resort since the 19th century, with pretty beaches and a promenade. This coastal town is also known for its close proximity to the famous Royal County Down Club golf course. Holidaymakers can look at vintage cars in the Route 66 American Car Museum or have fun in the Tropicana leisure pool.
The little town makes a great base for exploring the Mourne Mountains. There are three parks nearby, as well as several trails for walking, hiking or horseriding. Donard Park at the southern edge of town is a good starting point for climbing Slieve Donard (852m/ 2,795ft), the highest of the Mourne mountains. From here, the view stretches all the way to the Isle of Man, the whole of County Down and Strangford Lough with its landmark Scrabo Tower. To the north lie the hills of ►Belfast, to the northwest, ►Lough Neagh can be

Newcastle

← *Round tower and High Cross: the remains of the 5th-century monastery of Monasterboice*

The Mourne Mountains

made out. From the parking lot at Bloody Bridge, near Newcastle, the climb normally takes an afternoon. Around 3km/2 miles northeast of town, alongside the northern slopes of the Mournes, stretches extensive **Tollymore Forest Park**. The former 18th-century country seat has a conspicuous Gothic gateway. At summer weekends there are guided tours, and the Tollymore Outdoor Centre offers hiking, climbing and kayaking courses. A visitor centre has interesting information on the history of the region and its flora and fauna. (Opening times: park daily 10am–dusk; visitors centre June–Aug daily noon–5pm; Sept–May Sat/Sun noon–5pm.)

By Castlewellan village, further to the northeast, **Castlewellan Forest Park** is a good place to hire a boat, go fishing or hiking. The arboretum, laid out in 1740, has many different shrubs and trees and is well-known in the region (open: daily from 10am–dusk). Outside the park, Mount Pleasant Horse Trekking Centre offers hacks for beginners and experienced riders.

★
Mournes Coast Road

Annalong ►

Green Castle, Rostrevor ►

Warrenpoint ►

The coastal road leading south from Newcastle goes uphill, providing views out to sea on the left and, to the right, of the ever-changing backdrop of the Mourne Mountains, with its many rare plants. The sleepy-looking villages along the road live off fishing and agriculture. Annalong, Kilkeel, Rostrevor and Warrenpoint make a good stop-off point. From here, several side roads lead to the reservoirs of Silent Valley and the wild scenery around Spelga Dam. In the 18th century, the coastal stretch from Newcastle to the little village of Greencastle was infamous for smuggling; today, there are many old lookouts used by the coastal guard. High above the entrance to Carlingford Lough, 13th century Green Castle sits on a rocky ledge. Some 12km/7.5 miles further west, Rostrevor, the most beautiful village in the Mourne Mountains, hugs Carlingford Lough. The Victorian holiday resort owes its reputation to its colourful houses, mediterranean vegetation and pleasant atmosphere. The stretch of road leading from this seaport to Newry is very charming, its castle-like tower houses and ruins a little reminiscent of a trip down the Rhine. Particularly beautiful is the place where the canal meets the sea at the medieval Narrow Water Castle on the one bank, and the round tower of Clonallan Monastery on the other.

Newry

The old commercial centre and border town of Newry (pop. 23,000), between Dublin and Belfast, was established because of its strategic location at the Gap of the North, the gateway to Ulster. Reaping the rewards of the peace process, the locals have been improving the town and promoting tourism. Newry makes a good base for trips into the Mourne Mountains, to the coast, Slieve Gullion Park or the Cooley Peninsula (►Around Dundalk).

In terms of local history, the predominantly Irish-Nationalist Newry prefers references to the Cistercian foundation in 1144 rather than Sir Nicholas Bagnal. The Commander of the English garrison on Carlingford Lough financed the building of St Patrick's (1578), the first Anglican church on Irish soil. Up until the 1950s, brown coal was shipped on the Newry Canal (1740) from the western banks of Lough Neagh to Carlingford Neagh.

Mullet Peninsula

B 2

Republic of Ireland, province: Connaught ‎ ‎ ‎ ‎ **County:** Mayo

The lonely, boggy Mullet Peninsula, situated in the furthest northwest of Ireland, is only sparsely populated and hardly sees any tourists.

The peninsula's nearly barren western coast is exposed to the rough Atlantic weather, whilst the sweeping bays of the eastern side enfold Blacksod Bay, making it appear like a big inland lake. Both coastlines have pretty beaches, in particular at its narrowest point, along Elly Bay in the east. The main town, Belmullet, lies on a narrow strait connecting Mullet Peninsula with the main island. Belmullet is a good base for interesting drives along the 25km/16-mile the peninsula, as well as into the adjoining areas to the north.

Lonely peninsula

Mullet Peninsula is dotted with many ruins. Look out for the clifftop fortress at Doonamo Point (7km/4.5 miles northwest of Belmullet). The wall, 60m/197ft long and up to 5.5m/18ft high, stretches across the neck of the promontory jutting out to sea, enclosing three beehive huts as well as a ruined ring fort. In the southernmost part of the peninsula, at Fallmore, stand the ruins of St Dairbhile's Church. Enjoy the view from the peninsula's southern Blacksod Point, ► Achill Island to Slievemore Mountain. Looking west, the little offshore islands were inhabited at one point, and still show evidence of Early Christian settlements.

Scenic drive

5km/3 miles southeast of Belmullet, take the R314 northeast. From Glenamoy, take a detour to the north to **Benwee Head**, about 16km/

Other sights in the area

Towards Belmullet

10 miles away. The last kilometre from Portacloy has to be walked on foot. The massive jagged cliff walls rise up to 257m/843ft out of the sea, giving a fantastic view. A group of seven sea stacks, the Stags of Broadhaven, jut out of the ocean north of Portacloy.

Belderrig ▶ Continue inland on the R314 from Glenamoy inland towards Belderrig, 2km/1.2 miles south of the coast, with some more impressive wild cliff scenery. Alongside Céide Fields (▶ Ballina) 8km/5 miles away, this is the second important excavation site. The remains of a settlement and furrows excavated at Belderrig are, however, thought to date from c1500 BC. 6km/3.5 miles to the west, Glinsk mountain rises to a height of 310m/1,017ft. From the top there are views of the entire area.

Mullingar (An Muileann gCearr)

C 4

Republic of Ireland, province: Leinster
Population: 8,000

County: Westmeath
Information: Tel. (0 44) 4 86 50

Thanks to two large lakes nearby, Lough Owel in the north and Lough Ennell in the south, Mullingar in Westmeath is a popular leisure and recreation area. Large parts of the town are enclosed by the Royal Canal.

Between the waters This little rural town lies at the centre of a district mainly given over to cattle breeding. Dominating the town, the Catholic **Cathedral of Christ the King** (1936–1939) features a set of 42m/138-ft twin towers and houses an ecclesiastical museum. Worth seeing are also the Town Hall and the Courthouse, two imposing buildings dating from the 18th century, as well as the Military Museum in the Columb Barracks.

In Mullingar, the tradition of pewter production dates back centuries. There was a renaissance in the mid-1970s, and since then, objects have again been made from pewter here following old models. The premises may be visited; watch the artisans at work and buy their products.

Mullingar Bronze & Pewter Visitor Centre

Around Mullingar

The R394 leads north to Castlepollard, passing several lakes. At Crookedwood lies the ruined 15th-century church of Taghmon, with a fortified four-storey tower house. The tower and the nave feature vaulted ceilings. Take a minor road east of Crookedwood for 2km/ 1.2 miles to the 15th-century St Munna's Church, built in this beautiful location on the site of the 7th-century church dedicated to St Munna. Look out for the grotesque figure above the north window! Located 3km/2 miles from Crookedwood, driving west, Multyfarnham has a modern Franciscan college, standing on the site of a former 14th-century monastery with restored church. The Stations of the Cross in the college grounds are life-size.

Towards Castlepollard

Castlepollard also owns Tullynally Castle which has been the residence of the Pakenham family, the Earls of Longford, since 1655. The romantic castle (18th/19th century) has been altered several times. Closely connected to the estate are the Duke of Wellington and the novelist Maria Edgeworth (►Longford). Very nice is the park surrounding Tullynally Castle on the shore of Lough Derravaragh. (Opening times: the park is accessible all year round, the castle from mid-July–mid-Aug daily 2–6pm, and by appointment: tel. 044/ 611 59.)

◄ Tullynally Castle & Gardens

☉

Situated among hills some 4km/2.5 miles east of Castlepollard, the historical village of Fore is the site of a monastery founded by St Fechin in the 7th century. The church (c900) is preserved, along with a High Cross in the churchyard and the fortified »Anchorite's Cell« with mausoleum. In the 13th century, the monastery was replaced by a Benedictine priory, the ruins of which stand 400m/437yd apart. Of the priory, a church with two tower houses, parts of a cloister, outbuildings and the circular walls of a dovecote are still standing. Close by, in the fields, look for two gates of the former village fortification.

Fore

Carry on a few miles south of Mullingar on the N52 to Belvedere House and Gardens. The manor house takes its name from the beautiful view of Lough Ennell and was built around 1740 for the newly-

Belvedere House and Gardens

wed Lord Belfield. Soon the first Earl of Belvedere was accusing his young wife of committing adultery with his brother Arthur – and had both locked away for the rest of his life. In other respects, his lordship seems to have been equally belligerent, erecting the »Jealous Wall«, to prevent his other brother, George, who lived nearby, from looking in. (Park opening times: April–Sept daily noon–6pm.)

Locke's Distillery Whiskey lovers will enjoy a visit to Locke's Distillery in Kilbeggan, which has held its licence since 1757. After closing down in 1954, a museum of industry was planned, but eventually, in 1987, the place was taken over by the Cooley Distillery who are now maturing their whiskey here the traditional way, in casks. Join a guided tour of the restored distillery to learn how »pot still whiskey« is produced. Recently, a winery was added, showcasing the production of Irish sherry. (Opening times: April–Oct daily 9am–6pm; Nov–March daily 10am–4pm.)

Naas (An Nás)

C 5

Republic of Ireland, province: Leinster
Population: 8,500

County: Kildare

In the past, the kings of Leinster resided here in the North Mote. Today, Naas, 34km/21 miles southwest of Dublin, is a prosperous industrial town.

Town of kings and horses The Normans fortified the town, but it was raided in the 14th century. Parts of one of the castles were used in the rectory of the Protestant church. Naas borders the plain of Curragh (►Kildare), famous for horse breeding. The town is well known for the horse race on the Punchestown Racecourse 4km/2.5 miles south on the R411.

Around Naas

Maynooth The small town of Maynooth (pop. 8,500), around 24km/15 miles northeast, on the Royal Canal, has a branch of the National University of Ireland: St Patrick's College. The Institute was established in 1795 in the grounds of an earlier foundation by the English aiming to allow the Irish to train their Catholic clergy in their own country. It is currently the largest seminary in Ireland and the British Isles, now also accepting laypeople and women students. The imposing buildings, arranged around courtyards with lawns, date mainly from the 19th century. There is a church and a small museum with works of art and antiquities, documenting the history of the church in Ireland and its missionary activities. Next to the gateway of the college

St Patrick's College ►

stand the remains of Maynooth Castle (13th–17th century): a very large tower house, a gate house and parts of a curtain wall. Maynooth was held by the Earls of Kildare until a failed rebellion in 1534, when the castle fell to the English crown.

◄ Maynooth Cast

Take the N4 east to Leixlip. The name of the town is taken from the Danish and means »salmon leap«. Towering above what has, in recent years, become somewhat of a dormitory town for Dublin, is Leixlip Castle. Worth seeing is a barn about one mile southwest, on private property, which goes by the name of »The Wonderful Barn«. Lady Connolly of Castletown had this conical structure built in 1743, using rubble stone and tiles. Each of its five storeys could be serviced from the outside through hatches; a flight of steps runs in a spiral up to the top.

Leixlip

◄ Wonderful Barn

On the River Liffey, southwest of Leixlip, lies Celbridge. 4km/2.5 miles upstream stands spacious Castletown Housewhich has features of great architectural interest. Built in 1722 for the Irish Member of Parliament William Connolly by Alessandro Galilei, the central building, approached by a broad flight of steps, consists of three storeys as well as thirteen axes. The wings are connected to the central block by means of quadrant-shaped colonnades. The excellent stucco work inside, the staircase and the Pompeian Gallery are worth seeing. Today, the house is the seat of the Irish Georgian Society that endeavours to preserve as many buildings from the Georgian period as possible. (Opening times: April–Sept Mon–Fri 10am–6pm, Sat 11am–6pm, Sun 2–6pm; Oct–March Mon–Fri 10am–5pm, Sun 2–5pm)

★
Castletown House

The main attraction of Straffan, situated 6km/3.5 miles southwest of Celbridge, is a railway museum with a collection of rare models. (Opening times: June–Aug Tues–Sat 2–6pm; April, May and Sept Sun 2.30–5.30pm)

Straffan

Castletown House Plan

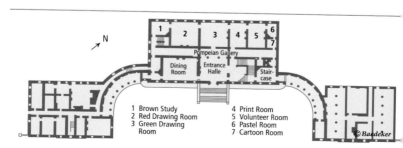

1 Brown Study
2 Red Drawing Room
3 Green Drawing Room
4 Print Room
5 Volunteer Room
6 Pastel Room
7 Cartoon Room

© Baedeker

Butterfly Farm

Butterflies are free to fly around the tropical greenhouse of Butterfly Farm in Ovidstown; various insects, spiders and reptiles are safely kept behind glass. (Opening times: May–Aug daily noon–5.30pm.)

Punchestown

Don't miss the very impressive standing stone of Punchestown, standing 5km/3 miles southeast of Naas on Woolpack Road, the medieval road from Dublin to Kilkenny. This menhir is over 7m/23ft high and tapering toward the top. When it toppled in 1931, a Bronze Age burial site was found at its foot.

Jigginstown House

Just under 2km/1.2 miles southwest of Naas, along the N7, look for the bulky torso of a building. Jigginstown House, begun in 1633 by the Count of Strafford as a summer residence for himself and King Charles I, was never completed, as Strafford was beheaded in 1641. The house's planned front length of 114m/125yd would have made it one of the largest manor houses in Ireland; it would also have been the first to be built completely in red brick. As it is, only the elegantly vaulted cellar and a few imposing rooms on the ground floor remain.

Robertstown

On the banks of the ►Grand Canal, reached via the R409, stands the old Canal Hotel of Robertstown, erected for ship passengers in 1801, at the highest point of the Robertstown Canal. Both the hotel and the waterfront of the village have had a makeover.

Navan (An Uaimh)

C 5

Republic of Ireland, province:
Leinster
Population: 3,500

County: Meath

Navan is the largest town in County Meath. The inventor of the internationally recognized scale measuring wind force, Admiral Sir Francis Beaufort (1774–1857), was born here.

Transport and industry

This little town lies northwest of Dublin in hilly terrain at the confluence of the Boyne and Blackwater rivers. There is a carpet factory here and, nearby, in the direction of Kells, the largest lead and zinc mine in Europe: Tara. The large motte on the western edge of Navan is a popular viewpoint.

Around Navan

Along the N51 towards Slane

Around 2km/1.2 miles northeast of town, in former monastic grounds in Donaghmore , stand a well-preserved round tower and a church. This is said to be the site of the first monastery St Patrick founded in Ireland. The 10th-century tower has a round-arched entrance door, situated at 3.5m/11.5ft above ground, with a relief of the Crucifixion. The church dates from the 15th century and the churchyard has some Early Christian headstones. On a rise further east, Dunmoe Castle comes into view. Two sides of the rectangular 16th-century castle with round towers survive.

◄ Donaghmore

◄ Dunmoe Castle

South of Navan, take a left turn 1km/0.6 miles past Bective to the 12th-century Cistercian abbey of Bective, a daughter house of Mellifont Abbey (► Drogheda). Some parts of the church, as well as the chapter house, are preserved. The pretty cloister, the tower house and the large refectory date from the 15th century, when the monastery was fortified.

Bective Abbey

Take the N51 west towards Rathmore. The village's ruined 15th-century church has remarkable figurative representations inside. To the left, just off the road towards Athboy, rises the Hill of Ward (117m/ 384ft), a very ancient religious site and meeting place.

Rathmore

Newgrange

►Boyne Valley

New Ross (Rhos Mhic Triúin)

D 5

Republic of Ireland, province: Leinster
Population: 5,000

County: Wexford

New Ross, on the steep banks of the River Barrow, is one of the oldest towns in County Wexford. Tourists enjoy coming to this town in the southeastern corner of Ireland, using it as a base for organized boat trips on the rivers Barrow and Nore.

Narrow, winding streets, occasionally narrow stairways only accessible to pedestrians, still give an idea of the medieval town plan. Small ships liven up the broad river and the port. Of the large early 13th-century St Mary's parish church, only the chancel and transepts remain. In the 19th cen-

 Baedeker TIP

Dunbrody Project

The SS Dunbrody took emigrants to the New World between 1845 and 1870. In the reconstructed ship a film tells its history, whilst an interactive exhibition brings to life the conditions aboard those ships. A database on Irish emigration to America allows some genealogical research.

tury, the nave had to give way to a new church. Look out for three delicately mullioned lancet arch windows in the chancel, as well as several medieval tombs. The Tholsel town hall, built between 1749 and 1804, is a pretty classical building with a domed clock tower.

Around New Ross

✱ **Kennedy Memorial Forest Park**

Drive a few miles south of New Ross on the R733 to reach the 250ha/618-acre John F Kennedy Memorial Forest Park. The park was opened in 1968, with finance provided by Americans of Irish descent in memory of John Fitzgerald Kennedy, the President of the United States assassinated in 1963. John F Kennedy's great-grandfather was born in Dunganstown village, to the west. 4,500 different kinds of trees and shrubs grow in the grounds, amongst them 500 varieties of rhododendron and 150 of azalea. Enjoy a good panoramic view from Slieve Coilte hill which can be accessed by car. The visitor centre shows a video and a permanent exhibition on the flora of the park. (Opening times: park May–Aug daily 10am–8pm; April and Sept to 6.30pm; Oct–March only to 5pm.)

On Hook Peninsula
✱ **Dunbrody Abbey** ►

Continue on the R733 to Dunbrody Abbey, the imposing remains of a 12th-century Cistercian monastery. The austere church has a choir, transepts, a nave and a 15th-century crossing tower. Of the monastic buildings, the library and the chapter house on the eastern side, the refectory and the kitchen on the southern side survive.

At Arthurstown, Ballyhack Castle stands off the road, at the water's edge. The five-storey 15th-century castle with vaulted rooms has been restored and is open to the public. (Opening times: July und Aug daily 10am–7pm; March–June and Sept Wed–Sun noon to 6pm.)

From Ballyhack, there is a passenger ferry across the broad mouth of the River Barrow to Passage East. Branch off the R733 past Arthurstown and continue south on a side road to get to the small fishing village of **Duncannon**, which has a nice sandy beach. On a promontory, the fort of guards the entrance to the mouth of the river.

The road ends in the south of the long peninsula, where on the eastern side 15th/17th-century **Slade Castle** occupies a picturesque position next to a fishing harbour. The beacon at the southern point of Hook Head peninsula stands on a 700-year-old round keep.

From Hook Head, take the road back 3km/1.9 miles north and make a right in Templetown towards Fethard-on-Sea, which also has nice sandy beaches. In 1169, where the headland of Baginbun extends south out to sea, the first Normans landed in Ireland. ◄ Fethard-on-Sea

East of the crossroads where the R733 and R734 meet, about 7km/ 4.5 miles north of Fethard, a signposted access road branches off to the right, for the ruins of the 11th and 15th-century Cistercian monastery of Tintern Abbey. ◄ Tintern Abbey

Omagh (An Omaigh)

B 4

Northern Ireland, province: Ulster   **County:** Tyrone
Population: 17,300

Tourists know Omagh most of all for its open-air museum, the Ulster-American Folk Park.

The place where the Drumragh and Camowen rivers come together is a great base for salmon-fishing. Hikes in the Sperrin Mountains are also recommended. Visitors who enjoy parks can also explore Gortin Glen Forest Park. The market town was in the news for all the wrong reasons in August 1998, when a car bomb planted by a splinter group of the IRA killed 28 people and injured another 200. Open-air history

Around Omagh

Head out north on the A5 from Omagh for 6km/3.5 miles, to reach the Ulster American Folk Park. This extensive open-air museum shows the history of emigration from Ulster to the US. The historical reasons behind emigration, the living conditions at the time (18th/ 19th century), are portrayed here, as well as the difficult trip across the Atlantic to a fresh start in America. The idea is to show the differences, but also common ground between the Old and the New World. There is a blacksmith's, cottages, a Presbyterian meeting house and much more, but particularly impressive are the reconstructed streets as you would have encountered them in an Ulster village and an American port city. ✹ ✹ **Ulster American Folk Park**

Whilst only some 4 million Irish live on the island, they are considered one of the major European population groups. Worldwide, around 78 million people are said to have Irish roots; as many as 15 US presidents are the descendants of Irish immigrants; of those, eleven have their roots in Ulster. (Opening times: Easter–mid-Sept Mon–Sat 11am–6.30pm, Sun 11.30am–7pm; mid-Sept–Easter Mon–Fri 10.30am–5pm.)

Situated more to the east, Gortin Glen Forest Park may be explored on foot or by car: there is a choice of three walking trails (2–4km/ 1.2–2.5 miles long); alternatively take a 9km/5.5-mile circular drive through the forest, with a chance of seeing Sika deer and other wild animals. Suitable for a longer walk is the stretch from Gortin Glen Forest Park to the Ulster American Folk Park. The trail, part of the Ulster Way, leads approx. 16km/10 miles along small roads and forest paths. On the way back, it is possible to catch the bus (no. 97). Pick up a trail map from the tourist office in Omagh.   **Gortin Glen Forest Park**

Every year, the border village of Strabane, west of the ► Sperrin Mountains, attracts some literary pilgrims following in the footsteps of Brian O'Nolan (aka Flann O'Brien aka Myles na gCopaleen). Flann O'Brien was born in the house on Bowling Green.   **Strabane**
Also of interest is Gray's Printing Museum in the former printing workshop where John Dunlop learned the trade. He was the first to print the American Declaration of Independence. (Opening times: Tues–Sat 11am–5pm.)   ◄ **Gray's Printing Museum** ☉

Portlaoise (Port Laoise)

Republic of Ireland, province: Leinster   **County:** Laois
Population: 3,600

Nothing remains of the original buildings of the old town of Portlaoise (pronounced »Purtleash«), which was destroyed in the 17th century, and most people associate Portlaoise only with the high-security prison for IRA prisoners on the outskirts, off the Dublin road, a fortress protected by barbed-wire.

Some 13km/8 miles northeast of town, near Emo village, look for Emo Court manor house. The house was built in the late 18th century for the Earls of Portarlington by famous architect James Gandon. Take a stroll in the park, with yew tree avenues, extensive lawns, rare trees and shrubs. (Opening times: mid-June–mid Sept Tue–Sun 10.30am–5.30pm.)   **Emo Court**

Take the N80 east of Portlaoise, passing after 5km/3.1 miles the Rock of Dunamase, a spectacular, somewhat sombre-looking ruined castle (10th–17th century). On the 60m/200-ft ridge, a tower house, bastion walls with turrets, gatehouses, walls and trenches of the old extensive fortification survive. There is a wonderful panoramic view of   **Rock of Dunamase**

← *After years of famine and poverty, Irish emigrants found*
  well-stocked shops with groceries and other commodities in America.

PORTALOISE

INFORMATION
James Fintan Lawlor Avenue
Tel. (05 02) 2 11 78
Open: June–Aug

WHERE TO STAY
► **Mid-range**
Killeshin Hotel
Dublin Road
Tel. (05 02) 2 16 63
Fax (05 02) 2 19 76
killeshinhotel@eircom.net
This hotel is a favourite with
business travellers.

the round tower of Timaloe to the south, the Slieve Bloom Mountains to the north and – on very clear days – even of the Wicklow Mountains to the east.

Around 12km/7.5 miles southeast rises the 12th-century, nearly 30m/100-ft round tower, all that is left of a **Timahoe monastery**. The Romanesque doorway is decorated with carved faces.

From Timahoe, drive 13km/8 miles southwest on minor roads to **Abbeyleix**. This pretty little town was established in the 18th century on the foundations of an earlier monastery, meticulously laid out by Viscount de Vesci. The Viscount's family seat, Abbeyleix House (1773), is set in a beautiful park. Heywood Gardens near Ballinakill, 5km/3 miles south of Abbeyleix, are also worth a visit.

Heywood Gardens ►

West of Portlaoise, the Slieve Bloom Mountains rise up to an altitude of 520m/1706ft. To access their beautiful valleys, take the scenic little roads from Mountrath.

Slieve Bloom Mountains

Mountmellick was founded in the 17th century by Quakers who, in 1677, opened their first school in Ireland in this little town, nearly completely surrounded by the Owenass River. 7km/4.5 miles further northwest, the Quakers established their first large cemetery in Rosenallis, at the foot of the Slieve Bloom Mountains. At Mountmellick, also look for one of the bizarre swarms of drumlins (mounds of gravel and sand created in the Ice Age) typical of the area. There is another one north of Portlaoise.

Mountmellick

★ ★ **Ring of Kerry**

D/E 1/2

Republic of Ireland, province: Munster   **County:** Kerry

The scenic drive around the Iveragh Peninsula has become famous as the »Ring of Kerry«. The road offers spectacular views of the coast, wild bogs and enchanting hill scenery.

Schedule a whole day to properly enjoy this extraordinarily beautiful landscape dotted with little fishing villages. The circular drive starts in Kenmare on the N70 southeast, carries on west via Waterville, and on to Killorglin in the north. Carry on inland on the R562 to Killarney and from there back to Kenmare. The overall distance is 158km/ 98 miles. If you are planning a detour to Valentia Island in the west, it adds at least 40km/25 miles to the tour.

Most popular tourist route in Ireland

Drive around the Ring of Kerry

The friendly town of Kenmare is situated where the Roughty River flows into the long bay of Kenmare River. High-qualitiy lace is produced here, and the woollen industry also has a good reputation. Today, the main source of revenue is tourism; but whilst much in evidence, tourism has not diminished Kenmare's nostalgic charm. The two main roads of Kenmare form an X, with a little park at the

Kenmare

Mountains to one side, the sea to the other: a Ring of Kerry panorama

top. Close by, to the west, on the banks of the River Finnihy, look for the Druid's Circle: 15 standing stones with a diameter of 15m/16.4yd and a dolmen at its centre.

Kenmare Kenmare is not only a good starting point for the Ring of Kerry, but also for the Ring of Beara, much less known and spectacular in its own way – well worth doing. The Ring of Beara leads around the Beara Peninsula south of Kenmare. (►Beara Peninsula).

Start the Ring of Kerry from Kenmare initially on the N70 going west, following the bay. On the right-hand side rise the foothills of the Macgillycuddy's Reeks.

The church in **Templenoe** dates from 1816. There is a viewpoint with car park at the ruined castle of Dromare.

After 6km/3.5 miles, the valley of the **River Blackwater** opens up to the right, where the river plummets through a deep gorge into the sea. Take a little path leading down off the road through dense, nearly tropical vegetation.

A little road leads north into the mountains, via a 250m/820ft pass to **Glencar** and Caragh Lake.

In **Tahilla** anglers can choose between freshwater fishing and high-sea fishing. Two of the main draws of Parknasilla are its scenic location and its year-round mild climate, favouring palm trees, pines, bamboo and jasmin.

! **Baedeker TIP**

Peak season

In peak season the Ring of Kerry can turn into one big traffic jam! It is recommended to start early in the morning in Kenmare – this avoids being stuck behind a coach all day. Coaches start in Killorglin.

Sandy beach on the Ring of Kerry

Sneem ► A bit further inland, situated on a narrow inlet, Sneem is a good base for fishing. The Protestant Church, which has seen many alterations since its construction in the 16th century, features an original weather vane in the shape of a trout. The mountains to the north and west, with a height of up to 660m/2,165ft, offer good opportunities for hillwalking and climbing.

✳
Staigue Fort After approx. 13km/8 miles, a very narrow road turns off to the right at Castlecove. Some 4km/2.5 miles on, a large stone fort of indeterminate date appears on a hill between two valleys. Staigue Fort is a round dry-stone building, 27m/89ft in diameter and over 5m/16ft high, surrounded by a ditch, and with chambers and stairs inside its 4m/13ft walls.

Back at the seashore, enjoy the drive with a view of the many small islands dotting the coast, and turn towards Caherdaniel, which offers opportunities for trout fishing, swimming and surfing. Nearby is a small stone fort.

Caherdaniel

Southwest of Caherdaniel stretches Derrynane National Historic Park. Take the sign-posted nature trail to explore the dunes, with a long sandy beach in front. At low tide, you can go across to tiny offshore Abbey Island. Themanor house was the home of »The Great Liberator«, Daniel O'Connell (1775–1847). Today, it houses a museum. (Opening times: May–Sept Mon–Sat 9am–6pm, Sun 11am–7pm; April and Oct Tues–Sun 2–5pm; the park is accessible at all times.)

★ **Derrynane National Historic Park**

The N70 leads up to the Coomakista Pass, rising 210m/689ft above the sea (splendid views!), and down to Ballinskelligs Bay. Lough Currane is to your right. Church Island, in this fresh-water lake, has a destroyed 12th-century church with a Romanesque doorway, remains of monks' living quarters, as well as several headstones with Christian symbols. Carrying on along the southern shore of Lough Currane, a sunken ruined castle is revealed. On the western shore lie the horse-shoe-shaped stone fort of Beenbane and the ruins of a beehive hut with thick walls.

Lough Currane

Waterville, Irish An Coirean (»little whirlpool«), lies on the small isthmus between Lough Currane and the bay. From here, two minor roads (later becoming one) lead right across the Iveragh Peninsula over the mountains and down to Killorglin, with very few tourists. Well worth doing! The southern route leads past various lakes with plenty of fish. West of Waterville, **Ballinskelligs Bay** has good beaches. Ballinskelligs village lies on the opposite shore.

! *Baedeker* TIP

Fishing

Waterville has everything: the sea, lakes and rivers teeming with fish make the village a popular base for freshwater and ocean fishing.

North of Waterville, a road branches off to the left, in the direction of Portmagee. Continue on a narrow side road south towards Coomanaspig Pass (330m/1,083ft) for a magnificent view of the bays and bird islands of this part of the Atlantic.

◄ Coomanaspig Pass

Portmagee bridge (1970) leads across a narrow sound onto bare, rocky Valentia Island, which offers opportunities for sea angling. Enjoy a splendid view of the Atlantic shore cliffs from Bray Head, 240m/787ft above the sea. There is a passenger ferry to the mainland leaving from Knights Town on the eastern side of the island.

◄ Valentia Island

A relatively recent tourist attraction on Valentia Island is the Skellig Experience, near the bridge. The visitor centre has good displays ► Skellig Islandson the life and work of the monks that lived there from the 6th to the 13th century. Another part of the exhibition is

★ **Skellig Experience**

dedicated to the local seabirds and the underwater world. There are regular boat trips from Valentia Island out to the islands jutting out of the water like the peaks of a sunken mountain range. The comfortable pleasure boats are only allowed to go around the Skellig Islands – a bird sanctuary since 1987. As the boat trips are not possible in bad weather, make sure to phone ahead: tel. (064) 316 33. (Opening times: April–Sept daily 10am – 7pm.)

Cahirciveen

The next stop on the Ring of Kerry is Cahirciveen. Opposite the little town, beyond Valentia River, the ruins of 15th-century Ballycarbery Castle can be made out. To the northeast, accessible via a minor road to the left of the N70, lie two ring forts: Cahergall, with a circumference of 32m/105ft, with two stone buildings within the walled enclosure, and Leacanabuaile (9th century) with stairs, chambers and subterranean rooms, on a hill-top.

Valley of Kells

Carry on northeast on the main road leading uphill through the broad valley of Kells. To the left, Knockadober rises 680m/2,231ft; the peaks of the mountain range to the right are of about similar height. In between there are beautiful views of the sea and mountains. Running along the foot of Drung Hill, in parts high above the sea, the road leads past an old stagepost. Carry on down to Glenbeigh, accompanied by a magnificent view of Dingle Bay and the Dingle Peninsula.

Glenbeigh

A small holiday resort in a scenic location, Glenbeigh will make anglers happy, whilst Rossbeigh, 2km/1.2 miles to the west, is the place for beach lovers.

Killorgin

Carry on for 15km/9 miles through moraine terrain to Killorglin. In this little town, the famous Puck Fair with horse and cattle market is held. Beyond the salmon-rich River Laune, the road forks. The N70 continues on via Milltown to ►Tralee, with, to the west, the ruins of 13th-century Kilcolman Abbey. The R562 turns off left to the east and continues on the Ring of Kerry along the river. Some 6km/3.5 miles past the fork in the road stands **Ballymalis Castle**, dating from the 16th century. The picturesque ruins of this four-storey castle lie on the shore, offering a view far across to the Macgillycuddy's Reeks.

! *Baedeker* TIP

Puck Fair
Good fun, featuring no small amount of drink, is the annual Puck Fair every 10 – 12th August, even attracting visitors from overseas. The origins of this fair are unknown but, at its height, a billygoat is crowned king of Ireland …

Continue on through the lakes of ► Killarney and, accompanied by splendid views, back towards **Moll's Gap**. A scenic route leads down to Kenmare, the starting point of the drive (Killarney to Kenmare 34km/21 miles).

Impressive scenery: the Macgillycuddy Reeks

A Detour to the Macgillycuddy Reeks

The Macgillycuddy's (pronounced »Maclicuddis«) Reeks, Irish Na Cruacha Dubha (»the black mountains«) rise up from the Iveragh Peninsula, partly wooded, partly bare. This ancient mountain range formed of red sandstone is the highest in Ireland: Carrantuohill (1,040m/3,412ft), Beenkeragh (994m/3,261ft) and Caher (960m/3,149ft). From its two highest peaks, the view stretches for miles: towards Dingle Bay in the northwest, the lakes of Killarney, and the mountains of southern Kerry. The view down to the nearby gorges, green valleys and small shimmering lakes is ample reward for the effort of making the climb.

Highest mountains in Ireland

There are two good starting points for climbing Carrantuohill: the youth hostel on the northern slope of the Macgillycuddy's Reeks or a car park nearby (situated approx. One mile from the youth hostel, in the direction of Glencar).

◀ Climbing Carrantuohill

The first part of the climb, through Hag's Glen, is also suitable for less experienced hikers and already gives a good idea of the scenery. Hiking up to Lough Callee, the mountain lake in a beautiful location at the end of Hag's Glen, takes about 1.5 hours. The second part of the climb leads via »The Devil's Ladder«. As the name suggests, this should only be attempted by experienced hillwalkers. Schedule another two hours for this.

◀ The climb

There is another way of climbing Carrantuohill: from the west, starting from Lough Acoose, a lake beautifully snuggled in the foothills of the mighty mountain. This route also requires some climbing experience.

◀ Alternative route

Roscommon (Ros Comáin)

C 3

Republic of Ireland, province: Connaught
Population: 1,700

County: Roscommon

Situated to the north of the town on a hill, the symbol of the town, Roscommon Castle, is a mighty Norman fortress.

Pretty town
Roscommon takes its name from St Coman who founded a monastery on this site in the 6th century. The Irish name »Ros Comáin« means something like »Forest of Coman«. The Dominican abbey close to this monastery was founded by Felim O'Conor, king of Connaught. A recess in the northern wall of the abbey church (altered in the 15th century) shelters the tomb of the founder (c1290), showing eight armed retainers.

Around Roscommon

Rathcroghan
Rathcroghan, approx. 23km/14 miles northwest of Roscommon, is said to be the coronation site of the kings of Connaught. A mound, probably a passage tomb, is the oldest part of the site. At the centre of a stone ring fort, a standing stone marks what is thought to be the burial place of Dathi, one of the last pagan kings of Ireland. Nearby there are more ring forts and Megalithic tombs.

Ballintober
Turning off right onto the R367, around 19km/12 miles northwest of Roscommon, brings you to Ballintober. There are the ruins of a castle built by the De Burgh family about 1300 and used as a residence until 1701, with a square ground plan, polygonal towers at the corners of the thick walls, two gate towers jutting out of the eastern wall and a moat that completely surrounds the castle.

Continue on the N60 towards Castlerea, a village with many leisure facilities (golf, tennis, fishing). Close by, look for **Clonalis House**, a 19th-century manor house surrounded by a park. Much earlier than that, the place was the seat of the O'Conors who provided several high kings and kings of Connaught. Various documents and exhibits in the house – furnished in Victorian style – serve as reminders of that time.

▶ ROSCOMMON

INFORMATION
Harrison Hall
Tel. (0 90) 32 63 42
Open: June–Aug

WHERE TO STAY

▶ **Mid-range**
Abbey
Galway Road
Tel. (0 90) 6 62 62 40, fax 6 62 60 21
sales@abbeyhotel.ie
Stylish hotel with nicely-appointed rooms.

Look out in particular for a copy of the »Brehon Law« and the harp of the blind bard Turlough O'Carolan (1630–1738, ► Carrick-on-Shannon, Around). There is good-value B & B accommodation here too. (Opening times: June–mid-Sept Tue–Sun noon–5pm.) 🕐

Roscrea (Ros Cré)

D 4

Republic of Ireland, province: Munster
Population: 4,400

County: Tipperary

Monastic town: Roscrea on the banks of the River Bunnow, has an interesting historical centre, but the main advantage of this small town is its location. Situated between Dublin and Limerick, Roscrea makes a great base for hiking tours into the Slieve Bloom Mountains.

Roscrea marks the spot where St Cronan founded a monastery in the 7th century. On the old monastic site, all that is still standing of the 12th-century Romanesque St Cronan's Church is the western façade with entrance gate and two blind arcades each. Above the entrance, the figure of a clergyman, probably St Cronan, can be made out. To the north of the church stands a 12th-century High Cross, on the other side, a round tower that has lost its conical roof. The 7th-century Book of Dímma, written in this monastery, is today kept at Trinity College Dublin.

★ **St Cronan's Church**

In Castle Street, look for the ruins of 13th-century Roscrea Castle. The castle had strong curtain walls, several towers and an ingenious system of stairs and passages to individual defensive positions. Within the castle walls, Damer House, built in the 18th century, is today used for changing exhibitions. Don't miss the beautifully carved decorations on the staircase. The Heritage Annexe next to Damer House has information on the history of the region. (Opening times: June–Sept daily 9.30am–6.30pm) 🕐

Roscrea Heritage (Castle & Damer House)

In Abbey Street, the grounds of the Catholic parish church holds the remains of a 15th-century Franciscan friary: a gate, choir walls and a bell tower, the latter's supporting arches forming the entrance to the modern church.

Franciscan Abbey

Near the golf links, 3km/2 miles east of town, the impressive ruined church of Monaincha (12th/13th century) was part of a monastery founded as early as the 7th century on a boggy island in a lake that was drained in about 1800. As in the case of many Irish lake islands, according to tradition this is an ancient sacred place.

Monaincha

Around Roscrea

Nenagh About 30km/20 miles southwest of Roscrea, the town of Nenagh (pop 5,500) lies in a fertile plain. The best feature of the town is the dungeon of Nenagh Castle, built in the early 13th century, a five-storey, round tower (30m/98ft) with walls up to 6m/20ft thick. Of the other towers guarding the Butler family's once pentagonal Norman castle, only one gatehouse tower is left. An unusual museum has been set up in the former prison, showing cells and an execution room from the 19th century. Using archive material, the museum tells the tragic story of 17 men who were executed. In the adjoining octagonal Governor's House, a classroom, a smithy, a shop and a kitchen have been recreated. (Opening times: mid-May–mid-Sept Mon–Fri 10am–5pm, Sun 2.30–5pm.)

National sheep shearing championships in Nenagh

Rosguill Peninsula

A 4

Republic of Ireland, province: Ulster   **County:** Donegal

Scenic Rosguill Peninsula is a small peninsula in the far north of Ireland.

Fascinating peninsula The peninsula reaches out between two inlets: Mulroy Bay to the east and Sheep Haven to the west. As in large parts of Donegal, Irish is still the main language here (Gaeltacht). This region is also home to a tweed mill.

Atlantic Drive Do follow the famous Atlantic Drive around Rosguill Peninsula. The starting point for this 20km/12-mile tour is Carrigart.

Tranarossan Bay Also from Carrigart, a narrow road leads uphill north, always hugging the western shores of the bay and, after 6km/3.5 miles, turning off west towards picturesque Tranarossan Bay. The road follows the Atlantic shore for a bit and then winds south, with views of Sheep Haven Bay to Downings, a holiday resort with a nice sandy beach. There is a tweed mill that is open to the public, selling Donegal tweed.

The Rosses (Na Rosa)

A/B 3

Republic of Ireland, province: Ulster   **County:** Donegal

The many bays of the Rosses on the northwestern coast of Donegal stretch from Gweebarra Bay in the south to Inishfree Bay in the north.

Round Trip

Overall, the landscape here is flat coastal land with grey rock, many lakes and small fields delimited by dry walls. Here too, Irish is the main language still (Gaeltacht). The only larger town in this region largely untouched by tourism is Dungloe (pop. 1,000), on the N56. To the southwest, admire some beautiful cliffs and several caves at Crohy Head. From Dungloe, use either the N56 northeast or a scenic road east leading directly to Gweedore (►Bloody Foreland). Take the R259 from Dungloe, hugging the Atlantic coast around the Rosses. Staying to the left-hand side, the drive leads along the shore, with good views onto many small islands, and across an isthmus between the sea and Lough Meela. Look out for Rutland Island, with the ruins of a harbour set up in 1796 stuck in the sand.

Dungloe

Carry on for another 8km/5 miles to Burtonport (pop. 280), an important fishing town. They say that more salmon and lobsters are landed here than in any other harbour in Ireland or the British Isles. Accordingly, several restaurants feature lobster and fresh-off-the boat seafood on the menu.

Burtonport and Aranmore Island

Lying just off the mainland shore, behind some smaller islands, Aranmore Island (also called Aran Island, not to be confused with the ► Aran Islands), is connected to Burtonport by a ferry service (in the summer hourly departures, crossing time approx. 20 min). Some 800 people live on the 13.5 x 5km/8.4 x 3.1-mile island. The main sources of income are fishing and tourism. The island's wild, heather-covered plateau ends at the western coast with cliffs and shore caves, nesting places for numerous sea birds. Further inland lies small Lough Shure, with plenty of rainbow trout. Sandy beaches can be found on the more protected eastern side. For bad weather, there is a choice of six pubs on the island.

The Rosses: stone walls dominate the landscape

Royal Canal

►Grand Canal · Royal Canal

Shannon (River Shannon)

B–D 3/4

Republic of Ireland

The river Shannon, 370km/230 miles long, rises in County Cavan. With its lakes, tributaries and canals, the Shannon forms a large intricate network of waterways, covering a fifth of Ireland's surface.

Longest river in Ireland

The Shannon flows through the country's inland lime plains before emptying into the Atlantic beyond Limerick. With the exception of a few larger towns, the shores of the Shannon are sparsely populated and are often lined by pastures. As there is no industry near the river, the light over the water is particularly clear. This idyllic environment is ideal for relaxing; floating on the longest river in Ireland in complete tranquility is one of the most beautiful holiday experiences in Ireland. Apart from a short non-navigable stretch upstream, the gradient up to Killaloe is so low that only six locks have to be traversed along the way.

Recommended routes

Between Battlebridge (Lough Allan) and Killaloe, the river has good tourist facilities. Even better, since 1994, the Shannon has been part of the largest boating area in Europe. A canal disused for over 100 years was restored and now leads from Leitrim, near ► Carrick-on-Shannon, to Lough Erne (►Fermanagh Lakeland) in Northern Ireland, giving amateur skippers 800km/500 miles of continuous waterways!

The following tours are recommended, depending on the schedule and where the boat has to be handed over: starting from ► Carrick-on-Shannon, you can explore Lough Key. More interesting, however, is to take the boat through the Lough Allen canal and then along the shores of the lake of the same name. Going in a southerly direction brings you to Lough Boderg; from here a detour explores the only partly navigable Mountain River. The canalized stretch via Lough Bofin downstream to Lough Ree, with Hare Island, also offers plenty of variety. To the

► SHANNON

INFORMATION
Airport, Arrivals Hall
Tel. (0 61) 47 16 64
info@shannondev.ie

north of ►Athlone the route also reaches Lough Ree. Most visitors will probably want to take the boat south to make a quick detour to the famous monastic settlement of ►Clonmacnoise, which can also be accessed from Banagher (►Birr). Lough Derg, with its pretty moorings at Garrykennedy, can also be reached from ►Killaloe. Unfortunately, the moorings are often full of people. Be careful on the two largest lakes in the Shannon area, Lough Ree, near Athlone, and Lough Derg, near Killaloe. Sudden winds can whip up a strong swell!

From North to South on the Shannon

Drumshanbo village is situated at the southern tip of Lough Allen. Every year in June, during the the popular Drumshanbo Festival of Irish Traditional Music, Song and Dance, the cabin cruisers stack up to a depth of several rows at the moorings. A nice idea is a bike tour around the lake on the 48km/30-mile, signposted Leitrim Scenic Lakeland Tour.

Lough Allen

Coming from ►Carrick-on-Shannon, most boats first head for the upper reaches of the river, or the Boyle River and its lakes. Don't miss pretty Lough Key (near the town of ►Boyle) with its wooded islands. Lough Key Forest Park, in the grounds of a former manor house, offers strolls on forest trails or in the bog garden, a restaurant and the opportunity to do some shopping.

Carrick-on-Shannon

Idyllic the Shannon at Shannonbridge

Lough Boderg, Lough Bofin & Lough Forbes

Going downstream from Carrick-on-Shannon, pass the Jamestown Canal with its lock. From here, consider a detour to Drumsna and Jamestown. Pass the lock to head for picturesque Lough Boderg, from where a narrow channel through the reeds leads to the lonely Carranadoe Lakes, a paradise for bird lovers and anglers.

There is a pretty little harbour, with mooring space for only a limited number of boats however, near Dromod, on Lough Bofin. The next stop, a bit further south, is Roosky with its quay.

Termonbarry, Lanesborough

Continue on between wooded river banks to Lough Forbes and, past the mouth of the Royal Canal, on to Termonbarry with its large lock. From Termonbarry (or Cloondara opposite), visit Strokestown and ► Longford . Further downstream, the extensive bogs are exploited by the Irish peat board Bord na Móna. At Lanesborough, a bridge with nine arches spans the Shannon.

Lough Ree

Here, the banks open up to the massive Lough Ree (»Lake of the Kings«). Several islands, such as Inchbofin, Inishturk and Inchmore, have remains of Early Christian monastic settlements. It is said that Inchclearaun (also called »Quaker Island«, after a 19th-century inhabitant of the Quaker faith), is the place where Clothra, sister of Queen Maeve, was killed by a stone slingshot from the shore.

To the south of ► Athlone and after passing through its lock, the river meanders through fairly flat countryside, until the towers of ► Clonmacnoise appear on the horizon. Arriving by water is the most beautiful way to approach the ruins of this monastic town.

Shannonbridge ►

At Shannonbridge (pop. 270), an old bridge with sixteen arches spans the river. There are also some relics of fortifications from Napoleonic times. Shannon Harbour was used in the past as the starting point for a boat trip on the ► Grand Canal to Dublin. The ruins of the buildings from that time give an idea of Regency-period elegance.

! **Baedeker TIP**

Discovering the bog

The Bord na Móna Blackwater Works to the south of Shannonbridge is the starting point, in summer, for tours into the bog. On a railway track originally laid down for transporting peat, a small train runs through the bogscape, passing numerous stops of geological, historical or botanical interest. You can also see live peat digging. Another tour, involving a guided walk, teaches visitors about the plants and animals that live here. (Tours late April–Oct daily 10am – 5pm.)

Below Shannon Harbour, the river widens, touching the old towns of Banagher (► Birr) and Portumna (► Loughrea). Only then does the Shannon flow into **Lough Derg** (► Killaloe), the largest of the many Shannon lakes, and one that has many small islets. The landscape changes now: the banks become more fertile, and there are more farm houses and settlements, signs of a certain prosperity. The southern tip of Lough Derg is surrounded by hills, whilst mountain ranges of very old red sandstone mark the horizon to both sides.

Shannon / River Shannon Map

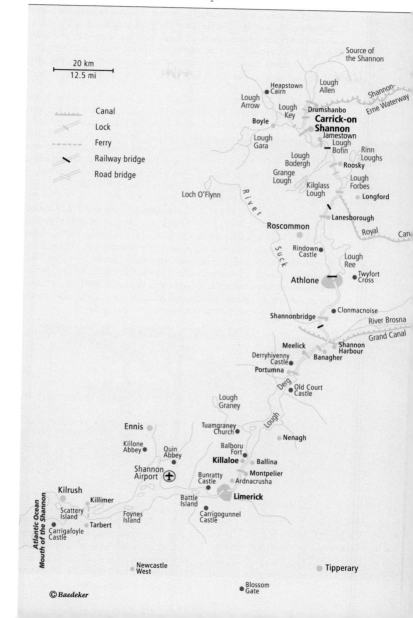

20 km
12.5 mi

Canal
Lock
Ferry
Railway bridge
Road bridge

Source of
the Shannon

Lough
Allen

Shannon-
Erne Waterway

Heapstown
Cairn

Lough
Arrow

Lough
Key

Drumshanbo

**Carrick-on
Shannon**

Boyle

Jamestown

Lough
Gara

Lough
Bofin

Rinn
Loughs

Roosky

Lough
Bodergh

Lough
Forbes

Grange
Lough

Kilglass
Lough

Longford

Loch O'Flynn

River

Lanesborough

Roscommon

Royal   Can

Suck

Rindown
Castle

Lough
Ree

Athlone

Twyfort
Cross

Shannonbridge

Clonmacnoise

River Brosna

Grand Canal

Meelick

Shannon
Harbour

Derryhivenny
Castle

Banagher

Portumna

Derg

Old Court
Castle

Lough
Graney

Lough

Ennis

Tuamgraney
Church

Nenagh

Killone
Abbey

Quin
Abbey

Balboru
Fort

Killaloe

Ballina

**Shannon
Airport** ✈

Bunratty
Castle

Montpelier
Ardnacrusha

Limerick

Kilrush

Killimer

Battle
Island

Scattery
Island

Foynes
Island

Carrigogunnel
Castle

Tarbert

Carrigafoyle
Castle

Atlantic Ocean
Mouth of the Shannon

Newcastle
West

Tipperary

Blossom
Gate

© *Baedeker*

Killaloe ▸Killaloe is not only known for its many interesting antiquities, but also for its yacht and motorboat marina. Killaloe is Ireland's water-skiing capital. For those who hired their boat, Killaloe is the end of the waterway. Boat owners are free to carry on. However, the following stretch can be difficult and risky. Whilst up to this point, the Shannon flows unhurriedly, over the next 29km/18 miles, the river develops a steep gradient.

Ardnacrusha Ardnacrusha is the site of Ireland's first and largest hydroelectric station, producing some 350 million kilowatt hours of electricity every year. The facility is open to visitors by appointment; access by car is possible either from Limerick or from Killaloe on the northern shore of the Shannon. In the huge lock chambers, the boats are lifted or lowered over 30m/100ft.

✔ **DON'T MISS**

■ Of particular interest in the hydroelectric station is the »fish ladder«, lifting salmon, in particular, up to the level of the upper canal within three hours.

▸**Limerick**, with docks and moorings for ships weighing up to 10,000t, extends mainly along the Shannon's southern shore. Soon, on the right-hand bank of the river, close to Limerick, Shannon International Airport ▸ Enniscomes into view. From here, the river broadens out to a width of nearly 100km/60 miles across, before eventually flowing into the Atlantic in a funnel-shaped estuary. Between Tarbert in County Kerry and Killimer in County Clare, a car ferry operates across the river (▸Kilkee).

Lough Derg is the largest of the Shannon lakes.

✴ Skellig Islands (Oileáin na Scealaga)

E 1

Republic of Ireland, province: Munster   **County:** Kerry

For many people visiting Ireland, a trip to the Skelligs, two small rocky islands some 14km/9 miles west of the Iveragh Peninsula off the southwestern coast of Ireland, is one of the absolute highlights of their trip.

However, you should have fairly good sea legs and be sure-footed. When the sea is rough, the crossing can be a bit dicey and visitors should be at ease walking on rocks and stone steps. In order to protect Skellig Michael – the only island that it is possible to visit – the number of visitors is limited. In the summer months, it is a good idea to book the boat trip ahead. Boats leave from Portmagee, Cahirciveen, Ballinskelligs and Derrynane (►Ring of Kerry).

Small rocky islands off the southwestern coast

Perfect scenery: Skellig Michael with the Stairway to Heaven in the foreground

Skellig Michael

The largest of the islands, Skellig Michael, has the remains of a monastic settlement. St Finan is credited with its foundation in the 6th century. Steps hewn into the rock (Stairway to Heaven) lead to a saddle between two rocky peaks (the highest: alt 217m/713ft).

At the monastic settlement, a guide greets the visitors and gives a short introduction to the history of Skellig Michael, before allowing visitors to explore the remains of the monastic buildings (on artificially created small terraces below the lower rocky pyramid) at their own pace. The six beehive huts are circular outside and rectangular inside; there are also two stone boat-shaped oratories (6th–9th century). Below those, the remains of a church (12th-century?) can be made out. The site also comprises a few little gardens, a well, tombstones, the remains of a sundial and enclosure walls bordering the abyss. Up to the 13th century, a community of 13 monks lived on the islands. As there is no well on Skellig Michael, they had to work hard to collect water in two small reservoirs. Later, many more pilgrims came here to perform a penance, climbing the highest point of the island to kiss the ancient stone standing upright in the rock. From 1820 to 1987 there was a permanent lighthouse keeper on Skellig Michael.

Little Skellig

Jagged Little Skellig is a bird sanctuary and cannot be visited. Many boats, however, go around the island to give their passengers the chance to see the birds (and sometimes seals too). Don't forget to bring binoculars! The most common bird here is the gannet. With over 20,000 pairs, the breeding colony on Little Skellig is said to be the second-largest in the world. Seeing a cloud of birds lift, drift apart and descend again is an optically and acoustically overwhelming experience.

Skibbereen (Sciobairín)

E 2

Republic of Ireland, province: Munster	**County:** Cork
Population: 2,000	

Occupying a charming position on the River Ilen, the market town of Skibbereen is one of the main towns of County Cork.

SKIBBEREEN

INFORMATION
North Street
Tel. (0 28) 2 17 66

The fishing harbour Skibbereen, near the southern tip of Ireland, makes a good touring base. This lively and friendly little town, founded in the 17th century by English settlers, attracts a fair number of tourists.

Around Skibbereen

The R596 leads southeast to Castletownshend, passing, after half a mile, the Liss Ard Experience. This is an area of around 16ha/40 acres with forest, flower meadows and little lakes on the banks of Lough Abisdealy. This was the place chosen by the German Veith Turske to create a natural, but also magical garden. (Opening times: ☉ May–Sept weekdays 9.30am–5pm.)

On the southwesterly edge of Castletownshend, the R596 leads to Drishane House, home of the 19th-century writers Edith Somerville and Violet Martin, who published their stories using the name Somerville & Ross. To the northwest, mighty Knockdrum Fort features a 3m/10ft-thick stone ring wall.

Leave Skibbereen in a southwesterly direction on the R595 to reach, after about 5km/9 miles, Creagh Gardens. In this romantic park right on the water's edge, look for camelias, magnolias, ferns and lilies, as well as many rare plants. (Opening times: March–Oct daily ☉ 10am–6pm.)

At the southern end of the road lies the friendly holiday resort of Baltimore, which has a sailing school and is well-known for its fishing.

Just offshore, Sherkin Island acts like a breakwater protecting the harbour. The island has the ruins of a castle and a 15th-century Franciscan friary. Further out lies Clear Island; its 150 inhabitants have preserved much of the old traditions alongside tourism. Irish is still spoken, and there are two colleges teaching Irish. The ruins of a 12th-century church and an old stone pillar with a carved cross are evidence of Early Christian settlement. The crossing to this, Ireland's most southerly island, takes only 45 minutes and is a particularly attractive trip for bird watchers.

Admire stunning cliff scenery at Fastnet Rock, the southernmost point of Ireland. There are boat services to both islands from Baltimore, and in the summer from Schull too.

On the drive back to Skibbereen, a minor road running east passes the clear saltwater lake of Lough Ine. Take a signposted path up to Hill Top (just under 20 minutes from the picnic area) to enjoy a fantastic view of the lake, as well as the sea, with its off-shore islands.

At Ballydehob, 16km/10 miles west of Skibbereen, the R592 makes a turn towards the southwest, leading to the small town of Schull (pop 580) and the local planetarium. There are several old copper mines in the area. Hiking up 400m/1,312-ft Mount Gabriel is fairly hard work, but the effort is rewarded by a great 360° view. There are passenger ferry connections to Baltimore und Clear Island.

It is definitely worth driving on to Crookhaven, with its sheltered seaport. A narrow path leads to Mizen Head; its highest point (230m/755ft) offers a great view of the Atlantic coast.

★ Sligo (Sligeach)

B 3

Republic of Ireland, province: Connaught
Population: 18,000

County: Sligo

On the banks of the wide Garavogue River, connecting Lough Gill with the Atlantic, lies the charming town of Sligo.

Nice town – all about Yeats

Sligo, Irish Sligeach (»river of the shells«), is not just the most important town in the northwest of Ireland, but also an important regional hub. This is the end of the line for the railway from Dublin, which makes Sligo the northern most railway station in the country. In and around Sligo, there is a lot to remind visitors of the poet William Butler Yeats (▶Famous People), who lived here for a while. Every year in August, the Yeats Summer School runs courses for Irish and foreign visitors.

Sights in Sligo

Memories: Yeats statue outside the Ulster Bank

On Stephen Street, north of the Garavogue River, visit the **Sligo County Museum**. The museum shows exhibitis from Pre-Christian times to the beginning of the Second World War, but the main draw is of course the Yeats Room, dedicated to Sligo's great writer.

On display are first editions of his works, manuscripts, letters and photographs of the Yeats family. The art gallery in the uppermost floor shows works by various Irish painters, including paintings by Jack Butler Yeats, the poet's brother. They say he was unable to paint anything without putting a bit of Sligo into it. (Opening times: April, May, Oct Mon–Sat 10.30am–12.30pm; June–Sept Mon–Sat 10.30am–12.30pm and 2.30–4.30pm.)

★ Sligo Abbey

From the County Museum, cross a bridge to reach the southern bank of the river. Stay to the left to visit the oldest buildings in town: the church, cloister and conventual buildings of Sligo Abbey. The Dominican friary was founded in 1253 by Maurice Fitzgerald and rebuilt in 1416 after a fire. The abbey suffered further damage during the Tyrone War in 1595 and once more during the troubles of the 1640s, but remained occupied until the 18th century. The church has a double nave; the choir dates from the time of the original foundation, whilst the transept is 16th-century. Look out for the canopied tomb of Cormack O'Crean (1506) on the northern wall of the nave with a Cruxifixion scene and additional bas-relief figures. Also look out for the O'Conor Sligo Monument (1624) on the southern wall. The sacristy and 13th-century chapter house abut the pretty 15th-century cloister, three sides of which are still standing.

Churches

In John Street, look for the Protestant St John's Church, built in 1812 in the neo-Gothic style, and on Temple Street for the Catholic St John's Cathedral, built in 1869 – 1874, in the neo-Romanesque style. These are the two main churches in town.

Yeats Building

Every year, the courses of the Yeats International Summer School are held in the Yeats (Memorial) Building on Hyde Bridge. The rest of the year, the local art gallery holds changing exhibitions, often with works for sale. (Opening times: Mon–Fri 10am – 5pm, Sat 10am–2pm.)

⊙

Excursions around Sligo

Drive around Lough Gill

To the east of town, scenic Lough Gill stretches for approx. 8km/5 miles; the lake is rich in salmon, trout and pike. Take a leisurely drive around the lake (37km/23 miles) or, equally rewarding, take a boat trip on the lake, joined, in the summer, by boats from Sligo and Parke's Castle. For an excellent view of the lake and its islets head for Dooney Rock, leaving Sligo on the N4 south, and following, after 500m/550yd, the sign pointing left to Lough Gill. Turning left again at the next crossroads brings you to the R287 and the viewpoint. Yeats immortalized the rock in »The Fiddler of Dooney«. Innisfree Island, near the southern shore, also the subject of one of Yeats' poems, attracts many literary-minded visitors.

 Baedeker TIP

Quirke's Sculptures

How do fairies, giants and other mythical figures come into being? At »Quirke's Sculptures« in Wine Street watch how simple chunky wooden logs and blocks are turned into works of art, carefully carved and inspired by Irish legends and folk tales. Of course these archaic-looking figures are also for sale
– an unusual, if not cheap souvenir.

Sligo *Plan*

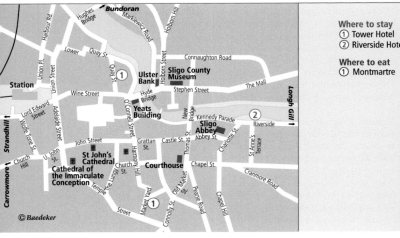

Where to stay
① Tower Hotel
② Riverside Hotel

Where to eat
① Montmartre

© Baedeker

Creevelea Abbey ▶ From the R287, drive east towards Dromahair and the ruins of the Franciscan abbey of Creevelea, founded in 1508, before the order was banned in Ireland. On the northern side of the monastery, the pillars have some figures worth seeing, amongst them St Francis with the stigmata, preaching to the birds.

★
Parke's Castle Driving on around Lough Gill leads to picturesque Parke's Castle, situated on the eastern bank of the lake. The castle is a three-storey rectangular structure with a large 17th-century courtyard. The unfurnished fortified manor house has been lavishly restored and may be visited. In the yard, the remnants of an earlier defensive structure have been excavated. The direct route from Sligo to Parke's Castle
⏱ runs west via the R286. (Opening times: June–Sept daily 9.3.0am–6.30pm; April, May and Oct Tue–Sun 10am–5pm)

Deer Park Court Cairn ▶ A little further on, a small road branches off to the right in the direction of Manorhamilton. Park the car after 3km/2 miles and walk to the impressive Deer Park Court Cairn, with three chambers (c3000 BC), lying on a wooded hill with a wonderful view of the lake.

Hazelwood House ▶ On a peninsula between the lake's nordwestern tip and the Garavogue River stands Hazelwood House, a handsome small manor house, built in 1731 in the Palladian style.

Carrowmore Leaving Sligo via Church Hill, following the road for some 5km/9 miles to reach the largest cluster of megalithic graves in Ireland, the passage-tomb cemetery of Carrowmore. Archeologists have found some 60 tombs here, many of which are, however, destroyed or damaged. Most of the tombs are a mix of passage grave and dolmen, with the oldest dating from between 3000 and 2500 BC. ⊕ (Opening times: Mai–Sept daily 9.30am– 6.30pm.)

Knocknarea mountain lies some 7km/4.3 miles west of Sligo. It is well worth the climb (30–40 min.), and not just because of the views. At the top sits a massive cairn, 11m/36 ft high and over 60m/197ft in diameter. A megalithic grave (approx. 2500 BC) is supposed to be under the cairn, and it is assumed that the legendary Queen Maeve of Connaught was buried here.

Knocknarea Cairn

Strandhill, 8km/5 miles west of Sligo near the airport, is a resort with excellent sandy beaches. The powerful swell makes Strandhill very popular with surfers, but the beach is too dangerous for swimming. At low-tide you can wade across to small Coney Island. Don't miss a visit to the award-winning »Seaweed Baths« with steamboxes.

Strandhill

The seaside resort Rosses Point, with its 18-hole championship links and sheltered sandy beaches, is also popular with holiday visitors.

Rosses Point

North of Sligo

The grandfather of the writer William Butler Yeats (►Famous People) was for many years parish priest at Drumcliff Church, 10km/6 miles north of Sligo. Yeats died 1939 in France, but had requested a grave in Drumcliff in his will, and was buried in the churchyard in

Drumcliff

◗ VISITING SLIGO

INFORMATION
Aras Reddan, Temple Street
Tel. (0 71) 6 12 01

WHERE TO EAT
► Moderate
① *Montmartre*
Market Yard
Tel. (0 71) 9 16 99 01
montmartre@eircom.net
The friendly staff of this restaurant, located near Sligo's municipal theatre, serve dishes influenced by French cuisine.

WHERE TO STAY
► Luxury
② *Riverside Hotel & Leisure Centre*
Riverside

Tel. (0 71) 9 14 80 88
Fax (0 71) 9 14 80 60
www.irishcourthotels.com
This new hotel with leisure centre offers many different activities, as well as a bar, a restaurant and luxuriously furnished rooms.

► Mid-range
① *Tower Hotel*
Quay Street
Tel. (0 71) 9 14 40 00
Fax (0 71) 9 14 68 88
www.towerhotelgroup.ie
Situated in the heart of Sligo, the Tower Hotel stands for comfort, friendly service and good food.

Yeat's Grave ▶ front of the church. His headstone hasthe following epitaph, composed by the poet himself: »Cast a cold Eye / On Life, on Death / Horseman, pass by!«. Along the footpath to the church, look out for a

High Cross ▶ High Cross, erected around AD 1000. Its east face depicts Adam and Eve, Cain and Abel, Daniel in the Lion's Den and Christ in Glory. The west face of the cross shows Christ Driving the Vendors out of the Temple, two figures and the Crucifixion. The rest of the High Cross is decorated with mythical beasts and ornamental interlacing.

Benbulben ▶ North of the village, Benbulben table mountain (517m/1,696ft) rises abruptly out of the plain. This weird natural formation features in many folk tales and stories. It was here that Queen Maeve and the hero of Ulster, CuChulainn, fought for possession of mighty bulls, and Diarmaid bled to death following his fight with the wild boar of Benbulben. However, a historical event also took place on the slopes of the mountain: the »Battle of the Book« of Cuildrevne (561), which resulted in Columba the Elder's exile. Part of the Dartry Mountains, Benbulben is of great interest to geologists and botanists. Visitors not put off by an ascent without a marked path can enjoy a great view across the plain and the Atlantic from the top.

! **Baedeker TIP**

Yeats Country

Whether or not you are interested in the works of W B Yeats, the drive through the Sligo landscape is beautiful – past a sandy coastline and spectacular rocks, through forests and along lakes and rivers.Just follow the signs with the quill ...

Glencar Lough A pretty area for exploring is Glencar Lough, stretching a few miles east of Drumcliff. At the eastern side of the lake, the waterfall in the middle of all that green is very romantic.

Lissadell House Some 6km/3.5 miles northwest of Drumcliff, Lissadell House, surrounded by parkland, was built in 1834 for the grandfather of Countess Constance Markievicz (1884–1927) and her sister Eva Gore-Booth. Countess Markievicz was active in politics in Dublin, taking part in the 1916 Easter Rising. Eva Gore-Booth was a writer. Yeats dedicated a poem to Constance and sometimes stayed at Lissadell House. (Opening times: June–mid-Sept Mon–Sat 10.30am–12.30pm and 2–4.30pm.)

»Pigeon Holes« ▶ Southwest of Lissadell a small peninsula juts into Drumcliff Bay. Look for the two »Pigeon Holes« near the fishing village of Raghly, open blowholes in the rock, where the sea, entering through subterranean channels, is pushed upwards with immense force.

Inishmurray From Grange village, north of Drumcliff, a by-road leads west to Streedagh. There is sometimes the possibility for foot passengers to join a boat to Inishmurray island (another access is from Mullaghmore, see below). The island, 7km/4.5 miles west of Streedagh was inhabited well into the 20th century. There is a particularly well-preserved Early Christian monastic site here. Founded in the early 6th century by St Molaise, the monastery was abandoned 300 years later following plundering attacks. The remains give a good idea of how this kind of monastery would have looked: a circular wall, 3–4m/10–13ft tall, with five entrances, around an enclosure in the shape of a pear, divided into four areas of different sizes. The enclosure holds various churches and huts: the Men's Church, the small Teach Molaise prayer house, the Church of the Fire, a beehive hut and blocks of masonry, like open-air altars. On top of one of those, look for the five famous Cursing Stones, round speckled stones used to place effective curses on enemies. Strewn all over the island are memorial stones and prayer stations that the pilgrims had to complete in a prescribed order. St Patrick's Memorial offers a particularly beautiful view of the mainland.

Burial mound at Creevykeel

At **Streedagh Beach**, only a few miles on, the Spanish Armada Memorial commemorates 6 September 1588, when three ships were wrecked here. The disaster cost 1,200 lives, 300 people were saved.

From Cliffoney, a minor road leads past Classiebawn Castle to the Mullaghmore peninsula, with a protected sandy beach, a harbour for boaters and opportunity for deep-sea angling. The Beach Hotel can arrange trips to Inishmurray Island.

At Creevykeel, near Cliffoney village, you will find an impressive court tomb, one of the most beautiful in the whole of Ireland. A wedge-shaped stone wall encloses an open court, behind which lies a double burial chamber, with two more burial chambers and the remains of a third behind it. The site dates back some 4,500 years.

✳ **Creevykeel**

South and East of Sligo

13km/8 miles south of Sligo, Collooney village lies on the Owenmore River, with the pretty 18th-century Markree Castle in the middle distance.

Collooney

In order to explore Lough Arrow

To explore the area around Lough Arrow, some 28km/17 miles southeast of Sligo, turn east off the N4 at Castlebaldwin; this road leads to the large Heapstown Cairn (probably a passage tomb) and then on to a small and fairly strange lake. With a diameter of around 300m/984ft, Lough Nasuil holds some 1 million litres/26.417 million US gallons of water. In 1933, the lough suddenly ran dry and stayed dry for three weeks, only to fill up again later, just as fast.

To the south, 16th-century Ballindoon Friary in its pretty lakeside location is a pleasant place to stop. After around 10km/6 miles you meet the N4 again at Ballinafad.

Carrowkeel passage tomb cemetery

Some 5km/3 miles north of Ballinafad, look out for the passage tomb cemetery of Carrowkeel, on a lonely hilltop in the Bricklieve Mountains. The site consists of 14 cairns that are all circular (with one exception), but inside show different types of chambers. It is thought that they were built around 2500–2000 BC. In the area below the tombs, look for the remnants of 50 round stone huts, maybe the living quarters of the people who built these tombs.

Lough Key Scenic site

Follow the N4 in the direction of Dublin to reach a wonderful viewpoint for Lough Key, on the border between the Counties Sligo and Roscommon. Across the road rises the imposing statue of »The Gaelic Chieftain«, commemorating the battle at Curlew Mountains in 1599. In Ballymore, 9km/5.5 miles further north stands an ivy-clad ruined castle with six round towers. From being constructed to being razed (c1300–c1700), Ballymote Castle was much fought-over.

Ballymote ▶

Sperrin Mountains

B 4/5

Northern Ireland, province: Ulster   **Counties:** Tyrone and Derry

The Sperrin Mountains (up to 670m/2,198ft) are a little-known haven for walkers and fishermen in the northeast of Tyrone. Walk for hours without meeting a single soul.

Lonely scenery

Covered in bog and heather, the Sperrin Mountains northwest of ▶ Lough Neagh are criss-crossed by an intricate network of brooks and small roads. The area, stretching across some 65km/40 miles between the towns of Strabane, Dungiven, Magherafelt and Newtownards, is very sparsely populated. Part of the mountain range extends south towards ▶ Omagh. Alongside the walking and fishing (salmon and trout), the area is good for biking, horse-riding and golfing.

★
Beaghmore Stone Circles

On the southeastern edge of the Sperrin Mountains, 10km/6 miles northwest of Dungannon on the A505 (signposted), look for the Beaghmore Stone Circles, seven mysterious stone circles and cairns dating from the Bronze Age. The site consists of further prehistoric monuments: twelve circular cairns as well as ten stone rows and other fragments, possibly parts of ancient collapsed stone walls. They were discovered during peat digging and it is assumed that the peat hides more stone witnesses.

The mysterious Beaghmore Stone Circles

Directly behind the **Sperrin Heritage Centre** in Cranagh, approx. 20km/12 miles northwest of Cookstown via the B162 and the B47, rises Mt Sawel (678m/2,2224ft). Displays and interactive animation show some of the history of the region, its environmental issues, as well as the gold found nearby, and exhibits on the influence of the local landscape on literature. If you are looking specifically for information on walking trails, this is the place, as the Ulster Way passes nearby (opening times: March–Oct Mon–Fri 11am–6pm, Sat 11.30am–6pm, Sun 2–7pm.)

Somewhat easier to reach is the An Creagán Visitor Centre, about half-way between Cookstown and Omagh on the A505. Here too, an exhibition explains the countryside and its people to visitors. There is information on walking trails and bike hire. In addition, a broad cultural programme stretches from Irish traditions such as music, storytelling, dance and crafts, to language classes, talks on history and archaeology, and guided walks. (Opening times: April–Sept daily 11am–6.30pm; Oct–March Mon–Fri 11am–4.30pm.)

An Creagán Visitor Centre

 Baedeker TIP

Family fun

Warm up with a cup of tea in the café of Sperrin Heritage Center and, weather permitting, try your luck panning for gold in the nearby brook – great fun!

Tara (Teamhair)

C 5

Republic of Ireland, province: Leinster

County: Meath

As a ritual site associated with the goddess Maeve, the Hill of Tara lay at the centre of the Irish-Celtic world, but the site already had religious significance in prehistoric times.

A spiritual place

Northwest of Dublin, take a left into a small side road at Tara village. The road leads slightly uphill to the famous mountain, from where you can see far out to the north and west. From the 3rd century onwards, Tara was the seat of lower-ranking priest kings, and later of the High Kings of Ireland. Every three years they held public gatherings here where laws were passed and and disputes amongst the tribes were settled. With the spread of Christianity, Tara lost its significance as a site of worship, but stayed the seat of the High Kings until it was abandoned in 1022. The region had to wait until 1843 for its next major event, when Daniel O'Connell made a speech during one of his mammoth meetings campaigning for Catholic emancipation in Ireland.

★ Hill of Tara

Walking across the Hill of Tara today, you only see flat grassy mounds. The ancient tombs and their ring-shaped earth walls can only be made out from the air. The impressive structures built in Celtic times from wood or wattle-and-daub are said to have had gates decorated with precious stones and inside were said to be furnished with tools made of gold and bronze. Of all of this, nothing has survived. The site is freely accessible at all times; there is no entrance charge.

Vistor centre

In order to get an impression of Tara's significance, watch the »Tara: Meeting Place of Heroes« video in the Tara Visitor Centre. The former Protestant Church is also where, in summer, recommended tours start, making the mythology and history of the place come to life. (Opening times: mid-June–mid–Sept daily 9.30am – 4.30pm; May–mid-June and mid-Sept–Oct daily 10am – 5pm.)

From the Hill of Tara the high kings ruled for a thousand years.

The central area of the site, the **Royal Enclosure** of the Irish High Kings, is surrounded by a large wall. Roughly at the centre of the enclosure stand the two walls of Cormac's House and the Royal Seat. In the past, the Stone of Destiny (Lia Fáil) coronation stone is said to have stood near Cormac's House. According to legend, the stone would roar when the right king was standing on it. Today, there is a memorial stone for the rebels fallen in 1798 on Tara on that site, erroneously called »coronation stone«.

To the north of the royal court, look for the Mound of the Hostages. In this passage tomb, dating from 1800 BC, the burnt remains of 40 humans were discovered. It is said that on ascending the throne, the kings of Tara took hostages from high-ranking families in their kingdom to ensure their loyalty. After their death – certainly not always of natural causes – the hostages were buried in the Mound of the Hostages.

To the north, the royal courtyard abuts the **Ráth of the Synods fort**, dating from the 2nd–4th centuries. Fortified at one time by a circular wall, this dwelling was partly destroyed in the early 20th century by over-zealous hunters of the Ark of the Covenant described in the Old Testament. Further to the north, two walls (30m/98ft apart) run parallel for some 180m/590ft, with a dip in the centre. Traditionally, these walls have been called Banqueting Hall. An early representation shows the dining table in the wooden structure, and the seating order of the guests of the High King, according to their status and profession.

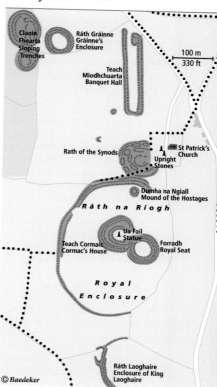

Hill of Tara *Plan*

Claoin Fhearta Sloping Trenches

Ráth Gráinne Gráinne's Enclosure

100 m
330 ft

Teach Miodhchuarta Banquet Hall

Rath of the Synods

St Patrick's Church

Upright Stones

Dumha na Ngiall Mound of the Hostages

Ráth na Ríogh

Ua Fáil Statue

Teach Cormaic Cormac's House

Forradh Royal Seat

Royal Enclosure

Ráth Laoghaire Enclosure of King Laoghaire

© Baedeker

Archaeologists think, however, that the walls might have formed a ceremonial entrance to a ritual site. To the west, there are two more earth walls that probably served as ritual sites: first **Gráinne's Fort**, and next to it the **Sloping Trenches**. Today, the Tara site is mired in controversy over the construction of the new M3 motorway close by.

A ritual site?

Around Tara

Some 800m/0.5 miles to the south, another hill is occupied by Fort Ráth Maeve. The fort with a diameter of 220m/722ft is surrounded by a wall and a ditch, but nothing remains other than this embankment. The name refers to the legendary Maeve, queen of the fairies and also a warrior queen and goddess who features in the cycle of Ulster myths.

Ráth Maeve

Thurles (Durlas)

D 4

Republic of Ireland, province: Munster
Population: 7,400

County: Tipperary

The old diocesan town of Thurles, 22km/14 miles north of Cashel, is the seat of the archdiocese of Cashel and Emly, though not only religious discipline is important here. Sport has also always found great support.

A cathedral with Italian flair
The keep of 12th-century Bridge Castle stands by the bridge over the Suir, and the smaller keep of the 15th-century Black Castle stands on the square. The cathedral, which was built in the Lombardian Romanesque style in 1865–1872, contains a 17th-century Baroque high altar by Andrea Pozzo originally from the Il Gesù church in Rome. In the chapel for the dead lies the tomb of Archbishop Croke (1824–1902), who was a great supporter of Irish independence. Among other things, he sponsored the Gaelic Athletic Association (GAA), founded in 1884, which is one of the largest amateur sporting associations in Europe today. The GAA stadium in Dublin, which has the status of a national shrine, is named after him. There is a small bird sanctuary on the island in the River Suir.

Around Thurles

✳ Holy Cross Abbey
The former Cistercian abbey of Holy Cross (13th–15th century) lies 6km/3.5 miles south of Thurles, on the right bank of the River Suir. Founded as early as 1168, the monastery was a much visited pilgrimage site because it owned a splinter from the cross of Christ. The restored church is three-aisled with two transepts and a mighty crossing tower built above. The 15th-century choir, with its east window and stone seats decorated with coats of arms, is particularly beautiful. The choir's vaults, the transepts and crossing are also noteworthy. In the northern transept a fresco – so rare for Ireland – has survived in part: a hunting scene with three hunters, a dog and stag are shown in brown, red and green. Between the two chapels in the southern transept there is a construction of pillars and arches, which was presumably used to exhibit the relic. From there a staircase leads to the upper storey of the monastic chambers. The chapter house on the east side of the cloister is not open to the public. The refectory on the south side has been destroyed.

Ballynahow Castle
Around 5km/3 miles north-west of Holy Cross stands 16th-century Ballynahow Castle, one of Ireland's rare round keeps. Two of the original five vaulted ceilings survive. The two lower floors were probably used for storage, the three above with larger windows for residential purposes.

Tipperary (Tiobraid Árann)

Republic of Ireland, province: Munster
Population: 5,000

County: Tipperary

Here in the Golden Vale, where the pastures are richest and the harvests most generous, lies Tipperary, capital of the county of the same name.

The town became famous for the song »It's a long way to Tipperary«, which was sung by British troops at the beginning of the 20th century and which entered the standard canon of English music at the beginning of the First World War. Jack Judge, the English author of the song written in 1912, never went to Ireland, so it is assumed that the word »Tipperary« was only chosen for its sound.

Industrial and market town

TIPPERARY

INFORMATION

Community Office
Tel. (0 62) 5 14 57

Only little survives of the old town. Of note is the choir arch in the 13th-century monastic church and the ruins of the primary school. Exhibits on the War of Independence (1919–1921) can be seen in a small exhibition at the eastern end of Main Street.

Around Tipperary

About 9km/5.5 miles east on the N74 stands the ruin of Thomastown Castle, which was built in the 17th century and extended in the neo-Gothic style around 1812. Father Theobald Matthew, famous promoter of abstinence, was born here in 1790. ►Cork.

Thomastown Castle

Turn right before crossing the bridge to reach the ruins of Ireland's largest medieval abbey, Athassel Priory (13th–15th century). It was founded for Augustinian monks by William de Burgh, who was buried there in 1248 The priory was in use until the dissolution of the monasteries in the mid-16th century, when the lands were given to the Earl of Ormonde. The remains cover an area of 1.6ha/4 acres. The church is 65m/70yd long, with a choir, an imposing crossing tower, and a three-aisled nave. There is almost nothing surviving of the cloister. All around are ranged the numerous convent buildings enclosed by a high wall. Once there was a bridge by the gate house, where it was possible to cross into the monastery from outside. There was a town here up until the middle of the 14th century, of which nothing has survived.

✱ Athassel Priory

Tralee (Trá Lí)

Republic of Ireland, province:
Munster
Population: approx. 20,000

County: Kerry

Tralee is not only the most important urban centre in the large county of Kerry, but also where the most beautiful Irish-born girl in the whole world is voted the »Rose of Tralee«.

Worthwhile stop

In spite of its relatively small population, Tralee, Trá Lí in Irish (»bay of the river Lee«), offers enough to make a one or two-day stop worthwhile. For most visitors, however, Tralee is the gateway to the historically rich ▶Dingle Peninsula, and the starting point for a tour of the famous ▶Ring of Kerry.

The town is also significant in terms of public services and especially for a range of shopping opportunities. Tralee is the headquarters of the dairy conglomerate Kerry Group, only founded in 1974, who export their products under the brand name of »Kerry Gold« to numerous countries around the world. Nothing survives from the old town because Tralee was burnt down by occupying forces in 1643 and 1691, to leave nothing for the enemy. There are however a few Georgian houses in the centre worth noting.

★
Kerry the Kingdom Museum

»Kerry the Kingdom« encompasses three attractions at the Ashe Memorial Hall: »Kerry in Colour« is a slide show that introduces the visitor to the scenic beauty of the region. The »Treasures of the Kingdom« museum shows the most significant archaeological exhibits and art pieces and brings to life the county's history from the Stone Age to the present with recreated scenarios; at the »Geraldine Experience«, eleven time-travelling vehicles take the visitor through the Tralee of 1450, complete with authentically recreated streets and squares. An effort is even made to replicate the sounds and smells of the era. This attraction is named after the Desmond Geraldines, one of the leading Norman families that ruled Tralee and the surrounding area. Opening times: March–Oct, daily 10am–6pm; Nov and Dec, noon–4.30pm.)

Siamsa Tíre

The Siamsa Tíre Theatre was built in the style of an Irish stone fort near the Ashe Memorial Hall. It is a national folk theatre dedicated to the preservation of Celtic culture and language. The programme is made up of music, dance and theatre (performances from May to September, usually at 8.30pm).

Blennerville Windmill and Steam Train

A narrow-gauge railway operated on the route between Tralee and Dingle from 1891 to 1953. It has been revived and travels from Tralee to the restored Blennerville Windmill at hourly intervals from

May to September, a distance of around 3km/2 miles. By car, the windmill can be reached on the R559 leading to Dingle. The Blennerville Windmill was built in 1800 and in service until 1880. It has been restored and the visitor can watch as the mighty mill stones grind wheat to flour. A multimedia show gives further insights into the history of the mill. As Blennerville Quay was an important departure point for emigrants, an exhibition is dedicated to the emigration waves of past centuries. (Opening times: April–Nov, daily 10am–6pm.)

Near the Steam Railway Station, the eye is caught by the interesting building of the Aqua Dome where an impressive waterworld offers

Aqua Dome

The Siamsa Tíre Theatre of Tralee cultivates Celtic heritage.

slides and wave pools, as well as a saunas and steam baths. (Opening times: April–Sept weekdays 10am–10pm, at weekends 10am–8pm.)

Around Tralee

Fenit   Fenit Seaworld at the harbour, around 10km/6.2 miles west of Tralee, allows the visitor to look all manner of sea creatures in the eye, from the smallest crab to scary-looking sharks. (Opening times: daily 10am–5.30pm; in the summer till 8pm.)

Ardfert   Drive 8km/5 miles north-west on the R551 to reach Ardfert, whose grounds boast significant remains of old buildings. Saint Brendan (483–578), born in neighbouring Fenit, founded a monastery here. The associated cluster of churches by the cemetery includes the castle-like cathedral (around 1250); the beautiful west porch and blind arcading of a previous Norman building (12th century) were used in its construction. The Gothic choir window and the lancet windows in the south wall are especially successful. The nave of the small Norman church Temple na Hoe can be found to the north-west, as well as remains of the 15th-century Temple na Griffin. A few hundred metres to the east stand the ruins of a Franciscan monastery (13th-15th century), with circular pillars and a beautiful south window in the church. The surviving sides of the cloister are covered by tiles.

Jutting out into the Atlantic, **Kerry Head** awaits past the quiet holiday resort of Ballyheige, situated further north on the R551. With a bit of luck, six-sided quartz crystals from the Kerry mountains can be found here, but Ballyheige's popularity stems from Banna Beach stretching out to the south. This is where in 1916 Sir Roger Casement (▶Famous People) had himself set down from a German U-boat to take part in the Easter Rising.

✶
Crag Cave   Crag Cave lies around 20km/12 miles east of Tralee. This impressive stalactite cavern was only systematically investigated in 1981, when it was established that this cave system is actually one of the largest in Ireland and almost 4km/2.5 miles long. (Opening times: daily 10am–6pm.)

▶ **TRALEE**

INFORMATION
Ashe Memorial Hall
Tel. (0 66) 7 12 12 88
tourisminfo@shannon-dev.ie

ACCOMMODATION
▶ **Luxury**
Ballyseede Castle
Southeast
Tel. (0 66) 7 12 57 99
Fax. (0 66) 7 12 52 87
ballyseede@eircom.net
Those with a passion for old castles can stay the night at Ballyseede Castle. Its history stretches back to the 15th century.

Trim (Baile Átha Troim)

Republic of Ireland, province:
Leinster
Population: 1,800

County: Meath
Information: Tel. (0 46) 3 71 11

The pretty and relaxing town of Trim has a great past, and film-makers (»Braveheart«) like to use the spectacular ambience of Trim Castle as a backdrop.

Hugh de Lacy, a vassal of Henry II, built a castle in the year 1172 precisely opposite the spot where Saint Patrick (► Baedeker Special, p.34) had founded a monastery in the fifth century. The castle changed hands several times and during the 14th century, the entire settlement was fortified around it with walls and gates. Several parliamentary meetings were held here in the 15th century. In 1649 the town fell to Cromwell. The film »The Power & the Glory« which can be viewed at Trim Heritage Centre, offers a good historical overview.

Small town with a great past

In the town centre on the south shore of the Boyne, the magnificent fortifications of Trim Castle rise up. It covers a surface area of about 1.2 ha/3 acres, which makes it the largest of Ireland's castles from the Norman era. The square keep is situated on the highest point in the middle of the settlement, with four small towers rising above it on the four corners of the main building, and fortified by four projecting towers, of which only three survive. In this way a design in the shape of the cross was formed. A wall fortified with (only partially surviving) semi-circular towers and a moat enclosed the grounds. A drawbridge was used at the tower gate on the south side. The battlement parapets connected with the town wall.

★
Trim Castle

Displays at Trim Castle provide information about life in the old days.

Today, the landmark of Trim is the **Yellow Steeple**, which is the all that remains of an Augustinian monastery on a bare elevation above the river. The almost 40m/130-ft tower stood at the north side of the former church. The 12th-century Augustinian abbey of St Mary's had been restored in 1368, and in 1415 parts of it were turned into an imposing manor house, which became known by the name of Talbot's Castle. Later a school was housed here, at which Arthur Wellesley (1769 –1852), later the Duke of Wellington, was taught.

Sheep Gate   A little further south from the Yellow Steeple (near the shore of the river) stands Sheep Gate, the two-storey ruin of the only town gate still to be visible today.

Black Friary, Maudlins Cemetery   The relics of the 13th-century Black Friary to the north are interesting, and so is the beautiful bronze statue of »Our Lady of Trim« in Maudlins Cemetery, at the other end of town. The statue of the Virgin Mary was made after the design of a wooden statue said to have once been at St Mary's Abbey.

Newton Trim   Barely a mile downriver, east of Trim, the ruins of Newton Trim standing by an old bridge once were a monastery dedicated to Saint Peter and Saint Paul. Only the choir, crossing and part of the nave survive of this once very large 13th-century cathedral, built for the Bishop of Meath. To the south, a few remains of the monastic buildings can still be seen. To the east stands a smaller 13th-century church with a notable double tomb from the late 16th century.

Tullamore (Tulach Mór)

C 4

Republic of Ireland, province: Leinster
Population: 9,300

County: Offaly

The most important town in the County of Offaly is well-known among whiskey lovers and lies almost exactly in the centre of Ireland.

Former citadel of whiskey   Until recently, the famous Tullamore Dew and Irish Malt Whiskey Liqueur were produced here. Tullamore, Tulach Mór in Irish (»great gathering hill«), served as the terminus of the ►Dublin Grand Canal until 1804, and experienced a boom as a centre for distilleries and breweries. In 1790 however, when Tullamore was still fairly small, the explosion caused by a large hot air balloon crashing destroyed most of the buildings.

Withy Tullamore Dew and Irish Mist are now produced in Clonnel, Tullamore has lost an attraction. But with the recent opening of the Tullamore Dew Heritage Centre in an old warehouse at Bury Quay, another attraction has been gained. Of course the focus is on whiskey production, but a Living History Museum also shows how people used to live and work, and highlights a few key moments in the history of the town, which, in around 1620, consisted merely of a castle, a windmill and a few huts. The strong drinks can be sampled at the end of the tour.

✱ Tullamore Dew Heritage Centre

> ! **Baedeker TIP**
>
> **Boat Tours**
>
> Why not take a boat tour on the Grand Canal, starting in Tullamore? Information about them can be found at the tourist office.

To the west of the centre, **Charleville Castle**, with its turrets and spires, seems like a Gothic folly. It was built for William Bury, later Lord Tullamore, at the turn of the 18th century, and designed by Francis Johnston, one of Ireland's most famous architects. A highlight is the dining room, furnished by Sir William Morris. The building is open to the public at present only as part of a rather expensive tour arranged by appointment, as restoration work is still proceeding. The castle is owned by a private educational institution.

Around Tullamore

A little north of Tullamore, in Durrow, there was once a monastery founded by Saint Columba in the 6th century. It became famous through the »Book of Durrow« which can now be admired in Trinity College Dublin. It was written and illuminated in the 7th century. A 10th-century High Cross also survives, adorned with fine figurative carving. The east side shows the Sacrifice of Isaac: Christ in Glory, to his left, David playing the Harp, and to his right, David Slaying the Lion. On the west side, one can see the Soldiers Guarding the tomb of Christ, as well as the Flagellation, the Imprisonment and the Crucifixion of Christ.

Durrow

East of Tullamore lies the picturesque little town of Edenderry (pop. 3,600). 7km/4.5 miles north stand the ruins of Carrickoris Castle, which used to belong to the O'Connor family and was the site of a massacre in the year 1305. In 1325, in penance for his father's crime, John de Bermingham had the small abbey of Monasteroris built for the Franciscans, 3km/2 miles to the north-west. There is a nice footpath leading from the town hall along the canal to the Downshire Bridge.

Edenderry

★ Waterford (Port Lairge)

D 4

Republic of Ireland, province: Munster	**County:** Waterford
Population: 42,500	

Waterford developed into a significant port due to its location. The town was founded by Vikings in 835 and later expanded by the Anglo-Normans.

Port in the south east

Waterford remained an English stronghold up to the 19th century, a position that was firmly established after Henry VII granted the town the motto of »Urbs intacta manet Waterfordia« (»Waterford remains untouched«) in 1487. Twice before that date the inhabitants had stood firm against rival pretenders to the throne. After Cromwell and his troops unsuccessfully laid siege to Waterford in 1649, the town wastaken the following year.

Many houses in the centre still date from the time around 1800, when the glass industry experienced its heyday in Waterford. There are many Georgian houses, especially on the Mall. An effort is being made to restore buildings that suffered during industrialization. The old Viking settlement is also being excavated. The town is also characterized by numerous hotels, restaurants and pubs.

Sights in Waterford

Town Walls

Waterford got its impressive town walls during the time of its foundation by the Vikings and its expansion under King John. Parts of them can still be seen in the Palace Garden by the theatre. In addition, several towers survive, such as the Half Moon Tower (Patrick Street), the Watch Tower near Railway Square, and Reginald's Tower.

★
Reginald's Tower

The impressive round Reginald's Tower stands at the point where Parade Quay makes a hairpin bend into the Mall. It is said to have already been part of an old Viking fortification from 1003. In reality, however, the tower in its present shape appears to be the remains of a 13th-century Norman construction. The town museum hides behind 3-m/10ft thick walls. (Opening times: mid April–Oct Mon–Fri, 10am–5pm, Sat, 2–6pm.)

The Mall

South of the tower, on the wide Mall, the town hall from 1788 survives in its original condition. The building also contains the Victorian Royal Theatre, which was built at the same time. One of Ireland's most beautiful town houses, Bishop's Palace, was built by Richard Castle (or Cassels), one of the major architects of 18th-century Ireland, who designed Leinster House and the Rotunda Hospital in Dublin as well as Powerscourt House and Westport House.

Waterford Plan

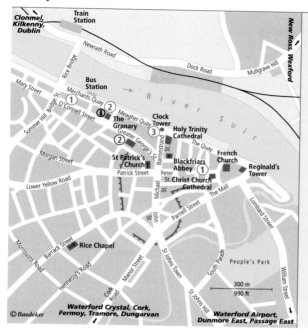

Clonmel, Kilkenny, Dublin

Train Station

Newrath Road

Rice Bridge

Mary Street

Summer Hill

O'Connell Street

Bus Station

Merchants Quay

Meagher Quay

The Granary

Greater George's

Morgan Street

Lower Yellow Road

St Patrick's Church

Patrick Street

Morrisson's Road

Barrack Street

Rice Chapel

Hennesy's Road

Cork Road

Manor Street

St Johns Town

St Johns Hill

Waterford Crystal, Cork, Fermoy, Tramore, Dungarvan

© Baedeker

Dock Road

Mullgrave Hill

New Ross, Wexford

River Suir

Clock Tower

Holy Trinity Cathedral

The Quay

French Church

Barronstrand St.

Blackfriars Abbey

Peter St.

Christ Church Cathedral

Reginald's Tower

The Mall

Michael St.

John St.

Parnell Street

Lombard Street

People's Park

South Parade

William Street

300 m
990 ft

Waterford Airport, Dunmore East, Passage East

Where to stay
① The Anchorage
② Dooley's
③ Granville

Where to eat
① Vine Vault
② T and H Doolans

Waterford's newest attraction is without doubt a small but fine treasury in The Granary, which is also where the tourist office is housed. These remarkable exhibits, including a Viking brooch (1100 BC) and a glass decanter from 1790, represent a trajectory reaching right up to the present time.

★
The Granary

Behind the town hall, Christ Church Cathedral rises up. A spacious interior contains two interesting tombs: the Rice Monument (1469) and the Fitzgerald Monument, made of Carrara marble.

Christ Church Cathedral

Continuing from here along Greyfriars Street, the remains of French Church stand on the right. Its origins reach right back to the foundation of a monastery in the year 1240. The nave was used as a poor house and hospital from the 17th to the 19th century, while the choir was used as a church by Huguenot immigrants and the Mary Chapel as a burial place for important families.

◄ French Church

Finds from excavations in Waterford and the surrounding area are shown in a church annex.

A church tower on the corner of O'Connell Street and Bridge Street is the only surviving part of the Blackfriars Priory Dominican mo-

Other buildings

nastery (1226–1541). Holy Trinity Cathedral (1793), with its rich interior decorations, as well as the Chamber of Commerce (1795) on St George Street, are by John Roberts, who also designed Christ Church Cathedral. Most notable in this classical building is the magnificent staircase.

Around Waterford

Passage East A good 10km/6 miles east of town, on the R683, lies Passage East, where the River Suir flows into the bay of Waterford Harbour. Strongbow landed here with 1,200 men in 1170 before taking Waterford. A passenger ferry runs to Ballyhack beyond the harbour.

▶ VISITING WATERFORD

INFORMATION

41 The Quay
Tel. (0 51) 87 57 88
www.waterford.tourist.com

The Granary
Merchants Quay
Tel. (0 51) 33 25 00

Waterford Crystal Visitor Centre
Tel. (0 51) 87 58 23

EATING

▶ Moderate
① *Wine Vault*
High Street
Tel. (0 51) 85 34 44
info@waterfordwinevault.com
The restaurant is housed in a customs warehouse dating from the 15th century. It offers wines imported from around the world and a rustic bistro menu, with a light modern touch.

▶ Inexpensive
② *T and H Doolans*
George's Street
Tel. (0 51) 84 15 04
One of the oldest pubs in Ireland, offering traditional music during both the summer and winter months.

ACCOMMODATION

▶ Luxury
③ *Granville*
Meagher Quay
Tel. (0 51) 30 55 55
Fax (0 51) 30 55 66
stay@granville-hotel.ie
This hotel dating from the early 19th century once hosted Charles Stewart Parnell. The rooms are all designed in individual traditional style.

▶ Mid-range
② *Dooley's*
The Quay
Tel. (0 51) 87 35 31
Fax (0 51) 87 02 62
hotel@dooleys-hotel.ie
This family-run business with comfortable rooms is in the town centre.

▶ Budget
① *The Anchorage*
9 The Quay
Tel. (0 51) 85 43 02
Fax (0 51) 85 69 79
kevinpjhayden@eircom.net
Centrally located hotel by the River Suir with comfortable accommodation in well-maintained simple rooms.

Back roads lead from Passage East to Dunmore East, which lies at the southern end of Waterford harbour. It is a pretty resort situated on a rise, complete with yacht harbour, beach and a rich selection of leisure activities.

Dunmore East

The R675 leads from Waterford to the coast and Tramore Bay. A detour of 4km/2.5 miles on minor roads in a westerly direction is an opportunity to see the beautiful Knockeen Dolmen, presumed to be 4,000 years old.

Towards Tramore

After about 13km/8 miles, the main road reaches the popular family resort of Tramore (pop. 6,540), with its attractive sandy beach, 5km/ 3 miles long. Other leisure activities on offer are fishing, horse-racing or golf. In the summer, in addition to the swimming paradise of »Splashworld«, another attraction is to be re-opened: »Celtworld«, where by means of holograms, lasers and computer graphics, among others, Celtic myths and legends are to be brought to life.

Drive upriver along the Suir from Waterford, initially heading west on the N25 and then in a north-westerly direction on the R680, to the former Quaker town of **Portlow**, reached after about a mile. Its tanneries make up the greatest part of Irish leather production. To the north-west lies Curraghmore Park. The mansion of the Marquess of Waterford stands amidst the magnificent estate, which also includes a shell house (only open on Thursday afternoons and bank holidays).

> ! **Baedeker TIP**
>
> **Waterford Crystal**
>
> Waterford Crystal, about 2.5km/1.5 miles south of the centre on the Cork Road, is one of the most highly regarded glass workshops. It is one of Ireland's most popular tourist attractions, and to avoid the crowds, it is best to take the morning tour and to book ahead during the main holiday season.

★ # Westport (Cathair na Mart)

C 2

Republic of Ireland, province: Connaught
Population: 4,500

County: Mayo

For many, Westport is one of Ireland's prettiest places. Tthanks to the abundance of fish in Clew Bay, it has also developed into a popular centre for sea fishing.

The narrow Carrowbeg River runs alongg the middle of the main road, the Mall, lined by lime trees and spanned by charming old bridges. At the southern end of the Mall lies an attractively designed square called the Octagon, where a statue of Saint Patrick depicts the

Pretty coastal town on Clew Bay

saint entangled in snakes. Designed for the Earl of Altamont by the English architect James Wyatt in 1780, the town was an important centre of trade before the arrival of the railway.

Westport House

✳ The entrance to Westport House on Westport Quay is reached by following the main road south from the Octagon square. Built by Richard Cassels in 1730–1734 and extended by James Wyatt, the seat of the Marquess of Sligo counts among Ireland's most interesting manor houses, even though little survives of the original interior. There are family portraits in the Long Gallery, and the Dining Room is decorated with stucco. Upstairs, landscape paintings depict scenes from the local area. Downstairs, a shopping arcade rather lacking in style has been installed. The beautiful park, designed in the English style, tempts visitors with unusual water features that make use of the tides. Children will love the small zoo. (Opening times: estate and zoo May–Sept daily 10am–5pm; in the summer till 6pm.)

Clew Bay Heritage Centre

Also on Westport Quay, near the manor house, Clew Bay Heritage Centre offers interesting exhibits and information on the region's history.

Westport House, with its beautiful furniture and art collection, is worth a visit.

Rockfleet Castle was a favourite base of Grace O'Malley's

THE PIRATE QUEEN

Probably no other woman earned the love of the Irish people as much as the »Pirate Queen« Grace O'Malley (1530–1603). Songs and legends claim her as the first Irish patriot.

The head of the O'Malley clan and ruler over **Clew Bay near Westport** was the only child and thus the sole inheritor of Owen Dubhdarra (»the Black Oak«).

The O'Malleys' livelihood depended on the sea: selling fish and piracy put food on the table. At an early age, Grace stepped into the footsteps of her father and, at nine years' old, successfully pestered him into allowing her to learn the trades of the sea. Her first marriage to Donal »of the Battles«, next in line as chieftain of the O'Flaherty clan, and the birth of three children, initially confined her to dry land. When Grace took to the sea again, her trading, pirating and war expeditions added more to the family's coffers than her husband. Soon, the O'Flahertys accepted her as the real clan leader.

After the death of her husband, Grace returned to the family home and, in 1566, was elected the **first female head of the O'Malley clan**. Her second marriage was a strategic one, giving her domination over the whole of Clew Bay. Celtic law gave her the opportunity to release her husband from the marriage after one year but hang on to his possessions.

Meeting Elizabeth I

With her **20 boats and 6,000 men**, Grace O'Malley soon dominated large parts of the west coast of Ireland, becoming the scourge of all merchant ships crossing the Atlantic. Getting on the wrong side of the Pirate Queen was not a good idea: when her lover was murdered, she destroyed the murderer's whole clan. The only power to best hers was England, which, under Elizabeth I, was increasingly laying claim to Ireland. Grace O'Malley gave in to the superior force, paying tribute to the English Queen, which allowed her to hang on to her possession as a fiefdom. In 1593 she travelled to London in order to ask Queen Elizabeth I in person for the release of her imprisoned son. It was this action in particular that made the »Pirate Queen« and feared clan chieftain into a legendary Robin Hood character and heroine of Irish freedom.

◉ VISITING WESTPORT

INFORMATION
James Street
Tel. (0 98) 2 57 11

FOOD

▶ **Moderate**
Quay Cottage
Harbour
(by the entrance to Westport House)
Tel. (0 98) 2 64 12
Fans of ships and all things nautical
will feel at home in little Quay
Cottage. The speciality is fish dishes of
course, but the vegetarian menu is not
to be sniffed at either.

▶ **Budget**
O'Malley's
Bridge Street
Tel. (0 98) 2 64 12
Not only young people meet in this
establishment, which offers dishes
from Mexico, Italy, India and Thai-
land.

PUBS

Big John McGing's
High Street
Tel. (0 98) 5 08 29
This lively pub is said to have the best
stout in Westport.

Matt Molloy's
Bridge Street
Tel. (0 98) 2 66 55
This belongs to the »Chieftains« flute
player. When he is around, he some-
times joins in with the music sessions.

ACCOMMODATION

▶ **Luxury**
Westport
The Demesme, Newport Road
Tel. (0 98) 2 51 22
Fax. (0 98) 2 67 39
reservations@hotelwestport.ie
Hotel in the middle of a park, just a
few minutes from the centre. During
the summer the bar offers evening
entertainment.

Baedeker Recommendation

▶ **Mid-range**
Westport Woods
Quay Road
Tel. (0 98) 2 58 11, Fax (0 98) 2 62 12
info@westportwoodshotel.com
A playground, tennis courts, and evening
entertainment are just some of the advan
tages of this house in a peaceful location.

National Famine Memorial Just a few miles west of Murrish stands the National Famine Memorial by John Behan. The artist designed it in the shape of a »coffin
ship«, one of the notorious ships on which the survival chances of
emigrants were very slim.

Around Westport

★ **Croagh Patrick** Ireland's holy mountain Croagh Patrick (753m/2471ft), rises suddenly out of the shore landscape south-west of Westport. The climb can
be made from a car park on the R335, at Murrisk. A small road ini-

tially leads to the white statue of Saint Patrick, and then goes up via a steep slope covered in quartz gravel (good walking shoes are needed). To reach the summit via the exhausting path requires a good two hours, but it is worth it, not least for the constantly expanding horizon. From right at the top, Clew Bay with its many little islands can be seen to the north, stretching away to the heights of the Curraun Peninsula and even further, to Nephin mountain, especially atmospheric at sunset. To the south, it is even possible to see the Twelve Bens of Connemara beyond the Mweelrea Mountains.

Each year on the last Sunday of July, there is a large pilgrimage up the mountain to commemorate the forty days of penance that Saint Patrick is supposed to have undergone here in the year 441. There is a chapel on its flat summit, where a service is always held on the day. Many pilgrims perform this pilgrimage barefoot, and the discarded shoes can be seen along the path.

The fishing village of Louisburgh, Cluain Cearbán (»Kerwan's Meadow«) in Irish, is especially popular with visitors due to its beautiful surrounding countryside. The plateau, traversed by many rivers rich in fish, is enfolded by Croagh Patrick in the east and the Mweelrea Mountains, up to 785m/2575.5ft high, to the south. The coast is lined by cliffs and beautiful beaches. To the north-east, the viewpoint of Old Head juts out into the bay. In the Granuaile Visitor Centre, discover everything about the legendary pirate Grace O'Malley. In

Louisburgh

Ireland's »holy mountain« Croagh Patrick

addition to historical documents, castle and ship models, there is also a video about her life. (Opening times: June–Sept Mon-Fri 10am to 6pm.)

Doo Lough Valley

The R335 leads from Louisburgh through the beautiful Doo Lough Valley, also known as the Valley of Delphi (► Connemara), though the road climbs gradually up towards Doo Lough (»dark lake«) until suddenly, the lonely lake opens up, with the Mwellrea Mountains behind. Salmon and trout can be caught here. When the sun is shining, the landscape appears bright green, though everything is cloaked in an opaque grey when fog banks draw in from the Atlantic. The cross by the side of the road recalls a tragedy that occurred during the Famine (1845–1849): 600 men, women and children set off from Louisburgh to Delphi Lodge to ask the then owner for food. He refused them, however, and 400 people died of hunger and cold during the return journey.

Killeen, Killadoon

A minor road heading south-west from Louisburgh leads to the Carrownisky River as well as to Killeen and Killadoon. The two isolated villages offer a wonderful view towards the sea and beautiful beaches.

Clare Island

The quiet holiday paradise of mountainous Clare Island lies off the coast, to the north-west. The island, still inhabited by 140 people, can be reached from Roonagh Quay, from where two companies operate small ferries (inquire locally for crossing times). During the 16th century, the island belonged to the legendary Grace O'Malley, and the castle on the small harbour is said to have been built by her. About 2.5km/1.5 miles south-west of the harbour stand the ruins of Saint Bridget's Church, dating from around 1500. Medieval frescoes displaying strange hybrid creatures of man and beast can be seen in the choir. The only character that is definitely recognizable is the Archangel Michael with the scales of justice.

Inishturk Island

Inishturk Island can also be reached from Roonagh Quay via Inishbofin. Nature lovers will enjoy the sandy beaches, beautiful walking trails and interesting plant and animal life here.

Newport and around

Newport is especially popular for the sea fishing in Clew Bay and trout fishing in the surrounding lakes. The landscape is characterized by the numerous drumlins (Ice Age deposits). Other islands in Clew Bay are also the remains of these gravel and sand hills that have sunk into the sea. North of Newport, situated on a quiet ocean bay, the imposing ruins of the former Dominican monastery of Burrishoole (15th century) can be found. The cloister and several memorial slabs have survived well.

Burrishoole Abbey ►

Rockfleet Castle ►

Just a few miles further west, left of the N59, the 15th century Rockfleet Castle – also known as Carrigahooley – stands on an ocean inlet. The four-storey keep with its single corner tower belonged to Grace O'Malley (►Baedeker Special, p.451).

12km/7.5 miles further on, in Mulrany, fuchsias, rhododendron and ◄ Mulrany
Mediterranean shrubs grow in profusion in the mild climate. There
is a golf course here and tennis courts. The R319 leads on to ►Achill
Island via the large Curraun Peninsula. It is worth driving around
Curraun Peninsula: on the south side a narrow road leads along a va-
ried coastline with views onto Clew Bay and Clare Island.

Wexford (Loch Garman)

D 5

Republic of Ireland, province:
Leinster
Population: 10,000

County: Wexford

**Situated on the most south-easterly tip of Ireland, Wexford has a
pretty quaint town centre with narrow winding streets typical of
the settlements established by the Norman conquerors.**

By the end of the 19th century, the previously flourishing port had   Lively town
silted up noticeably. In former times, the town lived mostly from agriculture, but today it is industry (the manufacture of farming equipment, among others) that defines economic life. Wexford is a lively
town with pretty pubs and a colourful art and cultural scene, as well
as being linguistically unique: the Yola dialect of earlier inhabitants
still colours the pronunciation of several words. Visitors can easily
get to know Wexford. Main Street runs roughly parallel with the
long quay at Wexford Harbour, and almost everything worth seeing
can easily be reached via its side streets going off to the right and
left.

Sights of Wexford

The local tourist office can be found on the semi-circular Crescent   Crescent Quay
Quay. This is also the site of a statue (given by the American government) of John Barry (1745 – 1803), who fought in the American War
of Independence and is regarded as the father of the US navy.

At the junction between Quay Street and Main Street, a small square   Bullring
is known as the Bullring, where the Normans once entertained
themselves with bull fights.

Westgate is the only surviving city gate; once there were five. Built in   Westgate Heri-
the 13th century, the tower has been restored and now houses the   tage Centre
Heritage Centre. An audio-visual show takes under half an hour to
present some interesting features of the town and region's history.
(Opening times: Mon–Sat 9.30am–12.30pm and 2–5pm, Sun,   ⏱
2–5pm.)

Selskar Abbey
Next door stand the ruins of Selskar Abbey, founded in the 12th century and destroyed by Cromwell's troops in 1649. A tower and parts of the 15th-century St Selskar Church survive.

St Iberius Church
St Iberius Church was built south of the Bullring on North Main Street in 1760, on the site of several earlier buildings. The best way to savour the beautiful interior is during one of the summer lunchtime concerts, held every Wednesday at 1pm.

Around Wexford

★★
Irish National Heritage Park
The Irish National Heritage Park was laid out in the middle of a swampy landscape near Ferrycarrig. In the grounds of the open air museum 9,000 years of Irish history are brought to life in recreations of settlements and buildings. Among others, there are dolmens, a stone circle, a Viking settlement complete with long boat, an Early Christian monastery, as well as a round tower. There is also a nature trail. (Opening times: March–Oct daily 10am–7pm, last entrance at 5pm.)

A reconstructed Crannóg

To the north, the Wildfowl Reserve is bordered by the broad bay of Wexford Harbour. Thousands of dwarf geese, as well as swans and 28 species of duck overwinter in the large bird sanctuary. There is a tower and camouflaged hides for birdwatching, and a visitor centre offers an overview of bird species.

Curragloe Beach, The Raven ►
(Opening times: daily 9am to sunset.) To the north, the dune-protected beaches of Curracloe Beach stretch out. In the nearby nature reserve of The Raven there are wading birds.

★
Johnstown Castle and Agricultural Museum
In a southerly direction, leaving Wexford for Rosslare, take a right on a signposted road to Johnstown Castle. It was built in neo-Gothic style in the second half of the 19th century using the remains of a castle dating from Norman times. The entrance hall can be visited, and a stroll around the park with artificial ponds and 200 different trees and shrubs is very pleasant. An agricultural museum has been installed in the farm buildings. (Opening times: park daily 9am–5.30pm; Agricultural Museum Mon–Fri 9am–5pm, Sat/Sun 2–5pm, closed at weekends Nov–March.)

Yola Farmstead Folk Park
Yola Farmstead Folk Park is located south of Wexford, on the road to the port of Rosslare. It is comprised of a reconstructed Irish village complete with 19th-century windmill. A craftwork shop offers trinkets and gifts to take home, and the Heritage Centre allows visi-

tors to research their family histories. (Opening times: May–Oct daily 10am–6pm, March, April and Nov Mon –Fri 10am–4.30pm.)
Rosslare, one of the sunniest and driest places in Ireland, is reached on the N25. A wide bay offers several kilometres/miles of sand and pebble beaches.

The well-known ferry port lies at the southern end of the bay. **Rosslare Harbour** is the point of arrival for connections from Fishguard (Wales) and Le Havre (France). It has an extensive pier and a ferry terminal that was completed in 1989. Almost all passenger ferry traffic from the European mainland is dealt with here, but Rosslare Harbour is also a significant freight port, and almost 10% of Irish exports are processed here. South of Rosslare Harbour, a narrow strip of land separates **Lady's Island Lake** from the sea. An island in the lake is connected to the mainland by a dam. The ruins of a monastery and 12th-century Norman castle can be seen on the island. 15th-century Rathmacknee Castle, reached by turning left off

 WEXFORD

INFORMATION
Crescent Quay
Tel. (0 53) 2 31 11

ACCOMMODATION
► **Mid-range**
Whites Hotel
George Street
Tel. (0 53) 2 23 11, Fax (0 53) 4 50 00
info@whiteshotel.iol.ie
Situated in the historic centre, the hotel is housed in a building from the late 18th century. It also has a fitness club, a good restaurant and the popular La Speranza Bar.

the N25 onto the R739, gives a convincing idea of what Irish castles of the 15th and 16th centuries looked like. Further along, the R739 leads to Kilmore and Kilmore Quay, a picturesque fishing centre off the beaten track at Forlorn Point. From here, consider a trip to the cliff islands of Saltee Islands (Little and Great Saltee Island). One of Europe's largest bird sanctuaries, with over 350 species living here, including cormorants, puffins, razorbills, and northern gannet, this is an inside tip. The best time for a visit is spring or early summer.

Wicklow (Cill Mhantáin)

D 5

Republic of Ireland, province: Leinster
Population: 6,500

County: Wicklow

The Vikings made use of the advantageous position of Wicklow's harbour. They settled at the 5th-century monastic centre of St Mantan and called it »Wykingio«.

Good beach base for mountain excursions

Wicklow stretches from the sea to the lower reaches of the Wicklow Mountains. The River Vartry flows into the Irish Sea here, after forming a narrow inland water stretching for 3km/2 miles.

Black Castle (12th century) once protected the old narrow streets of the town. Standing on a cliff promontory to the east, the Norman castle was frequently embattled in the 17th century. The remains of a Franciscan monastery in the parish garden date from the 13th century. The 18th-century parish church has a beautiful Romanesque porch. The most interesting place to visit, however, is surely Wicklow's Historic Jail. The former prison deals with the history of the penal system. (Opening times: daily 10am–6pm.)

Entrance to Black Castle

Around Wicklow

Wicklow Head

The viewpoint of Wicklow Head lies about 3km/1.8 miles south-east of Wicklow. The three lighthouses are rather unusual. Further south, the Silver Strand reaches all the way to Mizen Head via Brittas Bay.

✳ Mount Usher Gardens

Ashford, attractively situated on the River Vartry, is reached via Rathnew on the R750 and the N11 heading out of Wicklow in a north-westerly direction. This is where Mount Usher Gardens spread out on the shores of the lake. Originally designed as a small garden of no more than half a hectare/1.2 acres by Edmond Walpole in 1868, this garden landscape of exceptional beauty and rare trees, shrubs and sub-tropical plants now covers approx. 8ha/20 acres. It continues to be in private hands. About 5,000 different species of plants thrive in the romantic park landscape, providing an overwhelming palette of colour in May and the beginning of June, during the flowering of the azaleas and rhododendrons. (Opening times: mid–March– Oct daily, 10.30am–6pm.)

▶ WICKLOW

INFORMATION
Rialto House
Tel. (04 04) 6 91 17
wicklowtouristoffice@eircom.net

ACCOMMODATION
▶ **Mid-range**
Grand Hotel
Abbey Street
Tel. (04 04) 6 73 37, Fax (04 04) 6 96 07
grandhotel@eircom.net
Shining with renewed vigour: a recommended restaurant is attached.

Further up the Vartry Valley, a landscape feature worth seeing is the Devil's Glen. Water shoots through the densely verdant walls of a deep gorge before falling 30m/100ft into a rock basin known as The Devil's Punchbowl. Beautiful views of this natural spectacle are provided by well-maintained footpaths.

Devil's Glen

★ Wicklow Mountains

C/D 5

Republic of Ireland, province: Leinster   **County:** Wicklow

The Wicklow Mountains are an appealing mountain landscape of dark lakes and brown and purple speckled hills. Their peaks are often shaped like sugar cones and sometimes cloaked in shreds of fog.

Bog alternates with heather and deciduous forests with pine forest. The granite mountains begin south of Dublin and continue south through the county of Wicklow for a distance of around 60km/40 miles. To the east, they run towards the Irish Sea, to the west, they finish in the plain traversed by the River Barrow.

»The Garden of Ireland«

There are only two passes, Sally Gap and Wicklow Gap, that offer the possibility of crossing the mountains from east to west. Right up until the 18th century, the inaccessible upland valleys were a safe haven for the persecuted, outlawed and criminals. After the revolts of the 1890s, the English built a strategic road, the Military Road, in order to keep better control of the region.

Sally Gap, Wicklow Gap

Hiking information for the region can be found at the visitor centre at Upper Lake in► Glendalough. (Opening times: April–Aug daily 10am–6.30pm, only at weekends in Sept.)

Upper Lake
⏲

A Drive through the Wicklow Mountains

The drive from Rathfarnham (► Dublin) goes uphill towards the south. Half to the right, Kippure mountain (767m/2517ft) and its radio mast can be seen and, looking back, there is a beautiful view towards Dublin. Near the point where the road shortly turns off for Enniskerry lies the German military cemetery of Glencree. The R115 continues onwards to the south, passing two small lakes and crossing a highland bog.

From Rathfarnham to Laragh

From Sally Gap (505m/1641 feet), the road leads south through bare bog land, crossing several rivers that rise from the eastern flanks of the high mountains to the right (Gravate, Duff Hill and Mullaghclee-

Sally Gap

The soft Wicklow Mountains

vaun). Laragh is eventually reached via the road passing a waterfall in the boulder-lined valley of Glenmacnass; the waterfall is best seen from the valley side.

The R756 climbs in a westerly direction, past the famous monastic settlement of ▶ Glendalough, and back into the mountains towards **Wicklow Gap** (486m/1595 feet), located between the mountains Tonelagee to the north and Camaderry to the south. The latter lies in **Glendalough Forest Park**; the road following the park's borders. About 4km/2.5 miles past the top of the pass, a small road turns off to the right for Glenbringe youth hostel, located in an isolated valley basin.

After a further 6km/3.5 miles, a road turns half right towards the north and **Poulaphuca Lake**, also known as Lacken Reservoir. Covering about 2,000ha/5,000 acres, it serves Dublin's electrical and water needs.

The Piper's Stones ▶ About 2km/1.2 miles south of Hollywood, reached by the R756, a stone circle of indeterminate age near Athgreany is known as The Piper's Stones. Beyond the circle stands a lone stone: the piper.

✱ Russborough House North of Hollywood on the N81, the reservoir is reached once again, and after 6km/3.5 miles Russborough House, the seat of the Beit family. It was built by Richard Cassels and Francis Bindon in 1740–1750, in the Palladian style. The main building includes colonnades, wings and a large outdoor staircase. The interior contains good stucco work by Francini, as well as the Beit Art Collection, with works by Goya, Rubens, Velázquez and Vermeer, as well as Irish silver. ⏲ (Opening times: Easter–Oct daily 10.30am–5.30pm; May and Sept 10.30am–2.30pm.)

Detour into Glenmalure Valley and to Lugnaquilla Mountain Continuing south on the former Military Road from Laragh, after 2km/1.2 miles, the road turns right towards the mountains again, climbing up to a height of 386m/1266ft before leading down into the valley of Glenmalure. The terrain of Glenmalure Valley is frequently described as dark and haunting, but the scenic impressions offered by this rather isolated region are unique. At the hamlet of Drumgoff, at a small crossroads, a right turn soon leads to a car park, a starting point for Lugnaquilla Mountain (943m/3093ft). The 17km/10.5-mile footpath is not signposted, and the height differential is about 800m/2624 feet.

The R755 leads south-east from Laragh through the exquisitely beautiful landscape of the Vale of Clara , along the Avenmore River towards Rathdrum. The Avondale Forest Park (►Arklow) stretches out to the south. Turn off the R752 (leading to Wicklow) north onto the N11, to reach (►Mount Usher Gardens) Ashford. The R764, heading inland, passes the large Vartry Reservoir. At pretty Roundwood, change onto the R755 heading north.

Vale of Clara

Further along the road, the Great Sugar Loaf (501m/1644ft) rises up above the upland plain. It can be climbed from a large car park at the southern base of the mountain which, with a height differential of around 210m/689ft, takes about 45 minutes. A further stop along this road worth making is ►Enniskerry, and the magnificent Powerscourt Gardens situated nearby. From Enniskerry, the R117 leads back to Dublin (15km/9 miles).

◄ Great Sugar Loaf

Long-Distance Footpath

The Wicklow Way long-distance footpath was completed in 1983. About 126km/78.7 miles long, this signposted path leads south from Marlay Park (County Dublin: car park, bus service from Dublin) to Clonegal (County Carlow). There are car parks within range of the footpath, making it possible to only walk sections of the route.

Wicklow Way

The first section of the path leads along the eastern flank of the mountains and ends at the R759 at Luggala, between Sally Gap and Roundwood at Lough Tay. Continuing from Luggala, through the valley of Glanmacnass in the direction of Laragh, the path turns west and then south-west in the direction of Moyne via Drumgoff and Aghavannagh.

The last section leads south from Moyne to Clonegal, past the Ballycumber Hills and other ranges via Tinahely and Shillelagh. Leaving the region of the Wicklow Mountains, it is possible to continue walking from Clonegal to Graiguenamanagh in County Kilkenny on the South Leinster Way (40km/25miles). More details can be found on an information leaflet available from the Irish Tourist Board (»The Wicklow and South Leinster Way«).

Youghal (Eochaill)

E 4

Republic of Ireland, province:
Munster
Population: 6,000

County: Cork

Youghal (pron. »yawl«) is a historic market and fishing town in the south of Ireland. The Blackwater River widens to a lake and thus forms a safe harbour before running into the sea.

Cromwell's headquarters

Youghal, Eochail in Irish (»yew forest«), was a thriving town from the 13th century until 1579, when it was destroyed by the rebellious Earl of Desmond. Towards the end of the 16th century, Sir Walter Raleigh governed Youghal, later it was Richard Boyle. In 1649, the town fell to Cromwell, who installed his main headquarters for his campaigns in Ireland here.

To the west of the historic town centre, the 15th/16th-century walls and towers of the well-preserved town fortifications sweep towards the south-east for a distance of about 600m/650yd. Several houses in the town centre date from the 18th and 19th centuries. The main street runs parallel to the shores of the Blackwater River. Today, Youghal is a popular bathing resort due to its long sandy beach. Memories of John Huston's filming of »Moby Dick«, with Gregory Peck as Captain Ahab, still sustain the town a little, and it is also known for the original patterns of its traditionally produced needle lace, known as »Youghal Point«.

From the Middle Ages to today

Coming from the north, North Abbey, the ruins of a Dominican monastery founded in 1268, stands surrounded by a cemetery to the right of the main street. On North Main Street, look for the Red House, a typical Dutch building.

Fishing boats at Youghal Harbour

Several streets further on, William Street leads right to the Collegiate Church of St Mary's, with its free-standing tower. It was built in the early 13th century and rebuilt several times after that. Worth seeing in the interior are the oak wood carvings in the nave, the baptismal font and various tombs, including the tomb of Richard Boyle in the southern transept (1619). Northeast of the parish church stands Myrtle Grove, an imposing Elizabethan manor house that used to belong to Sir Walter Raleigh.

The five-storey Clockgate Tower at the southern end of Main Street, which was built to replace an old town gate in 1771, served as the municipal prison until 1837 and is home to a small museum today. Fox's Lane Folk Museum exhibits traditional household goods from the 18th century. (Opening times: July and Aug Tue–Sat 10am–1pm and 2pm–6pm.)

 **YOUGHAL**

INFORMATION

Market Square
Tel. (0 24) 2 01 70
Open: May–Sept

ACCOMMODATION

► **Budget**
Devonshire Arms Hotel
Pearse Square
Tel. (0 24) 9 28 27, Fax (0 24) 9 29 00
reservations@dev.arms.ie
Pleasant house with individually designed rooms.

Around Youghal

Drive north on the N25, and then head along the western shores of the Blackwater River, to reach the destroyed abbey of Molana, after passing the ruins of Rinncru Abbey and Templemichael Castle, an extremely picturesque group of church and monastic buildings located on the river.

Molana Abbey

To the west of Youghal, 12km/7.5 miles away, the round keep of 13th-century Inchiquin Castle is visible from the N25 near Killeagh. The road continues on to Castlemartyr, with its remains of 15th-century Seneshal's Castle. About 10km/6 miles further on, Midleton is a busy market town and commercial centre with a pretty 18th-century Market House and a church built after designs by the Pain brothers in the 19th century.

Towards Midleton

The main sight though is the Jameson Heritage Centre, installed in a mill house that was built as early as the end of the 18th century. From 1825 to 1975, there was a working whiskey distillery here. Various models, demonstrations and exhibits give an overview of whiskey distillation. (Opening times: daily 10am–1pm and 2.15–5.30pm. The recommended tours run March–Oct daily 10am–6pm, Nov–Feb, Mon–Fri around noon and 3pm.)

INDEX

LIST OF MAPS AND ILLUSTRATIONS

PHOTO CREDITS

PUBLISHER'S INFORMATION

Illustrations etc: 263 illustrations, 42 maps and diagrams, one large map
Text: Beate Szerelmy; with contributions from Birgit Borowski, Achim Bourmer, Rainer Eisenschmid, Dr. Peter Harbison, Odin Hug, Wilhelm Jensen, Dieter Luippold, Dr. Hedwig Nosbers, Matthias Öhler, Brian Reynolds, Dina Stahn, Jürgen Stumpp und Dr. Margit Wagner
Translation: Kathleen Becker; Natascha Scott-Stokes
Editing: Baedeker editorial team (Kathleen Becker; Natascha Scott-Stokes)
Cartography: Franz Kaiser, Sindelfingen; MAIRDUMONT GmbH & Co. KG, Ostfildern (map)
3D illustrations: jangled nerves, Stuttgart
Design: independent Medien-Design, Munich; Kathrin Schemel

Editor-in-chief: Rainer Eisenschmid, Baedeker Ostfildern

1st edition 2008

Copyright: Karl Baedeker Verlag, Ostfildern
Publication rights: MAIRDUMONT GmbH & Co; Ostfildern

Printed in China

DEAR READER,

We would like to thank you for choosing this Baedeker Allianz travel guide. It will be a reliable companion on your travels and will not disappoint you. This book describes the major sights, of course, but it also recommends hotels in the luxury and budget categories, and includes tips about where to eat, beaches, shopping and much more, helping to make your trip an enjoyable experience. Our author Beate Szerelmy ensures the quality of this information by making regular visits to Ireland and putting all her experience and know-how into this book.

Nevertheless, experience shows us that it is impossible to rule out errors and changes made after the book goes to press, for which Baedeker accepts no liability. Please send us your criticisms, corrections and suggestions for improvement: we appreciate your contribution. Contact us by post or e-mail, or phone us:

▶ **Verlag Karl Baedeker GmbH**
   Editorial department
   Postfach 3162
   73751 Ostfildern
   Germany
   Tel. 49-711-4502-262, fax -343
   www.baedeker.com
   E-Mail: baedeker@mairdumont.com

Baedeker Travel Guides in English at a glance:

▶ Andalusia

▶ Dubai · Emirates

▶ Egypt

▶ Ireland

▶ London

▶ Mexico

▶ New York

▶ Portugal

▶ Rome

▶ Thailand

▶ Tuscany

▶ Venice